IN THE RED AND IN THE BLACK

Debt, Dishonor, and the Law in France between Revolutions

Erika Vause

UNIVERSITY OF VIRGINIA PRESS
Charlottesville and London

University of Virginia Press

Printed in the United States of America on acid-free paper

First published 2018

1 3 5 7 9 8 6 4 2

Library of Congress Cataloging-in-Publication Data

Title: In the red and in the black : debt, dishonor, and the law in France between revolutions / Erika Vause.
Description: Charlottesville : University of Virginia Press, 2018. | Includes bibliographical references and index.
Identifiers: LCCN 2017061671 | ISBN 9780813941417 (cloth : alk. paper) | ISBN 9780813941424 (ebook)
Subjects: LCSH: Debt, Imprisonment for—France—History. | Bankruptcy—France—History.
Classification: LCC HV8651.F8 I6 2018 | DDC 346.4407/7—dc23
LC record available at https://lccn.loc.gov/2017061671

Cover art: *"Crédit est mort, les mauvais payeurs l'ont tué,"* François Georgin. Épinal drawing ca. 1850. (Author's collection)

CONTENTS

ACKNOWLEDGMENTS

As befits this topic, I have contracted no shortage of debts in writing this work.

First, I owe a huge debt of gratitude to the University of Chicago, where the research for this book began as part of my doctoral thesis. My dissertation chair, Jan Goldstein, and committee, comprising Leora Auslander, Paul Cheney, and Amy Dru Stanley, were instrumental in encouraging me to pursue this topic and in giving me feedback on the finished dissertation. Other University of Chicago faculty—including Françoise Meltzer and William Sewell—also contributed deeply to the early creation of this work. The lively culture of workshops, including Interdisciplinary Approaches to Modern France, the Law, Culture and Society Workshop, the Markets and Consumption Workshop, and the Modern European History Workshop, provided a welcome place to share early ideas for this book. During the two years I spent researching in France while in graduate school, Laurence Fontaine was a remarkably generous intellectual guide, as eager to help with scholarship as to offer hospitality. Claire Lemercier not only provided vital assistance in tracking down archives but also introduced me to the *séminaire* Histoire du crédit at the ENS. As economists, Jérôme Sgard and Pierre-Cyrille Hautcoeur provided totally new ways of viewing this information. Daniel Thuret, descendent of Isaac Thuret, made his family papers at the ANMT available for me. Funding from the University of Chicago, the France Chicago Center, the Georges Lurcy Foundation, the French Embassy (Chateaubriand), and the Woodrow Wilson Foundation (Charlotte Newcombe) helped pay for research and writing of the dissertation.

Since completing the dissertation, I have benefited immensely from additional opportunities for research and feedback. Talks given at the University of California, Berkeley, the University of California, Davis, the University of California, Santa Barbara, Northern Illinois University,

Washington University in St. Louis, George Mason University, Cornell University, Utah State University, Widener University, Tulane University, and Denison University as well as conference presentations at the American Society for Legal History, the American Historical Association, and the Society for French Historical Studies have sharpened my ideas. Previous versions of parts of chapters 1, 3, 4, and 5 have benefited from the comments of peer reviewers and editors of the *Law and History Review, Journal of Social History*, and *French Historical Studies* and the edited volume *Dealing with Economic Failure* (Peter Lang, 2015), where they have previously appeared. I also thank Clare Crowston and one anonymous reviewer from the University of Virginia Press—as well as two reviewers at Oxford University Press—for their extremely helpful commentary.

In addition to the opportunities presented above, Margrit Schulte Beerbühl helped introduce me to the rich conversation on the history of debt outside of France and America when she invited me to present work at the workshop Dealing with Economic Failure in Frankfurt, Germany, in April 2014. Rafe Blaufarb, who invited me to present my work at the Institute for Napoleon and the French Revolution's Bob Weider Workshop of Revolutionary Economic Practices at Florida State University in 2015, has been extremely generous in offering me advice and guidance both on the ideas in this book and on its publication. Thomas Luckett and Chia Yin Hsu of Portland State University have been instrumental in making me think about economic history in a more global way during the Richard Robinson Workshops on Business History that we have organized together. Discussions with other scholars of debt and credit, in France and elsewhere, including Alexia Yates, Tyson Leuchter, Nicole Mottier, Sergei Antonov, and Mischa Suter, have deeply influenced the way I have approached this subject. Stephanie Frank, although not a scholar of debt per se, has always managed to have brilliant insights about this project.

I have also benefited immensely from the financial and intellectual resources available to me at Florida Southern College. The College of Arts and Sciences provided me with a generous summer stipend for research in Paris in 2015. Jeff Zines digitized some of the illustrations from my personal collection that I have used in this book. My colleagues in a variety of disciplines, including H. A. Nethery, Colleen Moore, and Erica Bernheim, have provided emotional camaraderie as well as intellectual engagement during the years I spent revising the dissertation while simultaneously managing a busy work schedule.

My deepest debts, of course, I owe to my closest friends and family. I have been exceedingly lucky throughout the entire ten-year-long germination of this project to have enjoyed the companionship of great friends in Chicago, France, and Florida. Many of these individuals appear in the paragraphs above, but not all of them can be thanked at the length they deserve.

Emile Mufdi entered my life in the final stages of this project and made those much more bearable. Above all, I owe a huge debt of gratitude to my family, Marie, Alan, and Natalie Vause, without whom this work would be unthinkable.

IN THE RED AND IN THE BLACK

Introduction

What does it mean to fail? Upon hearing that her uncle had shot himself rather than face financial ruin, Eugénie Grandet, the naive heroine of Honoré de Balzac's eponymous 1833 novel, asked her father precisely this question. Félix Grandet answered his daughter with a violent tirade, characterizing *faillite* or bankruptcy as "the most dishonorable act that can dishonor a man" and judging a highwayman worthier of respect. The highwayman, he continued, at least "risks his life in attacking you." Rebuffing his pious wife's assumption that bankruptcy must be a "sin," Grandet inveighed against his brother in secular language, labeling the bankrupt a traitor to public trust and "a robber that the law unfortunately takes under its protection."[1]

The opinions espoused by Félix Grandet should not be taken as faithfully reflective of nineteenth-century beliefs on commercial failure. Balzac, no stranger himself to financial woes, quickly noted that Grandet's definition misleadingly assimilated all failures to frauds. However, in placing these words in his character's mouth, Balzac emphasized how closely related crime and financial loss were in the minds of many of his contemporaries and in the eyes of law itself. The France of Balzac's day was a tough place for borrowers. Each year, thousands of debtors found themselves arrested for commercial debts. Those who wished to escape debt imprisonment through bankruptcy sacrificed their honor—losing, among other rights and privileges, the ability to vote, to serve on a jury, or even to enter the stock market. If creditors discovered evidence of malfeasance or mismanagement in the bankruptcy, the debtor could face criminal charges entailing jail time or forced labor. Although bankruptcy itself was not a crime, precautionary measures were taken against all bankrupts. These measures presumed guilt rather than innocence and included the mandatory imprisonment of the debtor unless his creditors allowed him liberty.

Although the early nineteenth century was punitive for debtors, the lines between financial loss and crime were in a state of considerable flux. Between 1789 and 1867, debt imprisonment was abolished three times and reestablished twice. Meanwhile, a pamphlet war raged between its supporters and opponents. During the same period, reformers attempted multiple independent projects to change the bankruptcy law, which was alternately deemed too rigorous or too soft on the debtor. Contemporaries worried deeply about the implications of commercial failure: Was it fair that a debtor stood to lose his honor and his rights for circumstances often judged to be outside his control? Where could the lines be drawn between losses over which a debtor had no control and culpable acts of negligence? Should merchants engage their own liberty when borrowing money? Did the very rigors of the law push debtors into shady dealings with their creditors?

As the industrial and democratic revolutions fundamentally overturned age-old certainties, these questions proved a lightning rod for controversy. The French Revolution ushered in new ideas of individualism and liberalism. It promoted a social order based, not on title and blood, but rather on wealth as a supposed indicator of merit and productivity. It proclaimed the importance of the individual as the supreme moral actor. It dissolved a commercial world bound together by guilds and inaugurated an economy based on contracts made between free individuals. In acclaiming liberty as the highest good, it also ushered in the creation of the modern penal system under which the deprivation of liberty answered for infractions of the social contract. While the French economy of the early nineteenth century remained largely agrarian, with its industries focused on the small-scale production of luxury goods, an increased division of labor, limited use of mechanization, and substantial urbanization resulted in the rise of a self-conscious working class by the eve of the 1848 Revolution.[2] Nevertheless, contemporary French observers perceived the economic transformations around them less in terms of "dark satanic mills" than in terms of changes in finance capital—the evolution and proliferation of new firm structures, the growth of the stock market, and the increasing monetization of social relations.

For contemporaries, the relationship between creditors and debtors personified the contradictions of post-Revolutionary society more broadly. On one hand, observers associated credit with the individualistic pursuit of money and self-interest. On the other, access to credit depended on chains of trust and obligation, embedded in relations of hierarchy and dependence. The fascination of nineteenth-century authors and illustrators with such ostensibly dry topics as the circulation of bills of exchange and the depredations of usurers and bailiffs can in part be explained as a meditation on the parameters of an emergent market society. As with other widely debated topics of the age, including slavery and child labor, discussions about debt imprisonment and bankruptcy involved defining the relationship between liberty and property and delineating the role of the person in relation to the market. Legal efforts to reconfigure the relationships between creditors and debtors entailed profound impacts for sculpting the contours of the economic and the penal realms. The story of commercial failure during this period embraces external shifts in the relationship between economic activity and the law, but also internal shifts in the understanding of the commercial self engaged in and subject to these forces.

Like Eugénie Grandet, in writing this book I have asked what it meant to fail. The right to fail without being punished merely for failing is now deemed essential to the "creative destruction" of the market economy. Before the modern era, however, Grandet's presumptions were the rule rather than the exception.[3] How, at least in the eyes of the law, did failure and fraud become decoupled? What does this decoupling say about the relationship between the modern economy and modern penal system in an age that arguably gave birth to both? To answer this question, this book examines the history of debt imprisonment (*contrainte par corps*, literally translated as "bodily constraint") and bankruptcy (*faillite* and *banqueroute*) in nineteenth-century France. The story it tells—the story of how debt became detached from notions of the person, and at the same time disentangled from crime and dishonor—plays a central role in the development of a modern culture of capitalism, not merely in France but throughout the world.

The process by which this distinction occurred has been taken for granted rather than explored. The rich and abundant literature concerning debt and failure in the American context has focused instead on how debt both validated and troubled the liberal insistence on self-ownership.[4] As capitalism linked economic independence with notions of freedom, this literature has shown, it also introduced new forms of risk that threatened this independence and, in so doing, the very foundations of the self-sufficient citizen. Yet while previous literature has explored how the rise of modern capitalism encouraged and expanded risk taking, this book is interested in the simultaneous diminution of another type of risk—the risk of being confused with a criminal for having failed. Rather than viewing this risk reduction as merely liberatory, I argue that the decoupling of risk from the physical and moral person of the debtor constricted certain forms of risk taking while enabling other types.

This story is centered, as was so much of the debate about failure, on the "person" of the debtor. The laws enacted in the aftermath of the 1789 Revolution created a certain paradigm of the "person." A mixture of Enlightenment ideals of contractual individualism and a credit economy that remained deeply embedded in interpersonal relations, this notion of the person was simultaneously physical, a body to be thrown in jail for not paying a debt or for committing fraud, and abstract, a name on a bill of exchange or a reputation to be tarnished by the stain of bankruptcy. This "person," however, proved fundamentally unsettling for the liberal order, jeopardizing many of its foundational tenets. Reformers felt that it allowed access to credit for borrowers who should be excluded from the kind of economic independence allowed by the possession of private capital while confusing the lines between state, market, and household. At the same time investors faulted this model of the person failing to anticipate the needs of increasingly more complex corporations. The punitive connotations of holding the person responsible for the debt, moreover, drove many creditors and debtors to make arrangements in the shadow of the law and exacerbated the very problems of fraud and deceit that such rigor had been intended to repress. The struggle to redefine this "person" coincided with a new understanding of the relationship between the punitive state and the economy.

The three parts of this book follow the development of this commercial person through three different eras. In the first two chapters, Revolutionary and Napoleonic laws frame a highly individualistic but also honor-bound sense of the self. The next three chapters explore the contradictions inherent in this sense of personhood as revealed by the practices of credit and debt themselves. In the last two chapters, political reform, commercial practice, and philosophical speculation alike move toward a more collective and abstract notion of commercial selfhood.

Through tracing these developments, I argue that while we may think of the *owning* self as the one foundational to the modern economic order, the *owing* one in fact proved far more central to delineating its parameters.

The Law of Debt

Like many of his contemporaries, Theodore-Louis Troplong, perhaps the most celebrated French legal thinker of his day, believed not only that debt was intimately tied to the person but also that the history of debt law mirrored the linear and progressive trajectory of modernity itself.[5] In an 1847 speech to Paris's Académie des sciences morales et politiques, he posited that at the very origins of debt law "the person responds corporally, and principally, to contracted engagements. On one hand, insolvency is assimilated to crime. The debtor who dishonors his word in not paying his creditor differs little from a thief. In dishonoring his word, he has dishonored the gods whom he has taken as witnesses of oath; his body is therefore engaged by his offense; it belongs to its expiation. On the other hand, in order to make him pay with his possessions, the creditor must seize, first of all, his person."[6] Troplong argued that the more civilized the society, the more it relied on the debtor's property, rather than his body, as collateral for his debt. He happily reported that all that remained of such logic in the "civilized world" of his own enlightened age was the debtors' prison, the use of which in France had been increasingly restricted and ameliorated by successive reforms.

The real history of debt law was considerably more complicated than Troplong admitted in this short passage. Although both debt imprisonment and bankruptcy practices drew from Roman law, the nineteenth-century varieties could trace their direct genealogies in France only as far back as the twelfth and thirteenth centuries.[7] Even here, laws on debt were refracted through the complex patchwork of medieval customary practice, where practices against debtors varied widely among regions and cities. Beginning in the sixteenth century, a succession of royal edicts sought to regularize the treatment of debtors across the country, culminating with Minister of Finance Jean-Baptiste Colbert's Ordinance of 1673. This ordinance, upon which subsequent Napoleonic commercial legislation would be based, not only laid the groundwork for the procedures of debt imprisonment and bankruptcy but also established the critical difference between *faillite* and *banqueroute*.

The Ordinance of 1673 also clearly associated debt imprisonment and bankruptcy with commercial law by according jurisdictional authority over these cases to the *jurisdiction consulaire*. These merchant courts, which numbered around three hundred on the eve of the Revolution, had been founded by powerful guilds in the sixteenth century on the premise that commercial litigation required its own distinct legal system, a belief consistent with old regime corporate ideas of jurisdictional authority.[8] In these courts, merchant-judges elected by their peers adjudicated cases largely on the basis of precedent and customary practice. The law practiced in such courts belonged to the commercial or merchant law (*lex mercatoria*), a body of relatively analogous legal customs that had evolved more or less simultaneously across Europe with the revivification of commerce in the twelfth and thirteenth centuries.[9] By the eve of the French Revolution, the *jurisdiction consulaire* had successfully expanded its prerogatives in part because of its unique ability to handle the often extremely contentious litigation involving negotiable instruments, namely, bills of exchange and promissory notes, the usage of which was becoming more widespread by the eighteenth century.

The impact of the French Revolution on law strikes at the heart of the controversy about the nature of the Revolution's roots and its legacy. In its heyday, Marxist historiography on the Revolution, best exemplified by the works of Georges Lefebvre and Albert Soboul, insisted that the laws that emerged in this period represented the height of bourgeois triumphalism. The legal regime put in place by the Revolution's bourgeois victors broke decisively with its feudal antecedent (or, more accurately, given the plethora of old regime institutions, antecedents) in its embrace of contractual liberalism and individualism. Beginning with Alfred Cobban in the 1950s but taking root only in the 1980s, revisionist scholarship, including the works of François Furet and Keith Baker, has focused instead on the continuities between the Revolutionary project and absolutist law projects bent on centralization. Meanwhile, more recent accounts, such as those offered by Rafe Blaufarb and Suzanne Desan, have renewed the emphasis on the novelty of Revolutionary reforms, stressing the importance of Revolutionary discourse in the quotidian and concrete levels of daily practice of the law.[10]

Post-Revolutionary commercial justice provides an ideal and previously unexplored point of entry into this ongoing debate about the nature of the Revolution and its relation to the rise of the modern market. This debate, after all, has almost exclusively taken place in terms of the lead up to the

Revolution rather than what the Revolutionary legacy left behind. The character of commercial law, particularly its rules in terms of commercial credit, doubtlessly entails profound implications for the operation of the economy. An examination of this framework, as designed by Revolutionary legislation and the Napoleonic codes, suggests both continuity with old regime practices and a certain amount of discursive innovation, which justified the incorporation of an old regime corporate institution into the Revolutionary order. The regime of commercial justice that emerged from the Revolution both differed substantially from its prior iterations and yet, as I have suggested earlier, converged upon a notion of economic personhood that reformers and investors alike would find antithetical to the needs of finance capitalism. The transformation of this notion of economic agency took place not with the Revolution itself but in the relatively little studied but crucial years after the Revolution covered in this book.

First, however, we must understand the legal landscape of this time period. The Napoleonic codes reaffirmed a long-standing jurisdictional divide between commercial and noncommercial (or civil) debt cases. The Commercial Code, promulgated in 1807, provided an entirely different set of laws from the 1804 Civil Code to govern precisely those circumstances particular to merchants. Of the five books constituting the Commercial Code, the third book was devoted in its entirety to bankruptcy law, testifying to the critical importance of debt litigation in the overall understanding of commercial justice. Alone among the dense network of *prévôtés, sénéchausées*, and *baillages* that made up the beating heart of old regime justice, the *jurisdiction consulaire*, renamed the *tribunaux de commerce* (commercial courts), not only survived the Revolutionary attack on "private interests" but was enshrined into the Napoleonic codes. As Claire Lemercier has argued, the post-Revolutionary commercial courts maintained important features of their old regime structure that would allow them to "discipline" commerce in a France newly freed of guilds.[11]

While old regime notions of property were incredibly diverse, the distinction between movable and immovable property remained as crucial after the Revolution as it was before. For contemporaries, immovable property—of which land was the foremost example—formed the primary source of wealth and bestowed the most social status on its possessor. Transactions involving the collateral of immovable property presented a comforting solidity. The "masses of granite" that Napoleon had envisioned as the stable upholders of post-Revolutionary society were landed property owners, not merchants or bankers. Merchants, whose vocation involved the transfer of movable property such as money and merchandise, fit uncomfortably into a world that was still based on the supremacy of landed property. The French Revolutionaries, as Blaufarb has maintained, attempted to take the polymorphous conceptions and practices of old regime property and meld them into an abstract notion of property, the defining traits of which were its absolute and alienable nature.[12] Ironically, however, this notion of detaching people from property broke down when applied to the very people most commonly associated with the rise of modern capitalism: merchants. As one lawmaker said in creating the Commercial Code, commercial law was to be "concerned only with persons, an important distinction, derived from the nature of commerce itself, which, being only practiced on mobile objects, offers nothing for surety and guarantee other than the morality of persons."[13]

Nowhere did the connection between commercial justice and the person become clearer than when examining debt imprisonment and bankruptcy. Although the vast majority of *contrainte par corps* cases in the nineteenth century were for commercial debt, there were other forms of debt that could entail debt imprisonment, almost all of which involved some sort of preexisting illegality or suspicion of illegality. For example, an individual who mortgaged or sold property to which he had no legal title or a guardian who did not return the goods entrusted in the name of his ward could be held by *contrainte par corps* for the amount of the debt he owed, as could individuals sentenced by a court to pay compensation or who had committed poaching, hunting, or fishing violations. Apart from commercial debts, the only debts liable to debt imprisonment that did not involve some level of suspicion of fraud were those made by foreigners on French soil.

Commercial debt imprisonment, by far both the most common and the most controversial form of debt imprisonment in the nineteenth century, was the exclusive purview of the commercial courts. It belonged to a multifaceted legal landscape of creditors' tools for debt recovery, which included pay stoppages and the seizure of property (forms that could also be used on noncommercial debtors). Creditors who wished to obtain an arrest would first bring their suit before the commercial court, which almost always ruled in their favor, since all business credit transactions entailed the possibility of *contrainte par corps*. The creditor could then take the court order to the office of the commercial guards in Paris, or, in the provinces, to bailiffs who would perform the arrest. Although legislation limited the length of stay for debtors in prison according to the amount of the debt, the creditor paid for the debtor's detention for the duration of his stay. This expense would subsequently be added to the amount that the debtor had to reimburse.

Commercial debt imprisonment was integrally connected with bankruptcy, which was restricted to merchants and traders. Commercial courts adjudicated these cases. Aside from striking a private arrangement with his creditor (or by the failure of his creditor to supply a stipend for his upkeep), a commercial debtor could be released from incarceration only by a bankruptcy declaration. Thus, bankruptcy was implicitly built on the lingering threat of debt imprisonment for those who did not cooperate. Although only merchants were deemed likely to become deeply indebted through misfortunes beyond their control, bankruptcy laws sharply distinguished the presumed responsibility of a businessman for his failure. The debtor generally initiated proceedings, which ended with either a *concordat* rescheduling his debts or a *union*, a liquidation that seized and distributed assets on a pro rata basis. Although the status of *faillite* ascribed no wrongdoing on the debtor's part, it still involved the loss of certain rights and privileges as well as social opprobrium. Noncommercial debtors could be placed in a state of *déconfiture*, official insolvency, if their debts substantially exceeded their assets. A debtor in *déconfiture* could file for a *cession de biens*, a civil law procedure allowing creditors to divide an insolvent debtor's assets among themselves. In practice, the procedure of *cession de biens* was poorly defined in the laws and consequently seldom used.

Given the substantial differences between the treatment of commercial and noncommercial debtors, contemporary observers often commented that commercial justice represented a "state of exception," a legal code that ran parallel to, and in some respects outright contradicted, the law as it applied to ordinary French citizens. As such, a study of commercial justice invites comparisons with recent scholarship concentrating on "regimes of exception," whether these be applied to colonial subjects, felons, or slaves, in the creation of the modern liberal law.[14] This scholarship teaches us that, rather than being external to the "normal" operation of law, such spaces of exception are fundamental to understanding the operation of such laws. For some, the rapid pace and uncertain collateral of commercial transactions necessitated a justice set apart from ordinary justice. For others, it evoked similarities to the infamous revolutionary tribunals. Furthermore, commercial justice created within the citizenry a body of men who were to be judged differently from others when it came to credit transactions—namely, the *commerçant*. As Alessandro Stanziani has noted, "The existence of special law for trade was not linked to the French Ancient Regime nor did it express a simple state interference in economic matters," but rather "commercial rules were above all linked to the peculiar legal status of merchants."[15] To emphasize the particularity of this legal standing, I will be using the term *commerçant* throughout this book, since choosing one of its closest English translations, including tradesman, trader, merchant, or businessman, does not completely capture the broad scope of this legal term, which spanned all of these groups. The ideal of the *commerçant* as an individual set apart from the normal, putatively agrarian, Frenchman (or, even more exceptionally, Frenchwoman) and easily identifiable as such was anachronistic even as it emerged from the legislation of the Directory and Napoleonic periods. Created for a world defined by guilds, this notion of a distinct class of tradesmen seemed poorly suited to the complexity of property relations and the proliferation of new company forms at the dawn of the nineteenth century.

Not only did commercial law possess an anomalous position in relation to civil law, but the borders between criminal and civil law were also porous. The Napoleonic codes mandated punishment for gross negligence or mismanagement (in *banqueroute simple*) or outright theft and deception (in *banqueroute frauduleuse*). *Banqueroute simple*, adjudicated by the correctional court, could be applied in cases of erratic bookkeeping, speculation, extreme negligence, or where there was evidence that the bankrupt had continued operating his business long after he had become insolvent.[16] Conversely, *banqueroute frauduleuse* constituted a felony judged by the criminal court and punished by "afflictive and shameful" sentences including forced labor and years in prison. While in theory the proofs of either *banqueroute simple* or *banqueroute frauduleuse* distinguished them from an ordinary bankruptcy, in reality fraud was not easy to detect, and many of the indicators of *banqueroute*, for example, poorly kept books, were relatively normal business practices. In order to both clarify the legal definitions and also demonstrate the close relation between *banqueroute* and *faillite*, I will be using the terms *banqueroute* and *banqueroutier* (someone who commits a *banqueroute*) and *faillite* and *failli* (someone who undergoes *faillite*) when these specific categories are discussed in this text. However, when referring to failure in general, I will use the term "bankruptcy," thereby leaving open the potential for malfeasance.

The French Revolutionaries radically reformed the criminal court system, placing a much greater emphasis on juries and emphasizing friendly settlement over litigation. Napoleonic law enshrined criminal law in the 1810 Criminal Code. As opposed to the commercial courts, correctional courts (*tribunaux correctionels*) for misdemeanors and criminal courts (*cours d'assises*) for felonies were presided over by judges with official legal training. Major criminal cases, such as *banqueroute frauduleuse*, would involve a *juge d'instruction*, who would judge whether there was sufficient evidence to try a case and summon a jury, chosen from among eligible residents of the jurisdiction. Appeals courts (*cours de cassation*), whose decisions were final, heard cases referred to them by the lower courts.

The prospect of imprisonment arose at several different junctures in debt law: it could be used by a creditor for an unpaid commercial debt, it could be used against a bankrupt who had not been granted a safe-conduct pass by his creditors, and it could be used against a bankrupt found guilty of either *banqueroute simple* or *banqueroute frauduleuse*. Legally, these different types of incarceration possessed very different meanings. However, in the popular imagination, their meanings frequently overlapped. This phenomenon was particularly significant given the evolving connotations of prison in the nineteenth century. Before the latter half of the eighteenth century, the predominant use of the prison involved custodial imprisonment, such as that represented by *contrainte par corps*, in which incarceration was not a punitive measure but rather a means of detaining individuals. There are multiple explanations concerning why this shift happened. One school of thought, pioneered by scholars such as Douglas Hay, Michael Ignatieff, and Peter Linebaugh, stresses the importance of class discipline with the advent of the Industrial Revolution.[17] Although this body of work is largely focused on contemporaneous England, it emphasizes the importance of instilling a respect for property into the working class through the implementation of stringent laws and the creation of penitentiaries as sites of labor. Alternatively, Michel Foucault's seminal *Discipline et punir* famously traced how the prison replaced various inflictions of bodily pain, including execution, as the chief mechanism of punishment over the course of the eighteenth and nineteenth centuries.[18] For Foucault, the penal regime of the modern age entailed subtler yet pervasive forms of power that rendered the prison a model for the perfectly governed, perfectly surveilled society.

Subsequent research has softened the abruptness of the rupture between older and newer visions of the penitentiary and argued for significant discrepancies between the ideal of totalizing carceral institutions, such as those examined by Foucault and proposed by prison reformers, and the often disorganized and disparate realities of nineteenth-century prison life.[19] The term "prison" referred to a diverse group of institutions in post-Revolutionary France, ranging from cells in police quarters and cantonal jails to the great long-term detention facilities, the *maisons centrales*. Immense discrepancies existed between the treatment of prisoners not only among prisons but within them as well. In addition, there were multiple waves of prison reform movements during the period, led by activists who often bitterly challenged their predecessors' visions of the ideal penal environment. In this context, prisoners arrested through the process of *contrainte par corps*, who, outside of Paris, were frequently incarcerated alongside felons, appear less as an atavistic anomaly of the premodern age than as a testimony to the continuing diversity of prison life in a period of intense reform.

Tracing the history of debt imprisonment and bankruptcy over the first half of the nineteenth century reveals the interplay between the law as a contested, legislative ideal and its much messier application by ordinary men and women in the courts. Creditors and debtors alike regularly utilized the law—but also often chose to avoid it. The emergence of a new sense of commercial personhood during this period arose from litigants' attempts to maneuver a complex choreography of interests, which included maximizing their economic gains as well as other sorts of advantages. Although class played a substantial role in the reworking of legal subjecthood discussed in this book, the diverse socioeconomic backgrounds of those who were "punished" for their debt preclude any simple class-based explanation of this story. Additionally, while there is much in the account of debtors offered here that confirms Foucault's account of the shift toward a regime of orderly edification, this book stresses instead the lingering and perturbing importance of the putatively vestigial "person" of the debtor. Rather than the soul becoming a prison for the body, as Foucault famously put it, the body continued to arouse intense anxiety well into the golden age of penal reform. Much of this narrative's complexity can be attributed to the multiple and interwoven senses of debt involved in these legal battles.

The Many Meanings of Credit

In the opening chapter of a slim 1827 volume entitled *L'art de payer ses dettes et de satisfaire ses créanciers, sans débourser un sou*, the satirist Émile Saint-Hilaire presented his readers with a perplexing series of questions. "Who," he asked, "has been so fortunate that after these thirty years, after *assignats, mandats* and after the bankruptcy of the State . . . after emigrations, confiscations, requisitions, arrests, and invasions which have reversed every fortune, he has always been able to say 'I owe nothing'? Which people, sitting on a pile of gold today, could say, 'We will never be debtors'?"[20] Saint-Hilaire presumed that none of his readers would answer in the affirmative. He, like many of his contemporaries, not only viewed post-Revolutionary France, from the state itself to the smallest shopkeeper, as indelibly in the red but also saw these outstanding debts as symbolic of the rupture of more profound social and moral obligations precipitated by the Revolution. For Saint-Hilaire and others, debt and credit possessed far more than monetary meaning. The works of Dumas, Flaubert, and Balzac teem with references to usury, debt imprisonment, bankruptcy, and the importance of a good signature on a promissory note or bill of exchange. The most popular caricaturists of the day, artists like Daumier and Cham, devoted a surprising amount of time and ink to illustrating the mundane battles between creditors and debtors. In an era when factories remained small, relations of credit bound workers to employers, merchants to other merchants, and producers to consumers. They bound the cities to the countryside and the colonies to the metropole. Those who could not make good on their promises emerged as figures of continual anxiety, eliciting a myriad of reactions from pity to outrage. Concerns about credit and debt, as well as how borrowers and lenders should be treated, were not merely political or economic matters but cultural, social, and profoundly moral ones as well.

A vast body of research has depicted early modern France as perennially and extensively indebted. Given the scarcity of cash, individuals of all social ranks relied on credit not only to satisfy transactions that could not be undertaken in coin but also to forge social bonds through the dependency created by debt.[21] Debt in early modern Europe obeyed multiple logics, with economic calculation hardly being the preeminent among these. Lending was embedded in a culture of reciprocal gift giving, in which moral considerations about the character of the borrower often took a backseat to political and social considerations. For example, countless examples exist of objectively bad credit risks who continued to be extended loans over years and even decades. In early modern Europe, the identities of owners and possessions, of political power and economic property, were inextricably bound together.[22] As Clare Crowston has argued, under the old regime "the word credit . . . gives a name to everything historians already know about the operation of power in this period and shows, in addition, that contemporaries themselves were fully aware of how influence and reputation shamed access to political, social, cultural, and economic realms."[23] For Crowston, to understand credit in the pre-Revolutionary era is to situate one's self in an economy of regard, in which services, gifts, money, favors, and privileges all circulated according to one's access to credit. As such, credit before 1789 could not be disentangled from the political, economic, and social hierarchies on which ancient regime society rested.

Creditworthiness was closely connected with the concept of honor, a term that, while the subject of much recent historiography, has remained strangely vague. Historians have pointed to the desire to prove honor, and to avoid dishonor, as central to understanding many aspects of the eighteenth- and nineteenth-century experience, from dueling to gender roles to nationalism.[24] William Reddy has termed honor "an invisible code" that belied the era's supposed focus on self-interested and contractual relationships.[25] Indeed, while self-interest and the pursuit of monetary gain were seen as the antithesis of honorable behavior, honor—particularly in the form of credit—was essential to understanding commerce both before and after the Revolution. Scholars such as Amalia Kessler, John Shovlin, and Jay Smith have shown the importance of honor as a principal means by which commercial people sought to define their status in relation to the aristocracy in the old regime.[26] Over the course of the eighteenth century, intellectuals as well as merchants promoted new theories of honor that valued social utility and productivity and that raised the status of commerce at the expense of the aristocracy. As discussed in chapter 1 of this book, conceptions of honor, refracted now through the Revolutionary fixation with contract, became a central rhetorical point of the Directory. This same obsession with honor, which tempered the purported vice of self-interest with a sense of social obligation, continued to exercise profound influence in the decades after the Revolution, when, as Victoria Thompson has demonstrated, market inclusion and exclusion in the early nineteenth century revolved around gendered notions of honor.[27] Dishonor, by contrast, entailed a loss of standing in the community and formed an integral part of the criminal code both before and after the Revolution, thereby blurring the lines between shameful and unlawful acts.[28]

Not only was honor important to the merchant community in the abstract, it mattered to each and every merchant on a daily basis.[29] Access to financial credit depended on a merchant's reputation for honor within the merchant community. The very instruments with which commerce was conducted—promissory notes or bills of exchange—rested on the credit of those who used them.[30] Originally drawn up between anywhere from two to four parties, these transferable IOUs circulated in exchange for goods and services between holders by means of endorsement, the affixation of a signature onto the back of the bills, until their due dates. The list of signatures on the back allowed individuals to assess the creditworthiness of each link along the credit chain. Bill discounters would give money—or new bills—for these bills before their due date, with a cut of "discount" for the risk they ran in accepting the bills. The value of a discounted bill depended on the discounter's assessment of the credit enjoyed by the signatories. Even the terminology for these bills mixed financial interest with social judgment: A good borrower "honored" his engagements, whereas an unpaid negotiable instrument was "dishonored" and could be protested (officially refused). More broadly, merchants assessed each other's creditworthiness in terms of both promise keeping and tangible assets. Adherence to codes of honor created trust between parties and ensured promises without resort to cumbersome and expensive legal mediation. Trust in the upstanding nature of their fellow traders was often all merchants could rely on in a credit economy where there were minimal institutional safeguards and where knowledge of assets was generally local, unreliable, and intermixed with rumor. In such a context, the inability to uphold such standards, as evidenced in bankruptcy or debt imprisonment, not only constituted a source of shame but even implied that the debtor may have committed fraud.

Scholars have disagreed about whether and how much ideas and practices of credit and debt changed during the age of democratic and industrial revolutions. On one hand, the history of credit, recounted as the move from informal and personal credit to anonymous and institutional forms, seems like a promising heuristic for understanding the emergency of a "new" and "modern" world. In this vein, some scholars have suggested that, by the eve of the Revolution, credit had largely acquired its modern sense of detachment from networks of influence and regard and was increasingly understood to refer primarily to an abstract monetary sense of interest.[31]

The Revolution then marks the substantiation of a break between older "socially embedded" forms of credit and a new type of economic rationality. However, much recent research—and certainly much of the work on honor and dishonor in the nineteenth century—has suggested that the idea of a rupture oversimplifies the complex nature of credit. Scholars have critiqued the differentiation between "formal" and "informal" credit networks and revealed instead the multiplicity of actors involved in credit transactions both past and present.[32] Moreover, they have challenged the periodization of the narratives of modernity—demonstrating the existence of putatively "modern" forms of credit in the distant past and emphasizing the vitality of "traditional" institutions in the present.[33]

This book maintains that, rather than replacement of a "moral economy" of debt with a newly amoral, liberal one, the reality is more complex. The Revolution introduced radical ideas of economic individualism based around discretely held property sanctioned by contracts between atomistic actors and by the rule of law as meted out by a punitive state. These policies were designed to sever the chains of dependency central to the old regime, cemented by credit. Revolutionary governments imposed sweeping transformations of the economic order, including the reregulation of markets in many staple goods, the dissolution of the guild system, and the abolition of lending at interest and of debt imprisonment. These ideas soon proved perturbing even to the Revolutionaries themselves. Contemporaries saw the circumstances created by the Revolution as far beyond individual control, ruining even upright and competent businessmen, while at the same time unleashing self-interest unconfined by the monarchy's religious and legal constraints. Businessmen and politicians alike advocated strict commercial morality as a means of improving the circulation of credit in a society where new capitalist values and enhanced social mobility vied uneasily with aristocratic ideals of honor and reputation. Credit, which had provided the glue of social bonds in old regime society, was again invoked to strengthen the new society created by the Revolution. Nevertheless, even when returning in some respects to old regime practices—reinstituting debt imprisonment, capping interest rates, or reinforcing the vigor of old regime commercial laws in the 1807 Commercial Code—the Directory and Napoleonic regime marked a significant transformation in the ways that lenders and borrowers related to each other.

One way of understanding the discrepancy between the ideas embodied in laws about credit and the underlying social realities is by situating credit within the broader construction of the "economy" as a distinctive sphere of study during this period.[34] William Reddy has argued that the late eighteenth and early nineteenth centuries saw the rise of "market culture"—namely, "a set of (wrong) perceptions, a language through which these perceptions were formulated, expressed, and debated, and a set of (misguided) practices partially but imperfectly shaped in accord with these perceptions."[35] Reddy stresses that "market culture" never existed as a social reality, but only as theories upon which legislation was based. Contractual individualism constituted a particularly powerful aspect of market culture. For nineteenth-century legislators and economic writers, the move from status to contract represented a decisive break from a society of hierarchy and dependency to a society based on putative equality. These individuals refashioned old regime legal codes to the demands of a new order, putatively based on public virtue rather than on private honor, making the virtuous contract the centerpiece of their new meritocratic order. Yet the myth of the rational self-interested individual entering into egalitarian contracts based on mutual benefit belied a more complicated reality. Coercion, as evidenced in imprisonment of defaulting debtors, underlay the power of contractual individualism. Meanwhile, credit networks remained deeply embedded in relations of status and dependency.

This regime of debt based around the individual economic actor proved just as troubling as the previous regimes of credit had been. In fact, in nineteenth-century France, no figure better embodied the anxiety of this transitional moment or revealed the contradictions of economic liberalism better than the debtor.[36] Much of the controversy surrounding both bankrupts and debt prisoners had to do with anxiety about their social embeddedness as well as their physical embodiment. Even as post-Revolutionary reformers critiqued the inadequacies of measures implemented in the Revolution's aftermath to uphold "useful" investment and promote morality among borrowers and lenders, their criticism highlighted the fundamental contradictions inherent in their notion of economic personhood of those involved. The reality was that social connections as well as social status continued to constitute a huge and unmentioned form of wealth and property after the Revolution.

Credit lay in the interstices of property and social status, and its position there continually alarmed reformers who aimed to make credit completely dependent on the moral virtue of the borrower. Formed in part on a rejection of credit as it supposedly operated in the pre-Revolutionary world, creditworthiness was closely tied to the ideal of the independent, rational male head of a bourgeois household. This individual, in turn, transacted in an economy supposedly made up of bourgeois male household heads. However, the narratives of "bad" uses of credit that surrounded debt imprisonment or bankruptcy—whether of the virtuous man victimized by ruthless creditors, the wastrel dissipating his parents' inheritance, the usurer abusing the needy, or the conman defrauding his investors—belied this ideal and reflected the continuing importance of the social and political understandings of credit. For midcentury reformers, "bad" credit connoted not merely "backward" credit but also the credit of women and the poor. This credit supposedly rested on relations of power and dependency not only foreign to the idealized bourgeois male actor but often outright dangerous to his supremacy. Meanwhile, the almost constant comparisons that critics of debt imprisonment made with slavery (often labeling the institution of the debt prison "white slavery") demonstrated how uncertain they still felt the line between "persons" and "things" to be, even though the Revolution of 1789 had supposedly pried apart people from their possessions and rendered all property essentially alienable. Problematically, reformers increasingly understood that all these "bad" connotations of credit rested on the very notions of personhood central to the post-Revolutionary economy. The irony of the post-Revolutionary regime of credit was that, based on an ideal of an individual, abstract, rational, and assumedly male borrower, nineteenth-century financial life remained embedded in a thick network of social relations and utilized multiple kinds of collateral. Without wishing to present a teleological narrative, this story demonstrates how these contradictions ultimately led to the creation of a new type of abstract personality, one more in keeping with the new financial realities of elite borrowers and investors.

Accounting for Failure

In tracing this story, this book presents a narrative that portrays the history of debt as both a history of change over time and a history of continuity. It is a story that is sporadic, contested, and often wildly vacillating (as evidenced, for example, by the three abolitions and two reestablishments of debt imprisonment), but nevertheless it ultimately reveals a transition into a new paradigm. To tell this story, the book is organized more or less chronologically, beginning with the French Revolution, when debt imprisonment was abolished for the first time, and ending with a discussion of the practice's third and final abolition. This is a story of fits and starts, of political debate and negotiation. Ultimately, however, it points to the emergence of a new configuration of attitudes and practices involving the concepts of risk, failure, and crime, as well as a new construction of the legal person in relationship to the marketplace.

This book is also organized thematically, with each chapter interrogating one connection between debt and the law (particularly the law in its punitive form). Chapters alternate focus between debt imprisonment and bankruptcy, although the links between the two are stressed throughout. Chapters 1 and 2 explain the roots of post-Revolutionary law on commercial debt by examining the 1797 reestablishment of debtors' prison and the 1807 Commercial Code. This legislation, which underpinned post-Revolutionary practice and borrowed heavily from old regime precedent, nevertheless departed dramatically in terms of discursive justification. Chapters 3 through 6 investigate the increasingly problematic relationship between personhood and debt in the 1820s through the 1840s. Chapter 3 discusses the difficulties faced by writers, judges, and creditors in distinguishing between *faillite* and *banqueroute*, given that even *faillites* were generally believed to have not been truly blameless in their failure. Chapter 4 focuses on how incarcerated debtors, in forums as diverse as complaint letters to prison authorities to memoirs and newspapers, situated themselves within a discourse of honor and crime in which they occupied a category apart from "common criminals." Chapter 5 traces the growing campaign against debtors' prison as voiced in pamphlets, legislation, and popular literature. Chapter 6, focusing on the closing years of the July Monarchy, discusses how, in parallel ways, the bankruptcy reform law of 1838 and a body of court rulings on the bankruptcies of joint-stock companies (*sociétés anonymes* and *sociétés en commandite*) reflected changing notions of juridical personhood. In chapter 7, with the Revolution of 1848, ideas about credit as a social and political right laid the groundwork for calls to pronounce a moratorium on bankruptcies that had resulted from the Revolution itself. The epilogue gestures ahead to the subsequent separation of the person from the debt with the third and this time successful abolition of *contrainte par corps* in 1867.

When I first began working on this project as a graduate student, one faculty member said that I was attempting to tell the history of the French economy through the eyes of Balzac. In this book, I have tried to stay faithful to this vision, melding the gritty details of daily life with the emotional reactions of ordinary people while simultaneously exploring the legal and political realities in which these experiences were embedded. The proximity of commercial loss and fraud, as well as the prominence of debt in the daily life of French men and women, has bequeathed to subsequent scholars a rich source base, which often cuts across the disparate jurisdictions of the civil, commercial, and correctional courts. In writing this book, I have used a wide variety of archival and published documents from various courts in different regions of France, as well as legal newspapers (most prominently the *Gazette des Tribunaux*), government debates and official correspondence, pamphlets, personal papers, and the files of prison administrators. Nonetheless, some sources might seem notably absent. Political economy works, for instance, while present in the first chapter, vanish afterward, as concerns about debt imprisonment and bankruptcy stopped being as explicitly connected to questions of national political economy during the Restoration (although these connections will be reemphasized in 1848). In their place, I utilize a rich array of material from plays, novels, and caricatures to gain insight into popular concerns. In fact, owing to the sheer volume of evidence relating to debt imprisonment and bankruptcy, my selection of evidence has been guided by my interest in what these two practices reveal about the concepts of risk, fault, and personhood rather than by an attempt to provide an exhaustive account of either bankruptcy or debt imprisonment during this time period. Moreover, much of the evidence is partial to Paris and other large cities, reflecting the bias not only of data but also of contemporary attention. Statistical evidence tends to be fragmentary at best. While the state kept a close watch on bankruptcy rates from the 1820s forward, it only began to systematically compile data on the use of *contrainte par corps* in the 1850s. This makes it difficult to assess such crucial information as whether rates of incarceration fell or rose across the early nineteenth century, particularly since many regional internment records, including those of Paris's Sainte-Pélagie and Clichy debtors' prisons, have been lost.

The use of sources underscores an important methodological caveat for this work: It is above all a cultural history of bankruptcy and debt imprisonment. As such, it is guided by an effort to understand the connections between debates about the meaning of bankruptcy happening in legislative bodies with the fears and hopes of ordinary French men and women. I do not want to suggest that all relations between debtors and creditors in nineteenth-century France were as hostile as most of the cases presented here would indicate. I have decided to focus on certain elements of the archival evidence because they seemed symptomatic to contemporaries at the time, as evidenced by the massive literature critiquing debt imprisonment and bankruptcy. Nevertheless, we can still learn much about ordinary practice from these examples of imprisonment, prosecution, and debt negotiation. Indeed, often it is precisely in the rare but controversial cases that we are most able to make out such mundane details as the complicated extralegal transactions between creditors and debtors or food provisioning and the spatial arrangement of debtors' cells. By taking debt imprisonment and bankruptcy as indicative of widely felt tensions between the realities of credit at the ground level and the idealized way in which economic actors were interpellated by the law, this book aims at exploring how certain contradictions in legal subjecthood emerged from the Revolutionary period and how, through the largely unwitting efforts of legislators and litigants, new notions of personality emerged that would become fundamental to modern capitalism as we know it.

Part One

A REVOLUTION IN COMMERCIAL PERSONHOOD

1

Hard Contracts and Hard Money

Honor, Commerce, and Debtors' Prison during the French Revolution

In the spring of 1797, the play *Appel à l'honneur ou Les remboursements en assignats* debuted on the stages of Paris. Set during the previous year, the play centered on the moral dilemma faced by a merchant named Deslandes who had to choose between paying back his creditors in *assignats*, the Revolution's increasingly worthless paper money, and risking bankruptcy when the Revolutionary government decided to completely demonetize the inflated currency. Torn between the prospects of financial disaster and personal dishonor, Deslandes unwisely opted for the latter. This choice provoked a rift with his wise and virtuous wife, who compared repayment in *assignats* to guillotining his creditors. Deslandes, however, argued that he could not be asked to bear "the entire weight of the Revolution's ravages" on his own financial shoulders.[1] The merchant soon reaped the consequences of his unethical decision. The entire town turned violently against him and his family, outraged by his "crime" in repaying with "paper without credit" all those who had trusted him.[2] His daughters were attacked in the streets. Suitably penitent, Deslandes at last heeded the advice of his wife, who demanded that the family sacrifice everything in order to repay their creditors in metallic currency. Insisting that "children and creditors are in the same family," Madame Deslandes affirmed that "when, by the force of events, a man is placed in the necessity of sacrificing either his lines of blood or his lines of honor, he holds the contract of trust even more sacred than that of nature."[3]

This play, based on the true story of a commercial house in Lyon, was only one of many similarly themed theatrical pieces written between 1795 and 1798 as French citizens struggled to make sense of the massive inflation wrought first by the *assignat* and then by a brief-lived successor currency, the *mandat territorial*. Like *Appel à l'honneur*, works such as *L'agioteur, Les modernes enrichis, Tout le monde s'en mêle ou la Manie du commerce*, and *Les parvenus aujourd'hui* possessed edifying as well as satirical elements, simultaneously depicting and inveighing against the social ills of speculation during the paper-money regime. Bitterly aware of the significant gap between behavior that was legal and behavior that was moral, these plays often invoked the Revolutionary rhetoric of duty and civic virtue to curtail excesses attributed to the Revolution itself. In *Appel à l'honneur*, these stern dictums were most clearly enunciated by Madame Deslandes, who upheld the sacrifice of familial ties for the greater national good and assimilated economic contracts between creditors and debtors to the social contract that maintains the polity. There was little subtlety in the play's message: the good citizen placed his duty to his country above religious and regional ties, even as a creditworthy economic agent placed contractual obligation above personal self-interest or familial well-being.

While Madame Deslandes's counsel triumphed on stage through pure persuasive power, legislators sought to compel borrowers to honor their engagements through more coercive means. Sharing Madame Deslandes's insistence on the need to sacrifice personal gain for the public good, and largely indifferent to the dire straits into which the government's own financial behavior had placed many borrowers, lawmakers invoked the necessity of reestablishing debt imprisonment, which had been abolished in March 1793, as a means of reining in the purported excesses of Revolutionary individualism run amok. Combining Revolutionary discourse on contract with invocations of honor that recalled the old regime, legislators hoped not only to restore trust in the circulation of hard currency after years of economic turmoil but also to burnish the Directory's own shaky image as defender of an emergent moderate republican order in the aftermath of political instability and terror.

For several decades now historians have debated the novelty of the French Revolution: did it mark a fundamental rupture with the old regime and the beginning of modernity? Generations of scholars throughout the nineteenth and twentieth centuries certainly believed this to be the case. For liberals, the French Revolution ushered in the age of human rights and democracy. For Marxists, it represented the bourgeoisie's overthrow of the decadent feudal aristocracy. However, revisionist scholars have argued that instead of breaking with the past the French Revolution accelerated the monarchy's tendency toward centralization of key institutions and structures. For these scholars, the Revolution marked a radical break not in material conditions but in discursive modes for describing them: in short, the idea of revolution itself was the real novelty. More recently, historians have sought a middle ground between these two extremes. This move has coincided with a turn away from the Reign of Terror to its previously little studied aftermath. In examining the Thermidorean Convention and the Directory, a period when Revolutionaries turned away from the discourse of a radical break and instead sought to create enduring republican institutions, scholars find evidence of a much more complicated interplay between novelty and continuity.

This chapter follows the fate of one institution, *contrainte par corps*, over the course of the eighteenth century. A long-established feature of old regime law, over the centuries the usage of *contrainte par corps* had gradually become identified with commercial activity. As such it played an important role in the debates about commerce and honor stirred by the burgeoning economy of the eighteenth century, and it found both critics and supporters among Enlightenment thinkers. During the early years of the Revolution, opinion swung decidedly toward the hostile side. Condemned as an abuse of the old regime, debt imprisonment was abolished by the National Convention in March 1793 only to be reestablished in 1797 as the desire to encourage the circulation of the newly reestablished metallic currency inspired the Directory to reestablish what it saw as the norms of the pre-Revolutionary marketplace. The case of debt imprisonment is particularly revelatory not just for what it can tell us about the nature of revolutionary change at the structural level, but also because of the relationship between discourses, notably surrounding commercial honor and credit, and the material realities of finance that coalesced in the debates surrounding the procedure.

Like so many other developments of the Directory and Empire, it might be easy to dismiss the reestablishment of debt imprisonment as a return to the old regime past, or at least what was believed to be the old regime past, rather than a foundational moment in a new order. The economic historians Philip Hoffman, Jean-Laurent Rosenthal, and Giles Postel-Vinay have noted that although the Revolution transformed French society in deep and lasting ways, it had little effect on legislation involving credit.[4] The form of debt imprisonment reestablished in 1798 closely resembled debt imprisonment as it had been practiced for a century preceding its abolition in 1793. Moreover, the broader cultural context of debt seems to show more continuity than rupture with its old regime past. Corroborating Clare Crowston's claim that credit continued to be used well into the nineteenth century to signify social, political, and economic forms of reciprocity and power, critiques both of debtors and of debt imprisonment bear striking resemblances across the Revolutionary divide.[5]

This is not to say, however, that the Revolution changed nothing. Rebecca Spang has suggested that credit reveals a narrative of this tumultuous era that departs from the linearity of either the traditional story of the Revolution as rupture or the revisionist account of linear continuity. She argues that the Revolutionary period followed a "dialectical logic, in which the so-called 'modern' emerges only haltingly and only through sustained conflict with the old."[6] The case of debt imprisonment bears out such an interpretation. While the laws put in place following the Revolution may have resembled those of the old regime, they were new in several important respects. Primarily, they systematized a patchwork of dispersed customs and regulations into a coherent national approach to creditor-debtor relationships, and they solidified an understanding of debt based on notions of contractual obligation. Revolutionary legislators cast themselves as crusaders against both the supposed evils of old regime credit, with its incestuous links to political power and its corrosive connection to luxury, and the excesses of Revolutionary disorder, allegedly the result of unfettered individualism. In using notions of the social contract to uphold the rights of lenders in commercial credit contracts, legislators also created an understanding of debt imprisonment with penal implications.

No term featured more prominently in this debate than "commercial honor." Honor first entered into discussions of mercantile activity in the decades preceding the Revolution when Enlightenment pamphleteers appropriated this traditionally aristocratic virtue as a means of extolling the superiority of "productive" classes, including merchants, over idle and parasitic ones. Although during the early years of the Revolution honor took a backseat to the patriotic notion of "virtue," by the Directory "honor" again became the trademark of the good merchant. On the practical side, legislators desperately sought anything that could revive the languishing institutions of commerce after a decade of Revolutionary upheaval had severely threatened the trust on which they were based. As James Livesey has shown, many figures in the Directory adhered strongly to a doctrine of "commercial republicanism" that sought to reconcile the stern asceticism of Revolutionary practice with an appreciation of the benefits of commerce.[7] The use of force to encourage trust in the circulation of money and, consequently, in public credit resembled actions taken by the British government one hundred years earlier when the death penalty had been utilized as a means of instilling faith in the newfangled innovations of the Financial Revolution.[8] "Commercial honor" was not merely about words, or even about morality: it was about the very tangible value of money. Yet in inscribing the rhetoric of honor within the Revolutionary discourse of the social contract, according to which those who violated the obligations of honor could be equated to those who violated their patriotic duties, the Revolutionaries would create an apparent similitude between punishment and detention for debt that persisted into the decades that followed.[9]

Commercial Honor and Commercial Debt before the Revolution

In 1748, a half century before *Appel à l'honneur ou Les remboursements en assignats* graced the stages of Paris, Charles Secondat, Baron de Montesquieu, authored *L'esprit des lois*, a book whose influence on the French Revolution has only recently been fully appreciated by historians.[10] The reflections Montesquieu offered in this work on the relationship between commerce, law, and honor prove a particularly useful place to begin a discussion of the changing meaning of debt imprisonment across the century of the French Revolution. In Book 20, dedicated to the intersections of commerce and the law, Montesquieu expressed his support for commercial debt imprisonment, using incarceration to show where commerce demanded a different law than that of "ordinary" affairs. He wrote: "In matters that derive from ordinary civil contracts, the law should not entail debt imprisonment; because in these the liberty of a citizen is more important than the ease or prosperity [*aisance*] of another. But, in relations deriving from commerce, the law should find the public wealth [*aisance publique*] more important than the liberty of a citizen."[11] Montesquieu's praise of commercial *contrainte par corps* as necessary for the efficient functioning of commerce mobilized certain terms—public and private, wealth and liberty—that played a central role in Enlightenment understandings of commerce. On one hand, he linked commerce with liberty and believed commerce to be best cultivated under republican forms of government. However, Montesquieu argued against this freedom as a liberty that extended to the individual *commerçant*. Rather, he stated that "the freedom of commerce is not a power granted to the commerçant to do what they please" and, conversely, that "the constraint of the *commerçant* is not the constraint of commerce." Such constraints existed because commerce's justification was its link to the public good, public wealth, and public credit. In the chapter that immediately followed his excerpt on debt imprisonment, Montesquieu praised the "law of Geneva," which excluded the sons of bankrupts from public office, adding that under such a regime "the credit of the individual has still all the weight of public credit."[12]

Despite the amount of attention that Montesquieu famously lavished on explaining the emotional cores of individuals under republican, monarchical, and despotic regimes, he devoted little time to the internal motivations of merchants. Indeed, merchants seemed equally difficult to reconcile with Montesquieu's definition of either republican or monarchical governments. Republics were defined by virtue, consisting of voluntary subordination of personal interest to the greater good of country. Monarchies, on the other hand, were dominated by the principle of honor, a much more complex passion that excited men to great acts serving the public good, but did so out of an ambition for preference and distinction rather than out of self-renunciation.[13] In place of either of these two principles, the merchant was guided only by his self-interest, which in turn explained much in the long history of commerce. As indicated by his harsh attitude toward commercial debts, Montesquieu believed that individual self-interest could not be trusted to protect commerce by itself. Rather, the liberty of commerce demanded restrictions on the freedom of the individual *commerçant*.

Although Montesquieu separated commerce from honor, he belonged to an ongoing discussion in which many of his interlocutors came to argue for a close connection between the two. The century or so before the French Revolution witnessed not only remarkable growth in trade and commerce but also the emergence of the economy as a distinct subject of philosophical investigation and political concern. Attempts to compete with international rivals such as England and the Netherlands led French monarchs to copy their designs by carving out a commercial empire in the Americas and India. Colonial expansion enabled the import of raw materials as well as increasing wealth from trade in commodities like sugar and coffee. Spurred by significant gains in agricultural productivity and fed by the profits of oversea trade, urban centers became much wealthier. An ever-expanding variety of goods, particularly luxury items such as clothing and furniture, reached a widening spectrum of French society. With the expansion of trade in the eighteenth century, finance became an increasingly prominent part of this credit economy. The circulation of paper credit, in the form of bills of exchange and promissory notes, funded commercial transactions, while the state sustained its debts by heavy reliance on *rentes*, annuities bought up by private buyers. An increasingly heterogeneous assortment of investors pooled money into these loans, convinced of the long-term stability of the social order on which they rested. The rise of state-chartered joint-stock companies like the Compagnie des Indes tied an expanding number of people into a credit economy at whose heart was the state itself.[14]

These developments coincided with and reflected new ideas about the place and value of commerce in French society. Attitudes toward commerce prior to the late seventeenth century had been generally negative. Commerce was despised in equal measure by a Christian tradition that saw in moneymaking the antithesis of morality and by an aristocratic code that prized martial valor, landed property, and idleness. State officials also worried about merchants' alleged tendency to deceit and fraud. Commerce, moreover, was traditionally considered an activity without honor, fit only for commoners. Nobility involved in commercial activity could be stripped of their title through the process of *dérogeance*.[15] As Amelia Kessler has argued, "Commerce, in sum, was widely understood to be a public hazard, and as such it was appropriately the subject of public law—both administrative and criminal."[16] Even when commerce was looked on favorably, for example in the great mercantilist efforts of the early seventeenth century, it was glorified as an arm of the state. Not only did the police carefully monitor commercial activity in major urban areas, but guilds also effectively designated the boundaries of who could enter into commerce.

The valorization of commerce as a productive, useful, and even honorable activity, by contrast, became a defining feature of the Enlightenment. Albert Hirschman attributed this reassessment of the nature of commerce to the attempts of philosophers to create a stable social order by playing off the "interests" against "the passions." For these thinkers, so-called *doux commerce* (soft or gentle commerce) promoted peaceful and rational virtues linked to self-interest, which countervailed against man's other destructive tendencies. While not as traditionally manly or glorious as the bellicose desire for war linked to the feudal nobility, commerce had the virtue of suppressing the unruly passions of glory and pride that had wreaked havoc on Europe during the previous centuries.[17] The doctrine of *doux commerce*, perhaps best articulated in the writings of Montesquieu himself, valued commerce because of its public utility; by keeping men away from conflict and promoting general public prosperity, a *commerçant*, although individually guided by self-interest, nevertheless ultimately served the public good.

Montesquieu, as we have seen, did not associate commerce with honor, which for him largely retained its aristocratic connotations. However, commerce lay at the center of a certain middle-class sensibility that reimagined nobility based on the practical or utilitarian benefits of commerce to invert the traditional ordering of honorable and dishonorable. In his famous 1675 manual for commercial trades, *Le parfait négociant*, Jacques Savary provided an image of the ideal merchant far removed from the self-interested money-obsessed stereotype. In the decades that followed, other writers would expand on and sharpen his version of mercantile virtues. In 1757 Abbé Gabriel François Coyer authored a pamphlet entitled *Développement et défense du système de la noblesse commerçante*, which instigated a decades-long pamphlet war between those, like Coyer, who advocated expanding the role of the nobility in commercial activity and those who believed commercial values remained at odds with the traditional values of nobility. In arguing for the *noblesse commerçante*, meaning the aristocracy's right and even duty to participate in business ventures, Coyer simultaneously extolled the nobility inherent in these values. For Coyer and the pamphleteers on his side, honor belonged not to the traditional nobility, depicted as parasitic and idle wastrels contributing nothing to the national wealth, but rather to those who were useful and productive to society at large. Coyer's use of the word "honor," which in Montesquieu had been connected with martial exploits and opposed to the patient calculation of self-interest, marked a fundamental change in the meaning of the term. Coyer described the merchant's honor as being of another register completely from that of the warrior. It constituted an "other, less brilliant honor that consists of the knowledge of needs, the perfection of arts, application, economy, probity, public credit, enterprises that are useful to the state."[18] As opposed to aristocratic honor, which served only the interests of the individuals and families who possessed it, the less glamorous commercial honor, premised on self-interest, in fact served the interests of the state.

Coyer notably emphasized the relationship between credit and public credit and the good of the state. Ultimately, merchants became honorable by their acts that contributed to the general good. On the surface self-interested, they in fact contributed more to the public interest than those motivated by the desire for distinctions of rank and glory. To quote John Shovlin, in the writings of Coyer and others, "the merchant, long condemned as a selfish calculator, incapable of patriotism, increasingly emerged as a servant of the public welfare engaged not so much in profit-seeking as in the management of an important sector of the national interest."[19] Although the merchant's honor differed from military honor, advocates of *noblesse commerçante* frequently compared merchants to soldiers: both performed an honorable public duty, but both too were subject to stiffer penalties than their civilian counterparts when they failed to execute such obligations.[20]

Debt imprisonment epitomized this type of stiff penalty. However, as thinkers' opinions of commerce generally increased, the place of *contrainte par corps* in relation to commercial activity aroused greater ambivalence. Did the prospect of incarceration provide a crucial restraint on merchants, whose unfettered self-interest might otherwise lead them to cheat their creditors? Did it preserve commercial honor by only clearing the marketplace of those whose failure to meet engagements betokened bad faith? Or was it instead based on antiquated suspicions about commerce that ran counter to true commercial honor? The first published debate on the morality of *contrainte par corps*, unsurprisingly, was fought in terms of the *noblesse commerçante*. The debate, as Thomas Luckett has discussed, took place in 1760 in the pages of the *Journal de Commerce at de l'Agriculture*, a Brussels-based publication that catered to merchants, wholesalers, and political economists. In it, one writer, defending the debtors' prison, explained that "honor associates badly in the heart with interest, and interest, as you know, is the foremost divinity of the *commerçant*."[21] His opponent, meanwhile, insisted that honor and interest were not directly opposed in commerce because honor formed "the base and the solid foundation of the public confidence in the paper money that commerce circulates and reproduces endlessly" and "which is so deeply linked to his credit that one cannot interest one without the other nor attack honor without impacting credit."[22] Since any self-interested merchant could not hope to succeed in his affairs without credit, the writer insisted that interest and honor were in fact interchangeable for the merchant for whom honor was "more important . . . than life."[23] As with Coyer's explanation of honor, this anonymous critic of *contrainte par corps* linked self-interest and honor and showed how this constellation itself, rather than the threat of imprisonment, would encourage merchants to pay their debts.

Subsequent eighteenth-century attacks on debt imprisonment touched on related questions about the place of commerce in French society and the relationship between economic interest and commercial morality. In his 1788 pamphlet *Abus et dangers de la contrainte par corps*, Claude Gaspard Barbat du Closel d'Arnery, who styled himself a squire and who had already gained some notoriety as a minor Enlightenment thinker, focused not on whether debt imprisonment affirmed commercial honor, but rather on how it allegedly allowed a new class of self-interested merchants to effectively usurp the honorable place in society previously accorded to noble families. Although Closel d'Arnery also briefly decried other uses of debt imprisonment, such as the incarceration of indigent fathers for their inability to pay wet nurses and down-at-heel tenant farmers who could not meet the terms of their sharecropping agreements, he mainly desired to "show the evils that result from this condemnation when it is pronounced against bourgeois and gentlemen."[24] In his eyes, the greatest tragedy of *contrainte par corps* was that it encouraged young men from good families to effectively mortgage their patrimony for pleasure pursued at any price.

In *Abus et dangers de la contrainte par corps*, debt imprisonment essentially pitted landed property against money, much to the detriment of the former. Closel d'Arnery melodramatically bemoaned how the "zeal" exhibited by "our fathers for the transmission of hereditary goods" had been replaced by a new social order dominated by "new parvenus [who] owe their criminal opulence only to their abjection, their baseness, their depravity" in robbing the "sons of good families."[25] Clearly supportive of what he deemed to be legitimate commercial activity, Closel d'Arnery distinguished good and bad forms of commerce. Good commerce served the public interest. Bad commerce, on the other hand, served only the interests of a few corrupt individuals. Under bad commerce, the only type to utilize *contrainte par corps*, "even the most useful money becomes dangerous."[26] Closel d'Arnery's fears that young men were gambling their land and patrimony in usurious deals suggested a widely held anxiety that the rise of commerce had entailed a reconfiguration of the traditional balance of power between the two basic forms of property recognized by French property law: movable and immovable property.[27] These terms depended as much on cultural constructions regarding what types of property provided stability as they did on whether a given item could be physically moved.[28] Merchandise and money, for example, might be considered movable property and land and buildings immovable, but there were exceptions that defy any easy distinction based on what can actually move. *Rentes* were annuities, but were considered immovable. The political economist Anne-Marie Turgot identified even houses as movable property. Writers like Closel d'Arnery thought of immovable properties differently: they were linked to notions of solidity, family lineage, and permanence and ultimately related back to the quintessential form of immovable property: land. Immovable property, then, formed the basis of aristocratic society.

By contrast, movable property presented a troubling collection of practical and philosophical problems. First, there was its sheer mobility. Access to information was local and dispersed, and the whereabouts of money, furniture, or bills of exchange was often hard to ascertain. Indeed Antoine Furètiere's frequently cited dictionary of the time even defined mobile property precisely on the basis of its ability to be hidden or diverted.[29] Because mobile property possessed this capacity to flee, it also worried those who saw property as a hallmark of membership in the polity, including Turgot, who feared that those who held great stores of movable wealth held no land dear to their heart, possessed no constraint on where they would live, and, perhaps more urgently, could avoid taxation.[30] For Closel d'Arnery, debt imprisonment allowed those whose wealth rested primarily in landed inheritance to cede their fortunes to a new class of "parvenus" who built their wealth instead on movable property, namely, money itself. This prospect would sound the death knell of the upper class.

How had it come to pass that debt imprisonment permitted immovable property to be held hostage to movable property? Closel d'Arnery blamed the "murderous facility provided by the bill of exchange" for the plight of the nobility. Here too he reflected contemporary anxieties about commerce.[31] By the mid-eighteenth century, many shared d'Arnery's belief that the increased prominence of negotiable instruments such as the bill of exchange had begun to challenge a commercial order based on trust and close personal connections.[32] The bill of exchange, a form of IOU featuring a value giver, drawee, drawer, and beneficiary, could be transferred as payment for a debt between parties who might not know each other by means of a simple endorsement. When the bill fell due, the holder, would go to the drawee to obtain payment for the bill. Although these bills had evolved in the Middle Ages as a means by which merchants could undertake transactions in different cities through agents, by the eighteenth century the practice of transferring the bills through endorsement and of negotiating these bills, through discount, had increased the anonymity with which the signatories treated each other and the possibility for bad faith. They also might serve as covers for circumventing official prohibitions on usury laws. Closel d'Arnery spoke harshly of their use, claiming that "honest merchants" did not rely on bills of exchange. In signing a bill of exchange, he proclaimed, "men of all ranks and estates prostitute their fortunes, names, blood, and duties" to borrow money.[33] By using the word "prostitute," Closel d'Arnery connected *contrainte par corps* with an illicit sale of the body that damaged the honor of those who participated.

Lastly, Closel d'Arnery believed that the money borrowed by these young men from usurers was intended for "vice, luxury and debauchery." Far from being useful or necessary transactions, these deals allowed access to "easy credit" for illicit and immoral purposes.[34] D'Arnery's complaint echoed the charges leveled by critics of the supposedly degrading and immoral effects of luxury on commercial activity. By the 1780s writers habitually mobilized such charges to defend "true commerce" against a decadent and unholy alliance of financiers and aristocrats.[35] Indeed, on the eve of the Revolution, credit, exemplified by the yawning deficits of the French monarchy and the lavish expenses of aristocratic elites on luxury consumer items, appeared the quintessential embodiment of all the dangers of commercial society. French thinkers saw in the burgeoning of public debt and the expansion of the modern fiscal state an ominous tool of despotism.[36] They associated credit not only with the accumulation of luxury goods, which in turn were often connected to feminine consumption, but also with the porous boundary between gift exchange and power relations. Credit allegedly compromised the independence of the property owner, viewed by many republican thinkers as the ideal citizen. In place of a solid republican community, credit presented the dangerous possibility of an unstable imagination attached to visions of unlimited, but ultimately fictitious, wealth.[37] While d'Arnery's attitude toward the aristocracy appeared much more sympathetic, he shared the contemporary critique of credit as a corrupting and destructive force.

By the eve of the Revolution, multiple understandings of commerce, credit, honor, and movable property circulated throughout French society.

From political theorists to the merchants in the commercial courts who adjudicated conflicts over negotiable instruments, contemporaries emphasized the adherence to codes of honor as a means of mitigating the dangers posed by commerce, credit, and movable property. Merchants, they argued, could not be guided merely by their self-interest. Rather, they relied on codes of honor to create trust, which in turn allowed them to gain credit in the marketplace. Even if writers increasingly agreed on the honorability of commercial activity, they disagreed over the relationship of debt imprisonment to this code of honor. Some believed that *contrainte par corps* protected commercial honor by maintaining public trust in the speedy and fair operation of commerce and by punishing those merchants who failed to uphold their engagements. For merchants, debt imprisonment presented a practical means of minimizing the dangers posed by the fleeting and transitory nature of movable property. Yet by 1789 critics had also begun to attack it on the very grounds that it was too deeply imbricated in allegedly corrupt configurations of social and economic credit and did not serve the productive needs of commerce. They claimed that rather than promoting commercial honor, the debtors' prison presented a threat of coercion that undermined commerce's moral legitimacy, which was based on its link to free contractual agreement and peaceful civilization. Moreover, in practice, commerce did not rely on the threat of force to instill trust in its paper money, but on the good character of its merchants. This type of honor served as the foundation for private business and public credit.

Debt in Revolution

The French Revolution was, in certain respects, all about credit. It infamously began with the lurching deficits of the monarchy and the impending threat of royal bankruptcy. Its subsequent course was in large part directed by the desire of successive Revolutionary governments to avoid what Honoré Gabriel Riqueti, comte de Mirabeau, famously referred to as "the hideous bankruptcy," namely, default on the monarchy's old debts. Indeed, on the portentous day of July 13, 1789, the National Assembly pledged to "never pronounce the infamous word, *bankruptcy*."[38] The Revolutionaries proclaimed their fiscal as well as their moral divergence from the allegedly despotic past government by their unwillingness to deny the debts incurred by this government. Upholding its abstract commitment to property ownership, the Revolutionary government of 1789 would take on substantial additional debt to compensate former venal officeholders and beneficiaries of feudal rights for the property to which they had been legally entitled.

Yet despite proclaiming property rights sacred to the social contract, the Revolutionaries failed to settle the disputes concerning the possibilities and dangers of credit and commerce that had emerged in the later years of the monarchy. For many Revolutionaries, credit not only represented the lingering burden of past deficits on revolutionary action but could also constitute a force serving public good and private morality. As one legislator declared during the initial debate on the printing of the *assignat*, "The King's debt, which will become the Nation's, will henceforth have for its pledge the honor and loyalty of the nation itself and will be overseen by its representatives, the holders and trustees of the sacred treasure of the public faith."[39] Debt tied citizens to each other and the body of citizens to the national whole. The Revolutionaries imagined that the basis for lending between private citizens would also foster public-minded virtue and good character and replace borrowing that had been based on what Louis Sébastien Mercier termed the "feudal concept of honor."[40] Old regime credit built on dense networks of social knowledge and influence would be replaced by virtuous credit, serving the productive needs of the nation and accorded on the basis of merit and civic values. Indeed, Revolutionary governments from the Feuillants through the Girondins and the Montagnards were united by a belief in the capacity of supposedly natural markets to rejuvenate national character. Abbé Goutes, justifying the abolition of old regime usury laws in October 1789 (to which he had previously dedicated a similarly progressive work in 1780), went so far as to proclaim that "when two men deal with each other, to their mutual advantage and without hurting anyone, it is impossible that they sin."[41]

The National Assembly's decision to repeal old regime restrictions on usury reflected Revolutionary attitudes toward money more generally. Decriminalizing the money trade contravened centuries of secular and canonical regulation, yet the entire debate proved remarkably tame. Lending at interest was, after all, quite common despite the official interdiction. As one deputy remarked, everyone knew that moneylenders extended their loans to the Catholic Church itself.[42] More broadly, decriminalizing interest on short-term loans reflected the deputies' broadly shared belief in the virtue of nature and those activities supposedly based in nature. Free trade in all merchandise, whose price would be determined by the supposedly natural fluctuation of supply and demand, formed an integral part of this ideology. The deputies perceived what they were doing not as a revolutionary act but as a restoration of the natural economic order. In their eyes, "not law but nature made money something to be bought and sold."[43] The Revolutionaries' faith in the "meeting of free wills" in voluntary private contracts enshrined an idea of the rational self-disciplined economic actor at the expense, as Judith Miller has argued, of concerns about contractual equity.[44] Credit based in the processes of economic exchange itself, no longer embedded in networks of political power and social obligation, would ensure not only the purity of economic exchange but also the virtue of the state based on the sacred cornerstone of contractual obligation.

These attempts to refashion credit into a tool of civic virtue met their most dramatic test in the very instrument created to uphold public credit: the *assignat*. The *assignat* had initially been developed in 1790 as a bond payment on land confiscated from the church (and, subsequently, émigré aristocrats). However, it quickly replaced paper money as the debts and obligations of the struggling Revolutionary government mounted and the supply of metallic currency drained rapidly from the country. As Rebecca Spang has argued, the creation of this paper money presented a case study in irony. Unwilling to default on the king's debt, an action they associated with the excesses of despotism, the French Revolutionaries ended up absorbing the financial burden of the past even as their rhetoric promised the beginning of the new era. Revolutionary legislators had not embraced the *assignat* because it promised to be a radical new experiment, but rather the opposite: its firm attachment to land, deemed to be more "real" than the illusory value of money, promised to instill trust backed by tangible objects rather than the fictional promises of credit. Yet trust, as the *assignat*'s history showed quite clearly, proved much more difficult to instill, particularly in the chaotic context of the early 1790s. The uncertainty engendered by rapid regime changes stripped the *assignat* of its value at an alarming rate. Even as the government began to rely on the paper as its primary form of currency, slow inflation began in 1792, which was followed by substantial depreciation by early 1793.

Throughout this period, the Assembly and then the Convention stuck to a hard-line policy by which money was to be considered a type of merchandise like any other. Adherents to a free trade ideology that markets emanated from natural law rather than the actions of governments, the Revolutionaries more or less agreed that commercial virtue was best protected through thorough deregulation. On the streets, however, common people felt differently. As early as 1791, many tradesmen were refusing to grant credit given their fears about the depreciation of the principle, shipments of gold and silver were routinely intercepted in quest of "true money," and lenders were frequently subjected to violence from crowds of angry customers. From fall 1793 through summer 1794, the National Convention, dominated by the radical Montagnards, deviated from their previously unwavering adherence to a doctrine of free trade in money as a means of producing a creditworthy citizenry and rejuvenated polity. Pressed by their main constituency, the Parisian *sans-culottes*, the Montagnard government passed an increasingly emphatic series of laws intended to artificially uphold the plummeting currency. The *assignat* became the only legal tender, and hoarders, counterfeiters, and those who used other specie were subject to the death penalty.[45] In addition, lawmakers imposed the Maximum to cap the price of staple goods as well as wages.

During this period, lawmakers continued to insist upon a firm relationship between credit and virtue. Credit was to be made an explicit tool of the state to indoctrinate its members with republican values. In 1793 Minister of Finance Pierre-Joseph Cambon, who had proposed a written record of all the state's outstanding debts commonly referred to as the Great Book, further elaborated on this logic, explaining the effort not only as a financial expedient to improve the government's solvency but as a means of forming better citizens.[46] Debt, he argued, could forge new political loyalties. With a clean and regular accounting system, "the capitalist, who desires a king, because he has a king for debtor, and because he fears of losing his debt if the debtor is not reestablished, desiring the Republic, which will have become the debtor, because the capitalist will fear losing his capital in losing the Republic."[47] Whereas under the old regime credit had formed chains of dependency based on social hierarchy, under the new regime credit encouraged loyalty even from the most self-interested citizens.

From the early days of the Revolution, critics had attacked debt imprisonment as a process that corrupted and perverted the virtuous power of credit and submitted debtors to the tyranny of private whim. *Contrainte par corps* had appeared several times as an "abuse" in the *cahiers de doléance*—the lists of grievances submitted to the king by the French people before the convocation of the Estates-General in 1789.[48] The debtors' prisons had been an initial focus of attacks by the Parisian populace, who saw in them a vivid abuse of arbitrary power. During the tumultuous days immediately preceding the fall of the Bastille in July 1789 and the September Massacres of 1792, the Parisian populace had freed imprisoned debtors and thereby saved them from the fate awaiting their criminal counterparts.[49] Critics also found debt imprisonment incompatible with the new penal code of 1791, which identified prison as a fitting penalty for crime rather than as a place of detainment. Louis-Michel le Peletier de Saint-Fargeau, the code's guiding light, connected the loss of liberty through imprisonment with punishment for crime, saying that "one of the most ardent desires of man is to be free: the loss of his liberty will be the first quality of his punishment."[50] Moreover, each loss of liberty envisioned by the new code would force the criminal to work during his confinement to regain virtue in society.

Given this new emphasis on the prison as a place for work and rehabilitation as well as its increasing use as a place of a detention for enemies of the state, debtors seemed an egregious anomaly. In March 1793, during the course of a multiday debate that would more famously result in the formation of the earliest Revolutionary Tribunals intended to expedite the conviction of the nation's enemies, the National Convention voted by acclamation to end *contrainte par corps*. Considered by Georges-Jacques Danton to be "a shame for humanity and for philosophy that a man, in borrowing money, should mortgage his person and his safety," debt imprisonment emerged in Revolutionary rhetoric as a form of unnatural government intrusion into the private economic relationship between creditors and debtor. In separating the prison, as a public place of detainment, from the economic realm, members of the National Convention viewed debt imprisonment as perhaps just as problematically incompatible with the prison's new dedication to the punitive detention of so-called enemies of the fatherland.[51]

The fall of Robespierre in July of 1794 marked the return of what Rebecca Spang has termed a doctrine of "monetary freedom" and set in motion a chain of political and economic events that would ultimately inspire the reestablishment of debtors' prisons. In November 1794 the Thermidorean Convention abolished the Maximum, which had been widely ignored for several months. They returned instead to the insistence on the free trade in money whose value, being intrinsic, would presumably adjust to its natural price once laws impeding market transactions were removed. In 1795 the partial return to metallic currency combined with the Directory's massive printing of paper money provoked a staggering depreciation of the *assignat*. "The *assignat*, after saving the State, has lost it," declared the minister of finance, Vincent-Nougant Ramel.[52] By January 1796 the *assignat* had reached less than half a percent of its nominal value. Yet, as Ramel also noted, it was not easy to change "from paper which everyone despises, to metal currency which no one wants to give away."[53] The ceremonial burning of the *assignat* matrices in February 1796 did not signal an immediate return to hard money, since the amount in circulation was too small to compensate for the over 45 billion in *assignats* that had been in circulation.[54] For a period in 1796, the Directorial government issued a new land-backed paper money called the territorial draft or *mandat territorial*, promising that unlike the "fictional" value of the *assignat*, the drafts, backed by real land, would avoid depreciation.[55] Public confidence being at a nadir, the territorial draft soon followed the same fate as the *assignat*.

The depreciation of the *assignat* left intense and widespread suffering in its wake. Moreover, it exacerbated and reflected a nearly complete breakdown in social order. Nevertheless, many individual citizens profited from the *assignat*'s decline, and their completely legal but nevertheless universally despised behavior became symbolic of the corruption of the Directory itself. While most lenders and borrowers had initially believed that the *assignat* would be quickly replaced by a return to silver, as depreciation continued, only the most naive of debtors failed to take the opportunity to renegotiate pre-1790 debts in *assignat*. *Assignat* holders, on the other hand, offloaded their increasingly dubious paper money to borrowers, hoping that such debts would not be canceled out when stability returned to the nation's finances. Although borrowers must have been aware that their reputation—and hence their future ability to obtain credit—would be negatively affected if they took advantage of the rapid depreciation at the expense of lenders, as time went on such behavior became so widespread that this fear appears to have become irrelevant.

Once the bans on hard currency had been lifted, the scarcity of hard cash coupled with its value compelled many city dwellers to take advantage of the newly liberalized economy. The abolition of the guild system removed entry barriers to the many commercial and artisanal métiers, which had once been strictly controlled by corporate regulations.[56] Although concerns regarding the weakening of corporate control over workers dated far back into the days of the monarchy, the proliferation of commerce during the *assignat* period alarmed many observers. The struggles endured by small merchants and artisans in their efforts to make the *assignat*, issued in large and therefore impractical denominations, work for everyday transactions had further eroded the divisions previously enforced by corporatism.[57] With the return of metal coin, the hope of gaining currency through the sale of commodities motivated people from all walks of life to open up shops selling whatever they could, demanding metal in exchange.[58] Some bankers switched to using provisions as a stock instead of money, a trick that worked well as the price of food spiraled.[59] One poet quipped that "the fury of stockjobbing has transformed the people: the shoemaker sells string and the hairdresser cheeses."[60] Private residences transformed into makeshift boutiques. "On whatever side you turn your steps," wrote Sébastien Mercier, "you see the permanent fair of Paris, where traders are niched in the smallest holes possible."[61] With the price of staples already high, the cities were sellers' markets. Vendors demanded payment in hard cash from desperate consumers. Police reports testify to a veritable war between merchants and buyers, including ad hoc attacks against merchants who refused paper money. Legislators claimed that there were ten times more merchants and ten times less merchandise than before the Revolution.

As the value of paper money plummeted, the Directory's two legislative bodies, the Council of Elders and the Council of Five Hundred, passed laws by turns suppressing and then reinstating payments of debts, hoping to crack down on the debtors who deliberately profited from the plummeting value of paper currency in order to bilk their creditors. This continual legislative reworking of contracts disturbed lenders and borrowers alike. Some found themselves ruined as much by contract renegotiations as by devaluation, while those who were savvier, or less ethical, like Monsieur Deslandes in Appel à l'honneur, reaped sizable profits from speculation.[62] Both creditors and debtors besieged the government with petitions hoping to rectify the perceived injustice of their situations. Debtors, reflected one writer, "aren't demanding a simple reduction of their debts anymore from their creditors, it is all they owe that they want to make their creditors lose, they believe themselves entitled to justify all losses in saying that it is the discredit of the *assignats* that has caused their ruin."[63] Furthermore, the Directory's attempts to negotiate a revised payment scale based on the depreciation of the *assignat* were hampered by political as well as technical difficulties.[64]

Even while renegotiating private contracts, the government also attempted to solve the problems created by inflation by further liberalizing the trade in money. Overturning previous legislation passed in April 1793, in July 1795 the Directory abandoned caps on interest rates.[65] When it came to lending and borrowing money, declared the Directory, "every citizen is allowed to engage himself as he sees fit."[66] There was also money to be made in speculating on the declining currency, especially with the reintroduction of coin. In places like Paris's Palais Royal, speculators traded in paper currency, briefly provoking the closure of the stock market, the Bourse, in 1795.[67] The lifting of the ban on lending on interest was coupled with another development: the end of the official monopoly on pawnbroking previously held by the Mont-de-Piété. Believing that a free market in lending would help lower the interest rates more generally, the legislators shuttered the Paris Mont-de-Piété in 1796. When it was reinstated a few months later, the municipal pawnshop was forced to compete for clientele with increasingly voracious private lenders.

The dismantling of the Mont-de-Piété's monopoly coupled with the deregulation of interest led to an effervescence in the capital's pawnbroking industry. According to Parisian police, twenty or twenty-five pawnshops sprang up in Paris in 1796 and 1797, and by 1798 there were at least sixty-five pawnshops in the capital.[68] Even these numbers underestimated the amount of pawnbroking, given that many other businesses ran unofficial lending practices on the side. Interest rates at such places could be steep.[69] While commentators partially blamed Revolutionary immorality for the rise of these bill discounters, pawnbrokers, and moneylenders, observers also understood the risk these individuals ran in making their loans.[70] By April of 1797, many government officials had become convinced that an official monopoly on pawnbroking needed to be restored and interest rates capped again.[71] However, few thought such measures would eradicate the root of the credit market's problems. Distrust and self-seeking behavior, it seemed, were everywhere. The observant diarist Mallet du Pan wrote that there was "scarcely one fortune in a hundred which was not one by villainy or crime; scarcely one fortune in a hundred which has six months of solidity."[72] Commerce, noted one merchant, had become no more than a type of "brigandage."[73] The Revolutionary experiment in connecting credit more closely to virtue by supposedly freeing it from the restrictions of the state and the power of corrupting social bonds had failed. Having lost its honor, commerce had also lost public credit.

Both the government and the commercial community began to actively seek means of restoring confidence. On December 26, 1796, only weeks before the official demonetization of the *mandats territoriaux*, the ministers of finance and the interior conveyed a meeting of "extraordinary deputies of commerce," delegates elected from business communities in major French towns. The very term "extraordinary deputies" evoked the old regime practice of meeting with delegates from the country's commercial elite. The ministers assured the hesitant delegates that the government was above all concerned with putting commerce back on its feet after a period of what was euphemistically termed "violent crisis." However, "left to its own wisdom," they added deferentially, the government "would certainly commit errors."[74] Although the ministers invited the delegates to voice their thoughts on how to revive French commerce in the aftermath of the return of monetary currency, their main concern was more directly tied with the finances of the government itself: the ministers sought the approval of the commercial community in founding a national bank.[75]

The merchants, whose opinion was articulated by Jean-Baptiste Dubois, supported the free trade in money and distrusted government intervention in the economy. Dubois maintained that lending at interest, determined by convention rather than law, was "most necessary to the perfectibility of society and the growth of wealth, to the development of productive forces because it is the way by which industrious men can exploit to the best advantage the capital that would have remained idle in the hands of others."[76] A credit market free of legal restrictions and religious dogma had not inspired the financial crisis, which he attributed instead to the "force of circumstances" and, more precisely, to the government's monetary mismanagement. Dubois particularly detested the periodic meddling with private credit contracts, which, he argued, did more than erode business confidence. Rather, such intervention imperiled the essence of contract, the very organizing tenet of a free and virtuous society for Dubois as for most Revolutionaries.

Dubois wrote that "the first effect of such an abusive intervention is to enrich the debtor at the expense of the creditor, to substitute disloyalty for good faith, vice for virtue, and to quickly introduce the most unbridled corruption and the most revolting immorality into all classes of society."[77] Dubois claimed that this attack on contractual sanctity between creditor and debtor was closely connected to another: the 1793 abolition of *contrainte par corps*.[78] Without this surety against the malfeasance of debtors, he warned, "the very word 'bank' strikes Terror" into French hearts.[79] The capitalization of "Terror," linking financial devastation with the "despotism" of Robespierre, was hardly accidental. Dubois quickly proceeded to recall past "abuses of such power," including the Caisse d'Escompte and the Compagnie des Indes, which, "concentrating the property of many citizens in a small group of powerful and corruptible hands" had "devastated private fortunes and assaulted public credit."[80] He continued that the *mandats*, "the latest attack on property rights," allowed debtors to "pillage their creditors under the very sacred name of the law itself." Given that "credit is the soul base of its [a bank's] prosperity" and relied on "the morality of a debtor, the recognition of his facilities, the prudence of his enterprises, the state of legislation that protects and guarantees his property," Dubois argued on behalf of the deputies that the reestablishment of credit necessary for a bank rested on the reestablishment of debt imprisonment.[81]

The extraordinary deputies were not alone in calling for reestablishment. For the tradesmen and small shopkeepers who made up the municipal sections of Paris, the reinstatement of debtors' prison formed part of a vision of a renewed moral economy in which shifty speculators and con artists would be punished. On May 22, 1795, the Parisian section of Bonconseil had urged the Convention to respect property rights in its desire to restore government credit. It demanded the reestablishment of debt imprisonment, labeling it "the only guarantee of the honest man against thieves and bankrupts."[82] A few months later, a delegation from Bonne Nouvelle echoed this complaint, encouraging the reestablishment of debt imprisonment rather than the establishment of a business tax (the *patente)* as a means of distinguishing honest from dishonest businessmen.[83]

Even as initial discussion began about bringing back debt imprisonment against private debtors, the government itself defaulted on its debts. Over the course of the Revolution, indemnities, confiscations of property, and the forced loan (a tax aggressively levied on the wealthier part of the population to fund the war in December 1795) had meant that the government stood as debtor to many of its private citizens.[84] Many observers juxtaposed the government's relationship to its creditors to transactions between private debtors and creditors. The writer and businessman François d'Ivernois compared the government's reliance on paper money to a merchant's reliance on credit: "The *assignats* issued were but bills of exchange, drawn on the Revolutionary Tribunal and paid by the Guillotine, which Robespierre is said to have called 'an engine for making money.'"[85] The fiscal situation of the French state worsened so precipitously during these years that in September 1797, having purged grumbling royalists through a coup, the government itself effectively defaulted with the so-called bankruptcy of the two-thirds. By reimbursing *rentes* and state debts at two-thirds of their value in treasury bonds and consolidating the rest, the Directory reduced the deficit to 67 million francs from 250 million francs the year before.[86]

This process predictably provoked much unhappiness as well as accusations of hypocrisy from the state's creditors. One petitioner wrote that, were debtors' prison reinstated, "20,000 or 30,000 unfortunates" would be forced to flee the country to escape from the predatory grasp of "stockjobbers, so-called men of law."[87] Another pamphleteer, directly addressing the merchants who had made the reinstatement of *contrainte par corps* their "conditio sine qua non" for a national bank, asked them to remember the desperate plight of many of the state's own creditors. "You would want to punish with prison the unfortunate man who squirms below the forced delays that the government brings in liquidating its debt?"[88] he asked, adding that certainly the debt owed to private citizens by a republican government was "just as sacred" as debts made between two merchants.[89]

The debate around the reestablishment of *contrainte par corps* unfolded in two parts at the legislative level. The stakes for each part were slightly different. On February 24, 1797, Jean-Antoine-Joseph Debry presented to the Council of Five Hundred a motion for the reestablishment of debt imprisonment.[90] This debate was intentionally brief; the need to pass the bill was deemed sufficiently "urgent" to steer it quickly to the Council of Ancients, where it was also quickly approved.[91] Although this bill officially reestablished *contrainte par corps*, it furnished few guidelines about what the practice might look like in a legal landscape radically reformed by Revolution. A second law in 1798 ushered in an unprecedented nationwide centralization of the process with substantial protections for debtors (including prohibitions against arresting debtors while at home or during holidays).

On the whole, however, the debate does not seem to have pitted the left against the right, as other scholars have described in contemporaneous debates concerning debt legislation.[92] Nor did it break down evenly on the subject of free trade and the role of the state in the economy. Pierre Samuel Dupont de Nemours, who spent his youth befriending the likes of

Turgot and made his name popularizing physiocratic ideas, was undoubtedly one of the most indefatigable opponents of *contrainte par corps* in the Council of Five Hundred. But he found a vocal opponent in Jacques Antoine Creuzé-Latouche, well known for his opposition in the Convention to the regulation of the grain trade. Debry himself had supported a heavy progressive tax on luxuries and the creation of government workshops to help the poor only a few years earlier. Indeed, while legislators discussed *contrainte par corps* in painstaking detail in debates that continued for weeks in 1798, deputies across the political spectrum almost universally approved of the measure. The only scholarly account of the debates has argued that they were based on a fundamental error concerning the nature of eighteenth-century debt relations: namely, they saw debtors and creditors as two different classes rather than understanding the complex realities whereby debtors were often simultaneously creditors and vice versa.[93] Yet the members of the Council of Ancients and the Council of Five Hundred appear neither naive nor overtly partisan. Their central disagreement involved the meaning of commerce rather than its class implications.

The commission charged with studying Debry's proposal, which consisted of an impressive selection of men who would later spearhead Napoleon's efforts to codify French law, including Jean-Baptiste Treilhard, Jean-Jacques Régis de Cambacérès, and Emmanuel Pastoret, presented a report couching the argument for reestablishment in terms of property rights and the value of commerce. While the deputies considered themselves faithful champions of property, the meaning of "property" remained problematic.[94] In the debates that followed the commission's report, proponents of *contrainte par corps* for commercial debt argued for a fundamental distinction between commercial and noncommercial (often called "civil") life based on the kind of property involved. In civil life, property was relatively stable—which meant predominantly land based. However, in commercial life, they explained, "goods are mobile and, in a manner of speaking, fleeting."[95] Movable and immovable property, which deserved equal protection as the "base of the social order," demanded different kinds of securities. Immovable property was stationary: if an individual failed to pay a mortgage, one took the property he had pledged. Movable property, however, was trickier. A merchant who failed to pay a debt he had made on a bill of exchange might, in fact, have no property to seize. With nothing else to offer, a businessman pledged his name and his reputation when he took out a loan. Advocates of *contrainte par corps* believed that the person of the debtor who had made such promises should be held as collateral when a debt was defaulted. Even as legislators debated the virtues of establishing a national mortgage registry to better secure rights to immovable objects, movable property demanded the protection of *contrainte par corps*.

By providing security for movable property, legislators aimed at reviving the moribund state of commerce. They praised mercantile activity and distanced themselves from the suspicious attitude toward mercantile activity that they associated with Robespierre and the Terror. "We no longer live in the time where we praise ancient Sparta," proclaimed Creuzé-Latouche, articulating the common support of commercial activity.[96] For Pierre-Nicholas Perrée-Duhamel, one of the few men involved in the debate who had any actual business experience (before the Revolution, he had been a prosperous ship outfitter in Normandy), the abolition of debt imprisonment in 1793 reflected the Revolutionary government's dictatorial abuse of power over civil society. He reminded his audience that the people who abolished *contrainte par corps* had committed the worst excesses of Revolutionary violence. In abolishing *contrainte par corps*, Perrée-Duhamel added conspiratorially, the government had truly desired "the spoliation of properties and the destruction of all that stood in the way of their plan." Its plan had been no less than to subject commercial and civil society to complete and austere Jacobin control.[97] For Perrée-Duhamel, the abolition of *contrainte par corps* rather than its use constituted an illicit abuse of power insomuch as it deprived commerce of an essential protection. In contrast, the legislator added, the current government should enforce commercial autonomy in order to strengthen civil society.

Yet these men were no supporters of unrestrained commercial activity either. Indeed, in the minds of many deputies in 1797, commerce, despite its many blessings, represented a potentially corrupting force. Left to its own devices, commerce threatened not merely the social order but also markets themselves by undermining the trust necessary for transactions. Unfettered commerce evoked the specter of a society in which, as Debry's commission put it, "the longing for gain, ambition, the immoderate desire of all the vices destructive to social harmony" led its citizens "to stockjobbing and to ruin."[98] The preceding paper-money regime had been based on a system where one "renounced honor to have only those gains that involve the greatest risk and have no other rule but chance." Reestablishing concrete guarantees for commerce would distinguish such immoral speculation from true commercial activity that "made the country live." The current credit economy all but excluded small businessmen and artisans, those with nothing "but their bodies" to pledge as collateral, while allowing capitalists to charge usurious rates of interests for the risks they ran on loans. Rather than supporting a just social order, commerce without debt imprisonment actively undermined the public good.

Above all, restoring *contrainte par corps* meant restoring commercial honor. In the words of Council of Five Hundred representative Georges Desgraves, *contrainte par corps* only befell men who erred in "wanting to be too independent of the laws of honor, of morality, of forsaking everything, risking everything, above all the good opinion of one's fellows."[99] Similarly, another advocate of *contrainte* declared that it was "not contrary to the rights and duties of the citizen . . . it protects those individual interests, often still dearer than life and liberty . . . the honor of families and the honorable reputation of probity."[100] Citizens, he continued, needed to be taught the lessons of the freedom acquired during the Revolution. Libertinism could not be equated with liberty. Liberty implied suffering the consequences of those duties and obligations one had freely undertaken. The focus on honor would tie mobile property not only to a formal regime of securities equivalent to that of immobile properties but also to a similar code of social decorum.

Tellingly, these defenses of the use of punishment for failures of "honor" echoed much of the Revolutionary rhetoric of the social contract. For men like Desgraves and Perrée-Duhamel, *contrainte par corps* existed only when a contract had already been broken and a debtor wished to avoid the responsibilities involved in living in a contractual society. The language used almost directly recalled the idea of the revolutionary outlaw, the individual who not only violated the social contract but even attempted to make war on its very existence. Desgraves characterized the France of his day as a "state of war" in which the ubiquitous threats to commercial honor demanded a ruthless approach to those evildoers who failed to respect property rights.[101] For Desgraves, the "return to hard money" went hand in hand with the return to "hard contracts" reliant on the threat of debt imprisonment. If the circulation of money under the Montagnard regime had been infamously "backed by the guillotine," circulation of money under the new regime was to be backed by the threat of individual violence. No longer was the malefactor a political enemy to be excised from the national body because of his treason. Now he emerged as an enemy to the economic order who forfeited his rights to "not be a slave" as a punishment for his dishonor.

In addition to their belief that bringing back the threat of debt imprisonment would have a salutatory effect on merchants' moral behavior, deputies sought to restrain the potentially noxious effects of spreading commercial values with a highly defined division of labor in which commerce would be practiced only by certain individuals aware of both the legal and the ethical codes of the profession. They advocated a vision of commerce as a profession rather than as an act of exchange, which rejected both the Jacobin suspicion of commercial activity and the excesses of completely "free" markets. In their vision of commerce, businessmen were a special group, subject to different qualifications and duties, whose profession served the greater social welfare.[102] Echoing old regime discussion of the martial nature of the *noblesse commerçante*, Creuzé-Latouche compared merchants to the army and police. Like them, he reasoned, *commerçants* had to follow "particular laws that depart from general laws. They are subjected to more severe penalties than others." Those who served as intermediaries between producers and buyers fulfilled a public need, much as the police and army did. Like these public servants, *commerçants* lost the liberty they might have been entitled to as private citizens when their behavior infringed on their duty.[103]

Even as they extended these arguments, deputies maintained that they were fully in support of commerce as a liberal rather than corporate profession. The *commerçant*'s existence was justified by his service to the state and the public good, but he voluntarily chose to perform this activity. When Perrée-Duhamel asked, "Isn't the mercantile profession a liberal one? Doesn't everyone know the risks he runs in taking it on?" he suggested a definition of liberal that hinged on the distinction between professional and personal life. In postcorporate society, no one was forced to pursue or stay with any career.[104] A merchant's decision to enter commercial life was itself indicative of his willingness to be imprisoned if he failed in that capacity. Inside, commerce was dominated not by the lines of command and hierarchies of a guild, but rather by a democratic ethos that made it entirely compatible with republican values and also meant that businessmen would not make recourse to *contrainte par corps* unless forced. Representative Jean-Étienne-Marie Portalis declared that "commerce is essentially a profession of equals: because of this there exists between businessmen a kind of fraternity which excludes all harsh dealings . . . the common dangers to which they are exposed become for them new connections between each other."[105] Commerce was both democratic and special, subject to special duties and rules, and yet liberal and decidedly outside the corporate order.

Critics of reestablishment attacked both the conception of commerce and the conception of property inherent in its proponents' views. They were primarily concerned with the effects of granting to commercial loans securities and privileges that noncommercial lenders and borrowers lacked. In short, they were opposed to the vision, advocated by proponents, of commerce as a realm of exception. Representative Pierre-Charles-Louis Baudin argued that under the old regime *contrainte par corps* had been a kind of corporate protection given to the merchant class to balance out those privileges and protections accorded to other groups. With all other such privileges abolished in the new post-Revolutionary social order, there was no place for *contrainte par corps*.[106] Dupont de Nemours mocked comparisons of merchants to soldiers. Commerce, he argued, was essentially a peaceful activity. Moreover, it was an individualistic one. What army, he demanded rhetorically, would function if each soldier were guided by individual self-interest?

It followed for Dupont de Nemours that since commerce did not deserve special rules and privileges, merchants should be treated as any other citizen in terms of the law. Opponents of reestablishment treated debt imprisonment not as a separate commercial matter, but as part of a broader legal structure effecting both commercial and noncommercial individuals. Given their relative faults, asked Pierre-Toussaint Durand Maillane, should the state spend time and resources cracking down on petty debtors at a time when murderers and brigands roamed the country with impunity?[107] Guillaume-François Charles Goupil de Préfeln, departing from the views of his revered Montesquieu, whose bust he had ordered to be put in the Council of Five Hundred's meeting room, repeated that not only did the chaos of old regime jurisdictions make it impossible to merely "reestablish" such a practice but also that doing so without reference to new laws would lead to all sorts of violations of common sense. A convicted swindler, for example, could be sentenced to a shorter time in prison than an unfortunate debtor might face at the hands of a particularly heartless creditor. Dupont du Nemours connected *contrainte par corps* and arbitrary detention very explicitly. "We don't punish anyone on suspicion," he reminded his fellow legislators, "that only happened in the time of Robespierre; under our Republic, one needs to be convicted."[108] The legal differences between imprisonment for crime *contrainte par corps* must have been obvious to these men, trained as they were in law. Yet, by intentionally blurring the line between the two, they underscored the practical similarities between two processes that remained, in law, completely separate matters.

More deeply, opponents of reestablishment argued that *contrainte par corps* made human beings themselves a kind of property, one that they were allowed to alienate in making a loan. The deputies wondered whether a Revolution that had begun by enshrining human liberty should end by sacrificing it to monetary gain. Durand Maillane finished a comparison of the situation under the old regime with that in the post-Revolutionary context by declaring that "in the past, there was not as there is today a declaration of the rights of man, which says that the person of a citizen is not an alienable property."[109] In a similar vein, Dupont de Nemours eloquently explained the faulty logic of treating a debtor's "person" as his pledge. One did not find the qualities necessary to pledge in a borrower's "vile body, which is but a heap of needs," but rather "it is in the soul that one has those qualities that are respected and held accountable, that promise, that engage, that keep their word, that want, that act. . . . Are we machines, or movable properties, that one can stack as one wishes in a shop? No, we are intelligent and feeling beings, we carry in our breast an emanation of the divine."[110] Opponents of debt imprisonment maintained that far from giving movable and immovable property the same kind of security, *contrainte par corps* transformed human beings into movable properties.

The deputies' support for the reestablishment of *contrainte par corps* grew from a deep-seated disillusionment with the Revolutionary project and its "utopian" vision of mankind. Those who expressed doubts about the humanity of reinstating debt imprisonment opened themselves up to criticism that they were letting the "fancies of the heart overpower the lessons of experience."[111] Indeed, the bitter resignation to what were deemed necessary measures perhaps explains the marginal nature of objections to reestablishment: even among the opponents, few came out against the entire institution. On April 4, 1798, the Council of Five Hundred approved by acclamation a bill pertaining to civil and commercial debt imprisonment, consisting of three titles. The new rules stipulated maximum detention periods according to the amount of the debt, but set no minimum amount for which one could be imprisoned. They afforded protection to married women and minors, unless they were officially registered as *commerçants*.[112]

Eventually accompanied by several other pieces of legislation on imprisonment over the next decade, the law of Germinal An VI regulated the practice of *contrainte par corps* until the major overhaul in 1832.[113]

Paris police reports indicate nearly universal approval of debt imprisonment, especially in business quarters. Many hoped that other loans would receive similar security.[114] In Paris, the reestablished debtors' prison first reopened to Pierre Nöel, a wine merchant, on May 5, 1798, for a debt of 550 livres and 10 sous. He remained in prison for slightly over a year.[115] Until the reestablishment of well-defined commercial jurisdiction with the Commercial Code, numerous disputes arose that pitted various courts against each other and placed various law officers in jurisdictional conflicts.[116] Yet, despite the problems of its application, the reestablishment of *contrainte par corps* represented a victory not merely for a pragmatic approach to a credit crisis but for a particular interpretation of commerce within society. Although legislators continually emphasized the distinction between the commercial sphere and "ordinary" French society, they applied the terms of the political contract to the economic realm. By insisting that those who defaulted on commercial transactions violated the contracts they made with their creditors and therefore the social contract itself, they extended the implications of *contrainte par corps* far beyond its pre-Revolutionary meaning. As legislators struggled to intellectually justify the anomalous position of commercial justice in a regime built on legal equality, they arrived at an understanding of commerce as essential to public order but demanding different laws. These laws submitted the persons of those who practiced commerce to unusual constraints.

Conclusion

In 1803, six years after *Appel à l'honneur* had instructed Parisian audiences that obeying the terms of the social contract meant fulfilling the terms of contractual obligations to creditors, another dialogue posited a more complicated relationship between debt and contract. *Sur la contrainte par corps pour dettes telle qu'elle a été établie par la loi du 15 Germinal An VI*, written by an author described only as a "former commercial court judge," featured an interchange between two characters, called only "Traveler" and "Friend," about the merits of debt imprisonment. Although the ultimately victorious Traveler was a stalwart opponent of the institution and his friend an equally ferocious adherent, both sought to justify the practice principally in terms of the social contract. The Friend took the familiar line that a debtor who had "failed in his obligations to the conventions of the social contract, namely by failing to return the property of his creditor, a member of society," deserved to be "punished" because "by the social contract, all citizens guarantee to each one of its members the use of his property, as they guarantee his life and his liberty."[117] However, the Traveler asserted that such an opinion was based on a fundamental confusion between the values of "liberty" and "property." Liberty, the Traveler clarified, belonged to all citizens. Therefore only the collective power of the citizenry as exercised through the state, rather than through the actions of individual citizens, could lawfully deprive a citizen of his liberty. Unlike liberty, however, property belonged to each particular citizen and was not a fundamentally shared right. According to the Traveler, by treating liberty and property as if they were interchangeable, the law on debt imprisonment had created a "separation between particular and general interests." It had placed commerce outside the law of the social body and forced it to rely on coercion to uphold its private contracts.

This exchange between the Traveler and Friend, much like the debates that preoccupied the French government in 1797 and 1798, reveals the extent to which debates about debt imprisonment were also debates about the nature of contracts and the place of commerce in the new regime. In the years leading up to the Revolution, the growing importance of trade and the proliferation of luxury items had generated new and opposing viewpoints on how movable property and the merchants most closely associated with it could be reconciled with a social order built on honor and landed property. Some commentators believed that some merchants, guided by overweening self-interest, would defraud their creditors without the threat of debt imprisonment to make them honor their engagements. Others, however, felt that the very use of force entailed by the incarceration of the debtor violated the principles of *doux commerce*. Commercial honor, they maintained, regulated itself, free of the lingering threat to commerce. A successful merchant always needed to attend to his credit, which depended entirely on his honor. For many of these thinkers, debt imprisonment helped restrict commerce to the truly honorable. However, in the years immediately leading up to the Revolution, other writers argued that contracts must be based on the free will and true equality of adherents. The threat of debt imprisonment presented the specter of arbitrary and corrupt coercion rather than equitable commerce between contracting parties.

The French Revolutionaries believed strongly in commerce's public utility and justified maintaining the regime of commercial justice even as all the other jurisdictions of the old regime were swept aside. They sought to replace what they deemed to be the corrupt and arbitrary power of credit, associated with the excesses of the old regime, with a new and virtuous credit that stressed the importance of maintaining contractual obligations. Character and rational calculation, rather than power and influence, were now to form the basis of credit relations. Adherence to a strict code of honoring debts, including the debts contracted by the previous regime, underlay the Revolutionary experiment with the *assignat*, which was believed to have more credit than previous forms of money because of its basis in land. The massive depreciation of the *assignat*, precipitated by widespread distrust in the government and the species it issued, engendered instability on a staggering scale and further eroded confidence in commerce and the circulation of credit. By 1797, when the various paper species were entirely discontinued, the credit situation was grave and commercial trust at a nadir.

In the debates surrounding *contrainte par corps* in 1797 and 1798, legislators universally agreed on the value of commerce for the public good. Yet they recognized that certain elements of commerce, in particular those necessary to ensure public trust in credit, demanded that *commerçants* be subjected to a different and more demanding ethical and legal standard than ordinary people. "Commercial honor" entailed hard consequences. The Revolutionary lawmakers went far beyond their old regime counterparts: by not paying debts, one not merely dishonored one's self. One also failed in one's duties to commerce. Since commerce formed a vital branch of public credit and was seen as necessary to the public good, legislators believed that merchants who did not pay their debts, violating their private contracts, excluded themselves from the social contract. The reestablishment of debt imprisonment placed the institution in a new language: that of outlawry and fault. Careful to distinguish their treatment of the debtor's person from both the slave and the criminal, the Revolutionary legislators nevertheless perpetuated confusion by the implications of their laws.

Besides demonstrating the importance of Revolutionary political rhetoric in sculpting the post-Revolutionary credit economy, the reestablishment of debt imprisonment also represented a realignment of the state and the commercial community after years of tumult. Five years after the reestablishment of *contrainte par corps*, when the Gorneau commission was tasked by the Consulate with drafting a commercial code set about their work, they had first to grapple with the possibility that their work could be misconstrued as supporting a return to a corporate order. Instead they insisted that "if commercial legislation is composed of laws of exception, it is not for the benefit of the *commerçants* that it is done, but because the interests of all, because public wealth, prosperity and the happiness of citizens are attached to the prosperity of commerce."[118] What separated commerce's exceptional departure from the normal civil code was the objects that stood as guarantees for transactions: "The first [civil law] deals only with things, while the other concerned only persons, an important distinction, derived from the nature of commerce itself, which, being only practiced on mobile objects, offers nothing for surety and guarantee other than the morality of persons."[119]

For the Gorneau commission, as for the legislators who promoted *contrainte par corps* for commercial debts in 1797 and 1798, the exceptional nature of commercial law derived not from the privilege of a certain group but from the unique usefulness and dangers of commercial activity. At the same time, however, the reestablishment of *contrainte par corps* reflected a tacit agreement between the Revolutionary government and the commercial community. In 1800 the government succeeded in obtaining the cooperation of business elites in the creation of a national bank, somewhat along the lines of the ones proposed in 1796. This bank was essentially a commercial discounting bank and yet remained formally independent from the government itself, controlled instead by private shareholders. This uneasy alliance between state and commercial community would characterize subsequent decades. Successful at defining commerce as an activity that benefited society as a whole but that needed particular laws, business interests were able to maintain special processes for dealing with debt default and special courts, judged by other business people, to deal with these matters. In this way, the cautious and highly traditional society based on customs and family networks simultaneously mobilized liberal discourse to fend off regulation and called on state support when faced with threats to business order.

2

The Blessing of Being Judged

Bankruptcy and the Napoleonic Codes

On the morning of October 28, 1803, the creditors of the Marseillais grocer Martin Rambaud awoke to find his shop unexpectedly shuttered and Rambaud gone. It was not long before rumors of his bankruptcy began to swirl around town. Several witnesses reported having seen two women, presumably Rambaud's wife and daughter, moving merchandise into the homes of friends and relatives. Acting on what they saw as manifest evidence of Rambaud's bad faith, the grocer's furious creditors stormed into the offices of the Marseille police, arguing for a charge of *banqueroute frauduleuse*, the willful abuse of bankruptcy for personal enrichment, to be placed on Rambaud's head. Yet, following Rambaud's return and the discovery of the objects he had hidden, the creditors unanimously asked the police to drop the charges.[1] Frustrated by this flouting of the law, the police commissioner in Marseille wrote the minister of justice that he still considered Rambaud guilty of fraud.[2] Nevertheless, without the support of Rambaud's creditors, the case against the bankrupt merchant quickly crumbled, leaving the dismayed authorities to shake their heads in disgust.

Rambaud's case, which appears in the files both of the minister of the interior and of the minister of justice under the Consulate, was egregious in the level of illegal activity apparently involved. However, bankruptcies that skirted the boundaries of legality happened quite regularly in the opening years of the nineteenth century. Contemporaries, like the government officials in Rambaud's case, blamed the frequency of these events on the Revolution's noxious influence on commercial morality. The Revolution, with its attendant monetary instability and trade blockades, disrupted the relations of credit and debt that had stretched back over years, or even decades. The decade from 1789 to 1799 undermined the certainty with which average citizens imagined the future. In its place, Revolutionary upheaval inspired a credit economy built on distrust and the need for concrete collateral. Nor did this atmosphere suddenly change when Napoleon took command and proclaimed the Revolution over. Although Napoleonic institutions such as the Bank of France and the newly minted *franc germinal* provided some security to the financial market, the wars raging on the European continent continued to periodically upset commercial circles, precipitating chains of bankruptcies. The famous "masses of granite," the male property owners who were to ensure the stability of Napoleon's regime based on a highly individualistic notion of absolute property ownership, often proved to have built their fortunes on the shifting sands of credit and speculation.[3]

In this context of uncertainty and risk, debtors and creditors alike possessed manifold incentives to act with minimal concern for the niceties of the law. Given how many inducements Rambaud may have had to act illegally, it is impossible to know with certainty the mix of emotions and motivations that inspired his erratic actions. Did he scoff at officials' impotent efforts to curtail such acts of abuse? Was he confident in his ability to escape with impunity? Or did he act out of panic, afraid of the abuse his creditors, or his neighbors, might mete out to a bad payer? Whatever their motivations, debtors like Rambaud committed suspicious acts—fleeing, taking away objects from their businesses and houses, paying off particularly pressing creditors—with a frequency that deeply troubled government officials and common citizens alike. The actions of creditors like Rambaud's who, despite their initial anger, prioritized pecuniary self-interest over the demands of justice and chose not to invoke public authorities even more gravely damaged efforts at establishing the rule of law.

For many observers, such behavior by lenders and borrowers endangered faith in commerce as a whole. The Commercial Code, formulated in the immediate aftermath of a devastating series of bankruptcies that had rocked the capital in 1805 and 1806, was framed in a moralistic discourse. A member of Napoleon's Council of State, presenting the Commercial Code to Napoleon's legislative assembly, the Corps Législatif, in 1807, described in lurid terms how the Revolution had "shaken men, fortunes, classes, inspiring wild hopes as well as wild fears, limitless opportunities and bottomless abysses, putting in the place of real money a kind of paper whose rapid fall left nothing of fixed value and solid credit to nobody."[4] In this dire narrative, the dissolution of social bonds had unleashed a deluge of greed and self-interest, pushing crowds of unprincipled and ignorant men into trade in the hope of quick riches. As the legislator noted with distaste, under the Revolution "everybody was a *commerçant*; every house became a store, every first floor open to the street became a shop."[5] Widespread and brazen immorality had been the natural result. Under Napoleon, the councillor promised, commerce would return to the path of order and morality.

Scholars have generally portrayed the Napoleonic codes, of which the Commercial Code formed one of five parts, as the culmination of a centuries-long centralization project to reconcile and systematize the diverse laws and customs of old regime France into a uniform code.[6] Renouncing the Revolutionary ambition to regenerate man through the creation of ideal laws, the code's promulgators sought instead to "depoliticize" law, insisting that its only aim was to promote order, a vision that they filtered through an exceedingly negative view of human nature.[7] The crowning glory of the five codes was the Civil Code of 1804, defined by its insistence on absolute private ownership, which was to be ensured by a powerful state rather than left to the vagaries of natural right, and its support of a patriarchal family structure, which effectively overturned the Revolutionary commitment to egalitarianism.[8] The Civil Code became the most prominent example of civil law's top-down approach to justice. In the words of the legal historian Jean Hilaire, the Civil Code "affirmed the primacy of law and projected a strong suspicion of custom."[9] For the code's promulgators, precedent evoked the possibility of arbitrary decision making and irrationality, while codification promised the kind of universality and objectivity deemed necessary to social stability after over a decade of tumult.

The 1807 Commercial Code does not fit neatly into the image of Napoleonic law associated with the Civil Code. While the Civil Code is often regarded as one of Napoleon's landmark achievements, the few scholars who have examined the Commercial Code have generally dismissed it as regressive and derivative of the Ordinance of 1673. According to them, the promulgators of the Commercial Code not only ignored the signs of incipient capitalism but left substantial lacunas in regulating established aspects of commercial life.[10] The character of the Commercial Code contradicts many of the characteristics that defined the Civil Code. The Commercial Code, for instance, eschewed discussion of family units in favor of an overarching concentration on the individual merchant. By focusing on the fleeting nature of merchandise, it belied the Civil Code's insistence on absolute property ownership. Far more than any other branch of law, moreover, commercial law was a law of custom. For centuries, the elected judges of the *jurisdiction consulaire*, and subsequently the *tribunaux de commerce*, had based their rulings on a complex body of decrees and ordinances, legal precedents, and books such as Jacques Savary's *Le parfait negociant*. The National Assembly of 1791, in permitting commercial courts to operate while simultaneously sweeping aside all other types of old regime jurisdictions, affirmed the need for merchants to practice their own form of customary justice even as they minimized the importance of custom in other domains of French life. In many respects, commercial law fundamentally contradicted the aims of the Napoleonic legal project.

No single aspect of the Commercial Code more vividly embodied the anomalous nature of commercial procedure than bankruptcy. Although bankruptcy law retained many elements of old regime law, it was certainly the most innovative aspect of the Commercial Code. Bankruptcy attracted more careful attention than any other aspect of commercial legislation. The only sessions of the code's creation that Napoleon personally attended were those devoted to bankruptcy, and the regulation of commercial failure made up an entire book of the finished Commercial Code's five books.

When the code's creators considered how best to regulate bankruptcy, they struggled with defining the relationship of commercial justice to ordinary civil law. Was commercial law merely a law of exception to conventional law composed of specific incidents, as highlighted in the Ordinance of 1673? Or did it constitute its own kind of legal practice?[11] As the creators of the code realized, separating commercial from civil practices in a society no longer structured by guilds posed severe challenges. Moreover, merchants possessed identities other than their commercial selves: they were fathers and mothers, wives and husbands, and owners of real estate. In bankruptcy proceedings, these multiple identities came into conflict, provoking restrictions to be placed on the civil practices of merchants that distinguished them from ordinary citizens.

In addition to the tension between civil and commercial law, bankruptcy highlighted the tensions between formal law and customary justice. Howard Brown, in his study of the Directory, has detailed the "Hobbesian" anarchy of France in the 1790s. Organized bands slaughtered and pillaged throughout the countryside with impunity. Urban suicide rates reached staggering heights. For Brown, the problem of maintaining order in the

Revolution's aftermath resulted from a conflict between a kind of moral economy of justice defined by communal norms and customary practices and the codified laws enthusiastically implemented by Revolutionary legislators. Ironically, the Revolution strengthened communal forms of justice as a means of resistance to the Revolutionary state.[12] Although Brown's focus is on the endemic violence of French society in the 1790s, a similar state of affairs prevailed in the commercial realm. Many merchants apparently tolerated customary practices that verged on outright illegality in order to ease acute monetary shortages. Others, however, were outraged by these abuses. The Napoleonic regime attempted to curtail criminal abuses by recourse to tough penalties that were generally devoid of the element of shame and retribution that had featured so prominently in old regime law.[13] In handling bankruptcy, however, the promulgators were faced with a dilemma: commercial law was not criminal law, but the very informality of credit networks seemed to invite fraudulent practices. Moreover, none of the Napoleonic legislators viewed bankruptcy as a merely economic process from which the aspects of degradation and dishonor could be detached. They saw rigorous laws as necessary both to compensate for a moral system supposedly destroyed by the Revolution and to repress the long-established informal management of bankruptcy that years of instability had only strengthened.

In short, bankruptcy perfectly embodied the various conceptual, jurisdictional, and implementational problems involving commerce raised by the Commercial Code. While the Commercial Code systematized the treatment of commercial debt to an unprecedented degree, synthesizing and revising the patchwork of old regime ordinances, decrees, and edicts into a coherent framework, the promised return of order and morality to commercial affairs proved far more elusive. Despite the commercial community's successful resistance to the earlier attempts to criminalize bankruptcy, the 1807 Commercial Code struck many observers, particularly zealous public prosecutors and police officials, as providing no clear division between commercial and criminal jurisdictions. The early years of the code's application witnessed fierce disputes between prosecutors, police, creditors, and commercial courts about the implementation of its terms. Meanwhile, creditors and debtors quickly learned how to manipulate the law, frequently rendering it less suited to equitably managing default than to facilitating a complicated interplay of relationships motivated by power, greed, and personal enmity against the backdrop of both commercial and criminal courts. The professed desire of the Commercial Code's promulgators to make bankruptcy purely a matter of commercial law ran up against the realities of customary practice and the stratagems of creditors and debtors. While partly a product of the economic uncertainties of the time, the jurisdictional confusion also had its roots in the law itself: the person of the *commerçant* as defined by the Commercial Code could not easily be disentangled from the legal persons defined by the civil and criminal codes.

A Plague of Bankruptcies

Complaints about the bankruptcy process were nearly universal in the years preceding the enactment of the Commercial Code. In an 1801 pamphlet entitled *De l'influence du gouvernement sur la prospérité du commerce*, the commercial judge and banker Vital Roux began his chapter "Banqueroutes et Faillites" with the grim reflection that "a bankruptcy is no longer the last asylum of misfortune and the fateful refuge where the turns of fortune force the businessman."[14] Roux claimed significant experience in this regard. Born into a well-connected family of Lyonnais merchants, Roux moved to Paris, where he became a respected banker and witnessed firsthand the results of economic crises and poorly enforced laws.[15] In the dozens of creditors' convocations he had attended throughout his career, his shock at the "gullibility of creditors" was matched only by his astonishment at the "impudence and bad faith" of their debtors.[16] Roux attributed the deplorable state of affairs as much to "the inertia of the courts and the impotence of the laws" as to the state's poor example. Terming the government's payments to its creditors in paper money "more or less ruinous robberies, authorized by the law," Roux asked, "How can the courts be inexorable against bankruptcy when the creditors of the state are themselves so badly paid?" The Lyonnais judge did not see the country's ills as the ineluctable result of deregulation but nevertheless insisted that if government mismanagement had set the precedent for the lawless and shameless behavior of lenders and borrowers, then new laws must strike bankruptcy at its roots.

Historians have portrayed Vital Roux's pamphlet as a powerful reinterpretation of commercial doctrine in the wake of the French Revolution. In designating this body of law "commercial legislation" rather than "legislation of commerce," Roux indicated that commerce meant not the community of merchants, with its resonance of old regime corporatism, but rather a concept of commerce that was simultaneously more individualistic and more public.[17] In its appreciation of the power of positive law in relationship to commerce and its departure from natural right, his work also marked a significant departure from Revolutionary economic ideas.[18] As Rebecca Spang has argued, the French Revolutionaries had been guided by an ideology that equated political liberty with economic liberty. Instead of economic liberty leading to prosperity, however, this policy had further exacerbated the lack of trust in the stability of the government. In credit transactions, borrowers and lenders had negotiated their own arrangements in the relative absence of government oversight. Yet these transactions more generally led to a widespread sense of abuse rather than the creation of social harmony. Between 1795 and 1806, there were no limits on the legal rate of interest and usury did not exist as a criminal offense. Under the law, borrowers and lenders were free to contract at whatever interest rate they mutually agreed on. Yet contemporary accounts abound with condemnations of usury as a nearly universal abuse.[19] Likewise, Roux's reflections on bankruptcy represented a firm rebuke to the Revolutionary faith in private contracts between individuals. His critique focused not only on the way in which private citizens, left unsupervised, worked to the detriment of others but also on customary and communal practices of justice that circumvented the strict letter of the law. In theory, commercial failure during the Revolutionary period was regulated by the terms of the Ordinance of 1673, a document that contained only thirteen articles, each approximately a sentence long, devoted to bankruptcy. The lack of detail left merchants and commercial courts to regulate bankruptcy practices according to custom. Roux alleged that even the extremely broad terms of the ordinance were customarily disregarded: debtors did not even present their balance sheet or convoke their creditors. Although the ordinance stated that a bankruptcy began when the debtor fled or when seals were placed over his store, Roux noted that often merchants carried on as normal even after they had long stopped payment. Many continued to receive payments from their own debtors even after suspending payments to their creditors. If they even met with their creditors, they employed silver-tongued legal agents to persuade them to agree to paltry dividends. In *De l'influence du gouvernement sur la prospérité du commerce*, communal mechanisms for settling agreements produced flagrant inequities that undermined confidence in commerce itself.

Like Vital Roux, administrators believed that merchants too often ignored the few written laws that existed on bankruptcy in favor of negotiating among themselves. Officials regularly relayed to their superiors what they saw as the predictable fraud that resulted from informal debt settlement mechanisms. On December 11, 1805, for example, the departmental prefect reported that in Troyes in the previous two weeks alone, there had been five or six bankruptcies in which fraud was strongly suspected. One bankrupt had fled to the capital. Another, who had signed false endorsements on bills of exchange, had tried to poison himself, failed, and been found a few days later dangling from a noose in his barn. Another, with the help of his wife and brother-in-law, had hidden his merchandise.[20] Much as in Rambaud's case, creditors dispensed with judicial pursuits, fearing that such intervention would waste both time and precious assets. Although the number of bankruptcies from 1797 through 1807 seems to have been lower in Paris than it was in the final years of the old regime, with 190 declared in 1801 and 239 in 1802 compared to over 400 a year in the 1770s, state officials attributed this supposed decline to a widespread disregard for the law whereby both creditors and debtors desired to avoid official bankruptcy declarations.[21]

Even as magistrates focused on culpable collusion between debtors and creditors in their dispatches to the Ministry of Justice, creditors complained bitterly about how the laws and even the lawmakers themselves favored bankrupts over honest lenders. Petitioners decried magistrates who neglected to arrest those accused of fraud and even allowed them to actively flaunt their ill-gotten wealth.[22] Others protested that bankruptcy law sheltered the debtor from orders of debt imprisonment, which they portrayed as the only means of keeping fraudulent debtors in prison because officials failed to arrest them as *banqueroutiers*.[23] Even when officials actively pursued acts of fraud, creditors saw the legal system as thwarting their efforts at every turn. A half dozen creditors of two bankers in Angoulême, for example, wrote to the minister of justice bemoaning prohibitions against searching private homes, which they blamed for allowing the guilty bankers to avoid justice.[24] A former businessman claimed to have retired in disgust from commerce, avowing that he had not been a party in two bankruptcies in his life that would not have merited criminal charges against either the debtor, some of the creditors, or both.[25] In answer to one particularly strident denunciation of debtors, the minister of justice glumly admitted that "no matter how fraudulent their behavior, the magistrates must follow the law," however slow and ineffective this process might appear to some.[26]

For public officials, the private abuses in managing commercial failure could easily become threats to public order. After one businessman in the small southern town of Eyguières blamed his ruin on the improbable theft of some 15,000 livres in the night, the terrified mayor wrote that widespread suspicion of his tale had generated a "sort of popular effervescence." Believing the public suspicions justified, the mayor asked the public prosecutor to "take every means to stop the effects of the public indignation," up to and including pressing criminal charges, before it resulted in outright acts of violence.[27] For other officials, *banqueroute* marked the beginning of other crimes. In April 1806, one public prosecutor wrote to the minister of justice about a *banqueroutier* who had hidden in a prostitute's house, where he had shot and killed a notary, deeming his victim a rival for the lady's affections. The public prosecutor attributed the bankrupt's record of making violent threats to the same "burning passions" that animated his reckless spending. Moreover, according to the general prosecutor, the bankrupt-turned-assassin had "ruined himself at the Bank (the Lottery). Almost all the bankruptcies (and they are numerous) have no other cause but gambling," a passion that "inevitably led a man to homicide or suicide or both."[28]

The public appears to have been no more favorably disposed toward commercial failure. Public opinion, noted one pamphleteer in 1798, had become so enraged by the abuses that the "innocent bankruptcy" no longer existed. "In conversation," one writer explained, "the only question is what kind of penalty should be inflicted upon" the bankrupt.[29] Perceiving the "epidemic of bankruptcies" as a result of the breakdown of commercial morality, some writers suggested reviving the ritualistic elements of communal shame that constituted bankruptcy processes in the medieval period. One petitioner demanded that all bankrupts and their children should wear yellow three-cornered hats, evoking a color and fashion scheme that had formed an integral part of insolvency rituals in certain parts of Europe in medieval times, and that their names, addresses, and professions should be posted in town halls and stock exchanges for the public to see.[30] Another suggested that a *banqueroutier*, under penalty of perpetual imprisonment, should wear a red hat and have his carriage and horses painted red "so that people can better regard him as a ferocious beast to be feared."[31] Angered that insolvent debtors too easily avoided public notice, these writers aimed at ensuring that bankrupts stood apart visually from the rest of the community.

One of the most popular proposals, as judged by the sheer volume of such proposals received by ministerial offices, involved a return to the guild system, which its advocates upheld as a panacea for all commerce's ills. One proponent of this idea, a merchant named Vauchelet who wrote to the Ministry of the Interior in 1807, not only blamed bankruptcies and usury on the dissolution of the guild system but overtly connected the emperor's successes on the battlefield with the needs of the market, comparing the state of commerce "to that of a large army, defeated, dispersed. They are always soldiers, but no longer an army. The good ones suffer but the brigands . . . are given free rein. As soon as a strong hand comes to reassemble and reunite all these different bodies under one flag, all retake their places, the laws are followed, the security reigns where all was disorder et each one blesses the hand to which one owes this peace." If bankruptcy and usury were the most egregious signs of the evils of economic individualism, the solution to both was to harness self-interest to the simultaneously hierarchical and collective world of the old guild system.[32]

The upper echelons of the commercial community represented in the commercial courts and newly reestablished chambers of commerce shared many of Vauchelet's concerns. The Toulouse Chamber of Commerce suggested that the "upsurge of liberal ideas had been the bitter fruit of the Revolution" and in destroying "Catholic dogma" had created a commercial sphere deprived of all morality, driven completely by "covetousness and self-interest." Commerce was populated, furthermore, by upstarts "ignorant of the most fundamental principles of its functioning."[33] Yet the commercial elite proved staunchly unsympathetic to the reestablishment of the guilds promoted by men like Vauchelet.[34] While deploring the prevalence of bankruptcies, the Parisian Chamber of Commerce believed that a coherent body of law, rather than a return to the corporate order, would best ensure commerce's commitment to the public good. The merchants commented that the government could resolve the problem of commercial immorality by dealing with the laws on bankruptcy rather than by restoring the corporations.[35]

There was no clear consensus as to how the government should restore commercial morality. A possible solution lay in treating bankruptcy as a criminal affair and extending the government's direct oversight of the bankruptcy process. One writer to the Ministry of Interior named Legras proposed a system of salaried liquidators and curators around the country, who would take over the estates of those unable to pay their debts. These bankruptcy professionals, paid by the state, would ensure that a debtor's assets were well managed. Believing that "a bankrupt is necessarily an imprudent or wasteful man, incompetent or dishonest; and as the law intervenes in all cases of dissipation, incapacity and knavery," Legras affirmed that the state had every right to direct bankruptcy proceedings with a firm hand.[36] Indeed, he suggested that even more than women or children, groups deemed legally incompetent in most commercial matters, the bankrupt was incapable of managing his own financial welfare and should be taken under state protection. Vital Roux read Legras's ideas with interest. Although Roux believed too strongly in the independence of the commercial court system to support the idea of salaried liquidators, he nevertheless described bankruptcy in criminal tones, maintaining that bankruptcy was a "kind of public offense" and a "denial of the engagements that one has contracted with society."[37]

Legislating Bankruptcy

The year following the publication of his pamphlet, Vital Roux joined a seven-person committee, headed by Philippe-Joseph Gorneau, charged with creating a commercial code. Despite their deep experience in commercial law and practice, the task they faced must have seemed daunting: they were to take the diverse sources of commercial law found in decrees and ordinances, legal writings, and precedent, and create a new uniform law code. Several such projects had been attempted during the eighteenth century.[38] All of them had failed. The Gorneau committee's work would meet a similar fate, despite the committee's production of a second, revised version in 1803 after receiving biting criticism from the nation's commercial and civil court judges. Bankruptcy was the single most contentious aspect of the Gorneau commission drafts. Committee members shared with Roux the opinion that the legal ambiguities of bankruptcy law not only opened commerce to abuses but also undermined the government's very legitimacy as the sole dispenser of law. The commission admitted that the law itself encouraged abuses. Deeming the legal system confusing, arbitrary, and cumbersome, many creditors and debtors eagerly acted outside the government's aegis in making settlements. The extant laws offered inadequate means of controlling the potential for bad faith in these transactions. In the commission's opinion, even the newly reestablished right to imprison debtors was "an insufficient palliative" for the crisis, one that left the cunning debtor "in a dangerous independence."[39]

For the commission, the danger of this independence consisted primarily in the cooperative mechanisms devised by creditors and debtors to handle business failure outside the law. Their principle concern was to restrict the widespread practice of private settlements wherein creditors and debtors used notarized debt rescheduling to avoid the expenses and inconveniences of an actual bankruptcy and thereby the surveillance and protection of the commercial courts. In the eyes of the legislators, the willingness of both creditors and debtors to engage in informal settlements severely undermined the efficacy of the law. Yet, rather than rely on the commercial courts to respond to this abuse, the Gorneau commission favored dramatically expanding the direct power of the criminal jurisdiction over commercial failure. Deeming bankruptcy a "public affair" rather than one of "private interest," the commission suggested that an official, appointed by the municipality rather than by the local commercial court, supervise each commercial court to settle accounts between debtor and creditors.[40] This official would oversee almost all aspects of early bankruptcy proceedings, from the creation of an inventory of the debtor's possessions to the denunciation of fraud to the criminal court. When the Gorneau commission circulated its first draft of the new commercial code in 1801, judges from civil as well as commercial courts vehemently rejected the project for bankruptcy, believing it would create a caste of "bankruptcy professionals" who would prolong the length and paperwork of the proceedings in order to more amply pad their pockets.[41] The rejection of the Gorneau commission's bankruptcy reforms helped lead to the rejection of the entire project.

The Gorneau commission's two unsuccessful attempts at creating commercial legislation did not end efforts to criminalize commercial failure.[42] Following a financial crisis in 1805–6, which had been precipitated by the speculation of a group of highly placed bankers and tax collectors with government funds, Napoleon famously stated that "commerce has abused its liberty. It has a need now for the government to watch over it."[43] With work on a commercial code stalled, Napoleon's Council of State drafted an independent bankruptcy reform proposal in spring 1806. The draft, sent to eighteen of the country's largest chambers of commerce in June, proposed dramatic increases in the rigors as well as the amount of government oversight in cases of business failure. It presumed all bankruptcies to be fraudulent and placed all bankrupts under provisional arrest until inspection had been made of their accounts and balance sheets.[44] After the inspection, it got rid of all protections on a wife's claim to her dotal properties. Moreover, any bankruptcy where liabilities exceeded assets would be declared a *banqueroute frauduleuse*.[45]

As with the Gorneau commission's less punitive proposals, the chambers of commerce uniformly opposed the 1806 bankruptcy project. "Without question," declared the Nantes Chamber of Commerce, echoing the sentiments expressed in many other responses, "there have been a great number of fraudulent bankruptcies in the last several years. Yet there are even more bankruptcies due to inexperience or ignorance or the force of circumstances."[46] Many chambers worried that in replacing "a law too lenient with a law too strict" such regulation would provide incentive for distressed businessmen to resort to fraudulent means to avoid a bankruptcy declaration or flee rather than face up to their creditors.[47] Moreover, they argued, the Council's proposal failed to recognize the dire straits created by Revolutionary upheaval and constant war.[48] They also found the rules unfair toward small merchants.[49] The proposal, in short, not only tarnished all debtors with the same stain of criminality but also subjected commerce to the direct and constant surveillance of criminal courts.

With the government's proposals once again rejected by the commercial community, bankruptcy reform would be put off until the next year when Napoleon's Council of State set about the task previously entrusted to the Gorneau commission: the creation of a uniform commercial code. Despite the failure of previous efforts at increased criminalization, several members of the Council initially sympathized with petitioners' demands for the obligatory involvement of the state police in the early stages of a bankruptcy or even surveillance of the entire process by a public prosecutor. The emperor himself was a strong proponent of this viewpoint. At one point in the deliberations on Book III, Napoleon stormed into a Council session to declare that bankruptcy should be treated "as one does all cases where there could be a crime. He who kills a man, even by accident, during the hunt for example, is initially arrested and detained, then one examines him and if he is innocent one absolves him."[50] He added that no bankrupt should be allowed to remain with his head held high and that a few months of obligatory prison should be enough to "humble him."

Yet even as they carefully weighed the possibility of increased supervision, none of the councillors agreed with the emperor's draconian pronouncement.[51] "What is the Commercial Code, in essence?" one member asked. "It is civil law. One cannot handle a bankruptcy otherwise than in considering it a civil event."[52] Instead of attributing every failure to fraud, the Commercial Code specified three categories of bankruptcy: *faillite*, *banqueroute simple*, and *banqueroute frauduleuse*, respectively assigned to commercial courts, correctional courts, and criminal courts. Despite these different jurisdictions, the Commercial Code included basic regulations for both forms of *banqueroute* as well as *faillite*. The separation between *banqueroute* and *faillite* reflected a long-standing distinction included in the Ordinance of 1673 and was meant to divide those insolvencies that resulted from misfortune from those that originated in fraud or misconduct. The *banqueroute simple*, however, was new. It pertained to failure that was not the result of outright fraud but of the debtor's carelessness in keeping books, adhering to protocols, or managing his money. This new category aroused opposition on the Council of State. After some debate over whether it too harshly "tarnish[ed] with the name *banqueroutier*" those who were merely unfortunate, the councillors deemed the new category necessary in order to suppress what was seen as an epidemic of untrained businessmen who had flooded commerce since the breakdown of the guilds, yet it did so without assimilating all those who failed out of poor management to criminal offenders.[53]

Although the state council envisioned a firm line between criminal and commercial jurisdictions, they also sought to clearly delineate civil and commercial jurisdictions by restricting *faillite* to merchants alone and placing the process entirely under the supervision of the commercial courts. In theory, the councillors only reaffirmed prior doctrine on this matter. In reality, however, old regime notaries had routinely drawn up "friendly" bankruptcy arrangements, which then had lacked the oversight of the courts.[54] Meanwhile, debtors who were not really *commerçants* regularly filed for bankruptcy, and creditors successfully pressed charges of *banqueroute* against non-*commerçants*.[55] The councillors aimed to clarify the distinction between bankruptcy and insolvency by framing it as a distinction between commercial and civil law. Book III of the Commercial Code began by emphasizing the commercial nature of *faillite*. Article 457 read, "Every *commerçant* who ceases payments is in a state of *faillite*."[56] This single sentence not only attempted to define when a bankruptcy began, a subject that Legras and Gorneau had believed gave rise to fraud, but explicitly made only businessmen who could not pay their debts eligible for the bankruptcy process. These would automatically belong to the commercial courts.[57] Civil courts, meanwhile, would oversee the process of *déconfiture*, open to all insolvent borrowers.[58]

The 1807 Commercial Code reaffirmed the Gorneau commission's insistence that civil law, which "deals only with things," would be separated from commercial law, which, according to one promulgator, was to be "concerned only with persons, an important distinction, derived from the nature of commerce itself, which, being only practiced on mobile objects, offers nothing for surety and guarantee other than the morality of persons."[59] The Commercial Code was in one sense a set of laws about commerce and commercial practices. Yet the very first words of the code itself did not define "commerce" but rather defined the *commerçant* to whom the Commercial Code applied ("Article 1: They are *commerçants* who exercise commerce and make of it their usual profession").[60] Thus bankruptcy, as part of commercial law, centered on the debtor's person. As Councillor Emmanuel Crétet declared, "Without the bankrupt, there is no bankruptcy."[61] Book III contained several references to the "person" of the debtor. Article 455, for example, mandated that the "person of the *failli*" must be placed in a "debtors' prison or under house arrest" in the immediate aftermath of a bankruptcy declaration.[62] In presenting the bankruptcy law to the Corps Législatif, one of the code's promulgators, Jean Baptiste Treilhard, demonstrated how the Commercial Code's focus on the person of the individual merchant not only separated him from "ordinary" civil law but also connected him to criminal law. Explaining the need for precautionary imprisonment, Treilhard explained that "at the moment that a bankruptcy strikes, the person and the goods of the bankrupt are secured: the person, to respond to the offenses, the goods, to pay the creditors."[63] This formulation not only tied the person to the collection of the debt but also demonstrated that the criminal and financial aspects of bankruptcy were indissoluble.

By explicitly linking bankruptcy to the physical body of the debtor and the legal category of personhood, the councillors implied that companies where responsibility could not be individually assigned could not undergo the same processes. Thus while the Commercial Code permitted in Article 34 the creation of joint-stock companies (*sociétés anonymes*), which lacked any single responsible individual, it did not allow these companies to attain a *concordat* from creditors in the case of failure. Furthermore, the bankrupt had to be alive to be bankrupt. The estate of the deceased might be ruled insolvent, but unless the debtor himself had suspended payment, it could not be bankrupt. The actual wording of the Commercial Code treated bankrupts almost entirely as single, male individuals, with no explicit mention of female bankrupts and only a few references to bankrupts in joint companies and partnerships, such as Article 440, which declared that in case of the bankruptcy of such a company, the declaration had to indicate the name and address of each of the associates.[64]

Even as the councillors differentiated commercial law from civil law in making bankruptcy exclusively reserved for *commerçants*, other aspects of the code proved particularly tricky because the precautions necessary for preventing commercial fraud often seemed to contradict the rights of citizens, as guaranteed by the Civil Code. For example, the Civil Code famously insisted on the rights of private individuals to dispose of property belonging to them however they pleased. What did this mean in regards to a debtor? One particularly controversial issue in this regard was who should be able to manage the debtor's estate in the interim between the declaration of bankruptcy and the convocation of the verified creditors who judged the debtor's fate.[65] Previous laws had left the debtor in control of his own property after the declaration of a bankruptcy, since he was not considered legally expropriated. Critics like Legras and Gorneau had denounced this practice as a gateway to fraud and abuse. Some councillors suggested that the bankrupt's property be expropriated and sold immediately by the creditors in order to maximize the profit from any unsold merchandise. It was, as one member put it, "impossible to amass on one head the quality of debtor and that of property owner" since "the one necessarily excludes the other when the good one holds as property is at the same time the pledge of a debt."[66] Other Council members argued that immediately stripping a debtor of his possessions violated his property rights, "principles so much the basis of the social order that no other interest, even that of commerce, can be allowed to upend them."[67] The intervention of an official from the local criminal court, an idea proposed by others, aroused fears of repeating the fate of previous efforts at bankruptcy reform. The councillors ultimately agreed to avoid direct government involvement by letting the commercial court select agents from lists of reputable merchants and commercial judges to act as temporary trustees of the property. The commercial court would be the only judicial body involved in a bankruptcy, except in clear cases of fraud or gross mismanagement. Even commercial jurisdiction would be temporary: as soon as the creditors could legitimately elect their own representatives, the bankruptcy devolved into the creditors' hands.

Another area of conflict between the Civil Code and Commercial Code's priorities arose in the matter of secure creditors. For all of their suspicions about debtors, the councillors had little more confidence in creditors. The very nature of a bankruptcy presented the rather unique situation, as vividly illustrated by cases like Rambaud's, where all involved parties had multiple incentives to ignore the demands of justice or to manipulate the situation for their own ends. Moreover, the law, in privileging certain types of property and property holders, only added to the possibilities of abuse. The creditors included in a bankruptcy agreement were only the debtor's unsecured creditors, meaning those creditors who did not possess a mortgage or other legal priority for their claim.[68] Secured creditors, on the other hand, were those creditors who had a pledge or mortgage against an estate or other immovable property of the debtor. The legislators believed that, owing to the nature of commerce, unsecured creditors were more important to *commerçants* than secured creditors, and the latter were not included in bankruptcy agreements. Rather, secured creditors had the right to use the power of expropriation, which frequently entailed considerable expenses that depleted the assets available to pay off the unsecured creditors. To several members of the Council of State, the advantage enjoyed by mortgaged creditors seemed unfair, since the losses incurred by the unsecured creditors were, in the words of one councillor, "more often an inevitable effect of commercial circulation which should be protected."[69] The priority given to debts secured by land negatively affected the security extended to commercial creditors and might discourage commercial lending. For this reason, some on the Council initially proposed the idea of forming a body of mortgaged creditors parallel to that of unsecured creditors. In effect, if two-thirds of the mortgaged creditors formed a *concordat*, to be ratified by the civil rather than commercial court, they could proceed to have the bankrupt's immovable properties sold and the proceeds shared among the creditors according to individual claims. Mortgaged creditors under this system would only be able to pursue independent legal action for their debts if a *concordat* could not be reached. As envisioned by its proponents, this system would provide greater security for commercial creditors while simultaneously ensuring relative equality among mortgaged creditors.

The defeat of this plan testifies to the councillors' abiding belief that commerce represented a practice separate from normal civil society and inferior to it. Several councillors objected to the proposal on the grounds that *commerçants* were unlikely to hold vast amounts of immovable property, since they dealt first and foremost in movable goods. More problematically, this system created a legal order for noncommercial loans made to *commerçants* that differed fundamentally from the protocols surrounding loans in the Civil Code. It placed mortgages, loans backed by sacrosanct landed property, on the same level as commercial debts, a prospect that upended the deep-seated belief that land, as a property, represented a debt with priority over those of commerce.[70] The Council's powerful advocates of the primacy of landed property defeated attempts to set up a parallel *concordat* among secured creditors. The finished Commercial Code allowed mortgaged creditors to pursue their debt through expropriation unless they wished to join the unsecured creditors. Indeed, it went even further: Article 539 stipulated that mortgaged creditors who did not receive full reimbursement from the sale of immovable property would join with the unsecured creditors.[71]

Family property was another area where tensions emerged between the bankrupt's status as a *commerçant* and as an ordinary citizen. The Commercial Code envisioned the *commerçant* in almost exclusively masculine terms. Only Article 4 even mentioned the possibility of the female commercial person (*commerçante*) in specifying that women had to be recognized by local commercial courts (with the consent of their husbands) and that *commerçante* status required more than merely minding their husbands' counters.[72] Even though the code clearly imagined the bankrupt as the male head of the household, Book III devoted sustained attention to women. The legislators clearly reacted here to popular stereotypes in which the bankrupt's wife was virtually synonymous with the unsavory concealment of assets. Many contemporary writers, like Vital Roux, believed that the compliant wives of bankrupt merchants falsely claimed all their husbands' remaining assets as part of their dowries. One Belgian merchant, for instance, professed to be the creditor of five Parisian bankrupts all of whom had managed to squirrel away considerable sums under their wives' names. "Nothing is more frequent than 'separations of goods'—a certain sign of perfidy and bad faith," complained the merchant, "and nothing is rarer than separation of profits or of gains."[73] Napoleon, enraged by the rumors that swirled around the likes of Madame Recamier and Madame Ouvrard after their husbands' bankruptcies, demanded that a bankrupt's wife "share the sufferings of her husband" and that the law offer no protection to her claims.[74] Evidently imagining bankruptcy as a crisis of the very rich, the emperor went so far as to suggest that a bankrupt's wife should lose all her assets, except for a living stipend of up to 60,000 francs, to avoid the scandal of a bankrupt couple living in luxury off the wife's dotal properties.[75]

However, the councillors knew that wives could not be so easily separated from the legitimate operation of a business in a period when almost all businesses were based in the family.[76] The emperor's proposal, they countered, would not only destroy commerce, it would "condemn merchants to celibacy," a prospect that was not only physically and emotionally unappealing but potentially financially disastrous for the many small businesses where the contributions of wives were instrumental.[77] The finished Commercial Code attempted to crack down on alleged feminine fraud while still preserving the family's centrality to commercial enterprise. It contained several clauses in the section on women penalizing them as accomplices in *banqueroutes frauduleuses*. Article 554, for example, played on stereotypes of women who lived in luxury after their husbands' bankruptcies, stipulating that "all the diamonds, paintings, golden and silver dishes" belong to the creditors and that the bankrupt's wife should be left with "nothing but clothes and undergarments for her usage."[78] The Commercial Code substantially restricted the assets a bankrupt's wife could claim from her dotal properties to those belongings specifically mentioned in the marriage contract and also limited the kinds of loans she could put in her own name. Article 545 allowed the wives of merchants to regain possession of immovable property but only as immovable property and only if they could solidly prove their legal title. In terms of movable property, the councillors placed additional restrictions on women's rights: a woman married to a man deemed a *commerçant* at the time could take out no mortgage on any other debts, movable goods, or alienated goods during her marriage. This applied even to a woman who "marries the son of a *commerçant* having, at that period, no stated or fixed profession, who will become a *commerçant*" or a man who took up commerce within a year of marriage.[79] The difficulties posed by regulating the bankrupt's behavior with his creditors pointed to larger complications presented by starkly dividing commercial law from ordinary civil law. Merchants, after all, remained ordinary citizens, entitled to make property acquisitions and nuptial arrangements like any other citizen. When a merchant went bankrupt, these very same transactions suddenly presented multiple avenues for fraud and deceit. For the promulgators of the Commercial Code, the merchant's opportunity to declare bankruptcy, an opportunity denied ordinary civilians, necessarily entailed a divergent and more rigorous set of laws to govern even those property transactions not directly related to his commerce.

Although Book III of the Commercial Code borrowed heavily from old regime decrees on bankruptcy, it was not merely a wishful attempt to reassert the pre-Revolutionary status quo. Rather, it represented an uneasy means of reconciling newer understanding of commerce as exchange open to all with traditions deeply embedded in notions of personal collateral and corporatism. Bankruptcy law in particular challenged the code's insistence on commercial law as defined by the "person" of the *commerçant*. Legislators walked a fine line between suppressing what was seen as endemic fraud, on one hand, and criminalization, which had resulted in the rejection of previous efforts at bankruptcy reform. Nor was the conflict between criminal and commercial law the only point of strain on the new code. The tension between the Commercial and Civil Codes was brought into sharp relief by the Council of State debates concerning key aspects of bankruptcy law, from managing a bankrupt's property to the privileges of pledged creditors. Lawmakers sought to ensure commercial prosperity by providing as much security as possible to commercial loans, but they often found these provisions in opposition to the rights and privileges enshrined in the Civil Code. The Commercial Code's complex compromises surrounding the legal personhood of the bankrupt proved grounds for considerable ambiguity and confusion when it came to implementation.

Implementing the Code

Despite the Commercial Code's insistence that bankruptcy was a private commercial matter, throughout the Napoleonic period officials continued to believe that it constituted a very public affair. The Ministry of Justice carefully collected material pertaining to important bankruptcies in files alongside other matters that disturbed public order and opinion, including sedition, treason, and other rebellious acts. These files, today part of the French National Archives series BB 18, provide crucial insights into the challenges of implementing the prescriptions of the code in the decade after its promulgation. In bankruptcy cases small and large from all over the country, creditors, debtors, commercial judges, and district prosecutors combined the public and private, as well as political and economic, dimensions of bankruptcy. Although only documenting a small fraction of the total bankruptcies that occurred in these years, these cases were deemed worthy of note as potentially disruptive to social stability. Two aspects characterize these cases: first, the conflict between the law on *banqueroute frauduleuse* as applied by prosecutors and the belief systems of local communities of merchants, who often proved hostile to prosecutorial interference; and second, the conflation of criminal, civil, and commercial law. Not only did prosecutors call upon criminal law to repress what they perceived to be illegitimate customs, but, in the hazy boundaries between written law and informal practice, creditors and debtors manipulated the realities of business failure to serve their own purposes, calling sometimes on commercial law and sometimes on criminal sanctions.

The conflict between local commercial practices, often sanctioned by creditors and commercial courts, and Napoleonic officials appears repeatedly in the Ministry of Justice's files. Although the Commercial Code placed substantial limitations on the involvement of public prosecutors in the bankruptcy process, many officials, dissatisfied with what they saw as the apathy of the commercial courts in prosecuting fraud, took matters into their own hands. This often led to substantial and protracted resistance. In Marseille, where Martin Rambaud had frustrated authorities a few years earlier, an ambitious public prosecutor named Arnaud sought to crack down on the impunity enjoyed by *banqueroutiers*. He focused on the creditors who actively aided malfeasance through collusion or their own strategic bankruptcies. Provided with a golden opportunity to make an example out of the massive *faillite* of banker Simon Frédéric Rouvier in 1812, Arnaud seized not only his books but also the books of two of Rouvier's creditors who had gone bankrupt soon after the banker. The seizure of books, as the creditors complained, paralyzed the collection of assets not only for Rouvier's bankruptcies but for the two other bankrupts as well.

Owing to the inconvenience these efforts caused the creditors, Arnaud soon found himself at loggerheads with the Marseillais commercial community. The chamber of commerce wrote to the minister of justice explaining, somewhat inaccurately, that "before the publication of the Commercial Code opinion alone established a difference between *faillite* and *banqueroute*." The code, they insisted, while forceful against fraud, should "prevent private interest from being sacrificed to public vengeance [*vindicte publique*]."[80] Eventually the minister of commerce intervened on the side of the Marseille Chamber of Commerce, arguing that Arnaud had overreached his power and paralyzed the operations of the bankruptcy.[81] Rebuffed, the public prosecutor maintained that the affair demanded one pursuit against all three suspects, claiming that the suspicious nature of each bankruptcy indicated some form of conspiracy between the three.[82] The results of his painstaking pursuits further disappointed Arnaud: while finding Rouvier guilty on a commuted charge of *banqueroute simple*, the jury cleared his supposed accomplices.

Arnaud's predicament resembled those of many other officials who darkly noted not only the depressing frequency of bankruptcies in their jurisdictions but also the difficulties entailed in getting the commercial courts to report evidence of fraud. After a wave of bankruptcies erupted in the Languedoc region during late 1810 and early 1811, the minister of justice tasked the public prosecutor in Montpellier with investigating the basis of public rumors alleging fraud in these failures. Studying each bankruptcy individually, the prosecutor expressed his own confusion about the distinctions he had to draw between *banqueroute simple*, *banqueroute frauduleuse*, and regular *faillite*. This confusion, he argued, seemed understandable in light of the region's business customs, which skirted close to illegality. Indeed, almost every case the prosecutor examined, from that of François Rigaud, who dabbled in smuggling and gambling, to Jacques David, who failed to present his marriage contract to the court or separate his business from his personal expenses, to Pierre Gout, who had fled from Narbonne to Bayonne shortly after convincing his creditors to agree to a notarized debt rescheduling, could be considered a *banqueroute*. Yet each also appeared to be operating well within the customs of the region. A strict enforcement of the new laws, the prosecutor opined, would mean that all the debtors merited *contrainte par corps* or criminal charges or both.[83]

Creditors themselves often took the lead in rebuking the efforts of zealous public prosecutors to pursue bankrupts criminally. Sometimes, they appeared genuinely motivated by their faith in the debtor's innocence. The creditors of Blandeau of Angoulême wrote the minister of justice that none of them had pressed charges against him and maintained that the criminal pursuits initiated by the prosecutor had destroyed their initial hopes of repayment for some of their losses. They deemed this outcome particularly upsetting because "one has perhaps never found a bankrupt who has shown more probity and good faith." While Blandeau had so far avoided imprisonment, the public prosecutor now threatened him with the prospect. The creditors argued that Blandeau's arrest would place him in Angoulême's sole prison, which was, in their words, "too horrible and unclean even for criminals."[84] Officials generally attributed creditors' pleas less to a genuine conviction of the debtor's innocence than to a desire to protect what remained of the debtor's assets from being lost during the course of a criminal investigation. In Metz, the public prosecutor insisted on prosecuting one bankrupt for *banqueroute frauduleuse* over the vehement opposition of several creditors, who wrote the minister of justice about this administrative overreach. Rebuked by the minister, the prosecutor protested that he should be applauded "for the zeal with which I have pursued this shameless *banqueroutier* and the courage I have shown in unmasking the various intrigues that had given him impunity."[85] In response, the minister of justice insisted that the creditors be trusted on the actions to pursue against their debtor, whether or not they were impelled by good or bad faith.

In other ways the tactics of creditors occasionally replicated those of zealous prosecutors as the former exploited the laws that the latter attempted to enforce. For example, both prosecutors and creditors applied the broadest possible definition to bankruptcy. While the Commercial Code explicitly restricted bankruptcy to *commerçants*, creditors often lobbied to include property owners under this term, because the designation of a debtor as a *failli* allowed creditors to act on the debtor's person. The creditors of one landowner, who had fled his estate in the Dordogne with most of his liquid assets, claimed that he merited a charge of *banqueroute frauduleuse* because he had circulated bills of exchange. Having lied both about the mortgages on his land and about the extent of his share in his wife's property holdings, the landowner's carefully prepared disappearance gave rise to suspicions of fraud.[86] Unsurprisingly, debtors attempted to avoid being considered merchants. Xavier Rouillet, a former tax collector in Limoux who had signed and circulated letters of exchange on behalf of his son, a cloth manufacturer who went bankrupt in 1812, enlisted the local bishop to plead on his behalf. Seemingly conflicted about the elder Rouillet's acumen and morality, calling his business practices "imprudent" and "undesirable," the bishop nonetheless held that "he is a not a *commerçant* and thus he is not a bankrupt."[87]

Trials were no sure bet for the public prosecutors either. Even once authorities had secured the debtor's person, they often failed to convince juries, comprised of local merchants, lawyers, and property owners, to convict even those individuals who showed brazen disregard for the law. Despite what would seem to be overwhelming evidence against Jean-Pierre Giraud, who fled Narbonne in late October 1809, leaving a house stripped bare of everything of value from the silverware to the bedsheets, and whose commercial books, discovered a few days later buried in a pile of manure along the town ramparts, contained what seemed to be simulated sales of wheat in the days leading up to his failure, a jury decided to drop charges of *banqueroute frauduleuse* against him.[88] In Quimper in February 1809, the bailiff charged with detaining a merchant held on charges of *banqueroute frauduleuse* instead helped him flee. After the jury chose to acquit both parties, the judge, deeming the jury incompetent, fumed that the two individuals could not be brought to court again on the same charges.[89]

It is unclear exactly why juries tended to rule in favor of such individuals even with piles of evidence against them, although historians have noted that juries throughout the country chose to drop charges or to acquit criminal defendants at notably high rates during this period.[90] Magistrates and legislators alike saw in the lenience of juries a reason to doubt the new Revolutionary justice. Indeed, the Napoleonic Criminal Code of 1810 eliminated the *jury d'accusation*, which under Revolutionary law had decided whether there were sufficient grounds for an indictment. In the opinion of many observers, jury members were not sufficiently educated to follow the subtleties of the law, and they often had difficulty distinguishing between intention and motivation in assessing guilt. According to prosecutors' accounts, many of the juries were co-opted by the accused through threats or bribes. In 1810 the public prosecutor in Toulouse opined of *banqueroute frauduleuse* that "juries are so indulgent for this kind of infraction that if the proofs are not as clear as day (and they cannot be unless the creditors want to help me uncover them) it is probable that the charges will be dismissed."[91] The likelihood of acquittal encouraged both creditors and public prosecutors to refrain from risking their own money, or the treasury's funds, to pursue fraud.

Some creditors, believing that lower-level public officials had not acted fast enough to prevent fraud, appealed to higher magistrates, occasionally even insinuating negligence or outright malfeasance on the part of government officers. In April 1811 one creditor in Montpellier complained of being reduced to relying on public charity after the bankruptcy of the justice of the peace's brother, whom that official refused to pursue.[92] The banker Alexandre Morand wrote the minister of justice accusing the Parisian magistrate Grégoire Sainte-Hélène of culpable apathy. Morand had burst into Sainte-Hélène's office in Paris's Third Arrondissement at eleven in the morning one day in January 1808, demanding that the magistrate arrest the clockmaker Froissart *fils* on charges of *banqueroute frauduleuse* before Morand's own order of *contrainte par corps* against him expired at noon of that day.

When Sainte-Hélène insisted that Morand present viable evidence of fraud on Froissart's part, Morand accused him of stalling, even going so far as to suggest that Sainte-Hélène might be in league with Froissart's family, who were well connected in the town of Abbeville.[93]

Officials and creditors often found that bankrupts possessed powerful protectors within the social and political elites of their community. One enraged creditor in the town of Castelnaudry wrote the minister of justice about a merchant named Espinasse, "who should be in prison and is instead dining at his own house," allegedly because he had benefited from the protection of a cousin who was president of the town's criminal court. Espinasse had been cleared of charges of *banqueroute frauduleuse* at a trial where witnesses had mysteriously refused to appear or had stayed quiet. Moreover, "all of his accursed family" had similarly enriched themselves off their own bankruptcies.[94] Mathieu Barthelme Oduard, president of the commercial court of Montelimar, was removed from his position in 1811 when M. Salomon, creditor of Oduard's brother, accused him of complicity in his brother's *banqueroute frauduleuse*.[95] Oduard fought back against Salomon, alleging that the former Jacobin's rancor came not from his brother's actual wrongdoing, but rather from a political vendetta that had motivated Salomon to press for Oduard's bankruptcy in the first place. In Périgueux, multiple authorities became involved in the case of one Lacotte, who committed suicide shortly after his bankruptcy. The local tax collector filed a posthumous charge of *banqueroute frauduleuse* against Lacotte and accused the Périgueux Commercial Court of covering up evidence of Lacotte's fraud. He even alleged that the commercial court president had gone three times on the day of the bankruptcy to Lacotte's house to arrange privileged payments of his own debts in the bankruptcy.[96] Accusations of complicity in *banqueroute simple* and *frauduleuse* connected to this case reached all the way to members of the Corps Législatif.[97]

Public officials investigated charges of favoritism, but investigators themselves were not immune to the importance of social status. In one instance, François Roque, a cloth merchant and part-time banker in Brives, had almost obtained a *concordat* from his creditors when one creditor pressed a charge of *banqueroute frauduleuse*, claiming that earlier accusations has been dropped because of Roque's close connection with local officials. One allegation mentioned that Roque rented a house from the justice of the peace's sister. The public prosecutor in Corrèze, asked by the minister of justice to investigate the matter, verified that Roque rented from the official's sister but said he "could hardly believe this venerable magistrate, who has fulfilled his public duties for thirty years with honor and dignity and without a word of reproach against him" could possibly favor the bankrupt. Despite admitting that Roque deserved a charge of *banqueroute simple* for his disorderly bookkeeping, the public prosecutor did not press charges. Nor did he investigate rumors that Roque's family had paid off some of his more pressing creditors, including an unsuccessful attempt at paying off the one who had launched the accusation of *banqueroute*.[98]

Conflicts between departmental prosecutors and local commercial courts were particularly fierce in Paris. There, the prosecutor's tendency to drop in on assemblies of creditors and seize papers from the estates of debtors without official charges of *banqueroute* deeply irritated commercial court officials. They were particularly infuriated by the prosecutor's presence at bankruptcy convocations where, they argued, even silent, he dominated the proceedings, thereby giving the "impression of a criminal pursuit, and paralyz[ing] the liberty of the creditors." In 1811, immediately following the implementation of a new criminal code that replaced the Revolutionary jury system with an old regime–style inquisitorial system, the Parisian public prosecutor demanded that the commercial court furnish statistics on all bankruptcies in the past year and spoke to the police, "observing to them that a *faillite* establishes in itself possible grounds for an infraction." He also unsuccessfully demanded more judges to handle the criminal aspects of commercial cases.[99] The prosecutor's comments to the minister of justice revealed a tense relationship between the criminal and commercial courts, which the prosecutor believed were all too willing to turn a blind eye to criminal practices regarded as normal parts of commerce.

Prosecutors were not alone in accusing debtors of *banqueroute*, nor in their tendency to conflate criminal and commercial jurisdictions. Disgruntled creditors often shopped legal theaters in the hopes of extracting revenge if not reimbursement for their debts. In one instance, François Philippe Mondot-Lagorce, a Parisian banker, obtained a *concordat* from his creditors only to have two of them, Jean-Charles Ragoulleau and Martin Giberges, begin legal pursuits against him for *banqueroute simple*. The case quickly descended into charges of corruption, favoritism, and calumny, with Mondot-Lagorce alleging that Ragoulleau had been angered when he was not allowed to obtain preferential treatment for his debts. While Ragoulleau accused Mondot-Lagorce of having fled his house, the banker retorted that his creditor had convinced a complaisant bailiff to so ostentatiously and so completely blockade Lagorce's residence with seals that he and his family had been forced to take up residence elsewhere. Although Lagorce ultimately received a slander charge, the court of appeals upheld the banker's main argument that the commercial court's ratification of his *concordat* connoted its belief in his honorability. The court reasoned that to allow a conviction for *banqueroute simple* following such a judgment would create a scandal by implicitly criticizing the justice of the commercial court.[100]

The flight of delinquent debtors, a relatively common occurrence, also blurred the boundaries between commercial and criminal jurisdictions. Apprehending bankrupts on the lam often severely tested the coordination of civil and criminal authorities between towns, departments, and even countries. For instance, although an arrest warrant had been issued for one bankrupt merchant in Rouen, his subsequent apprehension in Angoulême was declared illegal because the justice of the peace had never received the warrant from Rouen.[101] In March 1812 authorities in Vienna apprehended a wine wholesaler who had fled Beaune several months earlier. His assets, however, proved far more elusive, despite the eager pursuits of Austrian creditors and authorities, themselves interested in the results.[102] Three military contractors, accused of bankruptcy in Paris, were discovered to have moved to Naples, where they claimed that their age and ill health made it unsafe for them to obey the warrants issued against them.[103] Border guards, meanwhile, sent information on suspicious individuals who had attempted to traverse the French border with old or false passports, but coordination between these officials and the bankruptcy officials was often ineffective.[104] When the deputy prosecutor of Doubs had Jean-Jacques Lathier arrested and extradited in Pontalier, Switzerland, in October 1808, Lathier accused the *département* of having overstepped the boundaries of its authority in treating him like a criminal.[105] Since neither commercial courts nor individual creditors possessed the means to apprehend a debtor who had run away, and since flight implied criminality in public opinion if not in the eyes of the law, this action predictably led to a confusion of criminal and commercial jurisdictions.

Given the difficulties in launching criminal pursuits, debt imprisonment served as an alternate means of preventing the flight of a debtor. Family members of incarcerated debtors often complained that their loved ones were treated like criminals. Nicolas Chevallot, who worked in the municipal tax office in Dijon, begged the minister of justice to expedite the trial of his twenty-two-year-old son, who had been held for complicity in *banqueroute frauduleuse*. Chevallot, also ruined by this bankruptcy, claimed that his son was held unjustly and arbitrarily and had been forbidden communication even with his mother.[106] At times, public officials seemed to have been overwhelmed by such demands. One public prosecutor snapped at a grocer's wife that it was her husband's fault if he had been detained for five months, since he had kept such disorganized books that the accusations of fraud leveled at him by his creditors proved nearly impossible to verify.[107] Precaution at any rate seemed preferable to liberty. Magistrates noted that granting bail to bankrupts accused of *banqueroute simple* generally had disastrous consequences. They demanded that bail be set at the entire amount of the bankruptcy and that agents be held financially and personally responsible if a bankrupt escaped custody before his trial.[108]

Friends and family of imprisoned debtors pleaded their loved ones' cases to civil and criminal officials rather than to recalcitrant creditors. The minister of justice regularly received letters from the friends and family of those pursued for bankruptcy or held in debtor's prison, pleading for the minister's intervention on the grounds of both clemency and justice. Basel resident Jean-François Kraus, for instance, implored the minister of justice to take pity on his daughter, accused of *banqueroute frauduleuse* in Besançon, because she had provided his only support while his son fought in the emperor's army.[109] The gravely ill wife and teenage son of one bankrupt, a fugitive from the police for the previous two years, begged both the emperor and the minister of justice for mercy, saying that "his life and his conduct had never put him in a position to merit abandoning his wife and child."[110] Debtors too wrote the Ministry of Justice asking for relief. Sentenced to ten years of hard labor in the *bagne* of Toulon for *banqueroute frauduleuse*, Nicolas-François Japiot begged the minister of justice to be allowed to serve out his time in Dijon instead. Fifty-six, in failing health, and claiming to be a wrongly condemned "unfortunate *père de famille*," Japiot could also marshal his creditors' support for a plan that allowed him to help them recover his remaining assets.[111]

Implementing the code was, in short, a messy process. In March 1811 a public prosecutor of the Paris civil court wrote a report detailing the application of the Commercial Code over the previous two years. On the eve of its implementation, he remarked, there was such fear of the new laws that struggling businessmen had hastened to file for bankruptcy prior to December 31, 1807, so as to be judged under the old laws. The prosecutor deemed the Commercial Code's provisions excessively rigorous because they presumed that "every bankruptcy is an assault on public order—a misdemeanor or a felony." The rigor of these measures led debtors and creditors alike to apply only those aspects of the new code favorable to their interests, thus "transforming by usage" the laws into ones far too favorable toward dishonest bankrupts. Appalled by the rise of bankruptcies, the public prosecutor regarded these failures, motivated "firstly by dishonesty, second by ambition and third by overconfidence," to be potentially ruinous to commerce unless the manifold abuses that allowed them to proliferate were quickly repressed.[112]

Despite his considered reflections on the roots of bankruptcies both in the failings of the laws and in the moral deficiencies of individual debtors, the prosecutor had few suggestions for remedying this state of affairs. In arguing that the punitive nature of the law encouraged illicit behavior, he merely returned the attention of the government to the problem that flummoxed lawmakers from their initial attempts to create a bankruptcy code. Unlike other sorts of illegal activity in which the interests of the perpetrators were directly opposed to those of the victims, creditors and debtors in bankruptcy cases strategically balanced the desire for justice with more pragmatic concerns about the possibilities of reimbursement. Sometimes these two goals, handled by two different jurisdictions, were at odds. In these cases, the creditors' desire to obtain as favorable an arrangement as possible generally trumped an abstract love of justice. Laws that were too punitive only seemed to provide further incentive to work on the margins of the law. Government officials, like the prosecutor himself, who attempted to vigorously prosecute debtors or creditors that took advantage of the complaisance of their counterparts, often found themselves sternly opposed by local commercial courts and chambers of commerce who saw such interventions as direct and unlawful intrusion into their jurisdiction. The early years of the Commercial Code, rather than resolving the tension between the criminal and civil components of bankruptcy, merely set the ground for a conflict that would continue throughout the following decades.

Conclusion

On September 3, 1807, when the comte de Ségur had presented the newly promulgated Commercial Code to the Corps Législatif, he introduced Book III on bankruptcy by asking the legislators, "a businessman who fails his engagements and goes bankrupt, should he, by his bankruptcy, be presumed fraudulent or considered as unfortunate?"[113] Ségur proceeded to tout the merits of the new laws over the old. While old regime law had erred too much in presuming the bankrupt's innocence, allowing him to pillage his creditors with the cover of law, under the Commercial Code the bankrupt was presumed "neither a guilty man, nor an innocent one, but as a debtor whose behavior demands a rigorous investigation and a solid guarantee."

In attempting to remove the legal category of bankruptcy from presumptions of guilt or innocence, Ségur distinguished the Commercial Code not so much from its predecessors as from practices and attitudes that flourished on the law's margins. From the later years of the Directory through the early years of the Empire, public opinion was scandalized by abuses perpetrated by creditors and debtors in equal measure. Early drafts of bankruptcy reform had envisioned a much larger role for criminal procedure in the bankruptcy process. Given the resistance these earlier drafts had encountered, the version that Ségur defended contained more moderate prescriptions in managing bankruptcy. Yet Ségur highlighted the rigor of the investigation and the solidity of the guarantee, underscoring that the presumption of fraud entailed by commercial default had not entirely dissipated.

The application of the Commercial Code in its early years flew in the face of Ségur's optimistic pronouncement that the new legal framework would resolve the problems of the old laws and that economic and criminal considerations would henceforth be firmly separated. Implementing the code's prescriptions in towns and villages throughout the country proved to be a much trickier and more confusing process than the code's promulgators had anticipated. The Commercial Code itself, based on a conception of the *commerçant* that extended beyond professional life to attach to the physical body and to his social ties and family, confused rather than sharpened the boundaries between jurisdictions. The new regime's insistence on contractual morality confronted engrained customary practices. The mobility of debtors' bodies as well as their assets convinced many creditors and government officials that criminal sanctions should be enforced even when fraud had not yet been proven. Prosecutors, frustrated by the continued willingness of some creditors to cooperate with blatantly illegal behavior, overstepped formal boundaries between commercial and criminal courts in the pursuit of debtors they judged to have committed fraud. The persistently deep connection between political position and economic power, reflected in the number of bankrupts intimately connected to important local or national political figures, complicated the process of separating the social from the financial implications of bankruptcy.

The treatment of bankruptcy cases under the code belies any clear distinction between civil, commercial, and criminal justice. The Napoleonic codes emerged in a period of radical transition. Government officials attempted to restrain communal forms of justice, which encouraged mechanisms for creating harmony that often ran counter to formal laws, even as they claimed that the Revolution's destruction of communal norms necessitated recourse to rigorous laws to restore morality. Commerce proved particularly intractable to efforts at centralization because commercial transactions rested on assessments of credit, which emanated from communal norms. Napoleonic legislators, like their Revolutionary predecessors, believed that the particularities of commercial law entitled it to a unique dependence on custom and communal norms. At the same time, in an atmosphere of chronic mistrust, these norms often engendered criminal behavior that undermined public faith in commercial practices. Bankruptcy in particular evoked this possibility. For this reason, the promulgators of the Commercial Code attempted to tie bankruptcy to the identity of the commercial person, an individual simultaneously conceptualized as a free, independent agent subject to prosecution for transgressions of the law but also as set apart from "normal" members of society and subjected to different rules and protocols. This notion of the commercial personality corresponded uneasily with the reality of individuals deeply embedded in networks of creditors, relatives, and friends.

After the Restoration, and the stabilization of the economy resulting from the end of the Napoleonic Wars, the criminal rigor that underlay attitudes toward bankruptcy in the first two decades of the nineteenth century faded. Unlike their Napoleonic predecessors, Restoration ministers of justice did not include files about bankruptcy among the threats to public order and decency. Many of the jurisdictional conflicts that set the commercial court and the criminal prosecutors at loggerheads were ironed out, generally to the satisfaction of the commercial courts. Yet because the Commercial Code was based on the person of the debtor, concerns about honor and concerns about the legality of a bankrupt's behavior continued to be closely intertwined. While government orators touted the "blessing of being judged" by a law that was universally believed to be just, compliance with this law remained erratic throughout the first half of the nineteenth century.[114]

Part Two

THE PARADOXES OF FAILURE

3

Risky Business

Banqueroute, Faillite, and the Culture of Credit

In June 1828, the Paris Correctional Court heard the arguments of Sieur Tessier, a bankrupt butcher, against Mother Lebret, a plaster and brick merchant, whom he accused of calumny for having called him a *banqueroutier* despite his offer to pay his creditors a generous 30 percent of his debts in a *concordat*. In her defense, Lebret, speaking with a "thunderous voice that had nothing feminine about it," did not deny calling Tessier a *banqueroutier* and justified her usage of a term that implied criminality and fraud. Explaining that she had lost over 40,000 francs of the "hard-earned product of her toil" in three bankruptcies, including Tessier's, Lebret described the privations suffered by her family, including a paralyzed husband and numerous children. The sight of the former butcher driving through town in his cabriolet while she had received "not a penny" of the dividends he had promised enraged the woman, who had been reduced to borrowing clothing from her relatives. After hearing the plaster merchant's heart-wrenching account, the jury dismissed Tessier's libel charge against her. *Banqueroutier*, they decided, seemed an understandable moral assessment in his case, even if Tessier faced no legal condemnation for his activities.[1]

The case of Tessier and Lebret vividly illustrates both the stigma attached to the word *banqueroutier* and the fluidity of the boundaries between *faillite* and *banqueroute* in popular usage through the early nineteenth century, despite the clear differences drawn between these categories in law. On one hand, the Commercial Code clearly distinguished *faillite* from the categorical list of activities that constituted gross negligence or mismanagement in *banqueroute simple* or outright theft and deception in *banqueroute frauduleuse*. Legal scholars, too, argued for firm philosophical differences between these legal categories based on the debtor's will. "*Faillite* is always necessary and forced," opined one writer, "it is the result of a loss, a misfortune or an accident independent of the will of the bankrupt. *Banqueroute* is always voluntary and the debtor's fault. The *failli* is therefore innocent; the *banqueroutier* guilty and punished by the law."[2] While there was almost universal acknowledgment of the innocence of *faillite* in the abstract, in reality the *failli*'s legal status appeared considerably more complicated. The Commercial Code took certain precautionary measures, particularly at the opening of a bankruptcy, which appeared to presume guilt rather than innocence. The code, as one legislator put it, regarded business failure from its outset as an abnormal state wherein the debtor, "merely for having gone bankrupt, is placed in a state of probation, is obliged to account for his conduct, to justify the causes of his bankruptcy."[3]

The evaluation of these causes, whether by the creditors at the convocation, commercial judges in ratifying a debt arrangement, or writers reflecting on the state of commercial morality, likewise challenged the idea of the truly innocent bankruptcy. Everywhere, *faillis* found themselves subjected to questions about their behavior and intentions. Why had they alone failed when others had managed, even in similarly trying circumstances, to uphold their engagements? Had they truly directed their affairs with the necessary prudence and foresight? Could their supposed misfortune have been prevented by wiser decisions? In a society of pervasive and perpetual indebtedness, why had their time run out? Many observers could simply not believe that failure to repay obligations could be truly independent of the will of the debtor. Businessmen themselves argued that the number of bankruptcies caused by misfortune was infinitely small compared to those caused by misconduct and imprudence.[4] Widespread doubt regarding the innocence of *faillite* did not mean that all *faillis* were considered *banqueroutiers* even in the loose sense of the term with which Lebret reproached Tessier. Opinions on bankruptcies varied, moreover, by region. As late as the early 1850s, the legal commentator Louis Geoffroy noted that although in Paris and other major urban centers public opinion accepted the notion of the honest failure, in the provinces "every bankrupt is still confused with the fraudulent bankrupt."[5] However, this doubt does help explain the civic degradation surrounding the *faillite*, in which even the debtor found fully excusable and truly unfortunate was stripped of some political rights and honorific privileges.

The fine line between *faillite* and *banqueroute*, as well as the punitive connotations attached even to innocent business failure, invites reflection about the nature of risk taking in early nineteenth-century France and its connection to the regime of personal responsibility embedded in the Napoleonic codes. Ever since David Landes's ascription of the "backwardness" of French industrialization to a deep cultural distaste for entrepreneurship, the image of nineteenth-century French commerce as profoundly hostile to risk has lingered despite the reevaluation of the scope and nature of the Industrial Revolution. Contemporary observers shared some of these beliefs. During his famous sojourn in the United States, for instance, Alexis de Tocqueville attributed the absence of a category comparable to *banqueroute* to the young nation's encouragement of even the most brazen risk taking.[6] Yet the direct correlation between bankruptcy laws, encouragement of entrepreneurship, and the innovativeness of an economy, while compelling, is facile. Not only did British laws, supposedly more "risk friendly," prescribe the death penalty for fraudulent bankrupts until 1820, but economic historians have argued that harsh laws toward debtors may in fact encourage risk taking under certain regimes.[7] More to the point, the rigor of bankruptcy laws does not indicate whether they were obeyed or enforced. In post-Revolutionary France, evidence from the bankruptcy dossiers, legal documents, and newspaper reports indicates that informal agreements and careful manipulation and adaptation of the law mattered more to the outcome of business failure than the strict letter of the law. Indeed, this reality explains a central paradox: despite nearly universal agreement that Napoleonic laws treated business failure harshly, contemporary sources unanimously criticized bankruptcy as an avenue for fraud.

Nineteenth-century intellectuals certainly believed that post-Revolutionary society encouraged risk taking, which they generally framed in terms of ambition. On one hand, ambition was emblematic of the Revolution's liberation of merit from the shackles of tradition and thus became the "liberal passion *par excellence*," infecting everyone from poets to statesmen who dreamed of glory.[8] Doctors feared that too much ambition could be personally and politically destructive: asylums overflowed with men who thought they were generals, emperors, and popes, victims of what Jan Goldstein has termed "the special monomania of the early nineteenth century," namely, "overweening ambition of all sorts, stimulated by the more fluid society that was the legacy of the Revolution."[9] While this type of risk taking seemed above all directed toward political and social advancement, as J. C. Martin has argued, merchants and artisans who sought to rapidly move forward in society also attracted the antipathy of their neighbors.[10]

This chapter examines how risks and culpability were assessed by looking at court cases involving charges of *banqueroute frauduleuse* and, to a lesser extent, *banqueroute simple.* Seeking to understand how arguments about appropriate risk taking were framed in an economy that was fraught with uncertainty and where the laws were not necessarily always applied, it draws primarily from the factums or *mémoires judiciaire*s of *banquerout*e cases. Regularly produced by lawyers and other court officials for major legal affairs throughout the nineteenth century, factums were printed explanations of the facts of court cases combined with arguments in favor of the litigants. Given that these documents were directed at judges (and sometimes circulated publicly), they had to combine mastery of the technical aspects of the case with persuasive moral rhetoric. Although it is impossible to ascertain the impact of these documents themselves or their moral arguments about failure in determining the outcome of cases, they do provide a revealing window into how judgments about a bankruptcy as a *banqueroute* or a *faillite* rested on holistic assessments of the debtor's person.

Commercial Culture in Nineteenth-Century France

Nineteenth-century merchants had good reason to obsessively dread the prospect of *faillite.* Scholars have estimated that in Paris in the late 1820s and early 1830s, approximately 2 percent of businesses went bankrupt every year.[11] Between 1,000 and 2,000 businessmen went bankrupt annually throughout France.[12] According to data compiled by Pierre-Cyrille Hautcoeur and Nadine Levratto, this meant that bankruptcies increased faster than the rate of new business growth.[13] The majority of these failures involved small industries, particularly clustered around wine and food and luxury goods, although there was also no shortage of spectacular bankruptcies involving sums over 100,000 francs.[14] Bankruptcy, in short, was an ever-present reality.

Practicing commerce in the post-Revolutionary era was fraught with risk. As one economic historian has put it, "In order to understand the period and the life of the business world as well as that of private individuals one has to conjure up a whole atmosphere of monetary shortage" wherein the "major recurring themes were obsession with repayment dates, the threat of bankruptcy, and the success of the moneylender."[15] In this commercial culture, social bonds both made and undid credit. Formal credit institutions played only a minor role in the management of most commercial credit during this period. Notaries generally confined themselves to long-term transactions.[16] Banks, insomuch as they existed, catered to elite clientele.[17] Personal relations between merchants mattered immensely. Every business functioned within a dense web of connections to other merchants, clients, and suppliers. Businessmen needed correspondents and associates as sources of capital and expertise, as well as people capable of providing information on nonlocal clients and recovering debts in other cities.[18]

Every bill of exchange or promissory note reflected these chains of credit. In addition to considering the credit of those from whom they directly took the bill, merchants scanned the names of endorsers listed on the back to see if they too were creditworthy. Too many signatures from notably insolvent or disreputable individuals might result in demands for additional securities, the mortgaging of collateral, or outright refusal of the bill. Bill discounters played a critical role in the circulation of credit, accepting commercial paper before its due date in exchange for a cut of the value. After appraising the strength of the credit network on each bill, the discounter took a greater or lesser cut in relation to the risks he ran. His task was fraught with danger: a discounter could be ruined by irregularities like forgery or accommodation paper, where bills were signed and circulated between complicit parties when no actual money or merchandise had been exchanged. The discount rate, considered a type of insurance premium for the discounter, was not subject to the same legal restrictions against "habitual usury" that could otherwise entail a prison sentence and a fine.[19] An 1837 survey of commercial discount rates divided these rates into seven categories, based on the selectivity of clientele whose bills were discounted and the corresponding discount level, with the lowest rates enjoyed by elite clientele in Paris and the highest by small provincial businessmen.[20] These rates also varied between individual businessmen. Those who enjoyed little reputation could expect to pay dearly for their bills.

Since the extension of credit often rested on strength of reputation as well as on social networks of family, friends, and associates, the stakes for a debtor not able to make good on his promises frequently extended far beyond the amount of the principal. However, the strength of such social bonds also meant that deadlines were often more flexible than the dates on promissory notes and bills of exchange might suggest. Bills could be renewed, although generally with a steeper rate of interest. Debtors and creditors frequently exhausted all other means of resolving debt disputes before taking matters to court. Even in transactions where personal ties were weaker, both sides remained deeply invested in preserving the harmony of their relationship. In a society where information was dispersed and difficult to obtain, maintaining a working connection often outweighed the benefits of finding a replacement for even a bad payer. Yet if they did not, the complex social webs in which credit was built could rapidly unravel, with each creditor seeking to secure his own debts as quickly as possible, even at the expense of other creditors. At this point, a debtor would be faced with all the methods of execution authorized by the law, including protests, seizures, pay stoppages, imprisonment, and bankruptcy.

Moreover, the same chains of commercial credit necessary for a merchant or artisan's prosperity could also precipitate his decline. The balance sheets of bankrupts included substantial sums that they had lost in other bankruptcies. Creditors routinely wrote off irrecoverable liabilities in these balance sheets. Businessmen ruined themselves attempting to help out their struggling friends or family members. Although credit helped build long-term bonds, constant indebtedness could make merchants particularly sensitive to France's periodic political upheavals. Shopkeepers who lent on credit to establish a customer base or artisans who supplied their clients with goods were devastated by revolutions, riots, and other disasters.[21] In an increasingly globally interconnected credit economy, international financial panics destroyed the fortunes of many businessmen.[22] To these types of risks could be added the continual threats posed by adverse weather conditions, fires, floods, shipwrecks, family or personal illness, and robbery during an age when few merchants had access to insurance.

In short, carrying out early nineteenth-century commerce was extremely risky business in which businessmen were in a constant state of indebtedness. In this atmosphere of pervasive fragility and instability, bankruptcy could devastate the chain of credit. Merchants dreaded and even hated bankrupts, even as their own precarious position made them sympathetic to the underlying causes of failure and in constant fear of facing the prospect themselves. As such, bankrupts represented the paradoxes of commercial credit. Émile Saint-Hilaire summarized the irony that "the more one owes, the more credit one has; the fewer creditors one has, the fewer resources." He added that "those who don't give credit infallibly go bankrupt [*faire banqueroute*], because the more one gives credit, the more one can borrow, the more one borrows, the more business one can do, the more business one can do, the more one makes money."[23] Saint-Hilaire's choice of the word *banqueroute* rather than *faillite* is telling; without credit, an individual would not only fail but would fail in a potentially criminal manner. Why did some debtors face this treatment from those who had previously extended them loans and discounted their bills? Why did others successfully weather the constant uncertainties that commerce faced? And why, given the difficulties faced by merchants on a daily basis, did the law insist on treating them with such rigor? The answer to these questions lies in an examination of the narratives that lawmakers, legal writers, and merchants themselves told about risk taking.

What Did It Mean to Go Bankrupt?

By the terms of the Commercial Code, a bankrupt, even one morally irreproachable in the eyes of his creditors, lost any number of political and social rights, including his right to vote, to wear the Legion of Honor, and to enter the stock market. Contemporary scholars hastened to explain that while a *faillite* entailed civic degradation, it could not be considered "an afflictive or infamous penalty" as was a *banqueroute*. Although *faillite* resulted in civic and political incapacities, one law book noted, it did not entail an *interdiction*, which stripped an individual of legal rights over his property owing to insanity, or a *conseil judiciaire*, the appointment of a special council to oversee property management often mandated for prodigals.[24] A *failli* remained a property owner; he was not to be considered expropriated in the seizure of his property, but only temporarily removed from the ability to direct his affairs. The restrictions placed on a *failli* did not impinge on a *failli*'s control of his property or over that of his wife and children.[25] Scholars realized that the legal consequences of a bankruptcy, however excusable, resembled both criminal and civil sanctions for crime, misuse of money, and irrationality and assured readers that such similarities remained merely superficial.

The legal stain of *faillite*, and its entailed loss of rights, could only be extinguished by rehabilitation, which required the full payment of the principal, interest, and expenses of the bankruptcy rather than mere satisfaction of the terms of the *concordat*. A debtor convicted of a *banqueroute simple* or *frauduleuse* could not hope for rehabilitation, nor, before 1838, could a *failli* who received a *union* rather than a *concordat*. Unsurprisingly given these barriers, few *faillis* ever managed to attain rehabilitation. The final and triumphal reentry of Balzac's bankrupt perfumer César Birotteau into the Paris stock market following his rehabilitation would have been one of only a few dozen rehabilitations each year, in contrast to the thousands of individuals who filed for *faillite*. Legislators believed that the small number of rehabilitated *faillis* demonstrated the integrity of the process and refused to make the process easier. Most *faillis* thus probably believed that their loss of political rights was a permanent one.

Opposition to the rigors of the law began soon after the implementation of the Napoleonic codes. In 1814 the lawyer Louis-Édouard LaMarre took the opportunity provided by the brief Bourbon restoration to the French throne to criticize the Napoleonic bankruptcy law. Prior to the code, he said, the absence of the intermediary category of *banqueroute simple* had led people to confuse *banqueroute* and *faillite*, "indistinctly giving all [bankrupts] the humiliating name of *banqueroutiers*." While this may have been harsh on the truly honest debtor, reckless and incompetent bankrupts sometimes received the benefit of the law, thereby dishonoring bankrupts as a group. Civic degradation made sense in this context where respectable and untrustworthy debtors were both considered *faillis*. However, LaMarre believed that the creation of the intermediary category of *banqueroute simple* had solved this problem. He pleaded that those who had filed for bankruptcy since the Commercial Code, whom he labeled as the "numberless victims of Buonaparte's government," should retain their rights as French citizens and not be "subjected to the penalties reserved for great criminals."[26] In 1827 the Paris Chamber of Commerce echoed LaMarre's criticism, comparing what they saw as the universally negative presumption of the bankrupt as guilty with the much lighter treatment of non-*commerçants* under *déconfiture*.[27] In 1835 a petitioner described the "shocking parallel and the flagrant contradiction" presented by the fact that an individual charged by the correctional court for fraud or disloyalty in his obligations regained his rights and privileges after his punishment, while a debtor universally recognized by his creditors as being of good faith nevertheless lost many of his.[28] Pointing to the disgrace attached to bankruptcy as a leading cause of suicide among honest but distressed traders, the petitioner asked for the legislators to revise the draconian principles of the code for debtors who attained a *concordat*.

For others, the problem with the punitive tone taken by the Commercial Code was not so much its injustice as the lack of incentive it provided for bankrupts to obey the law. An arbitrator at the Paris commercial court attributed the code's rigorous measures against all bankrupts to the righteous indignation of the code's promulgators at a few egregious abuses. Nevertheless, by the 1820s the arbitrator believed such measures increased the very frauds they sought to prevent.[29] Louis Geoffroy maintained that the debtors were often driven to criminal acts by seeking to avert the shame of a bankruptcy through dubious means. Worse, they were easily tempted to acts of outright fraud to hide their situation and then fled when they could no longer avoid ruin.[30] As one legislator put it, under the Commercial Code "rather than expose himself to such humiliation, the debtor forces himself, by consuming his last resources, to prolong a state of agony that opens him to all the temptation of despair; when it becomes impossible for him to dissimulate his situation anymore, he flees or hides."[31] Desperation sometimes explained or justified actions that elicited the charge of *banqueroute*.

Even as changing political and economic circumstances inspired some writers to question the bankrupt's civil degradation and the social opprobrium inspired by a bankruptcy, they led other writers to insist more strongly on the bankrupt's moral culpability. Jacques-Pierre Roret's popular 1829 *Code de commerce: Manuel complet d'industrie commercial* presented bankruptcy as an almost inevitable punishment for a merchant's unwise or recklessly greedy decisions and as a convenient foil for Roret's advice on being a good trader. He counseled merchants to be cautious and moderate in their desires, avoiding speculation and luxury and retiring from commerce once they had secured a satisfactory amount to live on.[32] By living simply, a truly successful businessman could proudly claim independence.[33] "Having too much trust in others is the ruin of many men," Roret added. True independence also entailed avoiding credit whenever possible. He included a list of commercial proverbs which included such pithy words of wisdom as: "He who goes to borrow money is seeking humiliation," "The second vice is to lie, the first to get one's self into debt," and "Better to sleep without dinner than to rise with debts."[34] In Roret's manual, the good merchant knew that the price at which he borrowed was always higher than the rate of interest.

The prospect of failure haunted Roret's depiction of successful commerce. Yet these dark possibilities were meant to reassure rather than disturb the reader: Business failure equated very neatly with failure to uphold his manual's practical advice and moral precepts. In two representations of bankruptcy, Roret showed how quickly professional incompetence and moral failings could lead to outright illegality. According to his account, most bankruptcies resulted from ignorance and temerity. They inevitably began when would-be merchants ascribed commercial success to chance or good fortune rather than to hard work and intelligence.[35] Those of humble

FIGURE 1. A bankrupt wearing a top hat that reads "Faillite" rides by his creditors in an elegant carriage in this print by Honoré Daumier originally published in *Le Charivari*. (The Daumier Register©, Noack Collection, www.daumier-register.org)

origins were especially susceptible to this misunderstanding, being easily misled by examples of meteoric rises.[36] Without the necessary skills and the ability to work hard, the ambitious young man who fancied himself a merchant was almost inevitably destined for bankruptcy. In haste, he rented a shop and employed a carpenter only to find himself petrified with boredom waiting for customers to arrive. When few arrived, the would-be merchant would watch in increasing despair as his rent fell due and his merchandise deteriorated.[37] After desperate efforts to secure funds through petty discounters and usurers, he would be forced to declare bankruptcy. Roret estimated that "a third of employees who populate the stores and shops of the capital are themselves former merchants forced to serve others by their own inability to master the principles of sale."[38]

For Roret, the line between this unfortunate but upright *faillite* and *banqueroute frauduleuse* was extremely fine. In the latter case, a young man, similarly bewitched by others' success and heedless of the dishonor of failure, set himself up in Paris's booming luxury trade and spent resources lavishly decorating his shop. Although never actually turning a profit, the young merchant became accustomed to a lavish lifestyle, including extravagant parties, fine carriages, and expensive gifts. Unable to make sacrifices and needing to pay the various suppliers, the merchant resorted to fictitious credit to stave off the inevitable. Eventually, he was forced to invite his creditors over for dinner "and, between the pear and the cheese," dupe them into agreeing to meager returns on a *concordat*.[39] Although Roret clearly distinguished between the morality of the *failli* and the *banqueroutier*, he portrayed them on a continuum. Merchants who lacked correct notions of the sacrifices, industry, and drive necessary to earn money honestly could easily be led from acts of incompetence and inexperience into outright breaches of the law.

Pierre-Sébastien Boulay-Paty, whose commentaries on the Commercial Code were regularly reprinted throughout the early nineteenth century, likewise doubted that failure could be truly innocent. The preface to a reprinted 1839 edition of his work began with the fatalistic pronouncement that "bankruptcies are an incurable plague on the social body." To believe otherwise, Boulay-Paty insisted, was to imagine a world in which all men were "prudent, wise and fortunate." In a less ideal world, bankruptcies were certain to arise from "incompetence, lack of order," or what he termed "fateful chance."[40] Accepting bankruptcy as part of the natural order of things, he consistently blamed individual failings in his descriptions of

FIGURE 2. *Banqueroutiers, Yesterday and Today*, from Henry Monnier, *Jadis et Aujourd'hui* (Paris: Delbache, 1829). (Open access image from the Davison Art Center, Wesleyan University, photo by M. Johnston)

individual bankruptcies. He argued that every father had a solemn duty to prevent bankruptcies by evaluating whether his son had the character necessary for a commercial career and, if he did, ensuring that he had the training necessary for such an endeavor. Like Roret, Boulay-Paty blamed many bankruptcies on those who attempted to make their fortunes too quickly, "creating daily in our great city luxurious establishments like veritable meteors, which shine for a moment and then vanish, crushed by their own expenses."[41] Shortly afterward, however, he opined more forgivingly that in commerce "a business solidly established today, perfectly solvent, can crumble tomorrow."[42]

Commercial judges, like the creditors who met in bankruptcy convocations, acknowledged that some of these bankrupts owed their failure to sheer bad luck. They could be ruined by unfair competition, burdened by personal or family illness, depleted by their inability to obtain payment from their own debtors, undone by a sense of duty and honor to their friends or family, or destroyed by political unrest or economic crisis. In general, however, commercial judges assessing the causes of bankruptcies aligned themselves rather closely with the analyses offered by Roret and Boulay-Paty, blaming the great majority of these failures on three factors: lack of sufficient capital, professional incompetence, and moral weakness. While these factors tended to be closely associated, insufficient capital and professional incompetence were more frequently noted among small traders, while the failure of large businessmen was often attributed to weakness in their moral fiber. The supposed lack of even a rudimentary education and basic accounting skills among small traders provoked continual complaints.[43] Chambers of commerce and commercial judges regularly bemoaned the alleged ubiquity of disorderly book and account keeping.[44] Unable to correctly record and evaluate their financial situations, these men also underestimated the amounts required to establish a business. Commercial court judges routinely pointed out the meager start-up capital of many bankruptcies in the Paris area compared to liabilities averaging over three times this amount.[45] Another commercial judge in the early 1840s declared that petty traders made up five-sixths of those who had failed that year, largely because their initial capital could never cover the basic operation of an enterprise.[46] The assets remaining from such bankruptcies frequently left nothing at all when divided among the creditors. The Paris Commercial Court, noted then-president Pepin Lehalleur in 1840, loathed agreeing to *concordats* in such cases.[47]

Yet if small merchants aroused the ire of the commercial courts for their presumption and recklessness, large merchants elicited even more blame for their failures. Commercial judges and creditors deplored the number of bankruptcies occasioned by the temptations of stock-jobbing and speculation that manifested itself in the playing of company stocks in boom years, overinvestment in railroad shares, and dabbling in construction projects and the real estate market.[48] In the eyes of many observers, even if speculating bankrupts had not stolen funds, they had misused the resources entrusted to them in the hope of obtaining rapid enrichment. The Chamber of Commerce of Metz, believing that the passion for stock market speculation was not a vice but "a crime because [the speculator] has thrown down the abyss other fortunes besides his own," even suggested that engaging in risky stock market speculation should constitute grounds for *banqueroute frauduleuse*.[49] One assembly of wealthy businessmen in 1839, worried about what they perceived to be a skyrocketing rate of bankruptcy, attributed this trend to "that fever for stock companies which has produced so many misfortunes."[50] Speculation was also linked to such marks of frivolity as exaggerated expenses of the establishment, overinvestment in luxury boutiques, and careless merchandise ordering.[51]

Judging *Faillite* and *Banqueroute*

Despite popular conviction that *banqueroute* was widespread, few bankrupts faced criminal prosecution. Several factors explain this low rate of pursuit and conviction. First, although commercial court officials could instigate criminal procedures against a bankrupt, it was much more likely that creditors would pursue charges of *banqueroute simple* or *banqueroute frauduleuse*. Sometimes creditors could gain the support of the trustee and most of the creditors for these charges, and the expenses could then be paid out of the estate. Often, however, the pursuits were entirely directed by one or two aggrieved creditors alone. There are many reasons why such complaints often failed to gain much ground among the creditors as a whole. First, *banqueroute* entailed imprisonment, meaning that a debtor would not be available to help his creditors recover debts or stay at the helm of an enterprise. Moreover, just as in the Napoleonic period, a *banqueroute* charge meant that criminal pursuits took precedence over the civil interests of the creditors. For example, creditors of Agnès Ribot, a shawl and thread merchant, accused her of *banqueroute* twice: *banqueroute frauduleuse* for reportedly hiding merchandise and *banqueroute simple* for keeping irregular books. As the trustee lamented, the resulting police seizure of her papers paralyzed the bankruptcy procedure by depriving the creditors of records necessary to recover debts.[52] Most creditors hoped to avoid such an outcome and could turn a blind eye to a certain amount of irregularity.

The situation could be even more trying if the trustees or the majority of creditors did not agree with one creditor's allegations of fraud, forcing the accuser to undertake a lonely and expensive investigation single-handedly.[53] Indeed, *banqueroute* charges often amounted to little more than an expression of creditors' resentment at their losses. In an economy where many creditors and debtors knew each other personally, those who sacrificed substantial sums of money could hardly be expected to react unemotionally to a borrower's inability to reimburse his debts. Creditors sometimes made charges against debtors only to drop them when they realized they stood little chance of winning. Although creditors brought charges of *banqueroute simple* or *frauduleuse* in roughly one in every six bankruptcies in the 1830s and 1840s, only a fraction of these were prosecuted as such.[54] Once a bankruptcy occurred, wrote one commentator, "the creditor is struck by one thing: his loss. He doesn't care if that loss comes from the fault or crime of the bankrupt, or whether it is the result of unfortunate events that no human foresight could have predicted, his sole interest is recuperating his money."[55] Most *banqueroute* charges seem to have ended with the creditor desisting once he realized that he could not prove his claim or that proving it risked jeopardizing the estate's remaining assets.[56]

Even if a case went to court, the likelihood of conviction was not high. Between 1825 and 1831, 695 people were tried for the crime *banqueroute* and only 312 convicted. Between 1832 and 1847, 1,999 people were tried and only 737 convicted.[57] This relatively low conviction rate could derive from the difficulty of proving fraud, although this was not always so hard. Leroux, a Parisian mercer, added in his account book a whopping 18,000-franc debt outstanding to a businessman named Bernard of Rhône, who, the trustees learned from Lyon's chamber of commerce, was so poor that he could not afford food.[58] The creditors of one Sabatino looked suspiciously at a balance sheet where the former tavern keeper attributed 100,000 francs in losses to improvements to his house, which was later auctioned off for only 48,250 francs.[59] Picard, a cloth cleaner in Yvetot, claimed to have been robbed a few weeks before his bankruptcy declaration, until a barrel containing 30,000 francs worth of indigo and another with 8,000 francs in cash turned up in a neighboring marsh. After unconvincing attempts to blame thieves, Picard faked insanity at his trial, arriving unshaven, holding a crucifix, and periodically chanting nonsensical Latin.[60]

On the other hand, almost all aspects of a charge of *banqueroute simple*, and even some evidence for a *banqueroute frauduleuse*, could be highly circumstantial. Although not considered a sign of fraud independently, excessive living expenses were sometimes included in broader allegations. For instance, when a provincial tailor filed for bankruptcy in 1833, his creditors pointed to his luxurious cabriolet of the sort possessed by only the most prestigious Parisian tailors, personal expenses coming to 13,000 to 14,000 francs per year, as well as extravagant sums spent on furnishing and embellishing his shop as adequate proof for *banqueroute*.[61] The creditors of Augustin Bernard, who ran a tanning business in Paris, fumed that the debtor and his wife had always been superlatively dressed, went regularly to the baths at Aix and Savoy, and possessed a richly furnished house.[62] To defend themselves against *banqueroute* charges, bankrupts had to account for even the most apparently frivolous expenses that might draw the eye of the public prosecutor. Gustave Perre, a blacksmith, attested that he only had two small rooms to receive family and guests in his country house with only three windows.[63] One *failli* accused of prodigality argued that none of his creditors had found among his possessions telltale signs of frivolous spending such as jewelry or bills for carriage makers. He added lightheartedly that the only lady's portrait in his possession was one of his mother, thereby casting down accusations of womanizing and high living.[64]

The Commercial Code left considerable discretion for both creditors and judges in deciding whether an act constituted *banqueroute* or not. Although some public prosecutors took bad or absent bookkeeping as an automatic sign of bad faith, generally both prosecutors and creditors alike were quite relaxed with such carelessness.[65] As one lawyer noted, when it came to prosecuting poor bookkeeping, "the law uses the word 'could'—it *can* raise the attention of the public minister but what the law is after is *the fraud*. If that isn't discovered then this simple presumption should vanish."[66] Even more apparently damning charges were left to the discretion of creditors and judges. While the Commercial Code said that an individual who circulated bills of credit worth three times the amount of his assets could be considered a *banqueroute simple*, in reality creditors recognized that this practice happened quite frequently in legitimate commerce. The judgment of a *banqueroute*, particularly a *banqueroute simple*, involved an assessment not merely of the particular facts of the case but of the morality of the person. The lawyer for one Joseph-Marie Sauvayre argued that the bankrupt cloth merchant, orphaned at a young age, had been forced to take up commerce to support his family too soon and had thus never learned the basics of business. So profound had been the young merchant's ignorance that he had been visibly astonished the first time he was shown properly kept books. Even his flight after his bankruptcy, which had originally pushed his creditors to invoke *banqueroute frauduleuse*, was cited as a sign of his irrational but forgivable character. Although admitting that the clothing merchant had committed numerous errors in his management of commerce, the lawyer's case demonstrates that at least some jurors might be counted on to feel pity, rather than disgust, at merchants like Sauvayre who "sailed without a captain on a sea full of perils."[67]

Banqueroute was frequently attributed to the desire to rise too quickly in society. This was certainly the case for Brassier *père*, a man who, having worked his way up from poverty to relative comfort as a domestic servant in the town of Clermont-Ferrand, helped establish his son in a weaving business. When his son ran up large debts from purchases made out of incompetence and inexperience, his father footed the bills with generous loans. Forced to declare bankruptcy, Brassier's son repaid the loans his father had supplied by smuggling merchandise into a room specially rented for this purpose. At his court hearing, prosecutors portrayed Brassier *père* as an ignorant but ambitious social climber whose reach exceeded his abilities.[68] Bankrupts themselves were aware of this prejudice. As one humbly born hardware wholesaler commented, a hardworking merchant was likely exposed to "envy, jealousy, and calumny when he rises quickly above the crowd: no matter how humble and modest his fortune, how noble and generous he is to his competitors, this man is almost always beset by unjust and implacable enemies both from those whose ranks he has left and from the class into which he has risen."[69]

This concern with the whole character of the debtor could also have disruptive effects on the image of the bankrupt as criminal. Louis Lambert, the trustee of Marseille businessman Jean-Joseph Giraud, and the principal proponent of a charge of *banqueroute frauduleuse* against the debtor, noted that while Giraud was evidently a "scoundrel" in his business operations, he was nevertheless "a good father and a noble man who seemed, by the advice he gave his son, to understand well his duties to nature and to honor." Bewildered that such a man could deceive his creditors, Lambert concluded that Giraud's actions "must be attributed to a lack of reflection and the chimerical hope he had conceived to repair his losses by risky operations."[70] Distinguishing fraud from failure in an environment of pervasive risk meant weighing a bankrupt's behavior against those of his counterparts, heavily favoring those who avoided risk as much as possible.

A Case Study: The Demiannay Bank

To illustrate exactly how legal and moral judgments involving a bankrupt's character functioned in tandem with each other, it is useful to look in detail at one case involving *faillite* accompanied by charges of *banqueroute simple* and *frauduleuse*: the case of Charles Demiannay, who had risen from peasant origins to become one of the most important bankers in Normandy in the 1820s. When his bank collapsed in November 1830, his nearly nine hundred creditors found his books absent or badly kept, endorsements on commercial paper from known insolvents, and over 3 million francs nowhere to be found. Over a million francs had been given to eighty-one creditors, among them relatives of Demiannay and members of the local judiciary, the day preceding the bankruptcy declaration.[71] The bank's de facto manager, Demiannay's nephew François, had fled the country. The Demiannay bank went bankrupt, and in the ensuing legal disputes, which would last nearly a decade, François Demiannay was charged and convicted of *banqueroute frauduleuse* while his uncle, Charles-Denis Demiannay, was charged and acquitted of *banqueroute simple*.

In several ways, Charles-Denis Demiannay's bankruptcy clearly could qualify as *banqueroute simple*. The bankruptcy trustees were shocked to discover the disorder of the firm's books: indeed it was hard for them to tell whether a man who had once managed nearly 100 million francs worth of funds annually had ever possessed a personal fortune. Erratic bookkeeping was only one of numerous irregularities the trustees faced. The well-placed creditors paid during the bank run resisted returning their payments, and many managed to keep them even after the opening of the bankruptcy was set back to November 20.[72] A substantial chunk of Demiannay's estate did not belong to him at all but, under the terms of a marital property arrangement, was under his temporary care until his three young children reached their majority.[73] Contrary to legal stipulations, Demiannay had not completed a property inventory after his wife's death in 1826, so it was difficult to ascertain what this share might be, although his relatives insisted it was considerable.[74] Moreover, the trustees found Demiannay uncooperative in arranging a *concordat*, instead he insisted that the creditors could hope for much more by pursuing the man he blamed for his bank's ruin: his nephew François.[75]

All of these aspects of Demiannay's failure highlight one thing: his bank, although one of the most important banks in Normandy, had remained a family business where the boundary between Demiannay's personal and professional lives was virtually nonexistent. His family members had been his primary employees; his nephew, whom he had accused of robbing him, had been driven as much by personal rebellion against a strict uncle as by greed. His recently deceased wife had operated the counter, as did many merchant wives of the era, and he had long relied on her much firmer grasp on bookkeeping. Demiannay had allegedly utilized his wife's dotal property, inherited by the couple's young children, as collateral for some of his bank's credit operations. Those to whom he lent and from whom he borrowed often carried dual identities as clients and as family and friends.

As they delved deeper into the bank's history before its fall, the creditors realized the extent to which Demiannay had absented himself from its daily operations. Preferring to occupy himself with real estate investment after the death of his wife, he had largely ceded control of the bank's financial operations to his nephew. Dreaming of transforming the Demiannay bank from a provincial to a Parisian enterprise, François had, independent of his uncle's clientele, an entire network of business correspondents, including James and Charles Rollac and Alexandre Cotman, many of whom were not officially acknowledged in the bank's books and were completely unknown to his uncle. Many of these individuals, moreover, likewise undertook risky business adventures, including the circulation of accommodation paper among friends. Then the July Revolution struck. Whether in panic or in disapproval of Charles-Denis Demiannay's public support of the new regime, investors withdrew some 3 million francs from the bank between late July and early November 1830, leaving the bank critically undercapitalized.[76] Even worse, the financial crisis set in motion by the Revolution hit François Demiannay's financial network especially hard. Demiannay and his correspondents were forced either to make still riskier speculations on merchandise or to procure funds from more established figures, such as the banker Isaac Thuret, who demanded steep guarantees for the risks they ran in accepting paper from such individuals.

All such measures were insufficient to ward off the Demiannay bank's impending ruin. The night that the first Demiannay bill was protested, François grabbed some money, which he used to pay off some of his more pressing creditors, and took a carriage for Le Havre, thinking to flee abroad. Charles-Denis easily convinced his creditors that the way to recuperate their funds was to pursue his nephew and his correspondent, whom he accused of stealing the bank's assets and betraying his trust. By the time François was found, arrested, and charged with *banqueroute frauduleuse*, however, almost everyone with whom he had been associated had gone bankrupt. The trustees of these bankruptcies were reluctant to comply with the Demiannay trustees and vociferously defended their bankrupts against the imputations of malfeasance leveled against them.[77] While François was brought to court on charges of *banqueroute frauduleuse*, the creditors and Charles-Denis attempted to pursue Thuret, the only member of François's network who remained solvent, for having received money from the Demiannay bank. Defending himself as a duped creditor of the Demiannay bank rather than the recipient of its stolen assets, an infuriated Thuret responded by charging Charles-Denis with *banqueroute simple* for not keeping proper books.

Although a typical *faillite* would have been adjudicated by a commercial court presided over by elected businessmen, the 158 criminal charges against François and his associates placed the trial within the jurisdiction of the penal court, and the charge of *banqueroute simple* leveled against Charles-Demiannay additionally rendered the case subject to a correctional court.[78] This meant that before the case came to trial, an investigating magistrate examined the evidence against the accused, interrogated witnesses, and compiled a report detailing the state's case. The trial itself, however, was in the hands of a jury of twelve and three professional judges to decide on the criminal charges against François and his network, with the judges alone ruling on the charge of *banqueroute simple*.

The first of what would be many trials in the "Demiannay Affair" opened in the Royal Court of Ile-et-Vilaine in Rennes on May 23, 1836. Rouen would have been the natural venue for the case, but over half of the town's magistrates were either Charles-Denis Demiannay's creditors or close relatives of his creditors, and the local press had shown itself hostile to the accused.[79] Assigning responsibility thus entailed presenting the abstruse financial transactions and complicated social networks that had precipitated the bankruptcy in terms comprehensible to a general audience. Out of the messy story of the collapse of the Demiannay house, the lawyers created narratives in which Demiannay and his nephew stood for divergent models of business management. As one account put it, under François, "there were, within the Demiannay house, two houses": the uncle's old-fashioned business and the more ambitious enterprises of the nephew.[80]

The image of Charles-Denis Demiannay presented to the court was carefully sculpted as the ideal businessman of a conservative land-oriented society. In the words of his lawyer, the famous politician and barrister Camille Odilon Barrot, Demiannay "wasn't a gambler, he was, on the contrary, cautious, he didn't manage his business grandly and as François said of himself '*à coups de canon*'—those are the habits of the new commerce: he was a merchant of the old school who left nothing to chance and did not advance unless escorted by guaranties. He had won his fortune bit by bit. He was prudent."[81] Demiannay understood his business not as pursuing material gain for himself but as acting as a custodian of public trust and an intermediary between consumers and producers. His lack of self-interest was demonstrated by his unwillingness to take risks with other people's money. Even Demiannay's rather remarkable rise from peasant origins offered proof of his obedience to social hierarchy. The banker, in explaining his business to the court, emphasized that he had taken over from Détancourt, for whom he had initially worked in the demeaning position of errand boy. Furthermore, he claimed that the money he had been given by Détancourt to start his own account in 1795 was collected from Détancourt's royalist clientele. Demiannay had indeed climbed far beyond his original station in life, but he had done so by insinuating himself into extant social structures rather than undermining them. Representative of "old commerce," he remained a faithful servant to the Rouen ruling class.

Demiannay stressed the values he shared with this class. For example, there was his well-known preference for landed over monetary wealth, a preference deeply shared among the ruling elite throughout France and particularly among those in Normandy. Demiannay saw money primarily as a means of obtaining land. Not only was his vision of the bank focused on property transactions, but he also used the proceeds from his bank for his own purchases of real estate. Additionally critical to Demiannay's presentation as a solid businessman was his familial role. Not only was family imagery likely to appeal to audiences who could not grasp financial complexities, but it represented a pure vision of social form as opposed to putatively self-interested alliances of profit-making endeavors.

Charles-Denis Demiannay's lawyers cast the banker as a dutiful and loving patriarch, betrayed by his faith in those familial structures. Demiannay played along. "I was good to my family: my family cost me more than 200,000 francs," he told the court.[82] He even expressed willingness to forgive François. "My nephew," he declared tearfully on the stand, "isn't what you'd think; he's unfortunate, he's a victim. He hasn't stolen anything, he hasn't got a *sou* . . . they told him he was Napoleon, they misled him with flattery."[83] Employees of the bank were assimilated to family, and had likewise treated Demiannay with gross ingratitude. Odilon Barrot pointed to one of Demiannay's clerks, whom the banker had "taken from the mud" and raised as his own child.[84] The clerk repaid Demiannay by hiding his nephew's ruinous operations and mocking the old man behind his back. Even Demiannay's errors, including his supposed inability due to grief to complete a proper inventory after his wife's death, could be attributed to this image of him as a model family man and head of his household.

In contrast to the Charles-Denis's abstemious and family-oriented existence, François's sexual escapades, often with women of lowly origin, were evoked continually throughout the trial, and had significance beyond whether the banker's nephew had dipped into the till every now and then to please his ladies' whims. The prosecutor's indictment began with the declaration that "François Demiannay had intimate relationships with many women" and pointed to "bundles of letters where cupidity is paired with the most disgusting libertinism."[85] Not only did such an association with high living provide possible motivation for François's deceit and theft, but it also emphasized the nephew's departure from the ideal of responsible male head of the household. In these letters, women possessed great power over the young man: François's lovers joked about informing his uncle if their expensive tastes were not satisfied. Charles-Denis's side used such behavior to cast doubt on the accuracy of witnesses' testimony. Ex-trustee Leblond's critical evaluation of Charles Denis was explained by the revelation that Leblond had once secretly sold François a diamond necklace for a mistress.[86] Charles-Denis's disapproval of his nephew's romances also offered him an explanation for the accusations of "severity" continually leveled against him.[87] In short, Charles-Denis had trusted in the bank's ostensible structure, which was family run and hierarchical, with employees and nephew owing primary allegiance to him. Trust was assured by the sense of allegiance that inferiors felt (or should have felt) to their superiors. "Commercial security," declared Odilon Barrot, "rests entirely on three or four great truths: the essential trust of a boss in his employees, the sacred obligation that links the employee and his boss, and the truthfulness of the employee's books."[88]

On the opposing side, the bonds between François's network emerged not from hierarchies of dependence but rather from social equality: they were not merely business associates but friends who attended the same parties and bought gifts for each others' mistresses. Their willingness to extend credit for business operations—even at considerable and ultimately disastrous risk to themselves and their own interests—was a by-product of their trust in each other. This relatively egalitarian image of business as a band of brothers trusting each other not out of obligation but out of self-interest was juxtaposed with a static vision of "old commerce," in which families bequeathed businesses down through generations.

The business model embraced by François and his commercial network seemed all too neat a fit into this model of an emergent speculative economy. As the public prosecutor described:

> The ambition to quickly make a fortune, that is the curse of our age, and in an epoch not too long ago, one judged it with a too great disdain. Then commerce was a hereditary profession. . . . One needed a man's lifetime, sometimes more, to found a fortune. The head of the family bequeathed to his children a wealth that was laboriously acquired but which had cost no sacrifice of honor. Nowadays, it is in a few years, and sometimes a few months, that one can become rich. These rapid elevations, too often followed by unexpected falls, should be signaled out as pitfalls to avoid. It is written elsewhere *he who rushes to riches will not be innocent.*[89]

What was particularly troubling about such behavior in the prosecutor's eyes was not the acquisition of wealth but the rapidity with which it was acquired. This rapidity was a sign of the ambition to rise above the traditional means of acquiring wealth. The prosecutor's feelings toward such ambition were not unmixed (he admitted, for example, that in the past the "disdain" for such an ambition had been "too great"). He was concerned, however, with the threat such ambition posed to the social order. He connected ambition in the financial realm, in its brusque pushing aside of time-honored protocols, with ambitions in the political realm, which pushed aside previous value hierarchies. Indeed, the July Monarchy was to become famous for the intertwining of financial and political power, with liberal Parisian bankers among its key supporters, while the landowning gentries, like Charles-Denis Demiannay's disaffected clientele, were begrudging toward the regime at best, openly hostile at worst. The financial aristocracy combined the worst excesses of challenging the social hierarchy by arriviste status with what was seen as a shameful focus on money and self-interest over honor.

The lawyers for François and his friends did not deny that two separate business models were reflected in the divergent mentalities of the uncle and the nephew. However, they questioned the relation each model had with the pernicious forces of individualism and speculation. In one official statement, James Rollac attributed Charles-Denis Demiannay's fall to lay misconceptions about the nature of commercial practice and a misplaced faith in the financial health of Demiannay's bank: "Everyone was so persuaded in Rouen of the immensity of the Demiannay fortune, that his fall could not be attributed to ordinary accidents of commerce aggravated by negligence."[90] The roots of Demiannay's fall lay in the economic crisis that had paralyzed confidence in 1830, in the Demiannays specifically but also nationwide, a crisis that had exacerbated the uncle's long-standing mismanagement of the company. François's lawyers claimed that many of the transactions made by François were perhaps poorly managed but nothing extraordinary for commercial practice, which had long exceeded the reach of commercial law. While François had certainly taken risks, he had done so in his role as the head of the bank, a position that almost all credited him with having and that the older Demiannay had never clarified. Many witnesses, who were not directly affiliated with the accused, testified that they dealt with François as the acting head of the Demiannay bank.

Furthermore, lawyers for François and his associates identified Charles-Denis Demiannay with the purported evils of the traditional credit system: high interest rates and an obsessive focus on land. Citing an 1824 usury accusation leveled against Demiannay, his opponents presented the banker as no more than a glorified loan shark, who charged steep interest rates to compensate for his democratic openness to many levels of clientele.[91] Demiannay's stewardship of the bank was attacked for being fictitious and speculative. The "true [cause] of the ruin of the Demiannay house," declared a legal brief for François, was that its wealth "only rested on credit and not real capital, thus its downfall was certain if the slightest disruption shook that credit."[92] Demiannay's wealth had only existed in the imagination: "he wasn't rich, he was only in error."[93] His obsession with land had been ruinous: it was expensive to acquire property in Normandy and the yearly returns were half of the amount that Demiannay paid in interest on the deposits.[94] Such investment also gave Demiannay the impression of being richer than he was. He had been severely undercapitalized; the moment his clientele lost faith in him, he lost everything.

Indeed, Demainnay's bankruptcy itself was read as a giant speculation, a calculated effort initially by the banker, then by his creditors, to profit off the gullibility of others. This speculation had made dubious use of the legal technicalities of the extant order as a means of acquiring and maintaining a fortune. François's defense trumpeted the testimony of Thézard, one of the original trustees, who spoke of the banker's air of "guilty calculation," explaining that "when a man is in business and he buys considerable property and spends considerable amounts of money on these properties, that man can only have one thought: 'If I succeed, I will be very rich, if I go under, I will still have my wife's possessions.'"[95] Demiannay and his creditors sought scapegoats rather than face that the bank had collapsed owing to accident combined with negligence. Such an explanation offered no chance at increasing the lot of the creditors. The substantial chunk of property that Demiannay's relatives were able to claim for his children also aroused ire. A brief for James Rollac remarked bitterly: "*ruined* by brigands, he would be able to administer, in the name of his underage children, a million francs in properties. . . . a fine position to be in after a *bankruptcy!*"[96] The trustees, in turn, were only out to pad their own pockets. Instead of trying to finish the process quickly with the highest possible return for the creditors, they embroiled the estate in lawsuits, thus further diminishing the remaining assets.[97]

Yet if each side hastened to paint its actions as honorable and those of its opponents as self-interested, neither rose to the defense of risk taking and speculation, even risk taking that ended more fortunately than François's transactions did. Instead, when the litigants wished to explain participation in speculative or risk-taking activity, they did so by demonstrating how this credit economy itself destroyed notions of responsibility. François and his network were portrayed less as active agents of speculative fever than as sufferers of a disease. Cotman's lawyer melodramatically declared to the jury that "you have been presented, in vivid colors, with the image of ambition tormenting spirits, the unbridled desire for riches depraving hearts, and, in the interest of public morality, one asks for condemnation that will give birth to a salutatory fear! But alas! How to impute to these young men the movement that seduced them and carried them away?"[98] The attorney Dubodan commented sadly that in "the unbridled desire for riches, like that for fame at any cost, there is the *mal du siècle*, there is the great social plague that demands a quick remedy." However, he saw François as a pawn of his own desires and social circles; "false friends had led astray his youth, they exploited his passions as they exploited his credit."[99] Once the "fever" of speculation had been hatched, it completely overcame the mind of its sufferer, thereafter merely its victim.

While the credit economy was thus criticized for concentrating too much power in the hands of the risk-taking individual who, intoxicated with his own liberty, would lose his ability to reason, it also created a type of social vulnerability that made even those who opposed its risk-taking tendencies susceptible to its repercussions. In defending Charles-Denis Demiannay of *banqueroute simple*, Odilon Barrot presented the banker both as the very archetype of the prudent businessmen and as a victim of what he called *force majeure* ("Ah! Recognize that there was a destiny, a *force majeure* from which Demiannay could not escape!").[100] Roughly comparable to the term "act of God," *force majeure* was invoked in both the 1804 Civil Code and the 1807 Code of Commerce as a means by which an individual could escape the legal consequences of a contract into which he had entered because extraordinary circumstances prohibited his fulfillment of his obligations.[101] Dubodan, also invoking *force majeure*, clarified that the grounds for the declaration were not natural causes—such as earthquakes and storms—but rather human ones: "One looks for an excuse in disasters one calls 'unforeseen' yet had been provoked, and then one presents one's self to one's creditors less in begging than as a master dictating strict conditions. . . . Because sometimes bankruptcies are inevitable, like lightning bolts, because commerce has its storms, like the ocean, would you then say that they are only merely misfortunes where only the chain of events can be blamed?"[102] Dubodan insisted that specific agents were accountable for the bank's ruin and yet the banker himself was nevertheless the victim of circumstances beyond his control. The bankruptcy had been "a vast conjuration against the fortune of a man whose limitless trust had delivered him to hardened defrauders."[103] Demiannay's trust had been his trust in the traditional social order. For this reason, he became a man incapable of seeing the future. "Ordinarily," declared Odilon Barrot, "something warns a businessman of the chances of ruin that menace him. If he has fitted out a ship, he knows that the ship may sink, if he plays the stock market, he should foresee the losses, but Demiannay!"[104] Demiannay did not make calculated guesses about the future: he had been content to believe and have faith. He could not be blamed for the general collapse of the very society in which he had put his trust into one of self-interested and calculating speculators.

After thirteen hours of deliberation, the jury declared Cotman, François Demiannay, and James Rollac guilty of most charges against them. The jury cleared Charles-Denis Demiannay of the charge of *banqueroute simple*. The Demiannay case provides a particularly telling example of the interplay between discourses about honorable, dishonorable, and criminal bankruptcy, on one hand, and the practicalities of bankruptcy, on the other hand. Pursued by a single creditor, who was interested in restoring his own name and clearing himself of charges of involvement in the bankruptcy, the bankruptcy of Charles-Denis Demiannay certainly had exhibited certain elements of a *banqueroute simple*. Yet by skillfully mobilizing cultural norms about what constituted a "good merchant," which were deeply vested in ideas about masculinity and moral economy, and juxtaposing these with the image of the speculator represented by his nephew, Demiannay, aided by his lawyers, succeeded in avoiding the correctional judgment attached to a *banqueroute simple*.

Conclusion

Although the Commercial Code had intended to draw a firm line between *banqueroute* and *faillite*, in practice these two categories remained porous throughout the early nineteenth century. The loss of honorific rights associated with bankruptcy compelled some observers to think in terms of punitive measures and to justify the loss of these rights with a search for the culpable causes for even innocent bankruptcies. For many contemporaries, who believed that a truly trustworthy individual would find credit with his community no matter the difficulties he encountered, the very idea of an innocent bankrupt verged on oxymoronic. In their eyes, *faillis* who did not commit brazen acts of illegality nevertheless met their fate by following a questionable moral code. Even commentators who attributed failure to misfortune realized that panicked debtors, dreading the shame of bankruptcy, frequently committed acts that bordered on illegality. Although public opinion conflated *faillite* and *banqueroute*, actual bankruptcies were largely characterized by their lack of punitive measures against the bankrupt. The realities of business failure and the bankruptcy process provided multiple incentives not only for debtors to cheat but also for creditors to agree to lenient terms. This, in turn, provided additional fodder for accusations that *faillite* constituted a form of robbery condoned by the law.

Banqueroute simple, which the promulgators of the Commercial Code had created in order to delineate the boundaries between *banqueroute* and *faillite*, exemplified the proximity between failure and fraud. Courts and creditors decided what constituted excessive expenses and when irregular bookkeeping crossed the line from customary practice to culpable mishandling of creditors' assets. As the Demiannay case illustrates, considerations of what constituted legitimate risk-taking behavior played a key role in decisions to press charges, as did the interplay of various interested parties battling to receive whatever compensation they could for their loss. In the arguments furthered by the lawyers of the uncle and nephew Demiannay, proper economic behavior was closely tied to adherence to proper gender roles and obedience to the norms of a conservative land-based society.

Bankruptcy demonstrated the central contradictions of the debt regime established by the Napoleonic codes. Credit relied on networks of social connections, and risk was a normal and innate aspect of these connections. The bankruptcy code, on the other hand, imagined bankruptcy in terms of the individual merchant, largely ignoring the complex social fabric of which he remained a part. If the evidence of bankruptcy dossiers and reformers' complaints can be believed, few nineteenth-century merchants followed the letter of the law to perfection in the practice of their trades. Furthermore, the rigorous prescriptions of the Commercial Code, meant to deter fraud, appear only to have encouraged reliance on arrangements that either manipulated the law or bypassed the laws all together, inspiring public outrage with a bankruptcy process that appears from the surface extremely strict. This reality also complicated the assessment of a bankrupt's actions. Rather than relying entirely on legal prescriptions to assess guilt and innocence in cases of *banqueroute*, these judgments also depended on the dynamics of his social fabric and on holistic assessments of the bankrupt's entire personality. Originally attacked for the cruelty of its criminal presumptions, by the 1830s Napoleonic bankruptcy law instead elicited criticism from legislators and reformers for the uncertainty and inefficiency introduced by tying the fate of a bankruptcy so closely to the person of the bankrupt.

4

A Palace of Debt

Constructing the Debtors' Prison

The late 1820s witnessed the emergence of many publications catering to the French public's insatiable curiosity for spicy stories involving crime, punishment, and prisons. Yet perhaps none were as curious as the *Pauvre Jacques: Journal philosophique, anecdotique et littéraire de Sainte-Pélagie.* The masthead featured the journal's namesake, a hapless coal peddler with his sack flung over his shoulder who was surrounded by several well-dressed gentlemen in the process of arresting him. Below, a caption read "Another businessman!" a scornful reference to the grounds for the humble coalman's arrest. As a "businessman," Pauvre Jacques had fallen subject to the most extreme rigor of commercial law, *contrainte par corps*, for unpaid debt. Those who wrote and edited *Pauvre Jacques* had faced the same situation. From within the confines of "La Petite Dette" at Paris's Sainte-Pélagie prison, they collected stories from debtors all over France to mount a powerful critique of debt imprisonment and the "incarcerating race" who used it.

Over the course of the following decade, this newspaper denounced abuses perpetrated by bailiffs and commercial guards during arrest, reviewed legal works on *contrainte par corps*, followed pertinent legislation, and critiqued the various financial and legal institutions connected to debt imprisonment.[1] Each week, *Pauvre Jacques* published a list of incarcerators, which served, according to one reader, as a "kind of pillory" that "stigmatize[d] those miserable people whom the law still protects, but public opinion will not absolve."[2] The newspaper worked in cooperation with charitable and legal aid organizations to benefit the debtors. Readers wrote in to the paper to offer money or inquire about the status of particular prisoners. Jacques Laffitte, Alphonse de Lamartine, and Victor Hugo were listed as subscribers. The Parisian paper's success inspired debtors in Lyon's Saint-Joseph prison to create a provincial counterpart, *Le Pauvre Jacques Lyonnais: Journal de Saint-Joseph*, which began its brief run in December 1830.

Pauvre Jacques provides valuable insights into the conditions of prison life on two different levels. First, the stories of unjust incarcerations and horrendous prison conditions recounted in petitions, letters, and editorials printed in the paper's pages illuminate how *contrainte par corps* worked in practice and underscore its impact on the lives of ordinary men and women. Second, the very existence of such a journal reveals the extent to which debt prisoners used their ambiguous legal position to protest and resist the conditions to which they were subjected. Indeed, *Pauvre Jacques* was one of several means through which debt prisoners contributed to the larger visibility of *contrainte par corps*, which also included petitions to ministries and legislative bodies, published life stories recounting the irregular and often scandalous circumstances of their own arrests, and speeches at trials which subsequently appeared in the pages of prominent legal journals likes the *La Gazette des Tribunaux* and *Le Droit*.

In his famous 1975 work *Discipline and Punish*, Michel Foucault briefly cited *Pauvre Jacques* and *La Gazette de Saint-Pélagie* as examples of the many calls for carceral reform during the first decades of the nineteenth century.[3] Foucault situated these journals, and the attacks on imprisonment they conveyed, within a wide-scale transformation of penal institutions starting in the 1770s and lasting throughout the nineteenth century. During this period, reformers pushed for the creation of a new national penal system in which the prison became, in Foucault's words, "an exhaustive disciplinary apparatus" assuming "responsibility for all aspects of the individual, his physical training, his aptitude for work, his everyday conduct, his moral attitude, his state of mind."[4] A novelty at the turn of the nineteenth century, mass incarceration rapidly became the chief means of punishment for criminal offenders, whose numbers eventually far exceeded the population of imprisoned debtors.

Yet *Pauvre Jacques* seems odd evidence for Foucault's story. It was, after all, a paper written by and for debt prisoners. These were men and, to a far lesser extent, women detained not for crimes or infractions but as a means of enforcing a contract at the hands of private creditors rather than the state. Although fascination with debt imprisonment grew in tandem with interest in the penal prison, these institutions differed fundamentally both in practice and as imagined ideals. While the state housed debtors, and state employees, either bailiffs or commercial guards, arrested them, creditors paid for the debtors' detention with funds to be reimbursed by their debtors. Penal prisoners, as conjured by the pages of Dumas and Hugo, spent long torturous years in confinement. Meanwhile, debtors' stays were so short, averaging under a month, that when the inspector counted the population in the debtors' wing of Sainte-Pélagie, he made sure to note the hour that he made the count.[5] Debtors were, in short, individuals over whom the state exerted no edifying power.[6] In general, prison reformers did not prioritize issues of *contrainte par corps*, nor did debt prisoners see themselves as sharing circumstances with other prisoners.[7] In the midst of the penal system's great transformation during the first decades of the nineteenth century, *Pauvre Jacques* spoke for these anomalous individuals.

Foucault's casual citation of *Pauvre Jacques* nevertheless invites us to consider the remarkable visibility of debt imprisonment in the early half of the nineteenth century in relation to the evolving idea of the penal prison during that epoch. Debt imprisonment, which relegated potentially productive members of society to idleness and fostered unequal living conditions based on financial circumstances, represented a stark contrast to the vision of prison as an orderly, uniform, and potentially regenerative space of confinement. As the existence of *Pauvre Jacques* indicates, the prison became central to a battle, led in part by the debtors themselves, to redefine the honor of credit relations and to paint the very institution, as well as those who made use of it, as dishonorable. Even as the peculiarities of debt imprisonment structured the concrete experience of everyday life, debtors not only regularly exploited their anomalous position to claim for themselves honorable identities but also used petitions, memoirs, and newspapers to reframe their stories. They drew upon and articulated a vision of debtors as distinct from other inmates and created hierarchies within the prison based on the supposed morality of their debts. By building and enforcing such separations, they attempted to distinguish themselves from criminals despite their physical proximity. They also aimed to reverse the stigma of disgrace from themselves to their creditors. Debtors were, in fact, far more proactive than prison authorities in enforcing boundaries between failure and criminality. In so doing, they helped create the category of debt prisoners as separate from, and morally superior to, criminals. They also challenged the way that financial failure degraded the person of the debtor in the same way that criminal transgressions did.

Locating Imprisonment

The prison loomed large in the imagination of French intellectuals and ordinary citizens of the post-Revolutionary period. As one historian of crime and punishment has summarized, "Never before had there been so much talk about these issues in the press and the political arena; never again thereafter (in France, at any rate) would there be such sustained and broad-based debate."[8] To debate the prison was in some respects to debate the legacy of the Revolution. For the Revolutionaries, and for the nineteenth-century liberals who followed them, individual freedom was the highest good. Those who violated society's laws forfeited their liberty. Yet this rational understanding of the prison was not the only, or even the dominant, mode of understanding the prison. While theorists published dozens of pamphlets about the ideal operation of the penitentiary system, and legislators debated whether to implement solitary confinement, readers of Balzac, Hugo, Dumas, and Eugène Sue delighted in these novelists' vivid accounts of brazen crime and long, sometimes unjust, confinement. Although statistics belied any dramatic uptick in crime or incarceration during the period, disturbingly high rates of recidivism sharpened fears that prisons created a dangerous and irredeemable underworld of career criminals. Anxieties about the effects of the explosive growth of cities like Paris coupled with an intellectual culture fed on romanticism and Catholic revival rendered the prison a key focus for the ambivalence felt about the Revolutionary project of reforming mankind.

Even as a political project, there was no singular definition of the prison. Penal reform was carried out less as a unified project than as a series of distinct ones, often with opposing ideologies, techniques, and goals. In France, the Revolution's humanitarian rationalism and Enlightenment abhorrence of torture had been enshrined in the Napoleonic Criminal Code, which had increased the number of crimes punishable by imprisonment rather than death. In 1810 Napoleon created the *maisons centrales*, long-term detention facilities that would become the heart of the new nineteenth-century penitentiary system. Yet specific attention to the quality of life within the prisons would wait until the early years of the Restoration, where it became the concern of newly established administrative bureaucracies, as well as charitable organizations, such as the Société royale pour les prisons. These associations principally aimed to reform the moral habits of prisoners, including problems of hygiene, gambling, and drunkenness, as well as providing moral and religious instruction, basic education, and work.[9]

In the early 1830s, a new generation of self-proclaimed social scientists, including prison inspectors Louis-Maturin Moreau-Christophe and Charles Lucas, rejected what they saw as the false philanthropy of earlier efforts at prison control in favor of a more scientific approach to the management of carceral institutions.[10] Their impetus derived from multiple sources. On one hand, the rise of an urban proletariat and periodic political unrest made wary social and political elites particularly interested in finding means of controlling an often unruly population. Furthermore, the developing science of statistics provoked efforts by observers to conceptualize human behavior itself as subject to quantification and then, possibly, to management. Inspired by the prison system in the United States, French reformers emphasized the importance of administrative regularization of prison conditions and cellular isolation of prisoners. It was during this period that the notion of total care replaced the disparate living conditions for prisoners in the early penal institutions. The prison was intended to preserve the extant social order and to rehabilitate the convict. Work formed a vital part of this dual role, with private entrepreneurs or the state itself compelling prisoners to labor for a submarket wage. By 1842 the French penitentiary system comprised 108,000 prisoners, including those held in *maisons centrales, maisons de justice, maisons d'arrêt*, cantonal prisons, and cells in police headquarters.[11]

Despite the dramatic transformation in penal institutions, dishonor remained a crucial role in the penal process to an extent often ignored by accounts like Foucault's. Before the Revolution, every aspect of criminal punishment had been steeped in the logic of degradation, in which the body served as the principal site onto which dishonor was inflicted. Gradations of punishment depended on the honor of both the assailant and the victim: a noble faced the more honorable death by the sword while the common thief would hang by the noose. Spectacular punishment had a ritualistic function of both upholding the righteousness of the current order and degrading the honor of the perpetrator. These included ceremonial aspects of sentencing, like the process of *amende honorable* in which a criminal, stripped to his shirt and barefoot, was led to a church with a rope around his neck and forced to beg pardon. While the post-Revolutionary criminal code putatively rested on the principles of natural rights and human reason, honor continued to be a crucial part of the process of punishment. Indeed, many honor-bound practices continued well into the nineteenth century. Civil death, for example, which remained in force through the 1850s, pronounced the death of the legal personality—including the dissolution of marriage, patriarchal authority, and the abolition of property rights as well as deprivation of civil rights—on all individuals convicted of crimes meriting penalties of death, deportation, or a lifetime of forced labor.[12] As Anne Simonin has argued, while under the old regime "indignity had the essential function of repressing the private disorders of families," the Revolution had connected dishonor to failures to serve the *patrie*. Throughout the nineteenth century, both private and public senses of dishonor coexisted. Violating the country's laws definitely entailed dishonor, as any casual reader can sense from the plight of ex-convict Jean Valjean in Victor Hugo's *Les misérables*. Yet whether committing dishonorable acts therefore implied criminality was much more debatable.

Nowhere was this conundrum more evident than in the debtors' prison. Commercial debtors who did not reimburse their creditors were deemed to have done something dishonorable, yet their dishonor could not be clearly compared to that of a thief or a murderer. Debt imprisonment placed debtors, and more specifically debtors' physical persons, in close proximity to criminally dishonored bodies. The image of the prison as a place of infection and contamination was widespread in the early nineteenth century. Despite the rise of the new hygienic cellular regime, prisons retained the connotation of miasma and disease they had earned in the centuries before. Many reformers believed that prisons produced moral contagion. So many corrupted individuals in close proximity could not but infect those less inured to a life of crime with the hardened attitudes of recidivists. Prisons were seen as a breeding ground for supposedly unnatural activity, such as homosexuality and tattooing.[13] Debtors, incarcerated out of sheer misfortune but forced to share accommodations with such corrupted members of the body politic, could be easily swayed, critics feared, to follow a life of crime.

Reformers concentrated on the damage done not only to the debtor's credit but also to his moral well-being by sharing an environment with those who had committed crimes. Closel d'Arnery's early attack on debtors' prison, discussed in chapter 1, began by evoking the image of the poor debtor imprisoned alongside convicts and other "loose and disreputable figures." "What sensitive heart," he asked, "does not shudder at the image of those slimy receptacles where the honest man and the vile criminal are surprised to find themselves together under the same roof, in the same room, even seated at the same table?" In evoking the sharing of food, Closel d'Arnery suggested bodily transmission of criminal behavior between convicted felons and honest but unfortunate debtors. Indeed, much of d'Arnery's imagery mixed the language of disease with that of crime. An imprisoned debtor was "forced to breathe for months at a time air doubly infected by diseases which are too frequently contagious and the redoubtable epidemic of crime." Moreover, he applauded efforts by prison reformers to separate debtors in Paris from criminals, arguing that "all form of communication is finally forbidden between the corrupt members and the healthy part of the political body."[14]

Nineteenth-century reformers stressed the contagious effects of criminal dishonor on debtors' reputations. One reformer argued that a released debtor was "not the same man and the opinion of others has also changed in his regard," adding that if he has "not lost honor one must nevertheless admit that he has been deprived of many social advantages whose loss is neither less painful nor less humiliating."[15] The formerly imprisoned debtor, said another, led an existence eternally "embittered by the memory of detention," constantly fearing that his humiliating secret would be exposed.[16] As such, he was in fact punished for his failure to reimburse a debt. "If nonpayment is an infraction, and debt imprisonment a punishment," the writer summarized, "we should regulate it according to the example of other punishments for other crimes."[17] Another writer added that to incarcerate debtors not only equated debtors with felons but also devalued punishment "to the point where it can be confined to the caprices of private interest," which would "enfeeble the moral resonance of penalty, because an individual who has spent several months in prison no longer has any horror of that state which separates him from the community of prison."[18] Introduced into the corrupting space of the prison, the debt prisoner rapidly adapted to his conditions. Released, he no longer feared committing crime.

Prison administrators shared these anxieties. From its reestablishment in 1797, debt imprisonment had been regarded as different both in practice and in concept from penal incarceration. Yet efforts at reforming the debtors' prison followed those of the prison in general, and the concrete realities of prison operation often meant that debtors and prisoners received similar treatment and accommodations. Responses to an 1819 inquiry into the state of the prisons revealed that there was "neither order nor uniformity" in the treatment of debtors, who faced myriad abuses including unequal and exorbitant rents, terrible food, and corrupt jailers.[19] Despite a subsequent 1820 decree that defined rights of debt prisoners and separated them from other prisoners, individual prison experiences largely reflected negotiations between debtors, creditors, and jailers at the local level.[20] Prison conditions differed markedly between and even within different regions of the country, in part because of the extreme difference in the number of inmates. The most accurate calculations on levels of *contrainte par corps*, made by Jean-Baptiste Bayle-Mouillard in his 1836 *De l'emprisonnement pour dettes*, showed that between 1823 and 1834, French prisons had imprisoned 25,307 men for private debts and 1,345 women. This meant that on any given day 1,269 people were incarcerated for debt.[21] The debt prisoners of the Seine consistently made up the largest single contingent of debtors nationwide, numbering some 7,588 out of the total 25,307 individuals incarcerated for debt between 1824 and 1833.[22] Paris alone had a true debtors' prison. From 1797 through 1834, Sainte-Pélagie housed male debtors alongside political detainees and juvenile delinquents. In 1834 all Parisian debtors were transferred to a former aristocratic mansion called Clichy, which was reserved for debtors alone. Female debtors, never more than a small portion of those incarcerated for debt, were first imprisoned in Madelonettes after 1797, then moved to Saint-Lazare, a prison mostly associated with prostitutes. Ultimately, they were transferred to Clichy, where they were housed alongside, though always separated from, their male counterparts.

Elsewhere in France, the small numbers of prisoners meant that there were no actual debtors' prisons and prison situations varied considerably. At the start of the nineteenth century, Rouen's Saint-Lô prison housed debtors alongside beggars, vagabonds, and convicted felons. In 1822 the debtors were moved to Bicêtre, where they enjoyed a spacious shaded courtyard, a large and airy building, a workshop providing some employment, and the possibility of obtaining food from outside.[23] Arrangements for food provisions, too, depended on the particular prison. The prison administration in Colmar in 1819 directly provided debtors with a generous supply of bread, butter, and broth, while debtors in Lyon and Bordeaux relied on the charity of local nuns for medical care and provisions.[24] In smaller towns, a debtor might be imprisoned alongside accused or convicted thieves and murderers. Even in larger cities where the number of debtors required a dedicated part

TABLE 1. Debtors held in Sainte-Pélagie prison, Paris, 1815–33

YEAR	NUMBER OF DEBTORS
1815	261
1816	254
1817	292
1818	396
1819	410
1820	333
1821	353
1822	585
1823	463
1824	396
1825	367
1826	517
1827	521
1828	N/A
1829	460
1830	438
1831	503
1832	402
1833	327

Sources: *Recherches statistiques sur la ville de Paris* (1815–23); and Bayle-Mouillard, *De l'emprisonnement pour dettes.*

of the prison, a large influx of prisoners could cause overcrowding. Debtors would have to be transferred to other parts of the prison or to other prisons entirely.[25]

Within the prisons, the treatment of debtors differed dramatically depending on their financial circumstances. Those with money could import the comforts of home. The German Prince de Kaunitz, incarcerated in 1830, sent his creditors taunting letters often written on the backs of his receipts from lavish meals he ordered in prison. "My lodgings on the rue de Clichy are like being in a country house," read one, "the restaurant is excellent, everyday there are truffles and champagne, I don't feel like I'm in prison."[26] Gabriel-Julien Ouvrard, the famous financier and bête noire of Napoleon, used his wealth to render his stay in Sainte-Pélagie agreeable. Although Ouvrard would normally have been forced to share a room with other inmates when he was imprisoned in December 1824, he instead purchased multiple rooms from cash-strapped fellow debtors. The financier handsomely furnished these cells with elegant carpets and new wallpaper, as well as an alabaster clock, and a few tables and chairs.[27] Such wealth gave a superficially appealing ambiance to the debtors' prison. When Adolphe-Victor Paillard de Villeneuve inspected Sainte-Pélagie in 1829 on behalf of the Société de la morale chrétienne, he declared that the prison possessed all the amenities of living in town.[28] Observers marveled at smoking dens, well-equipped libraries, and restaurants that served multicourse meals.[29]

For most debtors, who could not afford the opulence of an Ouvrard or Prince Kaunitz, prison conditions were generally miserable, whether they were lodged in debtors' quarters in Paris or in common cells elsewhere. Many prisoners could not even afford the *pistole*, the comparative luxury of a webbing bed, two small mattresses, basic linens, a small table, and two chairs. They instead opted for the *dépôt*, a spot on the floor of a cell that contained six or seven other people.[30] Debtors in Sainte-Pélagie complained of unsanitary conditions and insufficient ventilation. At one point, they noted, over a hundred debtors shared one latrine, which was "almost always covered with fecal matter" and emitted "wafts of infection."

The 1834 transfer of Parisian inmates to a new prison devoted to incarcerated debtors marked a critical moment in the ongoing struggle over prison space. The new prison, called the Maison de Clichy, was a former aristocratic *hôtel* noted for its beauty and situated in one of the city's more fashionable areas. The new prison seemed, in the words of one observer, "a veritable Eden, from which one would not wish to leave when one entered, possessing an immense garden where water and flowers left only enough sand to give necessary space for leisurely walks and games."[31] The prison reformer Moreau-Christophe predicted that this "palace of debt" would put an end to the "incarcerating race."[32] Outside the prison, he explained, the threat of *contrainte par corps* made life miserable for a debtor, a veritable "sword of Damocles" hanging over his head at all times. By contrast, Clichy provided a much more pleasant life than the debtor probably enjoyed outside the prison, making incarceration almost a reward.[33] Not only more pleasant than Sainte-Pélagie, Clichy also reflected a new attitude toward the purpose of a debtor's time in prison. As one commentator put it, "Sainte-Pélagie was the prison of the bad subject to whom, as one knows, leniency was rarely lacking; Clichy is a retreat destined for the meditation of faults or disasters that one must think of remedying; morality has gained something in this switch, poetry has lost everything."[34] In this first actual

FIGURES 3 AND 4. Two images of the Sainte-Pélagie debtors' prison: the café and the room of "an unfortunate debtor." From Victor Adam, *Album de Sainte-Pélagie*. (Author's collection)

space specifically destined for debtors, the debtors' prison finally started to approach the model of penitence already applied to criminal inmates.

Although contemporaries deemed Clichy considerably more appealing than its predecessors, the regime there was also considerably more stringent. While the movement of visitors in and out of Sainte-Pélagie and Saint-Lazare had been a subject of continual contestation, at Clichy visitation hours were strictly set at 10 a.m. to 6 p.m., and debtors could no longer share meals with their wives and children. Adding to this air of increased surveillance, Clichy had many of the same features as a prison, including high walls, solid bars, sentinels, and ramparts frequently patrolled by guards. Prison administrators ultimately decided that a limited and closely monitored official tolerance of certain games was better than the proliferation of informal gambling in the prison. In addition to the difficulties of suppressing gambling, some prison officials had become convinced that gambling created a limited form of wealth redistribution between wealthy and poor debtors.[35]

Nationwide, the transfer of the debtors to the Clichy regime also signified a turn toward a more disciplined and orderly approach to the debtors' prison, approaching that of the penal prison. New legislation on debt imprisonment in April 1832 ended many of the most flagrant abuses in arrest—including that of the elderly and of husbands and wives at the same time for the same debt. It also raised the minimum sum for which one could be arrested and, perhaps most consequentially for the debtors themselves, increased the stipend allotted to incarcerated debtors. Moreover, in October 1841 new penal regulation systematized the treatment of debt prisoners both within prisons and throughout the country.[36] It expressly forbade debt prisoners from associating with criminal prisoners. The law attempted to improve the morality of debtors: mass became mandatory for all Catholic prisoners, and prohibitions were issued against opposite sex cohabitation as well as alcohol consumption and loud noise. The law defined three distinct tiers for living quarters, thereby ending some of the freedom enjoyed by wealthier debtors.

The transformation of the debtors' prison as an actual space over the early nineteenth century runs parallel to the developments of the penal prison. Scholars have argued that early nineteenth-century prisons never lived up to the visions, conflicting as they often were, of prison reformers. The dream of the perfect disciplinary institution could not be realized overnight. Indeed, in certain respects, it never was. Yet if prisons remained heterogeneous institutions, how much more could this be said of debtors' prison. In a very real way, there was no actual "debtors' prison" until 1834, and even this space only housed a fraction of those arrested for debt nationwide. "Debtors' prison" represented more an idea than a physical place, and prison authorities and legislators shared no clear vision of what this idea might be. Thus, the experience of debt imprisonment differed radically between prisons and even between prisoners. Over time, administrators tried to make debt imprisonment resemble penal imprisonment. The relocation of Parisian prisoners to Clichy and the decree of 1841 represented a tentative attempt to instill the sense of morality into debt incarceration that penal reformers had long advocated for other prisons. Although the constraints placed upon state initiative in this regard by the very nature of civil imprisonment did not permit the kinds of thoroughgoing reforms seen elsewhere in the prison system, by the 1840s imprisoned debtors were both more systematically and efficiently managed and less likely to publicly denounce their conditions. Yet in reforming the abuses of debt imprisonment, officials only made prisoners more convinced that they were being treated like criminals.[37] Creating an actual physical place for the debtors' prison did not resolve the ambiguities inherent in confining individuals who had committed no crimes to institutions designated for those who had.

Negotiating Imprisonment

In the absence of any clear definition of the meaning of the debtors' prison, the concrete reality of debt imprisonment consisted of shifting negotiations between debtors, insistent that they be given more rights than normal prisoners, and prison authorities, who feared they would antagonize creditors by granting debtors more liberties. This aspect of debt imprisonment was not unique to France. Studies by Margot Finn, Bruce Mann, Joanna Innes, and Sergei Antonov, among others, have revealed a similar phenomenon in English, American, and Russian debtors' prisons, where, as Margot Finn has put it, the "protracted evolution of criminal incarceration allow[ed] the customary privileges and convivial conventions of the debtors' prison to persist (and even to expand) in the interstices of the emerging penal complex."[38] These studies have stressed two different aspects of the debtors' prison: first, the relative freedom and independence enjoyed by debtors both collectively and individually within the prison, and secondly, the prison reform movement's impulse to curtail these freedoms. Debt imprisonment epitomized the older, custodial form of incarceration with its wildly disparate privileges enjoyed by prisoners based on their social status, a model that penal reformers hoped to replace with a closely organized environment under uniform supervision and regulation. Surprisingly well-organized groups of inmates often negotiated the very conditions of incarceration.[39] Indeed, the image of the self-governing debtors' prison that has emerged has been so sanguine that other scholars have used the very petitions written by these debtor organizations to highlight the ugly realities of prison condition under custodial treatment.[40]

In nineteenth-century France too, debtors enjoyed a considerable amount of liberty and created effective civic institutions within the prisons, including newspapers, petition-drafting committees, and charitable organizations. Like their British and American counterparts, they produced an unlikely body of prison literature, of which the *Pauvre Jacques* was only the most remarkable example, testifying to their social status as men (and, infrequently, women) with at least a rudimentary education. Yet perhaps most striking in French writings is the close connection debtors forged between their individual creditworthiness and the perceived indignities of their surroundings. Couched in a language of wounded pride and sullied honor, debtors left myriad testimonies to their plight in which they strove to disassociate themselves from the taint of criminality associated with the prison. Denunciations of prison conditions accompanied denunciations of their creditors' behavior. While penal reformers envisioned the prison as a place of rehabilitation, debtors saw the prison as a stain on their good names and attempted to retell their stories as narratives of injustice and oppression.

Almost every aspect of prison life aroused complaints, largely on the grounds that it too closely resembled penal confinement. For instance, debtors resisted prison authorities' occasional efforts to control the importation of alcohol and food into the prison. For debtors, such contraband items constituted both a means of survival and a sign of autonomy. One debtor, a former soldier who had been incarcerated for five months in a room in Sainte-Pélagie with three other men and had a wife and four children at home, wrote to the inspector general complaining of the desk clerks who made it hard for him and his "companions in misery" to receive the bread and drinks brought by their wives.[41] Another prisoner spoke of living forty-eight days without a change of underwear because the overzealous concierge had confiscated previous bundles.[42] Given the difficulties in enforcing the laws, administrators often turned a blind eye to certain contraventions of decrees, such as those prohibiting hard alcohol.[43] This was a roundly beneficial abuse: the support of outside family and friends defrayed prison costs for the debtor, the creditors, and the state alike. Prisoners in several jails protested the monopoly held by jailors and official suppliers on the provisioning of food as well as the enforcement of order in the prison. Their complaints occasionally gained an official audience, and punishments were sometimes meted out to personnel deemed particularly abusive. In July and August 1845, prisoners complained that the prison administrator neglected the care of ill prisoners and allowed scandalous literature to circulate in the prison cells thereby "corrupting souls." Still worse, he collaborated with individual creditors to the detriment of debtors. Although the administrator apparently behaved this way toward debtors and criminal prisoners alike, only the debtors protested their treatment.[44]

Debtors also objected to the amount of money that creditors were required to provide at the beginning of each month to cover the costs of furniture, heating, and food inside the prison. Set at twenty francs per month at the dawn of the century, debtors avowed that the great majority of the money went into renting a bed and furniture, leaving only a small fraction to purchase food, clothing, and various toiletries.[45] An 1846 petition alleged that, as a point of comparison, "one normally spends fifty centimes a day on hunting dogs."[46] Many debtors also supported their families, frequently deprived of the household breadwinner, with money from the allowance.[47] The government granted the poorest debtors a pittance consisting of a small bowl of thin soup, some dry vegetables, and meat twice a week.[48] To receive the pittance, debtors needed a certificate of indigence requiring extensive scrutiny of their friends and family. At Sainte-Pélagie, the food was distributed in the middle of the courtyard, "as one feeds the kill to dogs."[49] Yet complaining about the stipend amount was a double-edged sword: every increase in the allowance increased the debt a debtor had to reimburse his creditor. Some inmates manipulated the rules about the stipend, which had to be delivered by 9 p.m. on the first night of the month or the debtor would gain his freedom. Debtors were thus not always unhappy to forgo their monthly stipend, and many used this loophole as a means of obtaining release from prison. Indeed, when one debtor reminded his creditor of his need to provide the next month's alimentation, the *Gazette des Tribunaux* commented on his "eccentricity."[50]

Conflicts regarding prison access highlighted debtors' efforts to distinguish themselves from criminals. In Sainte-Pélagie and subsequently in Clichy, prisoners could freely move around the prison in daytime. At night, cells were closed and locked more out of noise concerns than security fears.[51] The widely publicized death of a prisoner in Sainte-Pélagie in October 1821, attributed to "sanguinary apoplexy," not only provoked a full-scale government investigation into prison conditions but also gave debtors an opportunity to protest against the regulation of movement.[52] They alleged that the closure of cell doors at night had made it impossible for other debtors to come to the dying man's aid, and they were forced to listen to his "terrifying agony" through the prison walls. Escapes from the prison were in actuality quite infrequent, despite the relatively lax security. Maurice Alhoy, a former prisoner, explained in a guidebook on the prisons that the infrequency of escape resulted less from the "softness of the prison regime than the lack of resources awaiting a debtor outside the walls once he had escaped."[53] However, debtors were more likely to escape when transferred to the less vigilant care of a doctor. Creditors could hold doctors liable for the debtor's escape.[54] Judges weighed the reluctance of a creditor, fearful of losing his pledge, against the prisoner's genuine medical needs and the possibility of a public outcry. Newspapers denounced creditors who refused their debtors' heartfelt pleas to see dying relatives.[55] So obdurate were some creditors that, in 1832, at the height of the cholera epidemic that swept Paris, the imprisoned debtors of Sainte-Pélagie had to petition judges in order to get those infected transferred to a hospital following one death and several reported cases in the prison.[56]

Officials believed they had good reasons to place strict controls on the movement of debtors in the prison. Wealthy debtors allegedly hired prostitutes from their prison cells.[57] In other prisons, disputes about the paternity of children born while the father was locked away led to heavily supervised conjugal visits.[58] Many prisons restricted meetings between debtors and their guests to a specific parlor under the watchful eye of the desk clerk.[59] Police reports noted with unease the presence of debtors' families who lived in houses near Sainte-Pélagie.[60] Some families spent so much time with their loved ones at the debtors' prisons that fellow inmates complained of visiting children "beating each other" and "making messes" in the common spaces.[61] Other prisoners, like the imprisoned art dealer Jean-Baptiste Adam, adapted to these circumstances: he set up a makeshift school where his "companions in misfortune" paid him to teach reading, writing, and the catechism to their children.[62]

The spatial division inside the prison was highly contentious, with debtors continually drawing spatial boundaries between themselves and other kinds of inmates. While the character of provincial prisons made separating debt prisoners and criminals inconvenient, such separation was critically important to prisoners and officials in Paris. "The detention of a debtor is not a punishment like that of a fraud," said one prison administrator, "but a means reserved by the law for the creditors to be assured of their debt in the person of their debtor."[63] In the eyes of the prison authorities, the separation of the two groups not only facilitated the management of two separate prison regimes but also prevented the penal prisoners' bad morals from influencing the debtors. Officials fretted about placing female debtors in close proximity to prostitutes, since the formers' relative lack of education supposedly made them particularly impressionable to the allegedly corrupting influence posed by the prostitutes.[64] Administrators also tried to separate those incarcerated for different types of debt. As early as 1801, the prison directors of Sainte-Pélagie separated debtors for criminal fines and compensation from those who were imprisoned for commercial debts.[65] Criminal debt prisoners were also denied some of the privileges, including visitation rights and the ability to work in prison, occasionally granted to the commercial debtors.

Debtors actively enforced these divisions, which were to them as much moral as they were administrative. Indeed, commercial debtors described all alleged abuses of the prison regime in terms of confusion with criminal behavior. When the café in Sainte-Pélagie was shut down in February 1811, the debtors petitioned the government, declaring that that the manner in which they were forced to get food "humiliates us, in confusing us with prisoners punished for a crime, while, victims of unfortunate circumstances, we are worthy of the regard justly due to misfortune."[66] The debtors likewise decried the excessive surveillance at night by the desk clerks, which, they claimed, reduced them to the status of common criminals.[67] Prison officials, for their part, insisted that this vigilance was necessary given alleged orgies that had disgusted the "reasonable part" of the debtor population.[68]

Yet even as debtors objected to what they saw as the authorities' overbearing surveillance on the grounds that it reduced them to the status of criminals, they routinely ostracized other debtors arrested for less savory forms of debt, like stellionate (the selling or mortgaging of a property without legal title). In 1815 one debt prisoner ran afoul of prison authorities for circulating pieces of doggerel against two other prisoners, in debt prison for stellionate, including such lines as "To the pillory! Swindlers, knights of industry . . . monsters covered with infamy! You would do better there than at Sainte Pélagie."[69] The prisoner, like his comrades who chanted his song, appears to have believed that Sainte-Pélagie should be reserved for true victims of economic misfortune, while those whose debts implied less honorable intentions should be located elsewhere.

Few aspects of prison life more strongly divided debtors from criminal prisoners than their different ways of spending of time. Prison reformers encouraged the growth of manufacturing industries in penal institutions, promoting labor as having the capacity to "instill the virtues of the workplace; productivity, thrift, punctuality and order."[70] Even as the new model of the prison closely approached that of the factory, debtors did not form part of the labor force in most prisons.[71] Reformers considered the short duration of most debtors' stays impractical for long-term employment. Yet, perhaps surprisingly, at least some of the impetus for debtors' exclusion from prison employment came from their creditors. In Saint-Étienne, for example, a wine merchant named Claude Serre, who had caused to be imprisoned another wine merchant by the name of Denis Francon, addressed a series of letters to the prison prefect demanding that his debtor be forbidden from working in prison after Francon had refused what Serre described as an extremely reasonable arrangement including a reduction of his total debts by half and payment on an installment plan.[72] Although praising the local prison administrator's humanity, he found his own debtor undeserving of such charity. Arresting Francon had been "the only way to get *a part* of what I was owed," wrote Serre.[73] "It would be completely unjust for a creditor to nourish his debtors and that the latter be allowed to work for his own profit," he added, for such a practice "paralyzed the effects of the judgment," and the debtor, assured of food and lodging by his creditor, "would not hurry to leave."[74] Despite an apparently positive response from the prefect, several months later Francon was still working away, and an increasingly frustrated Serre demanded that the prefect take an official stance against work in prison for all debtors.[75]

Nevertheless, resourceful debtors found means of making money. The types of work they created, often practicing the same trades they had plied outside the prison walls, troubled administrators and creditors alike, since they afforded debt prisoners a disconcerting amount of independence. Imprisoned liquor sellers and restaurant owners, using goods smuggled into the prison by family and friends, established small canteens in their rooms where fellow debtors could pay to drink a leisurely cup of coffee or read an imported newspaper. Observers compared Sainte-Pélagie to a small town where "every morning, at the beginning of the day, the doors opened, the cells changed into cafes, restaurants, grocery or fruit shops, and reading rooms."[76] These small businesses competed with the official monopoly granted by the state to the prison canteens. As in many penal prisons, private contactors vied for the right to sell to the prisoners, a practice that many observers believed turned the prison into a veritable farm where prisoners were forced to pay astronomically high prices.[77] Prison administrators also feared that such makeshift establishments presented fire hazards and would lead debtors to take on financial risks beyond the limits of their solvency. "At this moment," wrote the inspector general of prisons in September 1824, "one Mr. Berthol maintains one such restaurant. In order to obtain objects that are hard to find, he makes debts and exceeds the means of his existence."[78] Debtors earned money by providing services of various sorts. Pierre Chamoron, a Savoyard peddler who died in Sainte-Pélagie in December 1832, amassed the 250 francs he had squirreled away under his mattress by running small errands for wealthier prisoners.[79] Prison authorities employed debtors as informants paid to keep track of troublemakers, a form of employment that carried grave risks if discovered by other inmates.[80] In especially compelling cases, administrators made arrangements to help out prisoners. When the administrators of the Saint-Joseph prison in Lyon heard the sad story of a furniture merchant with a sickly wife and seven children who had recently lost his house to his creditor, they hired him to manufacture prison beds and thus meagerly support his family.[81]

For the majority of debtors, however, the duration of their detainment was passed in idleness. Debtors sometimes bemoaned their enforced boredom. One prisoner, for example, wrote multiple requests to the prison administration asking to take up firearm practice, vowing that he had found an excellent and willing instructor, only to have his "need for exercise" rebuked by prison officials.[82] Indeed, ennui became a distinguishing part of depictions of the debtors' prison. One observer noted that debtors' alternately manifested "tranquillity and kind of resignation" were as an attempt to "blind one's self with songs and pleasantries" or a preoccupation with the necessities of material existence.[83] Another declared that while the debtors' lack of "absolute despair" differentiated them from penal prisoners, their optimism was eroded by the "deleterious effect" of imprisonment and lack of work on their mental faculties.[84] The financier Gabriel Ouvrard, imprisoned on two different occasions in Sainte-Pélagie, noted how the activity and business of the penal prisoners contrasted with the idleness of the debtors.[85] Prison officials worried about the possible consequences of this copious leisure time. While they had little authority to reform the debtors' behavior or compel them to work, administrators hoped to mitigate the debtors' purported penchant for "excesses" in order to preserve order in the prison and to avoid scandalizing the creditors.[86] The prison administration closely monitored political discussions, and the potentially acrimonious debates these might inspire.[87] Gambling particularly worried prison officials, who deemed it a "great scandal for the creditors" to see "men, deprived of their liberty for not paying their debts, play for 300 or 400 francs a night."[88] Perhaps more importantly, administrators believed that gambling encouraged fights among the prisoners and regarded all aspects of prison life with an eye to whether they might encourage the prisoners' "inveterate passion for gambling."[89]

The authorities' worst fear, namely, that discontent and leisure might end in open revolt, materialized on several occasions. News of the shooting of a debtor in Lyon's Saint-Joseph prison, after a small prison riot in September 1819, sparked unrest among the debtors of Sainte-Pélagie, who responded by insulting and throwing rocks at nearby military personnel.[90] On February 16, 1831, several debtors attempted to escape Sainte-Pélagie. When the director asked if their creditors or a police order had given them the right to leave, they replied, "Long live liberty! No more *contrainte par corps!*" The prison director called in the National Guard, which arrived to find the prison in a state of pandemonium with debtors shooting projectiles from the third floor. The National Guard resorted to bayonets to suppress the debtors, 150 of whom spent the night in a criminal prison.[91] A few months later an even more serious rebellion occurred when debtors, taking advantage of popular unrest in Paris, used a large beam to bash down a door before being quelled by the National Guard.[92]

On the whole, debtors found more success in gaining freedom by appealing to royal and private charities than by initiating rebellion. Kings Louis XVIII, Charles X, and Louis-Philippe all paid for the release of debt prisoners to celebrate various holidays and great occasions. Private charities, such as the Société pour la soulagement et la déliverance des détenus pour dettes, used their healthy endowment and political connections to procure the liberty of debtors whom prison administrators found particularly sympathetic.[93] Over a period of eleven years, the Société pour la soulagement et la déliverance des détenus pour dettes spent 90,000 francs freeing two hundred debtors and improving conditions within prisons.[94] The Société de la morale chrétienne, which worked on such causes as ending slavery and the death penalty, also took an interest in the debtors. Dismissing payment for the release of all debtors as a "pipe dream," the prison committee of the Société de la morale chrétienne tasked itself with easing the lives of the genuinely insolvent debtors, mediating arrangements with creditors and defraying judicial expenses.[95]

Perhaps surprisingly, debtors complained intensely about charity. To some, this philanthropy merely exacerbated a shameful state of dependency. One debtor claimed that the charities favored royalist prisoners while ignoring soldiers, poor workers, fathers of families, and, above all, suspected liberals.[96] Charity also might entail humiliating acts of obsequiousness or equally shameful declarations of poverty from the debtor or his family. Other debtors saw charity as encouraging more frequent use of *contrainte par corps*. The Martin Bequest, a 12,000-franc annuity bequeathed by Major Martin in 1824 to Lyon's Saint-Joseph prison for the purpose of liberating debt prisoners, sparked these types of criticism.[97] Although the bequest had released 203 of the 450 debtors held in the Saint-Joseph prison between 1830 and 1835, debtors themselves vociferously opposed the gift.[98] In one petition, they estimated that the donation had increased the frequency of incarceration in Lyon and its vicinity by a factor of ten.[99] Usurers, they argued, were now certain that a speculation on human liberty would be paid off by the major's generosity. Debtors recounted the release of a pregnant woman who had been imprisoned by a thread seller who had demanded reimbursement for expenses at twice the amount of the original capital, betting on the woman's gravid state as a means of quick compensation from the Martin Bequest.[100] The debtors, citing such abuses, argued that the money should be given to the debtors' families instead.

Occasionally, prison administrators or other officials received money to help release prisoners deemed particularly sympathetic. Faced with such a prospect from the prefect of the Loire, the prison administrators in Saint-Étienne drew up a table of all debtors, listing such aspects as "why the debtor might be of particular interest" and "conduct in prison" to choose from among the prisoners. The prefect chose to release Reynard, the father of a large family and a down-on-his-luck former baker forced to become a day laborer. No sooner had the prison authorities advanced the money than his creditor began to claim that the real amount of Reynard's debt came to some 1,500 francs more than the amount written on the internment record, much to the officials' consternation.[101] Debtors often preferred mutual self-help to the intervention of external institutions or individuals. In May 1828 the debt prisoners of Sainte-Pélagie elected a special committee to write petitions to the legislative chambers and the minister of justice. Prisoners also organized mutual aid societies to raise funds to aid fellow prisoners, but their efforts sometimes annoyed prison officials.[102] Shutting down one such effort in 1814, an administrator worried that the degree of organization among the prisoners involved in such a project made it "incompatible with the life of a prison." The steering committee had nevertheless managed to raise some 200 francs before the society was shut down, most of which, the police inspector noted dryly, might be difficult to redeem given the insolvency of the subscribers.[103]

Later mutual aid societies lasted longer and proved more successful. The society of L'Étonnoir at Sainte-Pélagie, for example, began as a social club but evolved into an internal philanthropic society. The society elected a committee of six administrators who served yearly terms working to maintain the rights of the prison population against the prison officials and to improve the material well-being of the prison, including the creation of a new reading room with a small library and additional baths.[104] The Étonnior, described by one debtor as "if not the best of republics, then at least the truest," drew up lists of those debtors particularly worthy of interest, provided free legal counsel, obtained books for the library, and held charity balls in the prisons.[105] The musicians were imprisoned debtors themselves, and proceeds paid for the release of other prisoners.[106] Such organizations also coordinated lotteries and raffles where debtors contributed small sums to help out their particularly unfortunate comrades. In April 1831, for instance, the debtors of Sainte-Pélagie held a raffle to benefit Charles Palmier, an indigent sixty-four-year-old butcher's assistant who had a paralytic wife and several children.[107] With the proceeds, the man came to an arrangement with his creditors and was released.

Without any clear aims and generally lacking even a clear spatial designation, debt imprisonment existed in terms of its opposite: namely, it was *not* penal imprisonment. The quotidian realities of imprisonment, which left debtors either idle or in an even more dangerous state of independence, seem to have supported an opinion on which critics and supporters of *contrainte par corps* tended to agree. The real power of *contrainte par corps* lay in the threat of incarceration rather than its actual implementation. Despite the centrality of debtors' physical bodies in debates surrounding the institution, the split powers shared by creditors and the state over these bodies rendered their actual incarceration strangely abstract. In this empty and vaguely defined space, debtors constantly negotiated the terms of their confinement, using the one certainty on which everyone agreed—that debtors were not penal prisoners—as an instrument for enlarging their sphere of freedom.

Reframing Imprisonment

Debtors connected their personal stories to their complaints about prison life through invocations of honor. In 1817, for example, Colonel James Swan, a debtor held in Sainte-Pélagie prison, addressed a pamphlet to France's Chamber of Deputies arguing for the rights of his fellow inmates. It was not the first time that the legislators had heard from this particular debtor. Swan's unusual history gave him a unique advantage as advocate for Sainte-Pélagie's victims of *contrainte par corps*. Swan was a foreigner, a Scottish immigrant who had made his fortune and name in America, where he had participated in the Boston Tea Party, risen to the rank of colonel in the War of Independence, and afterward made a fortune in land speculation.[108] In a tight spot with his creditors in America, Swan headed back across the Atlantic, dabbling in war provisioning and the buying and selling of *biens nationaux* in France.

In 1808 Swan ran afoul both of his former colleague Philippe-Herman Lubbert and of Napoleon's draconian laws on foreign debtors. Lubbert had Swan incarcerated for a debt of 250,000 francs. Swan not only denied the debt but also maintained that Lubbert was in fact his creditor and refused to pay so much as a bail bond.[109] Instead he accepted internment in Sainte-Pélagie prison, where he greeted Lubbert's periodic visits—Lubbert had "sworn to keep his debtor under lock and key until his death"—with a dismissive hand gesture.[110] Although Swan would appeal his sentence four times in court, losing each time, he would not negotiate. "Only considerations much superior to interest," Swan maintained, "can dictate such a conduct and make one prefer to his liberty an obstinacy directed by honor and the correctness of his own cause."[111]

For many, James Swan's "obstinacy" perfectly embodied the absurdity of *contrainte par corps*. Swan, a man who "had never presented the least threat to the public order[,] languished for 22 years in a prison."[112] For others, Swan was a swindler who speculated on others' trust, "a pirate of a new breed," whose rapacity could be reined in only by iron bars.[113] Indeed, Swan's story vividly represented to both supporters and opponents of debt imprisonment how closely bound the institution was with conceptions of honor. For his attackers, the disgrace lay in the "everyday scandal presented by the behavior of those wealthy prisoners for whom we are forced to provide."[114] For Swan's defenders, the aging colonel, who refused to pay out of "considerations much superior to interest," was a victim of the indignities of debtors' prison. Indeed, even on July 31, 1830, only three days after Revolutionary foment had liberated Paris's 228 incarcerated debtors, Swan returned to Saint-Pélagie, where he had by that time spent twenty-two years, preferring to go back voluntarily than to risk the indignity of being tracked down by commercial guards after Revolutionary tumult had cooled.[115]

Swan's long years in Sainte-Pélagie—during which time the prisoner penned multiple pamphlets posing solutions to the outstanding debt America had incurred to France in fighting the American Revolution—provided no clear revelation of his underlying motives. Incarceration neither chastised the "doyen" of the debt prisoners nor provided the money that Lubbert insisted he was owed.[116] Moreover, Swan used his legal limbo to render prison conditions themselves a space of contention. Whether drafting formal petitions to the legislative bodies disputing the legal technicalities of *contrainte par corps*, or attempting to expand the rights of prisoners, Swan exemplified how the rules around debt imprisonment provided ample means for manipulation at the hands of those savvy enough to know them.[117]

Debtors like Swan complained about, petitioned against, or otherwise attempted to resist the various means by which the prison administration more or less explicitly assimilated their lot to those of other penitentiary inmates. Yet their quest for recognition of the indignities of debtors' prison was also a fundamentally personal one. Debtors crafted narratives to justify their own arrests and clear their names and credit. Although we have limited access to how such narratives were constructed, one debtor named Jean-Baptiste Philippe Adam, an art dealer held in Sainte-Pélagie, left an important array of documents in which he constructed and reconstructed the circumstances of his arrest.[118] Born in Brie in 1776, Adam had moved to

Paris as a young man and established himself as a successful art dealer and appraiser in Paris's chic place Vendôme. However, his fortunes turned in the last part of the 1810s, and he spent nineteen months imprisoned for debt in Sainte-Pélagie. The experience continued to affect him a decade after his release, both socially and economically.

Adam provided four different accounts of the reasons for his imprisonment addressed to four different authorities, the first two written during his imprisonment in 1820 and 1821 and the last two in the 1830s when ill health impeded his ability to support himself. First, in a letter to the prefect of the Department of the Seine dated July 22, 1821, written from Sainte-Pélagie, he explained that after "considerable losses" in his commerce he had been forced to downsize his store. During the move, some of Adam's merchandise was lost in a fire. Barely able to make his payments, he was then slapped with a number of unpaid bills of exchange, none of which had yet been successfully recovered despite continued litigation against traveling merchants.[119] Owing to the construction at a nearby weaving factory, Adam could not open his doors to the public from March to October 1820. A broker robbed him of a bill of exchange. After divulging his tale of woe, Adam begged the prefect to temporarily stop the sale of his paintings by one of his creditors and to waive his unpaid back taxes.[120]

In his later narratives of his incarceration, Adam spared some details. In an 1830 letter to the fiercely reactionary and soon to be overthrown Charles X, Adam described his unflagging royalism during Napoleon's years as "the principal cause of the misfortunes" leading up to imprisonment, home inspections, and restrictions on his shop displays. Yet the immediate causes of the imprisonment had been unrelated to political designs; it had been the robbery of a bill of exchange by an untrustworthy broker and then a "*banqueroute* of 13,000 francs" by one client. Unable to pay off his debts and pursued by an "intractable creditor," Adam was thrown into Sainte-Pélagie, where the priest recommended him to the Société de bienfaisance, which arranged for his release. Adam left prison to find that "all that I possessed had been pillaged during my detention."[121] To make ends meet, he took up tutoring schoolchildren. In the late 1820s, his health failing, Adam was unable to continue with the lessons and resorted to begging the king for money. In subsequent begging letters he described his "most miserable existence assailed by all kinds of needs" and provided evidence of his sound royalist principles.[122]

For men like Adam, restoring lost honor could be as pressing a need as restoring their lost fortune. Adam highlighted the illicit nature of the dealings that had brought him to prison, as well as the social connections he had managed to keep before, during, and after prison, in order to validate his own innocence and good reputation. But how much dishonor did imprisonment cast on the names of those imprisoned? Indeed, nearly a decade after his release from debtors' prison, Adam's financial situation seems to have been much reduced. The 1,000-franc rent he paid for his Vendôme boutique had been replaced by a 35-franc rent for a store on the less well located rue de Loustry.[123] Sources corroborate that the disgrace of debtors' prison paled in comparison with to a criminal arrest. On one hand, "to have one's room at Sainte-Pélagie" was considered to be a calumny on the same rank with the term *banqueroutier* and fraudster.[124] Yet others held that debt imprisonment was indeed less shameful than other forms of collecting on debts. One debt prisoner, Louis de Marsilly, argued before the Paris Court of First Instance in 1838 that he should not suffer the indignity of having his mail perused by the clerks, stating, "I am neither condemned nor accused of any crime or infraction; I owe my creditor my person as a temporary guarantee of a debt. Having forfeited my liberty, I owe nothing to him nor to society." He added that, unlike a felon or a bankrupt, he still exercised his full civil rights and that "although detained for debts, if I were an elector or juror I could call upon the administrative authority to let me fulfill my civic and political obligations; since, as I said before, aside from my personal liberty, I am a citizen like any other."[125]

As Marsilly's comment suggests, debt imprisonment did not entail the same forms of legal degradation entailed by bankruptcy. At least one prison official considered debt imprisonment to be less feared by debtors than the seizure and sale of their possessions, adding that "if you consult the debtors themselves they will tell you that they prefer to be arrested as it remains almost unperceived because of the polite formalities of the commercial guards," whereas "a seizure by a bailiff who takes several hours to go through a lodging, who peruses all the possessions testing the patience of the debtors, their wives, children and servant and where the two witnesses in plain view of bystanders add still more to the scandal produced by the seizure and auction of belongings" was much worse.[126] Debt imprisonment frequently took place in stealth, lacking the highly public humiliation of bankruptcy or even property seizure.

On the other hand, debt imprisonment elicited cries of persecution and injustice among debtors that are largely absent from narratives of bankruptcy. In the accounts left by debt prisoners, critiques of creditors also function as critiques of the practice of debt imprisonment as a whole. One butcher's apprentice named Hulot published *Mémoir d'un prisonnier pour dettes détenu à Sainte Pélagie* in 1831, ostensibly an attack on debtors' prison as a whole, but largely focused on his own alleged mistreatment at the hands of his status-conscious father, "a former merchant butcher turned property owner."[127] Hulot *père*, beguiled by his new young wife, refused to help his son after forcing him to make an ill-fated loan to his brother-in-law. In the butcher apprentice's narrative, his father's lack of family feeling typified the pitiless behavior of creditors in general. A young law student named J. V. Blache, imprisoned in 1821, also spent most of his pamphlet against debtors' prison recounting his own tale of woe. Blanche alleged that his trusting nature and his willingness to help out his friends had made him the easy prey of an avaricious tailor. So hard-hearted was this creditor that he refused all attempts by Blache's friends to pay the debts, supposedly telling them, "100 écus are nothing in my line of business, I want him to do his five years. He will do them." Debtors shaped their accounts of prison in a language of both dignity and rights, attempting to show through their own cases of obvious abuse how the entire system was founded on such practices.[128]

The mixture of a systematic critique of prison conditions with deeply personal stories also typified the language of petitions sent by imprisoned debtors to the government in which the language of rights often accompanied effusively emotional descriptions of the unjust humiliation suffered by debtors. Swan's petition to the Chamber of Deputies evoked the horrors of prison life through unjust tales of imprisonment, including the story of a sixty-year-old father, nearly blind, imprisoned by his ungrateful children, and that of Portuguese sailor who despaired of seeing his beloved homeland again. Swan's petition, which found a sympathetic audience with the liberal royalist Jean-Guillaume Hyde de Neuville, helped spark the first legislative debate about the situation of the debt prisoners since the reestablishment of debt imprisonment in 1798. Nor was Swan's petition the only one that produced this effect; the debtors themselves provided much of the impetus for ongoing debates concerning *contrainte par corps*. The government regularly received petitions from debtors in prison across the country.[129] The banker Jacques Laffitte and the Yvonne deputy Claude-Joseph-François Jacquinot-Pampelune both claimed that direct inspiration from prisoners inspired their proposals for prison reform.[130]

The most dramatic of the debtors' attempts to reframe the meaning of debt imprisonment can be found in the creation of debtor-run newspapers, such as the *Pauvre Jacques* with which this chapter began.[131] The highlight of these papers was the weekly list of incarcerators—including, when possible, their names, professions, addresses, and the names of the debtors whom they had imprisoned at Sainte-Pélagie and later Clichy prison. A typical list of incarcerators would read something like this one, taken from the March 29, 1829, issue of *Pauvre Jacques*:

> M. Nicolas Friquet, rue Saint-Sébastien, n. 24, faubourg du Temple, has detained M. Vicaire, hairdresser, his cousin, for 15 months over a sum of 250 francs.
>
> M. Thomas Fatin, former lawyer, living in Bordeaux, Fossés Saint-Eloy, n. 32, has detained for three years M. Javerzat, his brother-in-law.
>
> M. André Guinet, rue des Boucheries-Saint-Germain, n. 49, condemned for the misdemeanor of usury by the correctional court of the Seine.[132]

The editors often added parts they deemed particularly shameful, such as using a "borrowed name" to have a debtor arrested, speculating on a debtor's family and friends by buying up bad debts from creditors and throwing debtors in jail, arresting a debtor for a small amount of money or a long amount of time, arresting a veteran, a relative, a family friend, or one of their own workers. Many creditors earned the title "usurer," implying that the bargain initially struck with the debtor had been on the shady side of the law. Eschewing its legal meaning, *Pauvre Jacques* frequently employed the term usurer as a synonym for creditor, implying that every creditor committed usury. At least some incarcerators did not appreciate such publicity; the journal's editors were charged with defamation and libel several times, while other merchants accused of using debt imprisonment wrote in claiming that the newspaper had confused them with other individuals of the same name or clarifying the causes that had led to their debtors' arrest.

Editorial columns offered additional room for ferocious and often deeply personal attacks on abuses perpetrated by bailiffs, commercial guards, and incarcerating creditors. Debtors used the forum to demonstrate

(CE JOURNAL PARAIT TOUS LES DIMANCHES.)

DIMANCHE

22 MARS 1829.

ON S'ABONNE A PARIS,

A Ste Pélagie, corridor dit le Palais-Royal, N° 81,

Chez Ponthieu, Ladvocat, Audin, libraires,

Poussin, rue de la Tabletterie, n° 9,

et chez les principaux Libraires de France.

N° 2.

Ire ANNÉE.

PRIX DE L'ABONNEMENT :

Pour 1 mois. . . . . . 2 fr.

Pour 3 mois. 6

Pour 6 mois. 12

Pour l'année. 24

Encore un Negociant...

Pauvre Jacques,

FIGURE 5. Masthead for *Pauvre Jacques*, March 22, 1829. Below the scene of the arrest, the text reads, "Another businessman . . ." (Bibliothèque nationale de France)

the inequity of their arrest. While lauding debtors' cunning resistance to capture, the paper consistently signaled out arrests obtained by trickery, force, or bribery against debtors who were arrested despite being sick, old, stark naked, or, in one case, the wrong person entirely. Debtors also hoped to restore their good names by explaining their side of the story. In its December 29, 1829, issue, *Pauvre Jacques* printed a letter from the British baronet Sir John Tasker, imprisoned in Bordeaux's formidable Fort Hâ, condemning as a "tissue of lies" a scurrilous pamphlet about the causes of

CE JOURNAL PARAIT TOUS LES DIMANCHES.

DU 6

SEPTEMBRE 1829.

(Une part des bénéfices est consacrée à soulager les détenus pour dettes les plus nécessiteux.)

ON S'ABONNE A PARIS,

A Ste Pélagie, corridor dit le Palais-Royal, N° 81.

Chez Ponthieu, Ladvocat, Audin, libraires,

Moreau-Rosier, rue Montmartre, n° 68.

Selligue, Imp.-Lib., rue des Jeuneurs, n° 14.

et chez les principaux Libraires de France.

N° 34.

1re ANNÉE.

PRIX DE L'ABONNEMENT :

Pour 3 mois . . . 6

Pour 6 mois. . . . 12

Pour l'année. . . . 24

Pour les départemens 1 fr. 50 cent. en sus par trimestre.

Toutes les réclamations doivent être adressées *franco* au bureau du Journal, à Sainte-Pélagie.

BAISSEZ LA TÊTE

PAUVRE JACQUES,

FIGURE 6. Masthead for *Pauvre Jacques*, September 6, 1829, showing an entry into the prison with the text "Lower your head." (Bibliothèque nationale de France)

his debts—namely, wastefulness and indolence—and advertising the publication of his military memoirs, the proceeds of which would go to benefit imprisoned debtors.[133]

The paper's editors devoted particular attention in full-length articles to those creditors who demonstrated particularly disgraceful behavior. Some, like the royal cloth merchant Pourrier, who imprisoned a tailor under the name of his valet rather than on his own account, were castigated for their cowardice.[134] Others earned mention for their cruelty. The January 24, 1833, issue of *Gazette de Sainte-Pélagie* rebuked Casenave, an apothecary, who not only threw Petit, a crystal carver, in prison for debts that the latter had partially paid but also confiscated and auctioned off all Petit's tools and materials, leaving the debtor's wife and four young children penniless and on the street.[135] One wine merchant aroused the ire of *Pauvre Jacques* for keeping his debtor in prison even as he died in the infirmary and after the prison director had personally asked for his release.[136] In its January 17, 1833, issue the *Gazette de Sainte-Pélagie* described how one English woman even had to suffer the confiscation of her loyal lapdog, now deemed a "pledge of her creditor."[137] The January 3, 1830, issue of *Pauvre Jacques* castigated a former debt prisoner who had someone arrested for debt three months after his own release, while the February 7, 1830, issue pronounced against a wholesaler who had gone bankrupt three times owing sums up to 275,000 francs and yet had incarcerated a struggling writer and father of four for a debt of less than 200 francs.[138]

The paper connected debtors' plights to larger demands for reform of prison conditions and for prisoner rights. Even as *Pauvre Jacques* mobilized certain norms about correct behavior in the moral economy of debt and credit to indict bad creditors and destigmatize good debtors, in actuality its goal transcended specific abuses. Indeed, in its vitriolic pages debtors mounted a full-scale assault on the entire institution of the debtors' prison. *Pauvre Jacques* regularly published petitions sent by debt prisoners from throughout France, including those in Grenoble, Bordeaux, Nantes, Versailles, and Lyon, who used its pages to address prison authorities or bring public pressure to bear on previous complaints.[139] It was in fact a premier venue for airing many of the complaints about prison conditions described in this chapter. Petitions described the squalid and cramped living conditions, inadequate food provisions supplied by corrupt monopolies, and the constant surveillance by guards that all but prevented visits from family members and creditors wishing to make arrangements. At the very broadest level, the paper linked prisoners' battles to regain their honor with the nation's struggle. The June 6, 1830, issue of *Pauvre Jacques* featured a small poem, written by a debtor, ending with the lines, "The oppressed can raise their brow/the oppressor should lower his head."[140] In the immediate aftermath of the July Revolution, the caption was changed to one more overtly political in tone, "Tyrants, lower your heads," thereby connecting the debtors' cause to larger goals of dignity and equality fought for by the Revolutionaries. In the newspaper's pages, debtors pleaded for the new government to remember those "victims of avarice and revenge" who populated the prisons of France.[141]

In highlighting the injustices done to them both individually and institutionally, debt prisoners reclaimed their rights as honorable men, fathers, citizens, and property owners and built movements inside and outside the prison to demand reform or abolition of the debtors' prison itself. By providing a venue for artisans and shopkeepers to defend their honor and shame those who had reneged on their financial as well as moral obligations, these forums acted both as continuations of disputes about creditworthiness between borrowers and lenders and as a potent means of disgracing the entire institution of debt imprisonment. They not only expressed the personal anxieties of such individuals but also attempted to define the nature of a new type of credit economy by those who increasingly felt themselves to be its victims.

Conclusion

The novelty of the penitentiary system in the early nineteenth century left considerable ambiguity as to detainment's precise meaning. The older custodial form of incarceration, intended not to punish but merely to detain and to coerce, persisted well into the era of carceral reform. Perhaps more so than in England or America, where debt imprisonment applied to many types of debt, the very use of the prison for debtors challenged the boundaries between failure and crime. Both criminal activity and the failure to reimburse debts entailed shame although not quite of the same type. With debtors incarcerated alongside felons in the country's prisons, however, this distinction could prove elusive.

Contrainte par corps became increasingly difficult to reconcile with the idea of the prison on the level of the practice as well as theory. The "birth of the penitentiary" had made the deprivation of liberty by the state the ultimate penalty for a crime or misdemeanor. The goal of penal detention was to train and rehabilitate the violator through work and education so that he might reenter society and become a valuable member of his community. With debt imprisonment, however, the state had limited ability to systematize and standardize the treatment of those who were incarcerated. Prison conditions varied radically throughout the country, where debtors were seldom separated from other criminals. Even within the same prison, a debtor's quality of life depended on his or her financial situation, thereby repeating within the prison confines the wide disparities between debtors outside prison doors. These economic disparities were exacerbated by the general lack of legitimate employment for the inmates. While penal institutions demanded productive labor of convicts, they excluded debtors from remunerative labor that might have paid off their creditors. Prison administrators worried that debt prisons fostered the very habits—gambling, sloth, and dissolute living—that had supposedly led debtors to insolvency in the first place.

Debtors shared prison officials' concerns with the separation of debt prisoners from convicts. Insisting that the resemblance to criminal confinement degraded them, incarcerated debtors contested almost every aspect of their imprisonment, from the arrangement of space and the movements of individuals in and out of the prison to the provisioning of food and resources. While penal reformers envisioned prisons as all-encompassing disciplinary institutions that retrained fallen men for society, debtors manipulated the legal ambiguity of their situations to obtain privileges and freedoms unthinkable in the kinds of institutions advocated by penal reformers. Debt prisoners led intensely personal struggles to defend their rights in which their efforts to regain their reputation and avoid the taint of association with the growing convict population was matched by their desire for a clean and comfortable prison space. In their graphic depictions of the trickery and cruelty that had placed and kept them behind bars, debtors' hoped to reframe a story that would cast them as the villains seeking to bilk their creditors. While few initially aimed at undermining the entire idea of debt imprisonment itself, ultimately their attacks, and the criticisms of the excesses of the marketplace they contained, provided an incisive criticism of the very institution of the debt prison.

In certain respects, the "debtors' prison" existed as an abstraction rather than as a reality. Unlike penal servitude, detainment for debt served no purpose in and of itself. In describing the lived experience of debt imprisonment, debtors regularly invoked the image of the pawnshop. Sainte-Pélagie, to one inmate, represented "the sad spectacle of a pawnshop of human flesh, in which living merchandise is randomly stockpiled without distinction of quality."[142] An imprisoned poet wrote, "Here we are walking packages in a depot/as in a pawnshop . . . jewels and rags together confused."[143] The actual application *contrainte par corps*, which literally translates to "constraint by the body," entailed very little attention to the body. This ironic absence can be explained by the fact that a debt prisoner found himself under the direct power of neither the state nor his creditor, but rather in a nebulous space between these two. If the justification for penal prison lay in depriving a malefactor of his most precious commodity, his liberty, debt imprisonment deprived a man of his liberty in return for a monetary transaction. Thus debtors compared their state not to that of criminals, whose degradation and dishonor they deemed justified by transgressions, but to slaves, whose bodies had likewise been commodified. The debtors' prison, as such, threw into vivid relief not only the uncertain nature of the prison, but also the limits of contractual agreement. Yet the way that debtors themselves formulated their opposition to debt imprisonment, which was directed by concerns about personal honor and resistance against supposed oppression, proved fundamentally at odds with the critique of debtors' prisons found in the influential tracts of middle-class reformers.

5

The Economy of Discredit

Jean-Baptiste Bayle-Mouillard and the Crusade against Debt Imprisonment

In the winter of 1833, during one of his biannual recesses from the Royal Court of Clermont-Ferrand, a young lawyer named Jean-Baptiste Bayle-Mouillard began what he would call "a great work, the work of my entire life perhaps."[1] The task: to prove, through painstaking and objective research, whether or not debt imprisonment was, as he termed it, a "useful" institution. For Bayle-Mouillard, gauging usefulness implied "not only knowing whether such an institution sometimes produced satisfactory results, which is obvious, or on other occasions [has] harmful effects, which is certain, but, by carefully comparing its inconveniences with its advantages, to come to a definitive result."[2] Armed with an impressive capacity for detail and equally helpful connections to local administrators, he began a journey through the country's penal system from the newly established Maison de Clichy in Paris to provincial jails where debtors were incarcerated alongside convicted felons. "One by one," he recalled, "I analyzed all those sad acts that enchain the liberty of a man."[3] At each prison, the young lawyer questioned inmates and officials, poured over the records, analyzed incarceration documents, calculated the duration of detentions, compared the professions of debtors and creditors, and, as he put it, only left a prison "after in some way exhausting it."[4]

Crowned with top honors by the Académie des sciences morales of Clermont-Ferrand for the results of his initial investigations, Bayle-Mouillard subsequently revised his thesis into a 420-page book entitled

De l'emprisonnement pour dettes: Considération sur son origine, ses rapports avec la morale publique et les intérêts du commerce, des familles, de la société. The book quickly became the touchstone work for debaters both for and against debt imprisonment. It differed from the many pamphlets that had preceded its publication in its extensive statistical analysis of how the debtors' prison affected French society. In addition to his textual explanation of his findings, Bayle-Mouillard included a lengthy appendix with all the meticulously tabulated data that had resulted from his months of research. The tables testified to the young lawyer's incontrovertible resourcefulness: exhaustive data correlated levels of debt imprisonment in regions of the country to everything from lottery participation to rates of illegitimacy. From this study, Bayle-Mouillard, who claimed to have begun his research with complete impartiality, reached one general conclusion: *contrainte par corps* was not only a useless institution but also an immoral and socially destructive one.

Although Bayle-Mouillard's work was widely applauded and cited in its time, and he went on to enjoy a long and honorable career as a judge and lawmaker, *De l'emprisonnement* today has been almost forgotten, aside from one recent article by the French economist Pierre-Cyrille Hautcoeur that largely just summarizes Bayle-Mouillard's findings.[5] Bayle-Mouillard's exhaustive volume, however, provides an excellent window into the tropes and questions that preoccupied the many writers who devoted time and energy to arguing about *contrainte par corps* in the decades following its reestablishment. Between the early years of the Restoration and the early years of the July Monarchy, scattered criticism of debt imprisonment cohered into a reform movement. In the 1820s and 1830s, writers published dozens of pamphlets both attacking and defending debt imprisonment.[6] Eminent legal scholars consecrated volumes to the finer points of applying *contrainte par corps*, with many an aspiring young law student defending his *thèse* on the subject. From the early years of the Restoration through the end of the Second Empire, legislators proposed multiple reform bills, as they struggled to balance the demands of commerce with increasingly vocal concern about the debtors' material and moral circumstances.

The fervor of the debate took contemporaries by surprise. One bewildered supporter of debt imprisonment proclaimed in exasperation that "the legislation on *contrainte par corps* was established a long time ago; no complaints, no criticisms were directed against it. Suddenly, violent declamations are leveled against it: the law has been accused, pursued, attacked on every point, as contrary to natural law, to humanity, to morality, to commerce."[7] Like other controversies of the time, including those surrounding child labor and slavery, the debate on debt imprisonment involved delineating the parameters of the marketplace. As lawmakers and writers worked to define an economy based on the notion of individual rational agents and separate gendered public and private spheres, they confronted difficult questions: Who should be allowed to participate in this marketplace? What kinds of goods could be bought and sold? What restrictions should be placed on economic agents in the name of morality? Although some commentators portrayed debt imprisonment as representing a backward old economy, for many others the possibility of engaging even one's self as collateral in a commercial transaction seemed closely connected to the broadening reach of the market.

Historians seeking to understand the nineteenth-century debate about debt imprisonment have rightfully looked at its relationship to the boundaries of the marketplace. Some scholars have embraced a teleological argument in which debt imprisonment was fated to recede before the forces of an abstract cash nexus. Describing the fate of debtors' prison in America, one legal historian has written that "the debtors' prison disappeared because it was obsolete. Reformers accelerated the contraction of creditor rights by pressing first for modifications in the imprisonment system and then for the abandonment of debtors' jail, but in the long run the institution would have disappeared anyway."[8] Others have advanced more complex theories concerning the connections between debt imprisonment and the creation of a modern marketplace. For Margot Finn, the British debtors' prisons did not vanish over the course of the nineteenth century but rather became associated with and governed by the disciplining of the poor. Debt imprisonment did not therefore stand in opposition to the emergence of modern marketplace practices, but paralleled and complemented them.[9] In Gustav Peebles's analysis of the rhetoric of British reformers, debtors' prisons gathered such opposition because they symbolized barbaric and traditional practices in the heart of the metropole itself that undermined Britain's claim to civilized superiority over the rest of the world.[10] Both Peebles and Finn see the reform of debt imprisonment not as a philanthropic endeavor but as a means of creating a liberal economy.

Bayle-Mouillard's canonical 1836 work supports a similar reading. Although Bayle-Mouillard self-consciously framed his research as a scientific and objective analysis of social phenomena that bypassed polemical and sentimental depictions of debt imprisonment and provided ideologically neutral truths about the institution, he in fact borrowed heavily from the contemporary tropes furnished by lawmakers, novelists, and pamphleteers. He shared his contemporaries' obsession with understanding whether debt prisoners qualified as *commerçants*, a fixation that distinguished the French debate on debtors' prison from similar conversations in the United States and Britain. This was on one hand a legal matter: in France, commercial debt imprisonment theoretically only pertained to merchants. In proving that non-*commerçants* regularly populated prisons, reformers merely pointed out a self-evident abuse of the law. Yet the ramifications of this concern transcended issues of the law's application to touch upon the changing boundaries of the marketplace.

While Bayle-Mouillard's findings refuted facile criticism of debt imprisonment as inappropriately applied, he affirmed a growing liberal consensus about the market as a space of total separation between private and public realms. Men, acting as free individual agents in the public space, contracted on the basis of their individual merits and resources with other men. A man's thick fabric of social ties, of which the family formed the most important, had to be excluded from his business dealings. This ideology led Bayle-Mouillard to characterize *contrainte par corps* as based on emotion rather than reason. He lamented its supposed reliance on dense webs of social connections, and he dismissed small commerce, where family life and business continued to be most closely interconnected and which, unsurprisingly, made the most use of debt imprisonment, in favor of big industries. With the seductive objectivity of his statistical analysis to support him, Bayle-Mouillard exemplified the viewpoint of a set of social reformers who perceived in debt imprisonment the embodiment of an illicit credit economy where the lack of separation between the public and private paralleled a similar lack of separation between failure and fraud. Bayle-Mouillard's highly influential study indicates that the decline of debt imprisonment owed itself as much to the emergence of a new imaginary about economic activity as it did to actual changes in economic life itself.

Defining Categories

Bayle-Mouillard's work must be situated both within the context of legislative reform concerning debt imprisonment and within an intellectual culture increasingly fascinated by a statistical approach to social problems. The young lawyer wrote his pamphlet in response to a contest proposed by the recently reestablished Académie des sciences morales of Clermont-Ferrand. The competition, which began in July 1833 with a submission deadline of December 1834, proposed a 1,500-franc cash prize for the best answer to the following question: How useful is *contrainte par corps* for commercial and civil debts? Candidates were also asked to address debt imprisonment's "relationship with public morals, the interest of commerce and the interest of families."[11] That the Académie chose the topic of debt imprisonment is hardly surprising. In 1832, a year before the Académie issued its call for papers, a reform bill had mandated fundamental changes to the function of debt imprisonment. Reform had been long in coming: the Chamber of Peers and the Chamber of Deputies had debated proposals to modify debt imprisonment in 1818, 1821, and 1828.[12] In the meantime, a vitriolic pamphlet war raged about the merits of debt imprisonment. Paris's Clichy prison, the first of its kind in France, was due to open the next year. Few topics more thoroughly engaged the intellectual circles of the July Monarchy.

Just as importantly, the Académie chose the topic of debt imprisonment because the subject seemed ideally adapted to statistical analysis. The reestablishment of *académies*, like the one in Clermont-Ferrand, during the Restoration after their abolition during the Napoleonic period had involved a new marriage of "science and power" in which savants were invited to consider the burgeoning "social question" in ways that posed minimal threat to the existing social order. Provincial académies, undoubtedly inspired by the example of the Académie des sciences in Paris, proved early converts to the popularity of statistical thinking that characterized the intellectual milieu of the 1830s. The contest that Bayle-Mouillard entered testifies to the Académie des sciences morales' interest in statistics. As Pierre-Cyrille Hautcoeur has noted, although the other contest submissions approached *contrainte par corps* from the standpoint of jurisprudence, the unanimous decision to award victory to Bayle-Mouillard's work owed as much to the rigor of the lawyer's analysis as it did to his methodological approach, which was predominantly statistical.[13] Eschewing what he saw as the "emotions and rhetoric" that had guided the works of pamphleteers on both sides of the debate about debtors' prison, Bayle-Mouillard vowed that he had begun his research with "complete neutrality" of opinion toward debtors' prison. He provided caveats about his own research, fearing that though he had attempted to be as objective and thorough as possible, the limitations placed on him by working independently on the project might interfere with the faithful representation of reality.[14] While at times *De l'emprisonnement pour dettes* reached a feverish pitch of moralism, denouncing *contrainte par corps* as a form of torture and slavery, much of the persuasive power that would make the book the touchstone of opposition to debtors' prison for decades to come lay in its self-consciously "objective" tone and its reliance on exhaustive compilations of data to prove its point.

De l'emprisonnement pour dettes testifies to the growing intellectual dominance of statistical thinking and ideals of scientific objectivity in assessing social phenomena. Historians have agreed that the increasing reliance on numbers marked a new strategy of communication and that "the idea of objectivity is a political as well as a scientific one. Objectivity means the rule of law, not of men. It implies the subordination of personal interest and prejudices to public standards."[15] For Theodore Porter, the reliance on objectivity and statistical thinking corresponded with the rise in both the centralization of states and the democratization of culture. Numbers, constituting a more broadly shared and supposedly transparent body of information, came to surpass arbitrary and informal knowledge, known only by elites. Other historians have focused on these supposedly transparent appeals as a mask for a larger bourgeois project.[16] Indeed, as Joan Wallach Scott has advised, "Statistical reports are neither totally neutral collections of fact nor simply ideological impositions. Rather they are ways of establishing the authority of certain visions of social order, of organizing perceptions of 'experience.'"[17] In the nineteenth century, these visions of order were almost always those of a certain educated elite. Heeding Scott's advice, we can read Bayle-Mouillard's report in two ways: First, it provides a window into the demographics of debtors' prison that, owing to the destruction of many archival records, are impossible to reconstruct otherwise. Secondly, as the canonical text in the abolitionist movement, it provides an entry into the ideological framework of the anti-imprisonment cause. Bayle-Mouillard's reality, as shown by my own attempts to simulate his research with the prison internment records from Lyon, was a product of the categories he used and the questions he chose to pursue, which were themselves created by his liberalism. *De l'emprisonnement pour dettes* is, in fact, a political statement, couched in the language of scientific objectivity. Despite Bayle-Mouillard's avowal of complete neutrality, his work contains a potent message not merely about *contrainte par corps* but also about the men and women most affected by it.

We can better understand Bayle-Mouillard's ideological agenda by examining the body of literature to which he believed his study belonged. In the introduction to *De l'emprisonnement pour dettes*, Bayle-Mouillard admitted the influence of the new statistical thinking, including the works of André-Michel Guerry and Adolphe Quetelet, on his research.[18] In studying debt imprisonment, Bayle-Mouillard borrowed liberally from these innovators' methodological approach in the study of deviance. Guerry's research in such works as *Statistique comparée de l'état de l'instruction et du nombre des crimes dans les divers arrondissements des Académies et des Cours Royales de France* of 1829 and his *Essai sur la statistique morale de la France* of 1833 focused on understanding the link between crime and other social variables such as illegitimacy rates, poverty, wealth, and suicide. He pioneered the use of graphic comparisons, in which regions of France were shaded to represent disparate data patterns, a technique embraced by Bayle-Mouillard. Quetelet, a Belgian astronomer who believed that the social world was governed by laws similar to the natural world, is best known for his theorization of the idea of the "average man." By classifying and categorizing his subjects by age, sex, education, employment, and social class, Quetelet argued that young, poor, unemployed, and badly educated men were more likely to commit crimes, a likelihood he measured by its level of deviance from the statistical norm.[19] Bayle-Mouillard not only borrowed many of Quetelet's techniques but also his conception of the social world as subject to recognizable laws and patterns whose causes could be identified by careful comparison with other social and economic factors.

While Bayle-Mouillard repeatedly referred to Quetelet and Guerry's work, Alexandre Parent du Châtelet's magisterial *De la prostitution dans la ville de Paris, considérée sous le rapport de l'hygiène publique, de la morale et de l'administration*, which appeared the same year as *De l'emprisonnement*, offers an even more revealing comparison. The result of eight years of sustained research, principally in police archives, Parent du Châtelet's tome not only shared Bayle-Mouillard's exhaustive statistical approach and transnational comparison but also ruminated on the material and psychological motivations for prostitution. As Victoria Thompson has argued, Parent du Châtelet's text linked unsupervised prostitution with unregulated economic exchange. He attempted to demonstrate, by means of painstaking charts and graphs, that although "women possessed a powerful form of capital in their sexuality . . . the deployment of this capital was either dangerous to society or without economic benefit to the women involved, who remained economically dependent."[20] Eager to avoid the impression that prostitution enabled the independence of women as market actors, *De la prostitution* associated the trade with poverty, desperation, and financial dependency and found it to be in direct opposition to the interest and well-being of the rational, self-possessed bourgeois male. Bayle-Mouillard's argument about debt imprisonment strikingly resembled Parent du Châtelet's argument about prostitution: for each man, these practices exemplified the dangers of unbridled laissez-faire that allowed market actors to engage any collateral they possessed, including their bodies, in economic transactions. For both Bayle-Mouillard and Parent du Châtelet, the results of an unregulated market in bodies undermined the foundation of the free, reasoning, presumptively male economic agent upon which economic liberalism was based.

Although he was as concerned as other statisticians in creating categories, Bayle-Mouillard also concentrated on dismantling the principal category of his study: that of the *commerçant*. Opponents of debtors' prison had long insisted that despite the official restriction of *contrainte par corps* for commercial debts to the *commerçant*, many of those arrested were not merchants, traders, tradesmen, or businesspeople even by the broadest definition. The portrayal of Sainte-Pélagie and Clichy as crowded with non-*commerçants* became so clichéd that in the section "Debt Prisoners" in the well-known panoramic sketch of French life *Les Français peints par eux-mêmes*, the only debtors in prison were "landowners, literary men, military officers, law or medical students, *rentiers*, water carriers, charcoal peddlers. . . . and other individuals also foreign to commerce, who, because of urgent need or a pressing momentary necessity, entered into an obligation improperly called an act of commerce."[21] Estimates of how many prisoners could actually be considered *commerçants* varied between the duc de Broglie's exceedingly low figure of four or five out of every hundred prisoners to more generous estimates of two-thirds or three-fourths of the debtors.[22] Legislators continually inveighed against the supposedly ubiquitous use of the "ultimate rigor of commercial law" against farmers and aristocrats.

However, while debtors' professions mattered intensely to both supporters and opponents of debtors' prison, no one could offer a comprehensive or precise definition of *commerçant*. Judges and legal scholars had long struggled to delineate the parameters of commercial law. While Jacques Savary in his 1675 *Parfait négociant* had defined the *commerçant* in terms

V.

Rapport entre la population et le nombre des détenus, dans chaque département, pour dettes envers des particuliers, le premier jour de chaque trimestre des années 1824 - 1833.

N°s D'ORDRE.	DÉPARTEMENTS.	NOMBRE D'HABITANTS fournissant 1 détenu.	N°s D'ORDRE.	DÉPARTEMENTS.	NOMBRE D'HABITANTS fournissant 1 détenu.
1.	Seine	117	21.	Seine-et-Oise	1,140
2.	Seine-Inférieure	466	22.	Aisne	1,158
3.	Cantal	515	23.	Isère	1,160
4.	Rhône	541		MOYENNE	1,283
5.	Calvados	596			
6.	Eure	657	24.	Lot-et-Garonne	1,309
7.	Aveyron	680	25.	Ardèche	1,357
8.	Doubs	727	26.	Alpes (Hautes-)	1,373
9.	Hérault	764	27.	Loire (Haute-)	1,446
10.	Ariége	783	28.	Orne	1,449
11.	Pas-de-Calais	814	29.	Rhin (Bas-)	1,526
12.	Garonne (Haute-)	848	30.	Jura	1,570
13.	Tarn	854	31.	Charente-Inférieure	1,584
14.	Lozère	871	32.	Saône (Haute-)	1,677
15.	Gard	886	33.	Ardennes	1,787
16.	Corse	1,062	34.	Aude	2,707
17.	Tarn-et-Garonne	1,063	35.	Marne	1,852
18.	Gers	1,083	36.	Puy-de-Dôme	1,879
19.	Lot	1,087	37.	Gironde	1,925
20.	Pyrénées (Hautes-)	1,114	38.	Oise	1,930

FIGURE 7. Example of Bayle-Mouillard's appendix tables from *De l'emprisonnement*. This table attempts to calculate the number of debtors per population in different *départements*. (Bibliothèque nationale de France)

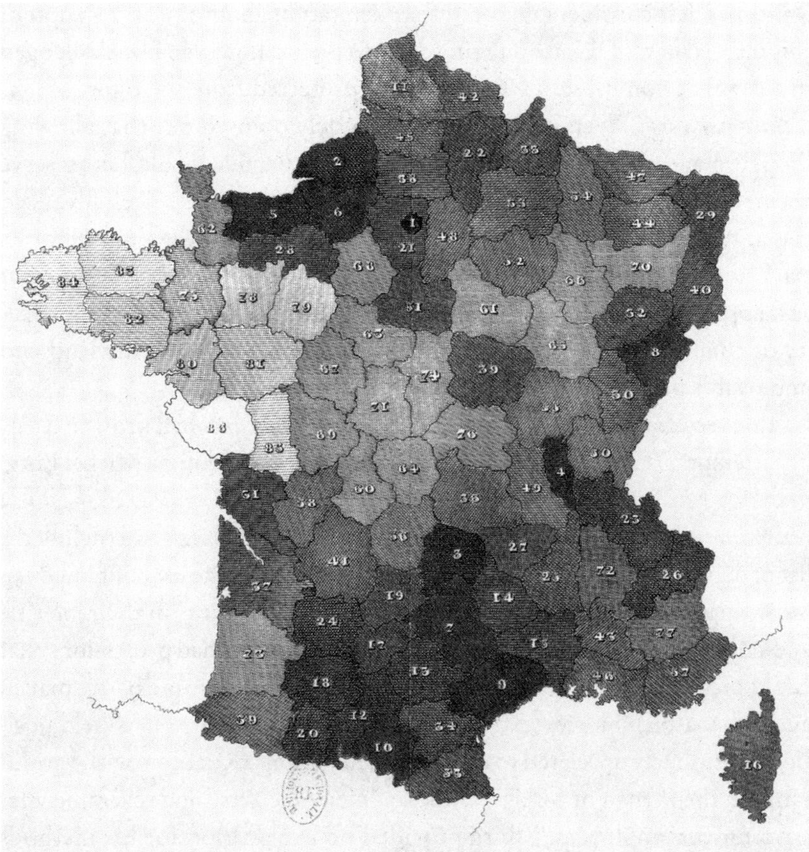

FIGURE 8. Bayle-Mouillard's map in *De l'emprisonnement* showing the rates of incarceration in different *départements* of France. The higher the per capita rate of debt imprisonment, the darker the shading. Paris and the South are the darkest on this map, while Brittany is the lightest. The Seine, however, is the darkest of all. (Bibliothèque nationale de France)

of membership in a merchant corporation, his views had become outdated by the eighteenth century as commerce increasingly proliferated outside the guild structure. Subsequent legal scholars argued that the definition of *commerçant* relied instead on the buying and selling of merchandise. However, this definition meant that even certain agricultural workers could be labeled *commerçants* and subjected to commercial law, a view that scandalized lawmakers.[23] The Commercial Code merely defined *commerçants* as those who "exercise acts of commerce and make it their habitual profession." The intentional vagueness of this definition, meant to avoid corporatist overtones, left considerable room for disputation about the application of commercial law.[24] Despite ongoing disagreements, however, few challenged the idea that non-*commerçants* should be protected from the rigors of *contrainte par corps*. Even pamphleteers who slyly pointed out that allowing shopkeepers and artisans to arrest delinquent clientele would better serve the needs of commerce than arresting *commerçants* themselves advanced this argument to demonstrate the law's hypocrisy rather than to call for its extension. By defending the line between *commerçant* and non-*commerçant* as it applied to *contrainte par corps*, commentators defended the abnormality of commercial activity from the normality of life tied to the land and immovable property.

This very concern with the arrest of non-*commerçants* had provoked earlier attempts at calculating exact figures of imprisoned debtors. Michel Burg, in the appendix to a blistering 1820 pamphlet entitled *Considérations sur la contrainte par corps, en matières de dettes dites commerciales*, had included a list of debtors in Sainte-Pélagie prison on May 1, 1820. The list contained 156 individuals, of whom only 18 actually included "merchant" in their job title and only four were listed as "businessmen." Another 21 had professions that could properly be called artisanal (including two tailors, one barrel maker, and one mason). However, the vast majority of Burg's prisoners held positions completely unrelated to commerce, including 48 debtors with various ranks in the French or foreign armies, 3 "men of letters," and several former government employees.[25] Burg provided no explanation for his methods for data collection, and his frequent use of identifiers such as "usurer" and "Jew" makes it highly unlikely that he had copied this information directly from internment records. Burg hoped that by merely laying out the sheer data on debt imprisonment, the case for reform or abolition would become transparent and obvious to everyone.

Bayle-Mouillard's findings on *commerçants* were considerably more nuanced. Although he frequently found debtors listed as property owners, *rentiers*, military officers, students, and employees in internment records, his evidence pointed to vast discrepancies in the imprisonment of non-*commerçants*, a term Bayle-Mouillard also never defined, in different regions of the country. In Paris, he discovered that their numbers were extremely high: between January 1831 and November 1833, for example, 665 *commerçants* and 557 non-*commerçants* had been arrested for commercial debts. While Bayle-Mouillard had not managed to obtain detailed information about professions from all major cities throughout France, he provided a chart of a few large cities, giving multiple caveats for the data. Nevertheless, he noted that in some places, like Saint-Étienne and Lyon, the imprisonment of noncommercial people was comparatively rare, while in other places, like Montpellier and Nîmes, such arrests were quite common.

Bayle-Mouillard returned to the considerable differences between cities in their incarceration of debtors in his next chapter, where he discussed the bill of exchange. The bill of exchange featured prominently in criticism of *contrainte par corps* because every bill of exchange, regardless of the profession of the signer, was subject to commercial law and immediately entailed *contrainte par corps* if unpaid. For this reason, critics widely considered it a tool for usury, while supporters believed that mandatory imprisonment for default gave it the same value as circulating currency.[26] Even lawmakers sympathetic to the plight of noncommercial individuals arrested for debt believed that distinguishing between commercial and noncommercial uses of bills of exchange weakened the power of this mighty form of credit. Furthermore, supporters of debt imprisonment feared that the speed with which bills of exchange circulated would be severely impeded if merchants did not know whether the signatory could be subjected to imprisonment for a default.[27] Vocal opposition from the chambers of commerce and commercial courts to restricting creditors' rights on pursuing bills of exchange helped explain the failure of early attempts at reforming debt imprisonment, including Étienne-Denis Pasquier's proposal of 1818 and the duc de Montmorency's proposal of 1821.[28] Although the law of April 17, 1832, specified that bills of exchange could not give rise to *contrainte par corps* if they were considered "simple promises" to pay rather than actual commercial

TABLE 2. Incarceration of commercial and noncommercial debtors, 1831–33

CITY	*COMMERÇANTS*	NON-*COMMERÇANTS*
Lyon	422	28
Marseille	42	14
Saint-Étienne	43	1
Avignon	16	9
Montpellier	56	42
Nîmes	41	22
Clermont-Ferrand	38	14
Total	658	130

Source: Bayle-Mouillard, *De l'emprisonnement pour dettes*, 188.

transactions, many suspected that commercial courts generally disregarded this alteration.[29]

Bayle-Mouillard's evidence seemed to substantiate these concerns about bills of exchange. After studying over three hundred financial instruments that had led to arrest, he doubted "that a single one of them was sincere."[30] Most bills were drawn not between major commercial cities but rather in isolated villages and hamlets that Bayle-Mouillard considered unlikely venues for genuine commercial transactions. The creditors involved were frequently landowners rather than merchants. Bayle-Mouillard believed that such transactions masked usurious exchanges between manipulative moneylenders and desperate borrowers. Extrapolating from his data, he stressed a connection between high percentages of arrests based on debts in bills of exchange and high percentages of non-*commerçants* imprisoned for supposedly commercial debts. What did this trend imply about the utility of *contrainte par corps* for commerce? Relying on data about regional commercial activity, including the per capita concentration of merchants (defined here as those who paid the government business tax or *patente*) and the amount of commercial litigation before commercial courts, Bayle-Mouillard insisted on a connection between high levels of commercial activity and low numbers of arrests for bills of exchange and of non-*commerçants*. That is to say, he linked commercial "backwardness" with the use of debt imprisonment on noncommercial individuals. On the other hand, he saw no link between commercial activity and the overall use of commercial debt imprisonment in a region: many of the most commercial *départements* in France had only middling numbers of debt arrests, while *départements* like Cantal, hardly a commercial center, had among the highest per capita usages of imprisonment. Bayle-Mouillard also found no correlations between economic crises and rates of debt imprisonment or bankruptcy rates and imprisonment.

Although Bayle-Mouillard's work refuted the claims of pamphleteers who had insisted that only non-*commerçants* ended up in debtors' prison, it confirmed another allegation routinely made by opponents of debtors' prison: that noncommercial creditors regularly utilized *contrainte par corps* to arrest *commerçants*. Bayle-Mouillard noted that in every city he studied, creditors who listed their professions as *rentiers*, property owners, and farmers formed a considerable percentage of incarcerators. In Lyon from 1831 to 1833, for example, he counted only twenty-eight debtors who were non-*commerçants* but a whopping 124 creditors whose professions seemed unaffiliated with commerce. When they did not live in the city where they incarcerated their debtors, they lived in the surrounding countryside rather than in major cities like Paris or Lyon. For Bayle-Mouillard, this fact suggested that the "businessmen, manufacturers, and merchants, those men who cover all of France with their social networks and who sell their products everywhere, who enrich the country with their labor, don't use *contrainte par corps*."[31] Only a parasitic and unproductive class of creditors relied on debt imprisonment as a means of payment.

Bayle-Mouillard held similar views on the debtors who were arrested. Although his data suggested that incarcerated debtors tended to be *commerçants*, he did not believe these *commerçants* formed an important component of their region's commerce. In cities where the number of *commerçants* arrested for debt vastly outnumbered non-*commerçants*, the imprisoned *commerçants* involved did not produce "anything that is essential to national wealth."[32] Lyon's Saint-Joseph prison held few individuals associated with the city's silk industry, whether these were the owners of silk factories, the *canuts* who manned them, or the cloth dyers and cloth finishers attached to those trades. Marseille's debt prisoners included barely a handful of the most characteristic industries of the maritime city of any class, whether ship outfitters or sailors, bankers or builders.[33] Bayle-Mouillard's debtors languished in prison for piddling sums. In estimates drawn from several provincial cities where he was able to spend a substantial amount of time between 1834 and 1835, Bayle-Mouillard put the average debt at around 1,440 francs, with more than three-quarters of all debtors arrested for less than 2,000 francs.[34]

Bayle-Mouillard took the small debts involved as evidence that most of these men, while listed as merchants, belonged not to the highest and most august ranks of the business communities, but rather to an unstable rung of the lower middle class. *De l'emprisonnement* somewhat condescendingly referred to the debtors who filled the prisons in Marseille, Lyon, and other towns as individuals engaged in "all the piddling forms of commerce which require neither skill nor education and form an industry for those who have nothing, an occupation for men who, too poor to do nothing, too lazy to work seriously, risk indiscriminately that little capital they possess, that which was confided to them."[35] Scanning internment records, Bayle-Mouillard discovered the same professions wherever he went: innkeepers, cabaret owners, wine merchants, leather merchants, café owners, tailors, and cobblers.[36] Such marginal businessmen were, in turn, likely to be imprisoned by individuals of the same professions. "In general," Bayle-Mouillard summarized, "the less a kind of commerce demands industry, the less it demands advances, the more those who exercise it are threatened with imprisonment. It is here that incompetent and luckless men take refuge. They want to escape poverty, and lose their liberty."[37] According to Bayle-Mouillard's data, the debtors' prison belonged to the least creditworthy realm of both borrowers and lenders. Furthermore, the professions most likely to imprison their debtors were also the most likely to find themselves in prison for debt. While debt prisoners were an eclectic lot, the groups egregiously absent from such places were workers in the country's most productive industries.

Through statistical analysis, Bayle-Mouillard attempted to solve the question that had long occupied so many of his contemporaries: Were most debt prisoners actually *commerçants*? Like almost all other observers, Bayle-Mouillard never actually defined the word *commerçant* nor devoted any time to considering the various ways in which commercial involvement might be categorized. For contemporaries, his research both indicated that the caricature of debt imprisonment as entirely used against non-*commerçants* had been significantly exaggerated and pointed to disturbing discrepancies in the application of the law in various parts of the country. From the standpoint of hindsight, however, a historian might find Bayle-Mouillard's unwillingness or inability to define *commerçant* at a more granular level disappointing. As major cities in France began to feel the effects of proletarianization, Bayle-Mouillard's analysis of the professions of incarcerated debtors poses as many questions as it answers. In one respect, however, Bayle-Mouillard drew conclusions with important implications for our understanding of the impact of debt imprisonment on social class. He speculated that most debtors belonged to the most precarious ranks of artisans and small shopkeepers consisting largely of the service industry. It was precisely in these groups where the connection between family and business, and between private and public lives, would overlap the most.

The Internment Records of Saint-Joseph Prison, Lyon

It would be impossible for a modern-day historian to repeat Bayle-Mouillard's impressive feat of the 1830s. Today prison internment records for debtors exist in only a handful of *départements*, and even these often provide only a fragmentary glimpse of incarceration over the early nineteenth century. Other pieces of evidence Bayle-Mouillard utilized in creating his book have vanished entirely. Nevertheless, examining the existent internment records can provide useful clues not only into the function of debt imprisonment but also into the choices Bayle-Mouillard made in framing his story. Internment record entries included the name, profession, and address of the debtor; the name, profession, and address of the incarcerating creditor; the arresting bailiff; the amount of the debt; and the way in which it was contracted. I have analyzed 318 of these entries from Lyon between 1835 and 1840, beginning three years after the passage of the law of April 17, 1832, but coinciding with the tail end of decades-long legislative debates about the debtors' prison.

Although Paris would seem the best place to study debtors' prison in nineteenth-century France given its share of the prison population, internment records for commercial debtors at Sainte-Pélagie, Clichy, and Saint Lazare do not exist, probably victims of the fire that destroyed so much of Parisian history in the 1870s.[38] While the absence of Parisian data is disappointing, Lyon can serve as a logical replacement. As France's second largest city during the period with a population of some 340,000 inhabitants, Lyon was at the forefront of the industrial production of textiles—as much as half of the labor force was involved with silk production in some fashion. It was also home to a precociously politicized working class, as was made abundantly clear by the urban upheavals of the 1830s.[39] After the Seine and the Seine-Inférieure, the Rhône, the department in which Lyon was situated, had the most litigation placed before its commercial courts.[40] According to Bayle-Mouillard's calculations, Lyon was among the leading incarcerators of debtors. Between 1824 and 1833, he counted 22 women and 781 men imprisoned for private debts in the department of the Rhône, making it the fourth highest per capita debt incarcerator (behind the Seine, the Seine-Inférieure, and Cantal).[41] The dominant role played by a single industry in Lyon's economy, its relatively representative nature as a large French city of the time, and its high incarceration rates make Lyon an ideal site for testing some of Bayle-Mouillard's findings about the activity of commercial people at a local level.

The first important fact revealed by the analysis of the internment records is the amount of money for which debtors were arrested. Bayle-Mouillard characterized debt imprisonment as overwhelmingly a phenomenon of the poor and marginal. In interpreting these data, we can assume that large debts implied a debtor had access to large credit in the first place and was therefore generally of a more affluent social position, whereas the prevalence of more small debts suggests the use of debt imprisonment by a lower socioeconomic class, in terms of both the creditors and debtors involved. On the other hand, an important factor to consider here is legal limitations: the law of April 17, 1832, had fixed 200 francs as the minimum debt entailing imprisonment. To put this sum in perspective, according to Louis-René Villermé's 1839 statistics, 200 francs equaled roughly four months' labor for a male textile weaver.[42] Of the 318 records analyzed, 41 were for debts under 300 francs (with 8 debtors arrested for 200 francs exactly). The law of April 17, 1832, also ordered that debts under 500 francs could result in a maximum of one year in prison—the prison records reveal that 143 of the 318 arrests were for debts under 500 francs, and 10 were for 500 francs exactly. Thus the majority of debtors were imprisoned for sums that were considered relatively low. On the other hand, some debtors owed very large amounts of money to their creditors. Two debtors, Antoine Ferlat, a merchant, and Pierre Ferrier, a businessman, were each arrested for 10,000 francs in running accounts owed to two different businessmen.[43]

In regards to understanding how imprisonment worked as a social strategy, perhaps the most interesting information revealed by these internment records involves the respective professions of debtors and creditors. Yet

TABLE 3. Debts entailing incarceration in Saint-Joseph prison, Lyon, 1835–40

AMOUNT OF DEBT (FRANCS)	NUMBER OF DEBTORS
<200	1
200–299	48
300–399	56
400–499	34
500–599	29
600–699	15
700–799	18
800–899	12
900–999	7
1,000–1,999	38
2,000–2,999	23
3,000–9,999	21
10,000 +	2

Source: ADR 2 Y 485.

making definite conclusions in this regard can be difficult. While some debtors were given almost impossibly specific professions—for example, one debtor was listed as a "merchant of lithographic stones"—thirty-one incarcerated debtors were unhelpfully called "merchant" and sixteen were called "businessman." Furthermore, a significant number of debtors were listed as having two careers, sometimes fairly complementary, such as "grocer" and "wine merchant," while others are quite detached from each other, such as "baker" and "joiner." It is unclear whether the debtor rotated from one career to another—many debtors are described as "former baker" or "former notary"—or whether he or she scraped together a living performing multiple tasks. In such cases, the debtors are considered by their first listed profession.

Despite these problems, some clear patterns emerge from the data. For example, eighteen debtors were listed as cabaret owners. Another five appeared as restaurant owners, five as café owners, and five as lemonade sellers. A total of fifteen debtors were considered wine merchants. Given the frequently porous boundaries between these professions, it seems that a substantial number of debtors (48 in all) fell into what might be called the hospitality and catering sector. Butchers and bakers, the given profession of eleven debtors each, also made up sizable numbers of inmates, but probably not disproportionate to their percentage in the general population. Haulers, on the other hand, numbering ten, do seem overrepresented, and perhaps were specifically targeted by their creditors because of the flight risk they may have posed. The number of artisans, including joiners, is notable, as is the number of coal peddlers and livestock or horse dealers. Forty-eight of the debtors provided a residence outside of Lyon or the surrounding communes (namely, Perrache and Guillotière), but most of these were from towns in the Rhône or neighboring departments like the Isère. Only nineteen debtors were female, and of these nineteen, six were widows and four were *desmoiselles* (unmarried women).

A sizable portion of creditors, 89 of the total 296, described themselves as "businessman" (*négociant*) rather than as "merchant" (*marchand*) or *commerçant*. While "businessman" could signify an ordinary merchant, it more typically referred to a wholesale dealer who bought merchandise from smaller suppliers, and thus generally implied a superior socioeconomic class.[44] Of those creditors providing more specific careers, only one described himself as a banker. Meanwhile, for transactions that were supposedly commercial in nature, the number of creditors who gave their professions as either

TABLE 4. Professions of incarcerated debtors in Saint-Joseph prison, Lyon, 1835–40

PROFESSION	NUMBER
Merchant	31
Wine merchant	15
Cabaret owner	18
Businessman	16
Building constructor	6
Lemonade seller	5
Grocer	10
Joiner	13
Innkeeper	7
Butcher	11
Baker	11
Cobbler	6
Tailor	4
Coal merchant	9
Animal merchant	9
Hauler	10
Café owner	5
Restaurant owner	5
Flour merchant	6

Source: ADR 2Y 485.

annuity holder (*rentier*) or property owner (*propriétaire*) is striking; they tie for the second most listed career at 26 creditors each. It is probable that these people, whose titles would imply that they were not commercial at all, in fact ran informal banking practices.[45] Wine merchants and animal merchants, abundantly represented among debtors, are also represented among incarcerating creditors. While innkeepers and tavern keepers were not as well represented among creditors as among debtors, "brewers" appeared among creditors' occupations but not debtors'. Overall, these connections between creditors and debtors seem to have largely been vertical rather than horizontal: creditors overall generally appear to have represented superior socioeconomic classes and debtors inferior ones. This is even more apparent in some of the individual relationships between creditors and debtors. When the debtor and creditor are in the same line of work, we often see the creditor holding a position of power, such as an iron merchant as creditor and the debtor a blacksmith. Strikingly, forty-five of the creditors provided their names in the arrest records as part of a company or a partnership.

Most typically, these took the form of two individuals or "So and So and Company," although on occasion debtors were arrested by a "father and son," "brothers," or, less commonly, "husband and wife." Lastly, creditors were much more likely than debtors to list a primary residence outside Lyon or the Guillotière. Fifty-four creditors were from surrounding towns in the Rhône or from other departments. Five claimed residence in Paris. Despite frequently publicized fears of women imprisoning men, only nine arresting creditors were women, not counting the two women who arrested a debtor in collaboration with their husbands.

A few preliminary steps can next be taken toward analyzing the social and professional proximity of debtors and creditors. Some debtors and creditors appeared to be connected by more or less explicit professional ties where the creditor probably supplied some sort of good or service to the debtor for which the latter owed reimbursement. Indeed, sometimes the merchandise in question is noted in the internment record. One example would be the arrest of Charles Luquet, a tanner, by Sieur Ronnaud, a leather merchant.[46] But in other cases there is no straightforward business relationship. While the debtor in such cases may have been borrowing money for his practice from a creditor, the two are not part of the same

TABLE 5. Professions of incarcerating creditors, Saint-Joseph prison, Lyon, 1835–40

PROFESSION	NUMBER
Businessman	89
Property owner	26
Brewer	5
Baker	5
Animal merchant	10
Wine merchant	15
Rentier	26
Grocer	8
Bookkeeper	4
Iron merchant	5
Merchant	5
Fabric finisher	3
Inn or café owner	4
Coal merchant	4
Flour merchant	3

Source: ADR 2Y 485.

or interrelated trades. For example, there is the arrest of Claude Bailly, a mechanic, by Jean Pierre Beard, an annuity holder who arrested two other debtors within the period I examined.[47] A third group exists where the relationship is particularly ambiguous: for example, the arrest of Sieur Beaume, a shawl finisher, by Sieur Tifrot and Company, coal merchants. Sieur Beaume may have been behind in paying his heating bills, but Sieur Tifrot and Company may not have supplied any such product to the finisher at all.[48] The conclusions drawn from this data must of course be cautious ones. Merely noting that a business relationship involving the actual purchase of goods or services could have taken place does not mean it necessarily did. Moreover, there are many types of social relations, for example, kinship lines and common membership in associational groups, that may have been as important as professional connections but that cannot be ascertained or even hypothesized by the available data. Despite these caveats, the prison records nevertheless reveal certain patterns of possible business relationships. The majority of these of creditor-debtor relationships, 142 out of a total 318, remain unclear because of the vagueness of the professional titles provided for either the debtor or creditor. Of those, where creditor and debtor provided more specific information, 81 indicated no clear business relation whatsoever, while 91 could be potentially have been part of a business relationship.

Although Bayle-Mouillard's analysis pointed to the great regional diversity between *départements* in terms of debt imprisonment, closely examining the types of evidence he used in one area is instructional in understanding not only the ways in which *De l'emprisonnement* functioned as a text but also the realities of imprisonment at the ground level. Certain elements of Bayle-Mouillard's study are supported by an investigation of the internment records in Lyon: for example, it seems that a large majority of debtors could be qualified, at least on the basis of their listed professions, as *commerçants*, whereas a larger group of creditors had noncommercial professions and lived outside the city of Lyon. On the other hand, the prominence of organized companies who imprisoned people as well as the strong indication that creditors often held a superior social class to that of their debtors seem to conflict with Bayle-Mouillard's portrayal of debt imprisonment as performed largely by members of the same social class on each other. Most problematically, however, the records suggest how difficult it must have been to categorize the careers of these debtors. The neat separation made by Bayle-Mouillard and many of his contemporaries between *commerçants* and non-*commerçants* appears to have been highly subjective.

The Morality of Debtors

The core of Bayle-Mouillard's argument about debt imprisonment, however, had less to do with the operation of the credit economy, where he perceived it to be peripheral, than with the relation of this credit economy to a particularly dangerous type of emotional economy. William Reddy has characterized the "emotional regime" that arose after 1815 as framed by "a sharp distinction between reason and emotion" in which the inevitable "failure of this distinction to apply to practice was understood as evidence for a highly pessimistic evaluation of the human capacity to reason."[49] The economic realm, much to the dismay of many contemporaries who bemoaned the triumph of money and self-interest over other values, belonged theoretically to the realm of reason. In economic transactions the bourgeois self was imagined simultaneously as an independent and rational individual who freely entered into economic exchanges based on putative equality and remained in a state of what Reddy has called "intense fragility," aware of the threat of dishonor and humiliation caused by the unfortunate variability of his emotional life. This division between emotion and reason mapped almost seamlessly onto another structuring division of nineteenth-century life: the separation between the public realm, a realm of competition and reason, and the private realm, characterized by harmony and emotion. In the aftermath of the Revolution, these realms became highly gendered: while women were relegated to the latter sphere, bourgeois men moved between the two, alternating their role as tough providers for their households with their role as stern but loving patriarchs.[50]

Nineteenth-century ideas about reason and emotion as they related to the economy were closely tied up with the idea of interest. While scholars like Reddy have depicted interest as diametrically opposed to emotion and honor in this era, contemporary observers expressed very ambivalent attitudes toward interest, which revealed their anxieties about the porous boundaries between feeling and reason. Although interest was envisioned as the glue that held the postcorporate social order together, almost all French philosophers agreed that interest did not suffice to give man a moral compass. The corrosive effects of self-interest intensely worried observers from Saint-Simon and Fourier to Tocqueville and Balzac.[51] Rather than worrying that self-interest was rendering the world crass and materialistic, as Albert Hirschman's work has suggested, many nineteenth-century thinkers believed that self-interest had not yet become rational and unemotional enough.[52] The continued concerns about the (frequently gendered) perils of consumption, for example, reveal the continued understanding that self-interest had at least two different but not always distinct meanings: one the rational self-interest that rested on self-discipline and foresight and the other immediate gratification of wishes and desires.

Bayle-Mouillard's central critique of *contrainte par corps* was that it encouraged this latter form of self-interest and in so doing destroyed the very foundations on which the former type of self-interest rested. *De l'emprisonnement pour dettes* depicted self-interest as an almost autonomous force that could possess and destroy people. In one particularly vivid denunciation, Bayle-Mouillard exclaimed that "*contrainte par corps* is an evil, because it makes men depraved: the debtor by his captivity, the creditor by his egotism: the first in accustoming him to contact with vice, the other in accustoming him to the aspect of suffering, in teaching him to satisfy his interest by the misery of another: both in substituting antagonism for union, war for peace, hate for love."[53] Bayle-Mouillard portrayed an inevitable path from legal process to emotional disorder to social disorder. Although he detailed the emotional degradation wrought by imprisonment, including how the enforced idleness of captivity eroded the ability to work and encouraged immorality, Bayle-Mouillard already considered debtors to be a morally dubious bunch. In his words, they were improvident and shiftless, "too poor to do nothing, too lazy to work seriously, risk[ing] indiscriminately that little capital they possess." Even more damningly, debtors were "masterless men"—former workers who, "unwilling to obey, had started up businesses with no capital."[54] Bayle-Mouillard condemned debt imprisonment for these individuals not because these faults did not deserve to be corrected but because *contrainte par corps* did not provide a means of doing so.

Bayle-Mouillard believed just as strongly that the possibility of incarcerating a debtor warped the bourgeois self of the creditor. Even as the reckless and lazy debtor who could use his body as collateral lost the ability to calculate his risks carefully, the creditor who could act on the initial impulse of annoyance he felt when a debtor failed to reimburse him could no longer "coolly assess the debtor's solvency." He instead became obsessed by "something that resembles the passion of a gambler who loses and wants to risk losing again to make up for what he has lost." No longer a self-disciplined capitalist, he was now a gambler. Reason quickly succumbed to the pull of emotion. A creditor "start [ed] by being hard" and "end[ed] by being furious." Nevertheless, even in his emotion-addled state, the creditor could be capable of a kind of self-interest, one that, in Bayle-Mouillard's account, inevitably permeated the sacrosanct divide between economic life and the private realm of emotion, harmony, and family. Instead of properly "counting only the debtor's resources," thereby limiting emotional transactions to the purely economic realm, the creditor now "calculate[d]" on the basis of the debtor's friends, family, and, most particularly, his spouse.[55] By gratifying his immediate self-interest, the creditor ended up undermining the entire liberal order, presenting the terrible inversion of emotions guiding reason and women's resources as surpassing those of men.

Deeply invested in the rhetoric of unemotional objectivity supplied by statistics, Bayle-Mouillard supported these allegations about the perverted emotional economy of debt imprisonment by attempting to demonstrate that the pronounced regional diversity in incarceration rates among *départements* correlated not to indicators of commercial activity but rather to other social variables representing passions and emotions. Relying on an ostensibly random assortment of social phenomena including illiteracy, homicide, and lottery participation as a kind of index for emotional disorder and lack of impulse control, Bayle-Mouillard argued that these diverse factors offered the clearest correlations with rates of imprisonment. He found, for instance, a strong connection between the number of illegitimate children in an area and that region's reliance on debt imprisonment, which he attributed to a lack of prudence and foresight. A similarly direct correlation held true for the frequency of crimes against property and people. He reasoned not only that creditors in areas with higher murder rates had less respect for "the dignity of man" but also that "homicidal mania is caused by pride, satiety, abuse of pleasures, disappointed ambition and unhappy love," factors which he also felt motivated men to take out loans that they could not reimburse.[56] Areas with high rates of debt imprisonment tended to be more literate and less prone to suicide. Bayle-Mouillard theorized that "men who are thinking of suicide rarely borrow money. On the contrary, educated men do borrow. The desire for self-advancement leads to hazardous enterprises."[57] He also noted that a similar "desire for advancement" perhaps explained the relatively close correlation between those areas with the highest revenues from the lottery and a high frequency of *contrainte par corps*. Bayle-Mouillard explained, "The spectacle of wealth excites desire, no one wants to wait, instead of acquiring fortune through work, one asks for it by luck."[58]

Bayle-Mouillard also condemned *contrainte par corps* for creating an illicit economy that rested on social connections and contradicted the image of the liberal economy based on the ideal of the individual actor. He agreed at least on some level with those who insisted that *contrainte par corps* offered a form of credit to those who lacked reputation or collateral, but he insisted that this form of credit did not benefit society or the economy as a whole. At one point in *De l'emprisonnement*, Bayle-Mouillard wrote with sardonic darkness that "if you have no resources, don't go to an honest capitalist . . . Don't go to a banking house . . . But descend lower, much lower . . . Go knock on the door of the usurer. It doesn't matter that you have nothing: if you have a wife who isn't completely despoiled, some well-off relatives, he will receive your person as a pledge. Go to him! He understands how debt imprisonment is a *means of credit!*"[59] Here, Bayle-Mouillard evoked a theme broadly shared in popular understandings of debtors' prison and perhaps best reflected in the ever-present figure of the *fils de famille*, the wastrel son of a good family who incurred great debts in pursuit of gambling, women, and keeping up with fashion.

Indeed, novels of the period teemed with young men who ended up in Sainte-Pélagie or Clichy on the orders of seedy bill discounters and avaricious usurers who hoped to be reimbursed by well-off relatives.[60] Maurice Alhoy's 1841 *La physiologie du créancier et du débiteur*, for example, recounts a kind of Faustian bargain struck between a young dandy and a usurer over a bill of exchange.[61] At the bill's due date, the moneylender approaches the young ne'er-do-well's family, informing them of their son's impending disgrace and the possibility of imprisonment. Terrified and scandalized, the parents not only offer the usurer payment for the debt but also thank him for his assistance and discretion. Balzac, who featured questionable uses of debt imprisonment in several of his novels, created a more complicated version of this trop in *Les splendeurs et misères des courtisanes*. The wily Vautrin suggests to Lucien Chardon, deeply indebted owing to his extravagant lifestyle, that he use the wealthy Baron de Nucingen's obsession with Lucien's mistress, the courtesan Esther van Gobseck, as a means of obtaining money. Vautrin has accomplices buy up the courtesan's debts and then threaten her with imprisonment.[62] The Baron de Nucingen comes to his beloved's rescue. These stories about wastrels, based loosely on some real-life cases, testified to public perceptions that the efficacy of debt imprisonment depended not on individual commercial honor but rather on mobilizing a debtor's network of family and friends.

Bayle-Mouillard devoted little time to analyzing the stereotype of the *fils de famille*, for whose existence his statistics provided scant evidence. On the contrary, he was deeply interested by the fact that these debtors were not generally young wastrels, but rather husbands and fathers of families well into their thirties and forties. The relationship between husbands and wives, rather than between fathers and sons, formed the centerpiece of Bayle-Mouillard's analysis of how debtors' prison mobilized social connections. Feminine virtue, rather than family name, proved to be the asset most imperiled by the threat of *contrainte par corps*. For Bayle-Mouillard

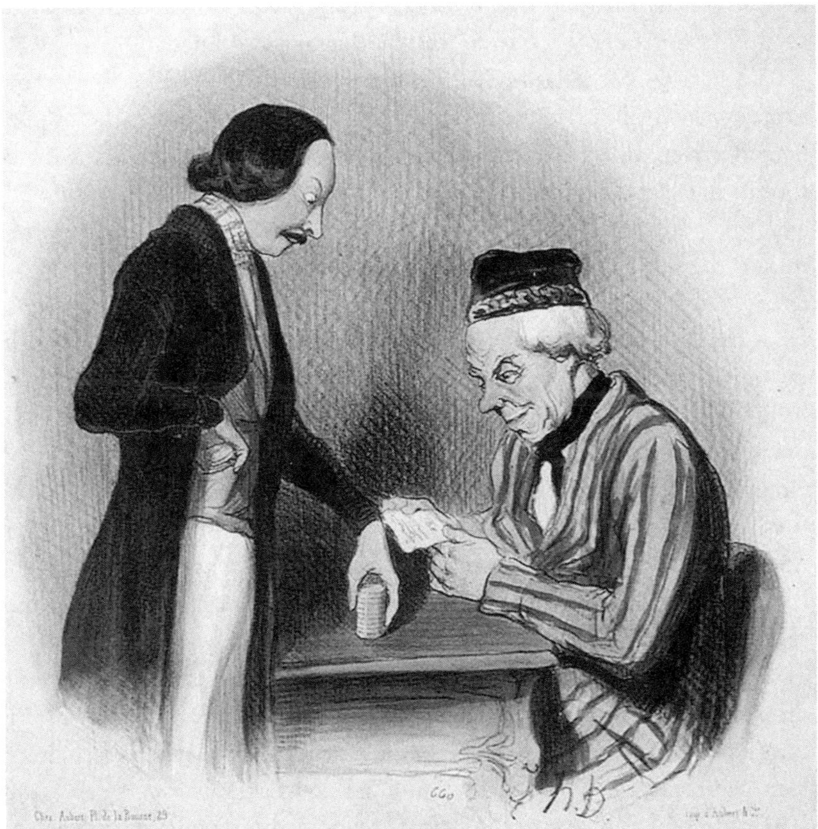

FIGURE 9. A young dandy approaches a usurer to discount a bill of exchange in Daumier's *Les beaux jours de la vie* (1845). (Indianapolis Museum of Art)

as for most of his contemporaries, the imprisoned debtor was always gendered male, an assumption based equally on the demographic realities of debt imprisonment (scarcely 10 percent of imprisoned debtors were female, according to his study) and on bourgeois ideals of merchant behavior. Given this premise, Bayle-Mouillard devoted little time to discussing the specific dangers faced by imprisoned female debtors, aside from one comment about their proximity to prostitutes in some jails. Instead, he insisted that *contrainte par corps* prevented the debtor from being "a good father and a good husband," duties that Bayle-Mouillard held to be a man's most sacred obligations to society.[63] Yet the damage was not limited merely to preventing a man's fulfillment of his "natural" obligations: debt imprisonment also "denature[d] the conjugal pact," which Bayle-Mouillard believed far more important than any contract between creditor and debtor. Indications of the "denaturing" of this pact, *De l'emprisonnement* alleged, could be found in the gender reversals precipitated by imprisonment.[64]

While Bayle-Mouillard relied mostly on anecdotal evidence to demonstrate how debt imprisonment imperiled the bourgeois categories of public and private by undermining gender categories, he also found evidence for this in examining the relationship between rates of debt imprisonment and the traditional form of dowry arrangements in different *départements*. The dotal regime, historically utilized in southern France (the *pays de droit écrit*), allowed for the wife's dowry properties to remain separate from those of her husband, while the communal regime, used largely in the north (*pays de coutume)*, entailed combining these properties under the husband's management. Although Napoleonic law had attempted to suppress these customary regional divisions by allowing couples to decide on either arrangement, Bayle-Mouillard insisted that the mindset inspired by these distinct regimes persisted in the regions where they had once been the legal standard. In examining the twenty-three *départements* with the highest per capita rate of debt imprisonment, Bayle-Mouillard found that seventeen of them were in regions that had traditionally used dotal regimes as a division of marital property, while only six of these *départements* traditionally relied on a communal regime. Among the *départements* with the lowest per capita use of debt imprisonment, the figures were reversed: nineteen had traditionally enjoyed communal divisions of property and only four had dotal regimes. In the *pays de coutume*, he explained, "people are accustomed to sharing their misfortunes," and the mere threat of debt imprisonment sufficed to motivate a wife to sell her property. Meanwhile, wives under dotal regimes, often at their family's prompting, attempted to hold on to their property, and creditors' threats alone could hardly move them. Although the Civil Code restricted a husband's ability to alienate his wife's dotal properties if their properties were separate, it did allow for this possibility in order to free a husband (or wife) from prison.[65] Although Bayle-Mouillard lacked concrete data that this ransoming of the wife's property took place regularly in southern France, he suggested that numerous husbands "willingly went to debtors' prison" in order to get their hands on their wives' property.[66]

While Bayle-Mouillard's evidence only implied that debt imprisonment threatened women's material interests, he was much more concerned about its impact on women's morality, as were many opponents of *contrainte par corps*. In one of the more dramatic examples of this anxiety, the legislator Hyde de Neuville, one of the earliest critics of debt imprisonment, regularly recounted the probably apocryphal story of a young woman whose ailing father had been arrested for debt by a merciless creditors. The beautiful girl borrowed money from an equally hard-hearted moneylender in order to release him. When she failed to reimburse the debt she had incurred in liberating her father, her creditor offered to accept payment in sexual services instead. Her chaste refusal of his lascivious advances earned her a spot in debtors' prison, where she contracted tuberculosis.[67]

Generally, women featured far less positively in abolitionist literature. Abandoning his wonted caution in citing the evidence of pamphleteers, whom he regarded as "polemical" and "emotional," Bayle-Mouillard liberally quoted piquant and dubious anecdotes from writers such as Loubens and Touchard Lafosse about debauched and heartless women who threw parties to celebrate their husbands' arrests and publicly professed the desire to see their spouses die behind bars. He quoted the prison reformer Benjamin Appert about the heinous pacts supposedly drawn up between adulterous wives and opportunistic creditors. Without even anecdotal evidence, he suggested that rebellious daughters regularly invited their lovers to buy up their fathers' debts under fake names and imprison their fathers so as to enjoy their romantic liaison without paternal supervision. Bayle-Mouillard believed that even a faithful woman could not be expected to maintain her virtue faced with her spouse's incarceration. A wife left "without her husband's guidance" and potentially subjected to the harrowing vulnerability of expropriation and eviction made easy prey for opportunistic philanderers who had lusted after her in secret. Furthermore, her love for her husband would wane because "one quickly ceases to love a man who has made one ashamed." From resentment over material sacrifices and the pain of losing her good name, a wife would inevitably stray from her marital vows as "indifference replaces sadness and then infidelity replaces indifference."[68] Without his wife's love, moreover, prison life corrupted the husband, making him forget his wife and children and participate in orgies.

In his insistence that debt imprisonment promoted a form of self-interest that distorted the fragile balance between emotion and reason, private and public, men and women, Bayle-Mouillard strayed considerably from his careful use of numbers and borrowed heavily from the polemical accounts furnished by other pamphleteers. At several points in his text, Bayle-Mouillard meditated on the contradictions inherent in his task. He asked his readers rhetorically, "How does one succeed in measuring by numbers the intensity of passions?"[69] Despite attempting to obtain such correlations through data on lottery participation, suicide, illiteracy, homicide, illegitimacy, and commercial litigation, Bayle-Mouillard believed that his most telling proof lay in the difficulty of predicting incarceration patterns. The correlations that he could find between the dotal marital regime and high incarceration rates led him to posit that debt imprisonment was favoring an economy radically antipodal to the kind it had been established to defend. Instead of organizing a moral economy based on the value of promises, *contrainte par corps* instead provided a means by which unscrupulous lenders and untrustworthy debtors could participate in the fruits of commercial prosperity.

Bayle-Mouillard's critique of *contrainte par corps* reads as an unconscious indictment of the precarious post-Revolutionary social order. Although *contrainte par corps* passed as a means of credit, Bayle-Mouillard insisted, it could "never be a true pledge, and thus by consequence it cannot be a real means of credit; by itself it pays nothing, guarantees nothing, confers neither preference nor privilege." Instead, he asked, "What is the person of a man deprived of fortune?" He was a being "without a home, without a fixed location, he has roots neither in the land nor in industry; he is lost in the middle of the crowd, and leave no trace after him. In some fashion he has neither country or family; he barely has a name."[70] The haunting tone of Bayle-Mouillard's inquiry underscores an irony of which the author himself was perhaps unaware. Although liberal individualism insisted on the primacy and equality of all individuals before the law, in his final understanding of what it meant to pledge the body, Bayle-Mouillard suggested that it was in fact impossible to detach the individual from all the historically contingent elements that gave his life meaning and value. For Bayle-Mouillard, the "person," as an abstraction, the abstraction touted equally as the basis of liberal individualism and of the system of *contrainte par corps*, almost ceased to exist.

Rethinking Failure

Bayle-Mouillard's volume was distinguished not only by the strength of its logic and its painstaking quantitative analysis of the nation's debtors' prisons but also by its careful attempt to provide an acceptable replacement for debt imprisonment. For Bayle-Mouillard, any alternative had to entail both a means of protecting creditors' rights and castigation for debtors' "fraud, imprudence and crime."[71] Although he had devoted considerable energy early in the book to attacking the British and American systems of debt imprisonment for their strikingly high incarceration rates, he nevertheless openly borrowed many of his ideas for fixing *contrainte par corps* from the common-law process of insolvency. Insolvency relief, as Bayle-Mouillard understood it, allowed debtors to petition a special court for release. The court would then perform a thorough investigation of the case and release the debtor after dividing assets between the creditors.

In Bayle-Mouillard's opinion, this process compared favorably to the closest approximation in French law, the *cession de biens*, not only in the number of debtors liberated but also in its cost effectiveness and its less humiliating procedure. He claimed that even those few debtors who could put forward the considerable sums imposed as expenses for a *cession de biens* often recoiled from the stigma attached to all the publicity. Moreover, Bayle-Mouillard saw *cession de biens* as a privilege accorded only to those debtors who could prove their misfortune and good faith, whereas insolvency relief belonged to common law, which assumed a debtor to be in good faith until proved elsewise. Insolvency relief thus allowed imprisoned borrowers a process, much like bankruptcy for *commerçants*, in which guilt or innocence could be assessed and punished if necessary.

Bayle-Mouillard went further than the English model, however, by proposing the abolition of the imprisonment that preceded the insolvency declaration and the establishment of a full process of civil bankruptcy in its stead. Under the proposed system, every non-*commerçant* who could not make regular payments to his creditors would undergo a court-ordered division of his remaining assets. Refusal to comply with court orders or evidence of fraud or gross mismanagement would be punished as fraud. No doubt anticipating critiques that civil bankruptcy treated debtors too lightly, Bayle-Mouillard proposed numerous accompanying precautions to prevent abuses. First, he insisted on the moral guarantee provided by a debtor's oath. This oath, if proven false, entailed the penalties and infamy attached to perjury. Although Bayle-Mouillard acknowledged that public opinion frequently forgave those who lied out of "blind pity or political passion" in the courtroom, it was "severe against those who perjure for monetary interests," for whom such perjury became "an indelible stain." This guarantee alone, Bayle-Mouillard argued, would be an effective deterrent for those debtors "who, in debt imprisonment, fear above all shame."[72] Moreover, while the debtors' prison allowed the debtor a haven from his creditors, the civil bankruptcy process entailed constant supervision. For Bayle-Mouillard, civil bankruptcy replaced the physical person of the debtor involved in debt imprisonment with the moral person involved in bankruptcy.

For non-*commerçants* who committed fraud, Bayle-Mouillard proposed punishments roughly corresponding to those of *banqueroute simple* and *banqueroute frauduleuse* for commercial debtors. Bayle-Mouillard's support of a civil counterpart for the process of *banqueroute simple* was particularly revealing. He argued that a non-*commerçant* who borrowed heavily to support an excessive lifestyle must be disciplined out of his bad habit, just as a commercial debtor would for similar mismanagement. To this end, he suggested amendments to the penal code to punish all debtors whose inability to pay their debts stemmed from prodigality or who had "abused credit in order to satisfy shameful passions and consummated their ruin by gambling or debauchery."[73] Bayle-Mouillard argued that this form of civil bankruptcy would be "more respected" by debtors than the prospect of *contrainte par corps*. Unable to evade the scrutiny of both his creditors and the legal system, a debtor would be "subject, for blamable actions, to shame and for punishable actions, not civil detention, but one of those condemnations that stains one's honor until death itself."[74] *Contrainte par corps*, which largely affected those who could not declare bankruptcy, provided no means of distinguishing guilty from innocent behavior. This reality particularly concerned him given the demographic realities revealed by his tables. The debtors who filled the nation's prisons belonged to an eclectic and economically precarious group of men and women, largely imprudent rather than crooked, whose resistance to orderly borrowing behavior nevertheless opened up the possibility of fraud. Rather than subjecting these individuals to the alleged torture of *contrainte par corps*, in which creditors probed for hidden assets, Bayle-Mouillard insisted that these men needed to be disciplined into becoming economic agents much like merchants were by the bankruptcy process.

Bayle-Mouillard's alternative to debt imprisonment closely resembled those suggested by other penal reformers and economic reformers. The era's two most prominent prison reformers, Charles Lucas and Louis-Maturin Moreau-Christophe, shared the belief that *contrainte par corps* did not adequately distinguish between two classes of prisoners: the "real delinquents," on one hand, who had committed acts of deliberate fraud, charlatanism, and swindling, and other individuals who had "fallen into their unfortunate positions through circumstances beyond their control."[75] Lucas demanded that judges be allowed to decide the good faith of the individuals involved on a case-by-case basis, and to incarcerate only those guilty of fraud. In his 1837 book *De l'état actuel des prisons en France considéré avec la théorie pénale du Code*, Moreau-Christophe argued against debt imprisonment as a method of execution—not merely on the grounds that it confused failure with fraud and played into the hands of usurers but also on the grounds of its futility.[76] He proposed that debt imprisonment, "an infamous method when it is not merely absurd," should be used solely as a means of coercing those debtors who refused to pay.[77]

Similar views could be found in the works of the lawyer and writer Alphonse Decourdemanche, who published a series of editorials on commercial law in the influential Saint-Simonian paper *Le Globe* in 1832 and 1833. Subsequently published as a book under the title *Aux industriels*, Decourdemanche's writings concentrated on the differences between the commercial and civil law regimes. According to him, these two systems divided the country into "two very distinct castes: *commerçants* and non-*commerçants*, governed by different laws and different courts." Decourdemanche argued that harsh commercial laws, of which debt imprisonment was the most extreme, assured that noncommercial lenders and borrowers enjoyed certain liberties not enjoyed by merchants. However, it also meant that noncommercial property, principally land, circulated much less rapidly and efficiently than commercial property.[78]

For Decourdemanche, the problem with debt imprisonment revolved around the problem of class. He used *commerçant* interchangeably with the words *industriel* or *travailleur* (worker), to refer to those who "possessed nothing but their bodies and their labor" and who had to work for subsistence. In short, by *commerçant* he meant some kind of proletarianized industrial workforce. In opposition to this group were the non-*commerçants* or "capitalists" who "possess either land or monetary values and speculate with the product of their wealth, thereby living off the work of others."[79] The central distinction between classes was not commercial or noncommercial but between those who owned capital and those who were obliged to work for it. Yet the laws lagged behind this new reality. They subjected those who labored to different standards than those who bought and sold. With bankruptcy and *contrainte par corps*, the average artisan found himself forced to pay his debts and suffered horribly "by his person" if he did not. Meanwhile, a non-*commerçant* could commit even acts of fraud without being prosecuted. If change was not made to the laws, Decourdemanche argued darkly, "there will come a time when the capitalists will find themselves in possession of all property."[80]

To rectify this injustice, Decourdemanche proposed extending commercial law to everyone. All property, particularly landed property, should be treated as movable property. By establishing a system of civil or consumer bankruptcy, Decourdemanche argued, creditors would not have to use debt imprisonment as a means of pursuit. In place of the Commercial Code, which pursued the person with great speed and efficiency, and the Civil Code, which pursued property with few guarantees, a new combined process would focus on property but also ensure adequate protection. Privileges enjoyed by certain creditors would be abolished in favor of the collective whole. Decourdemanche assured that "the *commerçants*, having prompt and efficient means for pursuing the payment of their products delivered to consumers, will no longer be exposed, as they are now, to see men of civil law taking with impunity the fruits of their labor."[81] The rest of the book elaborated his plans to replace the extant mortgage process with one better equipped to "mobilize" the land.

Perhaps the most telling justification Decourdemanche provided in advancing his new scheme was the comparison he made between debtors and corporations. Decourdemanche considered that any debtor, whether commercial or noncommercial, should be likened to "the manager of a joint-stock company that has failed. In providing a faithful account of the capital he had during his administration, the manager should be discharged of all future responsibility."[82] This assimilation of the debtor to the company, with a focus on the property rather than the person of the debtor as the main gage, would prove prescient in the years to come as creditors increasingly fought for the right to treat company debtors as regular debtors and legislation came to assimilate the two.

Decourdemanche's critique of debt imprisonment provides a fascinating counterpart to Bayle-Mouillard's because both writers implicitly underscore the transformed understanding of what it meant to practice commerce. Both analyses, in different ways, implicated *contrainte par corps* in the process of proletarianization, even if Bayle-Mouillard believed it allowed "masterless men" access to credit and Decourdemanche believed that property owners used debt as a tool against small artisans. Indeed, by the 1830s, calls for a system of consumer bankruptcy, allowing noncommercial individuals access to a process paralleling that of commercial bankruptcy, emerged from a variety of different perspectives. These calls were motivated by the widespread concern that debt imprisonment disproportionately affected individuals who could not be considered traders or merchants. For many thinkers, Napoleonic law, based centrally on land as an immovable property, no longer served the needs of a commercial society. Yet in envisioning the procedures potentially entailed in a consumer bankruptcy, reformers seemed less concerned with protecting unfortunate noncommercial debtors from the rigors of debt imprisonment than with controlling and punishing noncommercial debtors who abused the trust of their creditors or grossly mismanaged their money. At the heart of concerns about noncommercial debtors in debtors' prison was an anxiety about a realm where creditors and debtors avoided the law.

Conclusion

The decades-long controversy surrounding *contrainte par corps* raised profound questions about the relationship of the person to economic transactions. For liberal reformers like Bayle-Mouillard, debt imprisonment revealed the messy realities of a credit economy fundamentally at odds with their idealized vision of the market as a realm of independent and rational male actors who freely contracted based on individual character and personal capital. By permitting a borrower to leverage his freedom against the payment of a loan, debt imprisonment engaged not just the borrower's body but also his emotions and those of his family and friends.

Bayle-Mouillard's attack on debt imprisonment also reads as an attack on the class of merchants who used this practice both as debtors and as creditors. Here Bayle-Mouillard intervened in the debate about the meaning of the term *commerçant.* Despite the dissolution of the corporations, Revolutionary legislators had still believed that *commerçants* possessed certain distinguishing traits that separated them from the agricultural majority of France's population. Yet rather than specify the professions included under commercial jurisdiction, they defined *commerçant* in relation to the activity of commercial exchange. The persistent outcry against the arrest of non-*commerçants* for commercial debts throughout the first half of the nineteenth century reveals widespread anxiety about the growing range of people and things involved in commerce. In the words of one pamphleteer, "if by commerce we mean the transmission of all mobile things, intellectual or material," surely this "intrusion of commercial practices into the morals of civil life" in fact imperils the liberty of all.[83] Concerns about commodification paralleled concerns about proletarianization, as legal scholars and commercial judges found that the Commercial Code corresponded inadequately to the realities of work. Socialist thinkers like Decourdemanche depicted the opposition between commercial law and civil law as a form of class struggle between proletarianized workers, subject to the harsh terms of commercial law, and property owners, who benefited from the privileges of civil law.

Like Decourdemanche, Bayle-Mouillard's rejected the stereotype that debt imprisonment was primarily used against non-*commerçants*. His data revealed instead that both imprisoned debtors and incarcerating creditors belonged to the same kinds of unstable, downwardly mobile artisans and small shopkeepers. For these individuals, leveraging the threat of debt imprisonment had allowed the possibility of an economic independence that Bayle-Mouillard deemed both morally repugnant to the individuals involved and useless to the economy overall. Bayle-Mouillard's choice of statistical analysis, a methodological approach closely associated with the contemporaneous fascination with controlling urban deviance, reflects the disciplinary aspect of the abolitionist cause. Liberal reformers like Bayle-Mouillard objected to debt imprisonment not merely because they found it cruel, but also because they found it ineffective both as an economic and as a disciplinary instrument. The extension of commercial discipline to non-commercial individuals that Bayle Mouillard, like other writers, proposed in place of *contrainte par corps* reveals the growing frustration with the limits of economic personhood as inscribed in the Napoleonic codes.

Part Three

REMAKING COMMERCIAL PERSONHOOD

6

Bankruptcies without Bankrupts

Commercial Personhood in an Age of Speculation

In July 1833 Honoré Ardant, who had recently sold his broker's office in Paris, told his friend and former neighbor the Bishop of Beauvais that he was interested in placing his wealth in industrial investments.[1] The time seemed propitious for such a venture: the dawn of the July Monarchy brought with it a new energy toward commercial enterprises that would later lead Karl Marx to famously characterize it as a rule by bankers. Ardant initially had his eye on textiles, but when the bishop sang the praises of an enterprising widow named Madame Genthon, who owned a rapeseed oil factory not far from Paris, Ardant jumped at the opportunity. The bishop told the former broker that while Madame Genthon had filed for bankruptcy a few years earlier, she had only a few thousand francs in dividends left to give her creditors. Her main creditor, the bishop himself, had promised he would not claim the 40,000 francs he was owed in the bankruptcy settlement. Far from minimizing the importance of Genthon's bankruptcy in his pitch, the bishop made this prior commercial failure a point in the widow's favor. He knew that the deeply conservative Ardant, whose family had sheltered non-juring priests in the 1790s, would be moved by Genthon's ultimately unsuccessful courage in running her business during the Revolution of 1830.

Persuaded by his friend's ringing recommendation, Ardant entered into a joint rapeseed oil business with the widow. Yet even from the outset, Genthon's management of operations made him nervous. Funds appeared to be misplaced. The principal grain supplier, Monsieur Leborgne, an allegedly friendly merchant who was courting Madame Genthon's younger sister, seemed to deliberately delay grain shipments and demanded increasingly steep guarantees from Ardant before shipment. The young company soon faced severe financial trouble. When a single creditor pressed Genthon for payment, she quickly chose to file for bankruptcy again. Allegedly under the mounting financial pressure of her multiple bankruptcies, Genthon sold her factory and equipment to a distant cousin. Ardant, who regarded the factory as a pledge for his own investments, could not attend the creditors' meeting: a creditor, whom Ardant believed to be tied to Genthon, had incarcerated him in Paris for a 770-franc bill of exchange he had bought from other creditors. In Ardant's absence, Leborgne, now Genthon's largest creditor and his sister's fiancé, guided the meeting, convincing the other creditors of the hopelessness of their cause and buying up their supposedly worthless debts. Leborgne and several other family friends voluntarily renounced their privileges as mortgaged creditors in order to vote with unsecured creditors on the fate of Genthon's bankruptcy. In a final blow to Ardant, the bishop added his own substantial debt from Genthon's prior bankruptcy to the new balance sheet. His approval of the *concordat* proposed by Leborgne provided the critical majority needed to pass the arrangement among the creditors in Ardant's absence, with Ardant's debt written in as only 5 percent of the total.

Ardant would spend the next few years attempting to correct what he saw as the terrible injustice done to him by people he had trusted. He pursued charges of *banqueroute frauduleuse* against Leborgne, Genthon, and her sister, which they countered by pressing calumny charges against the ex-broker. Genthon had no sooner arranged with her creditors than Ardant challenged the arrangement. The courts for their part looked negatively at all parties involved. Not only was Genthon a bankrupt, a bankrupt three times over as it turned out, but Ardant's choice of business partners seemed imprudent or even "speculative."[2] Prior bankruptcy, in the court's eyes, suggested not only that the widow was possibly short on assets but also that her character warranted caution. For his part, Ardant seemed more upset at the bishop, who had led him into what he now saw as a trap designed to pay the creditors of Genthon's previous bankruptcy, than he was at Genthon and her alleged coconspirators. In a series of letters to his former friends, he juxtaposed what he saw as his own loyalty with the bishop's immorality in satisfying his debt. "I, who do not have the honor of being a bishop, have scrupulously fulfilled the obligations that were imposed on me," claimed

Ardant, adding, "Monseignor the Bishop, in this deplorable affair I can lose nothing but money, but, you, will you not lose something else?"[3]

While bankruptcies in early nineteenth-century France rarely involved the hostility of the Genthon case, they were dominated by the interplay of complicated social networks in which personal friendships, family connections, and professional relationships became muddled and confused. Creditors and debtors might be neighbors, friends, or family members of the bankrupt. Conversely, these parties might never have met each other in their lives or might have only passing acquaintance. Such networks were vital for the creation of businesses, yet they also made their collapses particularly difficult to handle. A mixture of conflicting motives, including self-interest and the desire to build and foster social alliances, guided creditors and debtors alike. Like Ardant, many saw bankruptcies as cleverly designed scams in which the bankrupt, with or without the collusion of some of his creditors, intended to make a profit. A bankruptcy, ostensibly a calm legal process designed to save all parties from the worst disaster, became a tug-of-war between the interests of those involved. In the memorable words of Balzac, in a bankruptcy there was "no legality or illegality, no truth or falsehood, no honesty or dishonesty. Any man is admired if he can *cover himself*: to 'cover oneself' means grasping funds to the detriment of the other creditors."[4] One newspaper article depicted bankruptcies as a rush to "take away indemnities from a shipwreck that had ruined so many others."[5] They were, in fact, scenes of wholesale pillage under guise of the law. "Every day, commercial practice and severe morality in accordance with the law are in opposition." A bankruptcy was "every man for himself."[6]

These laments were hardly original. As discussed in chapter 2, similar complaints had provoked the creation of the Commercial Code even as its implementation had done little to quell them. By the early 1830s, however, the demand for reform of bankruptcy law had reached nearly unanimous levels in the commercial community and government circles. Book III of the Commercial Code not only allowed and even encouraged both debtors and creditors to work in the margins of the law to maximize their gains, as seen in the Genthon case, but also seemed egregiously ill equipped to handle the realities of a burgeoning financial transformation that had begun in the latter years of the Restoration and continued into the July Monarchy. Investment-intensive projects such as the building of railroads and canals not only increased the integration of markets across France but also helped fuel the growth of new businesses and private finance. These endeavors demanded funds that generally outstripped even the deep pockets of the wealthiest individuals and inspired the growth of companies designed to pool investment and risk through shares. The spread of banking industries geared at providing easier access to middle-size industries, such as Jacques Laffitte's Caisse générale du commerce, used the sale of public limited-liability shares and the issuance of short-term interest-bearing notes to raise money for investment in industry and railroads. Around the same time, political economists and early socialist thinkers emphasized the importance of competition to the growth of this economy.

The growing importance of competition and the free market inspired widespread concerns about the negative side effects of an unregulated market.[7] Early socialist thinkers like Auguste Comte and Charles Fourier stressed the disharmony brought about by incessant competition and the relentless private pursuit of profit. Legislators shared many of their concerns about dishonesty and duplicity, and the 1830s saw the passage of many laws attempting to rein in the possibilities for fraud in the marketplace, including laws on weights and measures and on tainted food. Even as lawmakers perceived competition as the primary motivation for fraud, they also worried about collectivist patterns of association—for example, the growing number of joint-stock companies—as a vehicle for masking responsibility. In this context, the Commercial Code's focus on the individual person proved both inadequate in regulating the realities of collective vehicles of investment and a dangerous encouragement to unbridled individualism.

For lawmakers, legal thinkers, and political economists, no one aspect of the economy better reflected the dangers posed by these patterns in association and competition than bankruptcy. Meanwhile, creditors, seeking to maximize their protections in the case of business failure, grew frustrated with the limitations imposed upon settlements by the code's insistence on the debtor's personal responsibility for his debts. In 1838, after nearly a decade of committee studies and legislatives debates, legislators dramatically overhauled Book III of the Commercial Code in a bankruptcy reform bill whose practical measures introduced certain fundamental shifts in both the understanding and practice of bankruptcy. Meanwhile, writers of various political stripes, although critical of bankrupts, increasingly ascribed bankruptcy neither to accidents nor to moral failure, but rather to an economic system based on competition. Combined, these developments, which grew out of the complex social choreography of the bankruptcy process, worked to redefine what it meant to go bankrupt. From a process based on the honor of individual personhood, where the body served as the ultimate guarantee of a debtor's word, bankruptcy gradually became envisioned as an abstract process involving the most effective distribution of the debtor's assets. At the same time, while court cases and legal reform facilitated large-scale risk taking, small traders and artisans found their ability to seek refuge from debt substantially curtailed by these same reforms.

The Social Life of Bankrupts

From its implementation in 1808, commentators had criticized the Commercial Code's regulation of *faillite*. When the Chamber of Deputies finally appointed a special commission to examine bankruptcy reform in February 1835, after nearly a decade of fruitless discussion on the need for an overhaul of the bankruptcy process, the commission found widespread consensus among the commercial community and the nation's judges about the problems with the current code.[8] The principle defect of Book III, according to chambers of commerce and commercial courts nationwide, did not involve the law itself but rather its erratic and irregular application. The code's delays and expenses encouraged both creditors and debtors to seek questionably legal means of settlement that avoided the direct supervision of the law. Many respondents to government circulars felt that the code's harshness motivated debtors to seek alternative means of handling their financial difficulties. Instead, informal and sometimes outright illegal alliances with creditors both inside and outside the process of *faillite* made the Commercial Code, designed to provide rigorous state supervision of the bankruptcy, a travesty.

The disturbing aspect of bankruptcy in the eyes of judges and legislators lay in its double identity as a legal procedure and a social event; it was this second identity that often seemed to threaten the supremacy of the law. In an economy largely based on personal relationships, bankruptcies inevitably involved a complex choreography of actors by turns competing and allying with each other. The competition between debtors and creditors was so much a part of the way economic life functioned that caricaturists and satirists regularly produced poems, prints, and fake advice manuals about unexpected run-ins between borrowers and delinquent lenders.[9] The negotiation and competition inherent in the bankruptcy procedure not only compelled legislators to revise the code to make the process less dependent on the discretion of private citizens but also created new understandings of personhood as creditors fought to enlarge the scope of their protections and prerogatives. To examine the dynamics of bankruptcy operations, I have relied on two principle sources. The first involves the bankruptcy dossiers of the 1,314 cases of *faillite* registered before the commercial court of the Seine from January 1830 through December 1831.[10] The Parisian records are notoriously patchy, and there are notable lacunae in the collection of bankruptcy dossiers from the 1830s. Moreover, contents of bankruptcy dossiers vary enormously between cases, with some including detailed information about creditors, inventories of household and store goods, and the trustees' analyses, whereas others might contain only a few of these documents. The years 1830 and 1831, for which a complete set exists, were comparatively high years for bankruptcies in Paris, but otherwise seem representative of the pre-1838 bankruptcy process more generally. In examining these documents, I have particularly focused on the reflections left by the bankruptcy trustees as they discussed the difficulties they encountered managing an estate. Inevitably, these accounts reflect their perspective on the procedure, a bias I attempt to mitigate by incorporating a second body of sources in this investigation: legal factums put before criminal and appeals courts during the 1820s and 1830s that involved conflicts between different parties to the bankruptcy process. Of course not all cases left an extant criminal trail, but by studying the factums that involve trustees and creditors of bankruptcy, of which I have located fourteen, we can supplement the picture of bankruptcy provided by the dossiers.

Understanding bankruptcy as a social event necessitates first understanding the various actors involved, in both an official and an informal capacity, and how their competing interests could potentially determined the outcome of the process. After a debtor presented his balance sheet to the commercial court (or a commercial judge ordered his case open in response to creditors' requests or the "public notoriety" of a debtor's insolvency), the commercial court subsequently placed the case under the supervision of a commercial court agent, called the judge-commissioner. However, often charged with dozens of cases, these individuals played little direct role in the operation of the bankruptcy. Most of the decision-making power in the early stages of a *faillite* rested in the provisional trustee or trustees, who were typically elected from a list of creditors provided by the bankrupt and ascertained by the commercial court, although, particularly in larger cases, they could be complete strangers to the case, appointed and salaried by the commercial court. The provisional trustees managed the bankrupt's estate until the creditors listed on the bankrupt's balance sheet could be verified and were able to convene in the commercial tribunal's bankruptcy room, decide upon a *concordat* or *union* for the bankrupt, and elect permanent trustees to oversee the process.

Considering their responsibility in managing the bankruptcy, it is hardly surprising that many trustees were criticized for mismanagement and abuse of power. Multiple factums testify to the degree of animosity these figures could arouse. Some trustees reportedly openly favored the debtor, colluding with him to their mutual profit while the other creditors could only complain of such behavior to the bankruptcy judge at the commercial court. Others were accused of using these roles to enforce personal vendettas against the debtors. For example, Auguste Delalande, along with his father-in-law, Hébert, had placed a well-established merchant Martin Groult in bankruptcy on somewhat dubious grounds. As provisional trustee, Delalande not only raised charges of *banqueroute* against Groult but also depleted the creditors' assets by letting one of Groult's ships rot in the harbor rather than take care of insurance, not actively pursuing Groult's debtors, and losing property that belonged to the estate.[11] Another provisional trustee, the aptly named Prentout, persuaded several other creditors to put one Duroy into bankruptcy. Prentout then got himself elected trustee. It was only after the other creditors balked at the sum he had assigned as his due in the bankruptcies that they pored over the documents and learned that Prentout had called the bankruptcy as a means of obtaining money from Duroy's assets at the expense of his other creditors.

Even when a provisional trustee was not accused of outright corruption or abuse of power, the relationship between trustees and the other creditors was not always harmonious. This was partly due to the difficulty of the trustee's job in managing a troubled estate. After nearly two years of attempting to run Jacques Bestgen's cotton mill, the provisional trustees declared that the rent, taxes, heating, and pay for the foreman made it impossible to run the business profitably, and they suggested that it be shut down.[12] Trustees often went to technically illegal lengths to avoid bringing publicity to a bankruptcy, hoping not to scare off the clientele. This might include not obeying the legal stipulations to affix seals to the doors of a merchant's shop.[13] Collecting money owed to the debtor from his own debtors consumed much of the trustees' time and often left them with little to show for their trouble. In one instance, Marie Flory and her son Eugéne, who ran a bakery in Paris, reported nearly 10,000 francs in debts on their balance sheet. Of the over 5,000 francs owed by customers, the bakers had declared 2,309 francs as "good debts," 1,075 francs as "doubtful," and 2,308 francs as "bad." Despite spirited pursuits of the titles, the trustee barely recovered 100 francs.[14] The generally dire straights in which trustees found bankrupt estates doubtlessly contributed to the hostility many other creditors felt about their management.

The trustees also had to navigate and direct the complicated relationships between the bankrupt and the creditors and between the different groups of creditors themselves. Many creditors resisted surrendering their legal privileges against a debtor, including property seizures and *contrainte par corps*.[15] One of the trustees' first and most delicate tasks was to convince their fellow creditors to agree to share a common fate. When the provisional trustee Monsieur Maury, who represented a four of the seven creditors of Parisian animal feeders Jean François and Josephine Charlotte Mussé Collin, took over management of the couple's estate in February 1831, he found the situation deplorable: seven of the couple's cows were sick or dying, amounting to some 1,200 francs' worth of the couple's listed assets of 1,700 francs. A particularly relentless creditor, meanwhile, had thrown Jean Collin in prison for debt, and Maury found Josephine Collin "so distraught" by her landlord's pursuits for late rent that she too was unable to help him recover outstanding debts. Maury's private negotiations to get Collin out of prison failed, and getting a safe-conduct pass required several court battles. In order to save the family from eviction, Maury was forced to sell the couple's furniture and give the landlord the proceeds, thus severely diminishing the assets to be divided among the creditors.[16]

The trustee, as the representative of the unsecured creditors, faced frequent opposition from two groups of creditors outside the bankruptcy agreement whose debts trumped those included in the agreement: namely, mortgaged creditors and privileged creditors. This diverse group included not only landlords but also wives, whose contentious legal claims had aroused such passionate debate in the creation of the Commercial Code, and children, over whose property a bankrupt might only have usufruct rights if his spouse had died.[17] The Civil Code granted a host of other privileges to certain forms of debts, such as doctor's fees for costs of the last illness, domestic servants for six months of wages, and regular employees for a month's worth of wages, as well as the state for back taxes.[18] These claims not only trumped those of the unsecured creditors but also might be advanced by particularly aggressive creditors as soon as the debtor presented a balance sheet to the commercial court. Defending their own claims, the unsecured creditors sometimes allied with the bankrupt against his or her mortgaged and privileged creditors. The creditors of Elizabeth Grim, for example, joined with the widow to fend off her landlord's efforts to auction her merchandise and clientele *(fonds)* in order to pay the several months of back rent that she owed him.[19] While she merely wished to keep a cherished business that provided a degree of independence, they undoubtedly saw the company as their most lucrative asset. The bankruptcy trustees of self-styled businessman Chrétien Bruder regarded him as a "fraud," but fought on his behalf against both his estranged wife and a mortgaged creditor who claimed the right to his property in Batignolles.[20]

The trustees' provisional management lasted anywhere from a few months to several years. Subsequently, a meeting of verified creditors determined the debtor's fate. The creditors' convocation provided another fertile ground for attacks on the Commercial Code. Although few records exist of how creditors, assembling in the Salle des faillites of their local commercial court, decided upon a bankrupt's fate, contemporaries took an unsurprisingly negative view of the affair. One satire, called *L'art de s'enricher par la faillite*, depicted a bankruptcy hearing as inevitably including a speech by the bankruptcy trustee painting a picture of the bankrupt's career peppered with classical allusions to turbulent passions and immense losses. The bankrupt would then sobbingly declare that he and his family had subsisted on nothing but onions for weeks and convince all the creditors to take pity on him.[21] In Balzac's depiction of the creditors' convocation in *César Birroteau*, the trustees melodramatically declare to the assembled creditors, "We have taken our man apart like a shipwrecked frigate. The nails, ironwork, wood and copper have yielded three hundred thousand francs" for the effort; they added, "We vote that he should awarded a premium and a crown of laurel."[22] Balzac's trustees were not disinterested guardians. Instead, they portray the bankruptcy as catastrophically as possible in order to magnify their own role in salvaging the creditors' lot. In so doing, Balzac implies, they also hide whatever illicit benefits they may draw from the process. All that remains for the rest of the creditors to do is to blindly agree to the document that the trustees have devised. Criticism of the trustees echoed broader criticism of bankruptcy proceedings more generally. One legislator portrayed what many felt to be the typical outcome of a bankruptcy of any size: "When the rumors begin to circulate, the creditors arrive, fearing to not arrive soon enough, the safe is not completely empty: they find there a few *écus* . . . and the creditors, impatient to escape the shipwreck, seize it."[23] These actions, which favored the strongest, the largest, and the best informed among the creditors, mocked the equality of rights among creditors purportedly established by the code.[24]

Commentators also regularly complained that the outcome of the *faillite*, which was to end in either *union* or *concordat*, was determined not by the morality of the debtor but rather by financial practicality. Indeed, for economic as well as social reasons, creditors consistently preferred *concordats* to *unions* by a considerable margin throughout the early nineteenth century, even when they had sufficient reason to suspect the character and even the competence of their debtor.[25] Take the case of Adolphe Cailleux and Auguste Lefevre, wool manufacturers, who filed for bankruptcy in May 1831. The trustees first described the good character of the bankrupts: "They are young and ask for nothing more than to work. They are animated by the desire to make up for their losses."[26] Yet it was not such sterling qualities that persuaded the creditors as to the benefits of an arrangement. One trustee dismissed the possibility of liquidation by saying that "one must realize that the price of merchandise, the difficulty of obtaining payments, the immediate obligation to pay back the expenses of privileged debts, absorbed in great part the assets and reduces the dividends to almost nothing."[27] In view of these harsh facts, the creditors granted Cailleux and Lefevre a *concordat* stipulating that they pay the creditors 25 percent dividends over three years.

The decision to grant a *union* or *concordat*, however, was not merely about reconciling the interests of the creditors with the capability of the debtor to pay. It also entailed reconciling the interests of the unsecured creditors with those of the mortgaged creditors. Of the 1,849 bankruptcies that ended in a *union* or a *concordat* in Paris in 1842, there were 132 cases where payments to the mortgaged creditors swallowed up the entirety of the assets leaving nothing for the unsecured creditors.[28] Creditors definitely took this into account when making their decisions. For example, Clavery and Mouillon, the provisional trustees for a baker named Simon Auberton, had little praise to offer their bankrupt, whom they accused of "an absolute lack of order, a culpable carelessness, and glaring incompetence."[29] Nevertheless, their advice on a *concordat* or a *union* was a measured one. They admitted that the creditors' situation would be bad no matter which process unfolded. But then they coolly laid out the contours of their predicament, explaining that if the creditors voted to form a *union*, they would have to immediately sell the business and cede to the conditions of the landlord, who possessed a mortgage on the debtor's shop. Despite their reservations about Auberton's ability to responsibly run his own business, the trustees argued that a *concordat* would be a better option given the certain effects of a *union*.[30] Evidently persuaded, the creditors voted to give Auberton a *concordat*. Creditors generally preferred *unions* only if the debtor died during the bankruptcy process or if creditors deemed the debtor's mismanagement truly catastrophic. Owing to competition with secured creditors, dividends for *unions* were almost always lower than those for *concordats*, and a substantial number yielded nothing at all for the creditors.[31]

In general, and much to the consternation of the commission appointed to review bankruptcy law, creditors proved all too willing to agree to settlements, particularly when they felt they had little to gain from incurring further legal costs and delays. Balzac's César Birotteau, a prosperous perfumer, never appears at bankruptcy hearings, a practice he learned from a former employer who "had eventually found he was wasting so much time in litigation that he considered that the meager and uncertain dividend that might be received under a *concordat* was amply repaid by making better use of his time, instead of coming and going, negotiating and chasing after the excuses coined by dishonesty."[32] Indeed, small bankruptcies seem to have been handled with a good deal of complacency by creditors. Many debtors relied on this apparent indifference on the part of their creditors to start up new businesses and make up for their losses or even incur new ones. The Parisian wine merchant Jacques Caron went bankrupt in 1823 and had already started two other businesses, the first of which had also failed, by the time his initial *concordat* was signed.[33] After his June 1830 bankruptcy, the tailor Louis Ferdinand Blanchard, whose assets amounted to a mere 1,060 francs against liabilities totaling 1,663 francs, changed his Paris address from rue Coquillière to a new shop on rue Saint Antoine and began business again. Two of his old creditors, noticing their debtor's newly found prosperity, began pressing for reimbursement. Blanchard successfully petitioned the commercial court to reopen his bankruptcy case, with new assets amounting to 62,860 and debts at 23,510 francs.[34]

Such informal agreements between creditors and debtors were as common in bankruptcy proceedings as they were problematic. Many bankrupts considerably worsened their situations by taking out additional loans to fulfill informal agreements with some of their more insistent creditors before their bankruptcies. Rather than solving a debtor's problems, this often caused new ones. Monsieur Parisot, debtor to Monsieur Sauvan, made a written agreement on the eve of his bankruptcy, promising to pay back Sauvan in full. Technically fraudulent, this agreement proved to be impossible under the terms of Parisot's *concordat*, and Sauvan was forced to accept only half of his original debt. Soon after, Sauvan himself went bankrupt, and his trustees decided to pursue Parisot for the amount owed in the original contract.[35] Sometimes these informal agreements could be outright illegal. In 1839 Boullay, a manufacturer in Paris's Halle de blés, obtained a *concordat* with his creditors with 5 percent dividends. However, two recalcitrant creditors had refused to sign and received instead an agreement of dividends of 75 percent backed by Boullay, his wife, and his brother-in-law. When Boullay did not pay up, the creditors filed an unsuccessful charge of *banqueroute frauduleuse* against him.[36] Informal arrangements like these only intensified the fraudulent connotations of bankruptcy. In *Eugénie Grandet*, for example, the savvy and avaricious Félix Grandet, the same individual whose tirade against bankruptcy begins the introduction to this book, exploits informal agreements in just such a way. Rather than elaborate on this dubious plan in front of his guests and damage his reputation as an unworldly but miraculously successful businessman, he lets his acquaintances suggest a thoroughly unethical scheme for him. Félix Grandet saw a means of profiting from the insolvent estate of Guillaume Grandet, his recently deceased brother, by buying up the debts of the creditors at far less than their value. The scheme hinged on the creditors' preference for an informal liquidation procedure rather than the legal prescriptions of the code. In this underhanded scheme, Balzac alerted his audience, Grandet was exceptional less in his departure from legality than in his skill in skirting the law.

When commercial judges assessed the weaknesses of the bankruptcy process, they despairingly described the willingness of creditors to make arrangements because they believed it would be too difficult to force a debtor to acquiesce to legal requirements. In 1839 this reality provoked one commercial judge to declare:

> If the severity of creditors, which often attaches itself to honest and unfortunate bankrupts who they make cede to them everything they possess without caring that they are reduced to abject necessity, would apply instead to bankrupts who don't justify their losses, who often continue their affairs when they know they can't fill their deficits, if,

> instead of according *concordats* at five percent one saw them more inflexible in regards to bankrupts who don't deserve their good will, we would see fewer of these enterprises which offer no chance of success, and which are only created with the intention of living for some time at the expense of their creditors.[37]

Due to the inconveniences of legal pursuits, the bankruptcy process ended up disproportionately favoring debtors who knew how to manipulate both the law and their creditors' trust. Some even went so far as to establish businesses having no other financial base but advances from lenders that would never be reimbursed. At the ground level, bankruptcies were intricate social dances in which creditors and debtors alike carefully manipulated and negotiated laws in order to maximize their own profits in an apparently hopeless situation. Intended to unify all interests, bankruptcy instead often pitted usecured creditors against mortgaged creditors, trustees against the *masse*, family members against each other, and the bankrupt in shifting alliances with the opposing parties. They were, in short, extensions of the competition of the marketplace in an event that was supposed to entail cooperation and even sacrifice. This reality in part explains the frequently egregious discrepancies between procedures as they were spelled out in the code and the versatile ways in which businessmen and commercial courts actually negotiated commercial insolvency. This fluidity also accounts for much of the popular identification of bankruptcy with fraud.

The 1838 Bankruptcy Reform

Although there was widespread consensus among the courts and chambers of commerce that the Commercial Code's stipulations encouraged questionable machinations by both creditors and debtors, they disagreed over whether more leniency or more rigor might solve these problems. In 1827 the Marseille Chamber of Commerce noted the great discrepancy between the intentions of the Commercial Code's framers and the actual outcomes of the law. The code, they wrote, "prohibited secret arrangements and mandated stern punishments for *banqueroute frauduleuse* yet never had fraudulent agreements enjoyed such impunity."[38] The chambers of commerce were, in general, not kindly disposed to the bankrupts. Proposed legislation to end the obligatory imprisonment following a bankruptcy declaration aroused controversy. The Chamber of Commerce of

Boulogne-sur-Mer noted that "someone who has failed to honor one single commercial engagement can be imprisoned for debt. Why should the bankrupt, unable to honor all his engagements, be more favorably treated?"[39] Several chambers believed that the extant laws left dangerous loopholes in the treatment of bankruptcies after the declaration of a *union* that allowed debtors immunity from pursuits without necessarily having satisfied their creditors. Furthermore, the chambers articulated a widespread and general distrust of bankrupts' characters. The Chamber of Commerce of Dijon held that the number of bankruptcies caused by misfortune was "infinitely small" in comparison to those caused by misconduct and imprudence.[40] The Chamber of Commerce of Metz, believing that a merchant's passion for gambling was not a vice but "a crime because he has thrown down the abyss other fortunes besides his own," suggested that gambling be punished more severely under *banqueroute frauduleuse*.[41]

Despite complaints about the laxity of bankruptcy laws, the legislators were more concerned about facilitating the process than increasing its rigor. The minutes of the commission on bankruptcies, established by the minister of justice in 1833 and consisting of representatives from commercial courts, the chambers of commerce, royal and appeals courts, and members of the Chamber of Peers and of Deputies, reflect a broad consensus on the need to reform laws that most believed to have been "written in anger." While the minutes unfortunately do not identify which members of the commission advocated which policies, the summary of their conversation reveals that they felt that the glaring discrepancy between the letter of the law and the realities of business failure invited a potentially dangerous lack of respect for the law more generally.[42] Reformers specifically targeted the reliance on private arrangements, which, "immune to oversight and subject to numerous inconveniences," threatened the efficiency and justice of legal arrangements.[43] Yet this reform required striking a delicate balance between facilitating the process for creditors and debtors by removing some of the more cumbersome legal formalities and still maintaining protection against fraud. Although the minister of justice, introducing the first attempt at a reform bill in 1836, affirmed that the code's bankruptcy law remained undoubtedly "superior to all other nations," he admitted some major drawbacks.[44] The code's excessive severity and cumbersome regulations produced adverse consequences for both debtors and creditors. As one legislator summarized, "Rather than expose himself to such humiliation, the debtor forces himself, by consuming his last resources, to prolong a state of agony that opens him to all the temptation of despair; and when it becomes impossible for him to dissimulate his situation anymore, he flees or hides."[45] The code's rigor tempted debtors to fraud or flight, while creditors, dismayed by its cost and lengthiness, preferred outside arrangements.[46] As one representative put it, although "the interest of public vengeance is without a doubt superior to all others," when a legislator saw in every bankruptcy a matter of public judgment "at the expense of private interest" he not only overstepped his bounds but risked "all the private interests rising up against him and banding together to assure its futility."[47]

Perhaps the most dramatic innovations of the 1838 law concerned the forced closure of bankruptcies where assets could not pay for legal expenses. A closure meant that all the creditors regained their separate rights over the bankrupt, including the rights of *contrainte par corps*. The closure was introduced as a response to creditor complaints about debtors who managed to start up new business while the procedure of *faillite* stalled for lack of funds. For legislators these kinds of bankruptcies flouted the law and made *faillite* merely "an exemption from *contrainte par corps* and a means of deceiving new creditors."[48] At the time the bill was proposed, lawmakers estimated that half of the 12,000 ongoing bankruptcies nationwide had been stalled, many permanently, by inadequate funds.[49] The closure of a bankruptcy meant that the creditors could enter back into their individual actions, including debt imprisonment, pay stoppages, and seizure of property. By 1842, 1,203 of the 2,974 pending cases in Paris had been closed.[50] Some bankrupts, undoubtedly sensing that a particularly obdurate creditor waited in the wings, borrowed money wherever they could to prevent their bankruptcy from being closed.[51]

While the closure of bankruptcy for "insufficiency of assets" increased the scope of *contrainte par corps*, particularly over poorer debtors, another innovation of the 1838 bill restricted creditors' rights over debtors' bodies. The Commercial Code had mandated that all bankrupts be incarcerated in debtors' prison immediately after they had submitted their balance sheet to the commercial court. By 1835, when the committee debated the measure, few bankrupts ended up spending any time in prison.[52] In theory, creditors accorded safe-conduct passes, which allowed bankrupts freedom from imprisonment on the basis of the bankrupt's trustworthiness and good character. In reality, the code's lack of clarity about who could imprison and who would pay for imprisonment, as well as creditors' desire to have the bankrupt help them recover as many assets as possible, made imprisonment exceedingly rare. The arrest of bankrupts was so rare, and so confusing, that justices of the peace habitually released bankrupts arrested by commercial guards in Paris in the 1820s on the grounds that bankruptcy ended the creditors' right to enforce *contrainte par corps*.[53]

Surprisingly for a provision largely disregarded in practice, the end of mandatory debt imprisonment aroused several days' worth of debate among the commission members. Supporters of the provision held that creditors could not properly examine a bankrupt's character at the beginning of a bankruptcy. Given this uncertainty, it was best not to leave the debtor in a state of inviolability. According to one committee member, the possibility of imprisonment after the declaration of a bankruptcy instilled a "salutatory fear" into the debtor who took failure too lightly. He added that "a bankruptcy is almost always the result of faults or imprudence, and if one considers the evils it engenders, it is a kind of quasi infraction."[54] Abolishing mandatory imprisonment, this commission member continued, would have a "noxious influence on commercial mores." Instead, the government should enforce the laws in place. Yet most of the commission opposed this view, believing that imprisonment negatively affected the creditor.[55] They also questioned its legality: since the debtor had already been temporarily disposed of his property, it could not function as a form of *contrainte par corps*. Rather, it possessed a punitive nature, based on the presumption of fraud, which "would be unjust if applied to all bankrupts." Incarceration could never remain a private matter between creditors. Any incarceration would need to include accusations of *banqueroute*, since "any time a bankrupt is detained in a prison for debts it gives a character of crime or misdemeanor to his bankruptcy."[56] Despite the infrequency of incarceration in practice before 1838, the controversy aroused by its abolition underscores the profound symbolic importance that imprisonment held under the code. In choosing to remove mandatory imprisonment for bankrupts, the commission effectively ended the central role allotted to the bankrupt's physical person in securing his debts.

The abolition of mandatory imprisonment belonged to a broader reconceptualization of the role played by the person of the bankrupt in a bankruptcy. The 1838 reform also shifted bankruptcy law away from the person of the debtor in its treatment of bankruptcy after death. According to the 1807 Commercial Code, a businessman had to be alive, or at least to have suspended or refused payment while living, in order to be considered bankrupt. In 1835, for example, a Parisian wine merchant, referred to only as "P" by newspapers, perhaps to preserve his posthumous reputation, died two days after he ceased making payments but without having filed a formal bankruptcy declaration. Creditors accused his wife and nephew, who had transferred his shop and clientele shortly after his death, of complicity in *banqueroute frauduleuse*. Their lawyers, however, successfully maintained that the widow and nephew could not be charged as such, since the wine merchant "cannot be either a *failli* nor a *banqueroutier*," and they were instead charged with fraud and sentenced to two years imprisonment.[57]

The 1838 law, on the other hand, allowed for a bankruptcy declaration after a debtor's death. This innovation caused initial concern among the commission charged with reformulating the law. Opponents declared that "every bankruptcy implicated the person of the bankrupt and even supposes some degree of fault on his part" and worried that allowing the "stigma of bankruptcy" to attach to the dead would tarnish the reputations of those "not there to defend themselves." The commission nevertheless ultimately came down on the side of allowing the estate to be declared in bankruptcy after the debtor's death. Suicide, observers noted, was sometimes the most certain sign of impending failure. Perhaps more importantly for the commission, bankruptcy was established to give creditors greater ease in pressing their claims against the deceased's estate and succession.[58] In so doing, however, they opened the door to a fundamental reconsideration of the relationship between liability and commercial personhood, a relationship already being hotly contested in the nation's courts.

Persons and Partnerships

Although the debate on revising the Commercial Code had remained largely silent on the subject, the growing popularity of new forms of commercial association also helped redefine the nature of personhood involved in the bankruptcy process. Rather than being driven by legislative reform, the battles between creditors and debtors, and court rulings involved in settling these disputes, pushed forward new understanding of who and what could go bankrupt. In theory, the options for businesses in the early nineteenth century were fairly limited. The Commercial Code described three different types of commercial associations: the *société en nom collectif*, a partnership between two responsible agents; the *société en commandite*, a company headed by a director with sleeping partners; and the *société anonyme*, a limited-liability joint-stock company. Each of these forms entailed notions of responsibility that transcended the individual person envisioned by the code. By the late 1830s, commercial associations had achieved a considerable position in the French economy. Increasing numbers of such companies meant increasing numbers of company bankruptcies: of the 942 bankruptcies declared in Paris between 1838 and 1839, 101 concerned *sociétés*.[59]

The *société en nom collectif* was the most common of these forms, and the most closely tied to the logic of the person. In this type of business, each partner acted on behalf of the other partners. Each partner took responsibility for the debts of the entire association. Although the code recognized a single form of *société en nom collectif*, in practice these businesses ranged from enterprises where businessmen acted together but kept separate accounts to complete partnerships. Creditors, however, generally chose to place both partners in bankruptcy when one of them failed, no matter how distinct the two tried to make their operations. The numerous, and often acrimonious, court cases involving *sociétés en nom collectif* vividly illustrate the sometimes deleterious effects of association on the reputation of the other partners, as well as how deeply business associates cared about the value of their names in the business. The case of a Nantais timber merchant named Guérin-Chassi, who had formed a *société en nom collectif* with a merchant named Berchon, is a case in point. Berchon, tasked with paying off the sellers, fell behind in his account keeping. In response, Guérin-Chassi sent a series of increasingly desperate letters in which he closely linked his honor with that of his friend, and the value of his name to the value of his business. As the situation worsened, Guérin-Chassi demanded that Berchon stop signing in his name and that their signatures on bills be officially disassociated.

Although Berchon gave his word of honor to stop using Guérin-Chassi's signature, he continued to do so, leaving Guérin with no choice but to pay or lose his own honor. When the court placed both Guérin-Chassi and Berchon in bankruptcy later the next year, Guérin-Chassi sued his former partner, claiming that his goal "was less to win back the goods that were the fruit of long and hard work than to conserve intact a reputation for loyalty, frankness, probity and economy, acquired by all the acts of [his] civil and commercial career, and without which [his] life would be but an insupportable burden."[60] As Guérin-Chassi's poignant plea highlighted, a *société en nom collectif* did more than merely tie together the capital of two merchants. Instead, it tied together their reputations and their responsibility for losses, confounding the emphasis placed by the Commercial Code on individual responsibility.

The specific name attached to a bankruptcy was of crucial importance for both partnerships and other kinds of companies. When François Lecamus's bank failed in Paris in July 1830, the creditors struggled to determine whether he was the company's sole manager, thereby assuming the entire responsibility for the firm's collapse, or whether they should also include his brother Édouard, who apparently used the company funds as his private account without being officially a businessman. Creditors generally wished to pursue the broadest possible understanding of how responsibility might be assigned in a family enterprise, since that allowed them the best chances of recovering their losses.[61] The multiple identities of individuals involved in associations also challenged notions of a single uniform agent involved in economic transactions. For instance, in 1844 Monsieur Gounot was declared bankrupt in two capacities: first in his personal name for his own business, which ended in a *union*, and second as associate of a partnership, which ended in a *concordat*. An appeals court annulled the *concordat*, stating that "it is impossible to admit that the state and capacity of the same person can be divided into two contradictory positions, that of a debtor put back at the head of his affairs by a *concordat*, and that of a debtor placed under a contract of *union*."[62] Gounot's case demonstrated the difficulties of attempting to assign individual responsibility differently from collective responsibility in the case of bankruptcy. Judges struggled to reconcile the multiple identities that merchants might have when acting independently and with others.

Although the complexity of the family firm and the *société en nom collectif* both challenged the ideal of individual responsibility for debts on which the Commercial Code was based, the anxieties elicited by joint-stock companies, the *société anonyme*, and the *société en commandite*, were even greater. As Amelia Kessler has pointed out, difficulties in assigning responsibility in these kinds of associations date back to their origins in the seventeenth and eighteenth centuries. These new models broke with the ideal of the commercial association between family members or friends. Although natural rights theorists praised these innovations for enabling true egalitarianism, the *société anonyme* and the *société en commandite* aroused criticism for the unequal responsibilities they placed on their participants.[63] In the aftermath of the French Revolution, anxieties about the *société anonyme* and the *société en commandite* centered on how these forms concealed the agency and thus the liability of key actors. In a society where the juridical personhood of corporate entities had been destroyed, but where the corporal nature of liability lay at the heart of credit relations, the *société en commandite* and the *société anonyme* posed fundamental challenges to the legal framework of commercial debt.

The basic organization of the *société en commandite* consisted of a director, subject to unlimited liability, and passive or sleeping partners, who furnished funds either outright, as in the case of a *société en commandite simple*, or by means of shares, as in the *société en commandite par actions*. The company took the name of its manager. In theory, the *société en commandite* dissolved after the manager's death, although most companies included provisions in their charter to prevent the company's dissolution if the manager resigned or died.[64] Even as the *société en commandite* made the manager's name very noticeable, it also concealed other names from the public eye, just as it protected other individuals involved with the company from liability for the company's losses. In the nineteenth century, the *société en commandite* retained the reputation for subterfuge that it had earned under the old regime, where it had often served to mask the identity of nobles, who had been prohibited from involvement in industrial enterprises under penalty of *dérogeance*, the loss of their title.[65] As such, the *société en commandite* contained a hint of dishonor: in the shadows, individuals hid their identities and protected themselves from potential ruin, while sharing in the profits of the companies.

If the predominant concern about the *société en commandite* in the eighteenth century lay in its departure from a normative ideal of the cooperative merchant, the concerns of nineteenth-century observers revolved around the liability of the manager. The mid-1830s saw an explosion of *société en commandite par actions* that unnerved such pillars of the commercial community as the Bank of France and the great Parisian banking establishments.[66] These concerns reached their zenith around the same time that legislators were working on the reform of the bankruptcy laws. In popular works such as Frédérick Lemaître's *Robert Macaire*, critics portrayed the *société en commandite par actions* as a front by the sleeping partners, hiding behind the straw man they had appointed as manager, for embezzling guileless shareholders. These speculators, in the words of one particularly articulate opponent, placed in charge of the enterprise "an insolvent director, detaching themselves from the risks of the inevitable catastrophe."[67] Legally, creditors could hold the manager alone responsible in the case of the company's bankruptcy. Meanwhile, those truly morally responsible for the shareholder's distress, the speculators, could neither be criminally nor financially pursued.

The bankruptcy of these companies became a focal point of criticism. Bankruptcies, critics argued, allowed the sleeping partners to swindle gullible shareholders out of their fortunes. The economist and legislator Louis Wolowski noted that *sociétés en commandite par actions* rarely appeared on the registry of bankruptcies, explaining that these companies "ruin themselves, their capital is wasted, but they don't present their balance sheet" because the "entire weight of the disaster weighs on the managers, who are masters of ending the enterprise at the moment when they fear their subsidiary responsibility should be put in play."[68] Official management of a company, rather than a share in its profits, determined the degree of financial responsibility for the company's losses, which frustrated creditors unable to obtain dividends after a company failure. When one *société en commandite* with two managers failed a few months after its opening in 1838, the creditors wanted to include in the bankruptcy both the directors and the assistant directors, who had managed the society's affairs in the provinces in return for a substantial part of the profits they made there. A royal court declared that because these individuals were not personally involved in the management of the business's affairs they could not be held liable for the company's fall.[69] Liable managers faced stiff penalties for failure: in order to obtain rehabilitation from a bankruptcy, a partner had to pay not just his portion of the company's debt but rather the entire amount owed. As one lawmaker put it, "The social debt is the personal debt of each associate; honor and conscience oblige him to pay the entirety of the debt if he acquires the means of paying."[70] Although associated with appallingly lax liability, the question of personal responsibility for the *société en commandite* was in fact more complicated: the bankruptcy of these companies provoked questions about exactly to whom the company's debt belonged.

Generally, the *société en commandite*'s debt was exclusively linked to that of its manager. However, creditors who could prove that company shareholders or sleeping partners had been actively involved in the company's management could include these figures in the bankruptcy. The 1837 *faillite* of the Société des eaux de Montmartre, managed by Monsieur Chappe, threatened its creditors with complete ruin, since the manager was insolvent. However, when they proved that the shareholders had been actively involved in the management of the company, the creditors were allowed to make up for some of their losses through pursuing the shareholders.[71] In another case, D. Ibarrart, manager of a shipping outfitter in Nantes, was declared bankrupt in 1840. While Ibarrart believed his associates and the company itself should be placed in a state of bankruptcy, his associates argued that the company would be fine with a new director and that the bankruptcy was Ibarrart's alone. Furthermore, they argued that Ibarrart was only seeking to avoid payment of his initial investment.[72] In these cases courts had to carefully reconstruct the exact amount of responsibility held by agents in the operation of a *société.*

Sleeping partners who never reimbursed the price of their shares further tested the limits of personhood and responsibility in the *société en commandite*. During the 1838 liquidation process of Mesnard and Company, a bitumen processor, the company's creditors discovered that a sleeping partner named Lingeret had never paid for his fifty company shares and promptly invoked their right to *contrainte par corps*.[73] The Paris commercial court considered him a *commerçant* and declared that commercial law could not support having "on one hand, a manager [who is] responsible in an unlimited and bodily manner for the execution of the engagements of the society" and on the other hand, sleeping partners who reaped the company's profits "but are held [responsible] only by civil means which are often illusory." A royal court, however, sided with Lingeret, proclaiming that a shareholder was merely "a lender of funds who does not deal with the business's operations [*operations sociales*]" and thus could not be judged by commercial law.[74]

On the other hand, in 1841, for instance, the royal court of Grenoble ruled that during the operation of a *société en commandite*, creditors could only pursue the manager for the company's debts, but in bankruptcy, creditors could also pursue shareholders who had not paid for their initial investment. This obligation would be considered a commercial debt even if the shareholder did not qualify as a *commerçant* because the investment was intended for commercial purposes.[75] The ultimate decision to shield shareholders from commercial law might seem at odds with the general trend of furthering creditors' rights through decoupling the person from the debt. However, in protecting shareholders, the courts applied this separation of person and debt more broadly; although the shareholder was responsible for the debt, creditors were denied the right to pursue him by his person. Despite the problematic nature of *sociétés en commandite*, they remained closely tied to the centrality of the person and to the kinds of close personal relations that lawmakers saw as the hallmark of the enterprise *en nom collectif*. The issues faced by companies in getting sleeping partners to pay for their initial investment in the case of a bankruptcy underscored the continued importance of family and friendship ties in the operation of such businesses. Likening the relationship of managers to sleeping partners with those between company partners and family members, commentators insisted that conflicts in the case of a bankruptcy be resolved by the same arbitration processes used to solve other interpersonal disputes.[76]

While courts and lawyers disputed the exact parameters of liability throughout the 1830s and 1840s, courts produced notions of legal responsibility that were both narrower, insomuch as they excluded sleeping partners and shareholders from commercial debt imprisonment, and more abstract, in the sense that they treated companies themselves as entities rather than as associations of individuals.[77] The *société anonyme*, by contrast, proved much more difficult to reconcile with notions of personhood embedded in the code.[78] In the *société anonyme*, no single individual carried responsibility for the company's actions. These organizations required government authorization, accorded only after a thorough assessment of the company's solvency and public utility.[79] While the titles of other types of societies contained the name of one or more of the persons subjected to unlimited liability, the title of a *société anonyme* contained the name of its commercial activity rather than of a person, hence the term "anonymous society."[80] The absence of a name tied to the company correlated with the absence of a person to be held liable for paying its debts. For some, this raised the question of whether such a company could even undergo the normal bankruptcy process. In 1843, for example, the director of one insolvent fire insurance company argued that declaring his company bankrupt violated the terms of the Commercial Code because to "declare the bankruptcy of a *société anonyme* is to recognize a bankruptcy without a bankrupt."[81] Although judges overruled the company director, his suit underscored the problematic nature of applying the terms of bankruptcy to companies where no one could answer for the company's failure.

The bankruptcy of the Loire Railroad Company, a joint-stock company established to build railroad infrastructure in the Rhône, provides a particularly vivid example of the complicated nature of these cases. After the company's failure in 1836, the result in equal measure of the impracticality of its design and a series of storms in the region the previous year, the bankruptcy trustees had proceeded as one normally did with such a company:

namely, with the liquidation of all the company's assets and the pro rata distribution of dividends among the creditors. Dissatisfied with the trustees' handling of the estate, several creditors, former railroad engineers, sought instead to obtain a *concordat* with the bankrupted company. This was an unconventional choice. As the trustees' lawyer argued, for a *société anonyme* to lawfully agree to a *concordat*, "it would be necessary above all to find a person who had the legal character to present these propositions, who consents to be responsible for their fulfillment and who is morally interested to accomplish them in order to have the right to excusability and rehabilitation which the law, in its enlightened protection, potentially offers to a faithful and unfortunate bankrupt."[82] For a *société anonyme* like the railroad company, the code's prescriptions seemed not only impossible to fulfill but even absurd to envision. For a start, the lawyer said, there were no "responsible and seizable managers." No one could be arrested for failing to make good on his debts. Furthermore, he continued, the company's shareholders "do not owe the amount for the best of reasons, they owe nothing, it is their initial investment that owes." As such, the lawyer finished, "there are no bankrupts, or the bankrupts are none other than the capital, the coffers of the company."[83] Could a company's capital face arrest? Were there legal means of recourse against a person, impoundment of belongings, imprisonment, pay stoppage, if the *concordat* was violated? Given these differences between individual debtors and limited liability corporations, the trustees' lawyer insisted on the inapplicability of the *concordat*.

Yet the engineers ultimately won their case. Acting as the defunct company's administrators, they proposed a *concordat* to the other creditors. Rescheduling its debts, the company continued to operate and, backed by substantial government investment, ultimately prevailed as the Reconstituted Railroad Company of the Loire. The creditors' victory in this case testifies not merely to the growing importance of companies like the Loire Railroad Company but also to the redefinition of the meaning and nature of bankruptcy. If the Commercial Code, with which the trustee's lawyer sought to uphold the necessity of a *union*, was built on the logic of personhood, increasingly creditors and legislators alike pushed for a definition of bankruptcy linked less closely with the flesh-and-blood person of the debtor than with needs and the desires of the unsecured creditors.

Pushed along as much by a desire to ensure creditors' property rights as by the hopes of ensuring debtors' compliance with legal prescriptions, the aspects of bankruptcy proceedings that most clearly resembled the penal realm began to disappear in the 1830s and 1840s. This era witnessed continuous attempts to reconcile the legal notions of personal responsibility for commercial failure enshrined in the Commercial Code with the challenges posed by complex firm structures to legislative reform. Efforts to expand creditors' rights gradually created a bankruptcy process more lenient toward debtors. They also endowed fictive corporate entities with rights and capacities comparable to actual persons with whom creditors could negotiate in the case of commercial failure. In so doing, investors and judges alike increasingly undermined the close connection between the actual person of the debtor and his legal personality.

Rethinking Bankruptcy

Even as judges and legislators debated how best to adapt bankruptcy law to the realities of emergent patterns of investment pooling and commercial association, political and economic thinkers of both socialist and liberal stripes examined bankruptcy as a means of comprehending the challenges and realities of an emergent capitalist order built on individualistic competition and collective risk. In 1837 Horace Say, the son and intellectual heir of the great political economist Jean-Baptiste Say, contributed to the debate on bankruptcy law with a pamphlet entitled *Avant-propos à la discussion d'une nouvelle loi sur les faillites*. Say's several years as a commercial judge and several decades of involvement with the export business in the United States, Brazil, and France, provided a practical foundation for his theoretical commitment to French liberalism, a school founded in large part by his father. He viewed the problem of bankruptcy reform through the dual lenses of abstract theories of competition and association as outlined by the French liberal school and in terms of the concrete realities he saw in cases presented before him at the Commercial Court of the Seine. His pamphlet simultaneously displayed a firm grasp on legal technicalities and the ability to situate the debates about bankruptcy reform in the context of broader economic developments.

For Say, Book III of the Commercial Code lagged substantially behind the commercial dynamism that had marked the first half of the century. Say found the first proof of this discrepancy in the situation where, to "avoid individual pursuits of his creditors and obtain a safe-conduct past, a spendthrift officially stops payments with the commercial court clerk. The court cannot refuse to put him in bankruptcy; nevertheless, despite the acts of commerce that the spendthrift has undertaken, according to the law he is not really a merchant."[84] Say's use of the word "spendthrift" to describe non-*commerçants* who could not fulfill the contractual obligations of a bankruptcy reflects a deep mistrust of those who took on substantial amounts of debt without the demands of commercial operations. Echoing many critics' claims about *contrainte par corps*, Say argued that commercial courts should be more careful about allowing such pursuits against noncommercial individuals. He believed it to be unjust to the creditors that these spendthrifts could find "refuge in these generous and protective dispositions of the law designed to help unfortunate and honest merchants." Say approved efforts to allow bankruptcies where the debtor could not pay for the costs to be reopened to the individual pursuits of the creditors.

The status of joint-stock companies represented an even thornier problem for Say. He argued that these companies formed "fictitious entities distinct from the person of each of the associate managers" who must independently answer for debts. To Say, this situation represented a conundrum: while the company was the "only direct debtor of its debts," each associate individually could be considered as security for the company and liable for its debts in case of the company's failure to pay its creditors. He explained this as a principle of solidarity between the company and the company's managers, which meant that a bankruptcy extended to all the associate managers of the company as well as to the company's assets. Yet, for Say, this led to an illogical impasse: on one hand, associates were declared twice bankrupt, once in their own name and subsequently in the name of the company. But on the other hand, the overriding importance of an individual's status as a *commerçant* clearly meant that a merchant involved in such a bankruptcy could not be allowed to retain his good name. Say's concern with this paradox reflected his unease about the challenges posed by collective entities more generally. A strong believer in individual economic actors yet also aware of the benefits permitted by the *société*, Say hoped to reconcile these two ostensibly opposing agents.

Say felt that in order to maximize the benefits for creditors of a *société en commandite*, bankruptcy law needed to more clearly delineate the role and responsibilities of joint-stock companies, particularly the *société anonyme*. He noted that a *union* was the only option open to a *société anonyme*," because this company "is nothing but a fictitious entity, which cannot present itself in person to an assembly of creditors, who therefore cannot accord him a safe-conduct pass, for the reason that he cannot be apprehended by body; he cannot be declared excusable and, in short, that he worries little about rehabilitation."[85] Say believed that in many cases *concordats* might be a better deal for the creditors in these situations, and saw the person-oriented nature of the Commercial Code as impeding the most profitable resolution to commercial distress. In Say's opinion, only a thorough revision of the Commercial Code, reflecting the tumultuous changes to the economy that had taken place over the preceding years, could make bankruptcy law more effective.[86] Yet he admitted that such a revision posed fundamental challenges to the individualistic nature of the law, which he generally applauded.

While Say's work demonstrated the problematic nature of more abstract associations and the expanding boundaries of commerce for economic liberals, early socialists saw in bankruptcy an example, not of the problems posed by a burgeoning financial section, but rather of how financial capitalism operated more generally. In a pamphlet entitled *Observations sur les faillites et banqueroutes* published the same year as Say's, Paul-Émile Laviron presented very different ideas about the reforms necessary to bankruptcy law. Only twenty-six at the time of the pamphlet's publication, the Besançon native had barely finished his law degree but had already adopted the militant brand of Fouriest socialism that would guide him through the rest of his turbulent and politically engaged career. Building on the ideas of Charles Fourier himself, who had written several pieces mordantly categorizing bankruptcies into such groups as "goose bankruptcy" and "Attila bankruptcy," Laviron, like his teacher, believed that bankruptcy embodied the terrible realities of an economy based on competition in all its messy contradictions.

Laviron scoffed at reformers' attempts to fix flaws with bankruptcy regulation. Under a system that protected competition as a natural right, he reasoned, victory inevitably belonged to those willing to use the most ruthless and mendacious means of getting ahead.[87] The honest merchant, who sold only high quality goods and paid his employees fairly, would be consistently outperformed by his unscrupulous competitor because the latter would cut costs at every turn. In an environment where probity meant poverty and dishonesty reaped profit, honest merchants were driven either to dishonesty or to bankruptcy.[88] Laviron believed that honest bankruptcies were incredibly rare, because bankruptcy generally served as a means by which wily merchants enriched themselves at their creditors' expense. For this reason he made no distinction between *faillite* and *banqueroute*, referring to them as *faillite-banqueroute* and considering all bankruptcies where the debtor did not deprive himself of all assets in order to reimburse his creditors the maximum possible of their debts as a form of theft and trickery.

Contrary to the 1838 reform bill, Laviron's proposal addressed the problems with bankruptcy through radical alterations to the commercial system. He called for establishing guild-like "monopolies of commerce" requiring all goods to be made essentially the same and, when possible, marked with a special mark from state inspectors. Not only would these guilds reduce bankruptcy, Laviron assured his readers, but they would also assure consumers of quality. Under a system of "limited competition," honest men who eschewed mercantile professions out of well-founded fear of the ruthlessness of free trade would feel confident starting their own businesses. Although Laviron believed bankruptcies would be far less frequent under his system, those that did occur would be easily distinguished from fraud. He explained that under such a system a merchant could not successfully hide merchandise or make up expenses. It would moreover be "easy to determine the limits" for necessary expenses of an enterprise because, among other reasons, "an opulent appearance would no longer be useful to gain clientele and credit."[89]

According to Laviron, under his proposed system no rational trader would opt for a bankruptcy rather than continuing in his business, given the meager reward for his cunning and the certainty of punishment for fraud. Every bankrupt would be treated as a *banqueroute*. Echoing the language of Napoleon, Laviron argued that bankruptcy should be treated in the same way that "the mutilation of a body supposes murder, like taking away an object presumes theft."[90] Extending the metaphor, he added that under such a system it would be "up to the person who mutilated the corpse or who took away the object to prove that these facts are the result of excusable imprudence or *force majeure*." While admitting that under the current economic system it was not possible to judge bankruptcy with such legal rigor because the evidence of a possible crime was too confused by the vagaries of the market itself, once the system of limited competition was implemented, such legal justice would be possible.

Charles Fourier's more notorious disciple, Alphonse Toussenel, expanded on Fourier's ideas about bankruptcy in his *Les Juifs, rois de l'époque* of 1845. Toussenel was a journalist and writer who worked for the newspaper *La Paix* before founding the Fourierist *La Démocratie Pacifique*. Subsequently identified as the founder of modern anti-Semitism, a view strongly articulated in *Les Juifs*, he was equally well known in his lifetime for his works on natural history. Toussenel's argument about bankruptcy in *Les Juifs* must first be contextualized within the anti-Semitism of Toussenel's views toward commerce more generally. The fundamental premise of Toussenel's work posited a conflict between "productive" labor, connected to the Christian majority of France who worked the land and to "true" artisanal trades, and the "parasitic" practices of buying and selling, which Toussenel believed to be largely, but not exclusively, undertaken in France by the Jews.[91] Importantly, however, he alternated in his text between considering the Jews as a separate race and conflating them with commercial people more generally. The book began in the latter vein with a long tirade against the Dutch and British as commercial peoples before arriving at the Jews as the element of the population in France dedicated to corrupting the country through trade and speculation. For Toussenel, commerce manifested the essential qualities of Jewish identity including deceitfulness and the lazy desire to acquire wealth without hard labor. The Jews constituted a commercial nation, akin to the British or Dutch, in the interior of France itself and surreptitiously worked to corrupt the rest of the nation with their speculative practices.

For Toussenel, bankruptcy and usury highlighted the deep resemblances between commerce and theft. Although economists justified speculative commercial credit because it encouraged risk and allowed enterprising individuals to make great fortunes, Toussenel believed that these fortunes inevitably resulted in other people's losses. He envisioned the economy as essentially stationary and believed that "real productive wealth," meaning the wealth produced from the land, could not be generated but only transferred. All "speculative" wealth constituted a transfer of resources from the generally honest majority to a dishonest elite.[92] Bankruptcy constituted a primary means for the transfer of this wealth; ruining good, hardworking families with their risky speculations, financiers grew wealthy from gambling with others' fortunes. For Toussenel, commercial credit equaled "the right to go bankrupt," which, in turn, was the equivalent of both theft and usury and represented the "privilege of stealing with impunity." Toussenel remarked that "in principle, bankruptcy is never excusable; it is always a *banqueroute*, unless in the case of a *force majeure* like a robbery which has left one completely bereft, a shipwreck, a fire, or a flood."[93] While Toussenel's hardline approach to bankruptcy echoed the rhetoric of the early nineteenth century, his attack was far more systematic: as in Laviron's account, far from representing emergent capitalism when it failed, bankruptcy characterized the fundamental approach of "financial feudalism" toward the accumulation of wealth.

Say, Laviron, and Toussenel differed profoundly in their understandings of how bankruptcy embodied the paradoxes of a capitalist economy more generally. For Say, bankruptcy manifested the deficits of the Commercial Code in managing an economy that had evolved considerably since the dawn of the nineteenth century. In particular, the process highlighted the confrontation between a legal system based on individualism and the realities of collective risk. Both Laviron and Toussenel, on the other hand, believed bankruptcy exemplified the chicanery of the market economy more generally, with Laviron seeing it as the natural result of unbridled competition and Toussenel as a speculative means of transferring wealth from producers to parasitic classes. For all three men, however, the individual character of the bankrupt mattered far less than the structure of the credit economy that created bankruptcy. Indeed, even Toussenel and Laviron, who depicted bankrupts as almost universally fraudulent, did not hold these individuals culpable for their actions.

As the following chapter will discuss, in 1848 bankruptcy became one of the most egregious signs of the need to radically reorganize the credit system in its entirety. The result of market causes often completely obscure to their authors, bankruptcy had the potential to devastate a wide range of individuals—from workers to smaller shopkeepers, from domestic servants to the industry owner himself—connected by webs of trust and obligation to the bankrupt. As such, for many reformers bankruptcy would become the perfect symbol of the defects of the socioeconomic status quo. This vision in turn owed much to the legal and political developments of the 1830s and 1840s, when new laws on bankruptcy and new rulings by courts transformed bankruptcy from a category tied deeply to the person of the bankrupt to an abstract state of a business's solvency.

Conclusion

Although the promulgators of Book III of the Commercial Code intended to restrain the arrangements made between debtors and creditors to those under the surveillance of commercial courts, bankruptcies continued to operate as both social and legal events throughout the nineteenth century. Bankrupts and their creditors by turns allied and competed with each other, hoping to maximize their gains from a generally hopeless situation. With the expansion of capital-intensive enterprises in the 1820s and 1830s, creditors, using bankruptcy laws centered on the person as a means of pursuing their debts but at the same time frustrated by the constraints placed by the code's requirements, prompted court rulings that significantly broadened the interpretation of the code. For legislators, the creative uses debtors and creditors made of the law provoked considerable consternation. Would increased leniency or additional rigor ensure compliance with the legal requirements of a bankruptcy? Although the reforms of 1838 generally sided with less rigor, even voices within the commercial community felt that the dangers of speculation necessitated the imposition of more discipline on the commercial order. Following the enactment of the 1838 bankruptcy reform law, no less prominent a figure than the president of the Paris Commercial Court declared the need to "conserve for French commerce the morality that distinguishes it from that of many nations where bankruptcy is approached without shame and too commonly."[94] He suggested that before a bankrupt could start his business again, he should be forced to prove his credit and morality before a jury composed of elite businessmen. The president acknowledged that neither political economists nor legislators would seriously consider his plan. Yet even these opponents recognized the formidable challenges posed by an age of speculation.

The innovations of the 1838 reform, which frustrated the likes of the president of the Paris Commercial Court, had profound effects on the meaning of bankruptcy. Ostensibly minor aspects of the new legislation, including the official end of the seldom-followed mandatory imprisonment for the bankrupt and the declaration of a bankruptcy after death, reflected a profound rethinking of bankruptcy which contrasted starkly with the code's insistence on the centrality of the debtor's person. Both contemporary commentators and subsequent scholars have focused on the law's more generous attitude toward debtors, with Pierre-Cyrille Hautcoeur and Nadine Levratto calling it a "decodification" meant to "encourage the spirit of enterprise."[95] Yet the abstract interpretation of the company contained in the new legislation would have long-lasting impact. Rather than defining the company by the name and physical body of its owner or manager, a company became an abstract legal entity in its own right. Even as the 1838 bankruptcy law helped create a vision of the company divorced from the centrality of the debtor's person and therefore more practical for large-scale enterprises, it had a very different impact for smaller businessmen. The process of "closure," which allowed creditors to pursue debtors who lacked even the means to pay for the legal expenses of their bankruptcies, created a two-tiered process. Utterly insolvent bankrupts, generally taken from the lowest ranks of merchants and artisans, would be subjected to increased market discipline, while bankruptcy continued to protect those companies and individuals with assets large enough to maintain the expense of a bankruptcy process.

These developments in legislation were complemented by innovations in practice. Judges in commercial, royal, and appeals courts increased creditors' rights even at the expense of the hallowed notion of the debtor's person as the pledge of his debt. In a variety of decisions, they also insulated shareholders from the full impact of market discipline, enshrining more deeply the idea of limited liability. The decoupling of bodies from companies, visible in the treatment of *sociétés en commandite* and *société anonymes* in the 1830s and 1840s, added to the popular anxiety surrounding these forms and testifies to the growing importance of negotiable stocks in forming capital for industry over the traditional form of family or individual money. In liberal and socialist schools of economic thought, attention shifted away from the character of individual bankrupts. Instead, diverse writers saw bankruptcy as representative of the larger reconfiguration in notions of association and competition as the financial sector expanded and diversified. On both a theoretical and practical level, the 1830s and 1840s represented a critical phase in the detachment of failure from individual responsibility and the person and its association instead with systematic problems and collective institutions.

7

A Discount on the Future

1848 and the Remaking of Financial Responsibility

On the morning of February 24, 1848, a crowd surged down Paris's boulevard de la Madeleine. Violence had been brewing in the city since the cancellation of a protest banquet two days earlier. That morning, King Louis-Philippe scrambled to form a new government after his hasty dismissal of the unpopular Guizot administration. As the crowd passed the debtors' prison of Clichy, a voice cried out, "Free the debt prisoners!" A group of five or six hundred people broke down the doors of Clichy prison, where news of the revolt had already excited the debtors to force their way toward the doors.[1] Liberated, the insolvents took up arms with the militants, distinguishing themselves from their counterparts, according to one journalist, "in their maintenance of order and their opposition to looting."[2] By the end of that long February day, the crowds had taken the Hôtel de Ville, the Palais-Royal, and the Tuileries Palace, burning their looted contents at the place de la Bastille. The royal family had fled to England. Tepid efforts to establish a regency had failed, and a republic was provisionally proclaimed. The February Revolution, as it became known, kindled similar outbursts of unrest across Europe.

That revolutionary crowds saw debt prisoners as victims of the prior regime's injustice was hardly unprecedented, yet the February Revolution took up the problem of credit scarcity and defaulted debt in a far more systematic manner than had previous revolutionary regimes. Historiography on 1848, heavily influenced by Karl Marx's canonical accounts, has largely focused on labor history, perceiving in it the first articulated signs of working-class identity. The crucial role played by credit and debt in the events and debates of 1848 has been largely overlooked. Discussions of bankruptcy and debt imprisonment that occurred in 1848 were part of a broader rethinking about the meaning and place of debt in French society. The year 1848 became a key moment in the history of responsibility for failure, when what had been an intensely private shame became, for a brief amount of time, legally suspended and ascribed to forces beyond individual control. In this way, 1848 helped to redefine the nature of credit and commercial personhood more generally.

The Second Republic explicitly linked private credit concerns with fundamental questions about the social order itself.[3] The Revolution of 1848 was born amid a credit crisis that the political instability exacerbated. For both ideological and economic reasons, legislators linked the stability of public credit to the credit status of individual merchants. In the space of only a few months, the provisional government introduced numerous new institutions and financial instruments designed not only to revive credit but also to expand access to it across the French population. Many of these measures would long outlast the Second Republic itself. Although intended as an immediate reaction to overwhelming circumstances, the government's efforts to reshape the credit market were not merely pragmatic. Across the political spectrum, politicians and political thinkers realized that the gradual development of an industrial economy had inextricably connected the ordering of civil society with the organization of the financial system. Thus, it symbolized not only the weaknesses of the extant order but also an area of potential rebirth. The prominent socialist thinker Louis Blanc, for instance, deemed credit in and of itself "an excellent thing." Yet under the current "system of isolation and individualism" it was quite frequently disastrous, since

> a worker, happy enough to have the chance to earn his daily bread and that of his family by the sweat of his brow, sees himself abruptly forced back into the most extreme misery. Who does he blame? His boss? But it is not the fault of this last individual that has caused the downfall of the workshop that had provided for the laborer. A workshop closes in France because a large firm has gone bankrupt in England; a large firm has gone bankrupt in England because of some fraudulent transaction in America![4]

For Blanc, credit exemplified the cruel paradoxes of capitalist society. It was an omnipresent yet arbitrary force, it connected individuals in relations that they were largely powerless to control and yet from which some reaped unmerited rewards and others suffered unfair punishments. According to Blanc, the current financial system gave "strength to the strong, riches to the wealthy and credit to those who have the least need of it."[5] This inequality on the socioeconomic level sapped political promises of their force and integrity. Others corroborated Blanc's views. How free was your average small tradesman or petty trader, asked the Fourierist socialist and deputy Victor Considerant, when this class was constantly "eaten by worries and anxieties, not succeeding, despite Sisyphean efforts, in meeting their engagements, in making ends meet in their business, in filling the bottomless pit of their deficits, ceaselessly decimated by reciprocal bankruptcies?"[6] Debt, that continual burden of past engagements, weighed heavily on the capacity for future freedom and rendered hollow those promises of liberty inscribed by law.

Yet Blanc and Considerant, like many of their contemporaries, believed that credit, a potent symbol of the old order's economic injustice, had the potential to transform society for the better. Rather than chaining borrowers and lenders in hierarchical chains of dependence and obligation, a reorganization of the credit system could restructure such relationships on a more egalitarian plane. Such a reconfiguration was viewed as being not on the margins of a political agenda but at its heart: without such a "republicanization of credit" the Revolution's political goals would remain unfulfilled. For many observers, credit needed to be transformed from a system of debts that tied Frenchmen and women to their past to a system of hopes that allowed society, newly united, to progress toward the future.

These ideas in turn gave birth to substantive efforts at reform of the bankruptcy code as well as a short-lived abolition of *contrainte par corps*, which this chapter will situate within the broader context of an ongoing financial crisis as well as debates about the proper nature and function of republican credit. Differences concerning how and in what form to revive commercial credit, and consequently how to treat commercial debtors, became increasingly divisive battles between dueling economic visions of the left and right, pitting those who merely wished to revive trade and industry in its current form with those who hoped to use credit as a means of redefining French society. Much in the way as they had during the Revolution of 1789, discussions of private credit and discussions of public credit became inextricably linked. In 1848, however, reformers challenged rather than affirmed economic individualism and attributed the distress of private borrowers to the catastrophic state of public credit. They aimed to revive the economy by democratizing access to credit and relieving borrowers of much of the burden of their failure, whether in modifying the laws on bankruptcy or abolishing debtors' prison.

Ultimately, the February Revolution's more radical measures did not even see out the short-lived Second Republic. Yet their temporary nature belies the conceptual significance of such measures. The complex and interconnected nature of a commercialized economy suddenly struck by political crisis demanded a reassessment of the nature of personal responsibility in the financial realm. The creation of the *liquidation judiciaire*, a process in which business failure was separated from the civil and social consequences that adhered to debtor's person, marked a fundamental reconceptualization of the relationship between the debt and personhood.

The February Revolution

Events transpired with astonishing rapidity in the early days of the Revolution. With the Orleanist monarchy overthrown and a republic declared, the provisional government's immediate preoccupations centered on restoring order and adequately provisioning the capital after days of upheaval. Yet such concrete concerns did not prevent the new government from pushing through measures intended to quickly sweep away what were seen as the previous regime's most egregious abuses. On February 25, the provisional government guaranteed work for all male citizens and proclaimed the right of workers to associate. Newly established national workshops provided employment on public works projects, such as digging canals, constructing railroad stations, and planting trees. Other progressive reforms soon followed: the death penalty was abolished on February 26, universal manhood suffrage was declared on March 2, and slavery was abolished on March 4.

In the spirit of these decrees, on March 9, 1848, the provisional government abolished *contrainte par corps*, describing it as an "ancient debris of Roman legislation which, in putting people on the rank of things, is incompatible with our new public laws."[7] Three days later, debtors remaining in the country's prisons were released. Despite the decree's bold proclamations against debtors' prison, the government always intended for the elected

National Assembly to review the decision. Moreover, commercial courts continued to pronounce *contrainte par corps*, with the execution of these orders pending a formal review.[8] This legal limbo would persist long after the Assembly's election in May 1848. The manifold problems facing the young republic pushed *contrainte par corps* away from the order of the day. Meanwhile, the commercial crisis deepened, and calls by businessmen and chambers of commerce to reinstate *contrainte par corps* grew increasingly vehement.

The widespread calls for swift government action stemmed from a credit crunch that had paralyzed trade. This financial crisis, which was to be one of the Second Republic's most pressing and complicated challenges, had roots deep in the previous regime's financial norms as well as in the workings of an increasingly transnational economy.[9] During the economic boom of the early 1840s, companies had taken on substantial debt. Many had speculated on stocks, particularly railroad stocks. Beginning in 1845, a recession, triggered by agricultural shortages, forced companies to delay payments. The stock market bubble in railroad stocks burst. The draining of currency from the Bank of France, much of whose bullion had been invested abroad during the 1840s, further aggravated this situation. The events of February 1848 crushed a tentative recovery. Panic about governmental stability, a slump in the stock market after it was reopened in early March, and a sudden rush to retrieve currency led to a crisis in negotiating letters of change. Bill holders, even those at the upper echelons of the commercial community, found themselves unable to discount their bills, as worried lenders feared the onset of another profoundly unsettling revolution.

Certainly, the immediate aftermath of the Revolution gave the elites much to fear. Observers unsympathetic to the fledgling government spoke of a "general panic" that forced great capitalists to make hasty concessions and officials to put forward "erroneous and even absurd" proposals to placate the populace.[10] The prospect of mob violence terrified property owners, as did the new government's apparent social ambitions. Not only were great financers like Baron de Rothschild badly hurt in the pocketbook by the decline of key stocks, like railroad shares, and by the instability of the government bond market, but they also faced popular hostility, sometimes bubbling over into overt displays of violence.[11] Bankers found themselves labeled members of the "financial aristocracy" by a growing chorus of writers. Undoubtedly, many feared they would soon join the fate of the "feudal aristocracy" during the previous great Revolution of 1789.

All of this was bad news for credit circulation. Between February and April, 250 banks across the country suspended payments. Among the hardest hit were banks such as the bank of Gouin, Ganneron, and Baudon, which had served as intermediary third signatures allowing many medium-size manufacturers to have their commercial paper negotiated at the Bank of France.[12] Inspired by Jacques Laffitte's Caisse générale du commerce et de l'industrie, these banks had flourished in the decade before the Revolution, enlarging access to credit to medium and small businesses, but they had always remained critically undercapitalized, taking on engagements that often surpassed by twenty or thirty times their own funds. With the failure of these banks and those of many small private firms, the Bank of France took the unusual and desperate step of pursuing the endorsers of bills for payment, as so many of the borrowers had ceased or suspended payment. By August 1848 the bank held some 60,000 francs' worth of unpaid negotiable instruments in its vaults.[13] Periodic bank runs also dangerously depleted the money supply. As specie drained from the bank, it was forced to stop reimbursement on its bills. The provisional government reacted on March 15 by making bank bills legal tender, not exchangeable in specie, and allowing the Bank of France to issue new bills in larger denominations, effectively creating a form of paper money. Shortly afterward, this privilege was expanded to departmental banks.[14]

The credit crunch grew acute on the popular level as well. With the collapse of businesses, unemployment spread. In cities across the country, men and women lined up to receive alms and food and to work at the national workshops. On February 25, when the government allowed anyone who had placed an object worth ten francs or less at the Paris Mont-de-Piété to receive their pledge back for free, seventy national guardsmen had to keep order while the line wrapped around the twisted streets of the Marais.[15] On March 9, a crowd of small merchants and artisans gathered outside Paris's Hôtel de Ville to request a month-long prolongation of the due dates on commercial effects. While newspapers put their numbers at around eight hundred, Countess Marie d'Agout wrote that some three thousand people pressed their demands on the national government. Backed by the Bank of France, the minister of finance refused to countenance these demands.[16] Infuriated, one merchant supposedly lashed out in response, "You boast to us of your people! We will make you see what your people are! Tomorrow we will close our workshops, our stores: we will throw our workers in the streets . . . you will see then if it's better to concern yourself with them or with us and if they will content themselves for long to have you celebrate their patriotism!"[17]

Yet if the government would not cede to such requests, it did modify the rules applied to negotiable instruments. A decree on March 20, 1848, granted a delay on pursuits by creditors. Another law soon followed that prolonged the amount of time a holder had to press his claim for payment.[18] A decree on March 23 suppressed several of the costlier aspects of the protest, abolishing the need for witnesses and substituting a simplified system of all-inclusive expenses for the despised return account.[19] The crisis, however, demanded more radical reforms as well. The government, at the behest of the Bank of France, sought new institutions to provide the essential third signature necessary for discount by the bank. Between March and November 1848, the government set up sixty-seven new discounting branches throughout France.[20] Although the July Monarchy had made similar efforts in the crisis of summer 1830, these branches met with opposition from the banking elite and most had collapsed shortly after their creation.[21] In 1847 the thirteen remaining branches were severely undercapitalized and hardly useful in alleviating the crisis.[22] The new discounting branches, supported by government and municipal bonds as well as by private shareholders, witnessed a burst of activity. Businessmen were called upon to act as shareholders in these enterprises.[23] Some even proposed that commissions of merchants collect money from private individuals for the sake of commerce, stressing that patriotic and commercial duty were one and the same.[24]

Yet the discounting branches did not adequately meet the needs of smaller enterprises, whose difficulty obtaining credit had long preceded the Revolution. The Revolution, in exacerbating the financial situation, merely accentuated the weakness of the extant system. Furthermore, officials of a government that based its legitimacy on popular sovereignty sought to strengthen such claims by pressing for financial reforms to increase access to credit. In March 1848, Minister of Finance Louis Garnier-Page proposed the creation of a warrant system, in which a businessman deposited merchandise at a warehouse, received a receipt acknowledging his goods' worth, and could then circulate this receipt by endorsement as a form of credit.[25] The idea, borrowed from the English dock system, served two purposes simultaneously: facilitating credit, it also helped reduce overstock. Despite certain drawbacks, the warrant system generally succeeded in its mission, and warrants remained in use after the crisis of 1848 had passed.[26]

Another government effort to alleviate the credit crisis centered on the foundation of sub-discounting bank branches, organized by trade, to negotiate commercial paper from small businessmen and artisans.[27] While the discounting branches previously formed by the government needed two signatures, the sub-discounting branches took paper with one signature and permitted the use of warrants as collateral. The sub-discounting branches gave small companies in these trades easier access to discount at the Bank of France. If their popularity and the glowing reports of newspapers are to be believed, the sub-discounting branches, established in every city with a discounting branch, enjoyed resounding success. During the first eleven days of operation, over 4,000 businessmen and artisans discounted over 11 million francs' worth of commercial paper. On March 30 alone, more than 1,200 people discounted bills totaling around 2 million francs, of which 400,000 francs was discounted in Paris.[28]

In attempting to revive credit and commerce, the provisional government walked a thin line between protecting private property and resuscitating the economy. Government officials, caught in the middle of an increasingly contentious political battle between a nervous bourgeoisie and an insistent laboring class, hesitated to intervene too directly in private credit contracts. On March 15, for example, a delegation of Parisian business people demanded that "deposits made into the hands of powerful property owners be retired by at least a half in order to found a discounting branch."[29] Armand Marrast, mayor of Paris, denied the government's right to enter into private affairs "which are regulated by contracts which the government cannot change."[30] Marrast affirmed the government's sympathy with the plight of commerce, particularly small commerce, but also emphasized that the government could not compel private creditors to be similarly generous.

Despite this conservatism, officials saw the rapid expansion of credit institutions not merely as a pragmatic reaction to a crippling financial crisis but also as a part of a redefinition of the role and purpose of credit in society. Administrators and petitioners alike spoke of the need to "republicanize credit." This term entailed broadening the accessibility of credit to small and medium-size companies and rendering its institutions more open and egalitarian. Yet hidden beneath the financial vision of a more stable economy was that of a peaceful social revolution. There was, as the printer Louis Hachette declared, something profoundly egalitarian about these loans in which the government extended money "on a thorough appraisal of the morality, the skills and the financial position" to petty borrowers who might otherwise be turned away for lack of social standing.[31] For Marrast, as for Hachette, discounting and sub-discounting bank branches were profoundly democratic institutions. "You sell to your neighbor," he told a delegation of small businessmen, "he writes you a bill and at that very instant, you can take that bill to the discount branch which will accept it." With the new branches, "all business people become shareholders in some manner."[32]

This vision of shareholder democracy had guided the very birth of the branches themselves. At the official opening of the National Discounting Bank, Director Laurent-Antoine Pagnerre declared trust to be the only source of credit. Although he argued that no revolution should inspire "more legitimate trust" than the one of 1848, instead the struggling republic had found itself battling years of mismanagement by its predecessors. "To overcome the disasters of our past," declared Pagnerre, "to assure the prosperity of our future, we need to turn to the paths of morality, to profoundly modify the very bases of credit. From institutions founded on egotistical interests, for the exclusive profit of a small number of privileged individuals, one must substitute institutions founded on the interests of all and for the profit of all, that is to say, democratic institutions that universalize, that republicanize credit."[33] Pagnerre's vision of republican credit transcended mere democratization of its institutions and called instead for a reform in the meaning and morality of the word "credit" itself.

Credit and Republican Society

"Republicanizing credit" may have been the new state policy on financial matters, yet government officials had hardly invented the idea, nor were they the most systematic advocates of its application. Alongside the expansion of public institutions, a parallel private efflorescence likewise imagined banks as key vehicles for economic democracy. These pamphlets took part in an explosion of periodicals that occurred after the lifting of previous restrictions on freedom of the press. Tackling diverse aspects of French life, ranging from the colonial slave trade to religion and representing a wide variety of political beliefs, these pamphlets complemented the information provided by long-established papers. Discussions of credit featured prominently in this literature. A later writer would describe 1848 as a year when "everybody spoke of Credit."[34] As with the various political visions of the young Second Republic, however, visions of regenerated credit were diverse and sometimes conflicting. In 1848 alone, there were as many projects for banks proposed for *société anonyme* status as had been proposed during the entire eighteen years of the July Monarchy.[35] These institutions were designed for a wide variety of purposes and targeted different clienteles, but generally focused on those sectors that had encountered the most difficulty in accessing the credit market; namely, workers, small commerce, and small rural landowners.[36] These plans, while copious, probably reflected only a fraction of all the attempts devised in the period to change the credit system. Indeed, hundreds of pamphlets were published in 1848 proposing ingenious methods of organizing credit in order both to revive commercial and public credit and, quite frequently, to restructure society on a truly republican basis.[37]

The political and financial goals of these pamphlets were closely intertwined. Writers perceived the precariousness of the previous credit economy as symptomatic of its roots in an unjust social system. Credit, which depended on trust, could not thrive in a society where lenders and borrowers contracted as unequal competitors for their own selfish interests. The Fourierist representative Victor Considerant spoke for many reformers when he asked, "How could that former society reconstitute itself, how could aristocratic credit be reestablished: that credit so fragile, so unstable, that the smallest crisis, the tiniest wind of revolution that blows on the face of the water, topples it like a house of cards; so cowardly and so lifeless that the slightest apprehensions suspend it in its own insecurity, freeze it in its own selfishness?"[38] Credit could certainly not be reestablished in the same way that it had been previously constructed, since this configuration had proved inherently unstable.

Despite the diversity of the goals expressed in the pamphlets of 1848, their critiques of the status quo and their proposals for reform shared certain common elements. First, they generally linked private credit concerns with fundamental questions about the social order itself. The usurer and the miser were not merely private evils, but fundamental to understanding the faulty nature of circulation and exchange in a hierarchical society. At the same time, the credit crisis vividly demonstrated how the gradual development of an industrial economy over the previous decades had inextricably connected the ordering of civil society with that of the financial system. Not only socially unjust, credit was economically inefficient: a veritable house of cards where "the slightest apprehensions suspend it in its own insecurity, freeze it in its own selfishness."[39] Credit as it existed was private and therefore antisocial, independent of human agency and anarchic.[40]

Pamphleteers argued that so long as credit continued to be unequal the political goals of the Revolution would go unfulfilled. While "the equality of political rights exists for all citizens, inequality reigns in the institution of credit," wrote one pamphleteer.[41] Bankers avoided taxes and held no allegiance to the land. Others compared the banking elite to an exclusive gambling club. One author wrote that the government "destroyed the lottery and all public gaming, only to permit the development of a more dangerous form of speculations . . . the Stock Market, the ruin of small capitalists to the profit of the great financers who, after a few years, have all come to disdain actual commercial affairs."[42] Leo Fontarive argued that a financial aristocracy who controlled the stock market, lacking the knightly graces of earlier nobility, ruthlessly exploited "the toil of the people, the fortune of the middle-class and the budget of the State."[43] The financial aristocracy, parasitic and idle, appeared as a logical replacement for the landed aristocracy of the 1789 Revolution.

For some writers, the evolution of a new credit system was not merely a political necessity, it was also a logical inevitability. In his 1848 *Histoire philosophique du crédit*, Victor Avril divided the history of credit into four phases. In the first stage, loans were "backed by the blood, life, flesh of the debtor." Following this came two overlapping epochs dominated by monetary pledges, deposit banks and pawnshops, and then what he termed the current "unhappy era" in which credit was backed by work but paper money and discount banks de facto ruled the country. The promised fourth era would be the "reign of good mortgages" in which the full liberating potential of credit would be realized. Over the course of these four stages, Avril noted, credit became increasingly detached from "capitalist impediments and usurious language" and moved toward the "splendid horizons of mutuality."[44] The arrival of the republican regime meant that the "monarchy of usury" would be abolished once and for all, ushering in a new era of credit. On a more practical level, Louis Langlois argued that the financial crises that had struck all the major financial powers in the past decades were evidence of a disconnection between modern capitalist societies and the laws. Wealth had become increasingly liquid, and as individuals "are free and without patronage, all men are obligated to take upon themselves the risks and perils of contract," but laws regarding property were rooted in a time of "slavery and servitude" when "rights and interests were given only to the few." Reforming the credit system entailed bringing the legal system in line with economic realities and creating a science of private credit just as there was a science of public credit.[45]

Not everyone spoke so glowingly of these efforts to reorganize the financial system. In the eyes of opponents, the dangers posed by the ideological ramifications of these projects far outweighed their supposedly misguided practical consequences, which some likened to those of John Law's bank scheme and the *assignat*.[46] For conservative Charles-Louis-Gaston Audiffret, the provisional government, "partisans of an envious democracy," had "officially declared war on the aristocratic power of capital" by means of credit.[47] In so doing, they undermined the very bases of capital accumulation on which economic recovery rested. Gustave Puynode opined that credit was very beneficial to the poor when correctly lent, but feared overt state involvement.[48] Even those resistant to the state's plans accepted the need for reform. The financier Baron Benjamin Delessert, whose family belonged to Paris's banking elite, conceded that the unjust nature of the current credit system, left unreformed, threatened oligarchic control of the country.[49]

These more conservative voices were not incorrect in their assessment of the radical political agenda of many attempts to reform credit. Indeed, the most vocal supporters of the republicanization of credit in the government certainly aligned themselves with the left. Among these was the Commission du gouvernement pour les travailleurs, popularly known as the Luxembourg Commission, which received direct input from workers themselves. In a report given to the National Assembly on April 26, 1848, Louis Blanc, who cochaired the committee with worker Albert Martin, laid out what the delegates saw as the most pressing problems facing the laboring class and suggested remedies. While the report is generally remembered for its advocacy of the right to work, credit also played an essential part of the committee's analysis of working-class difficulties.

For the Luxembourg Commission, the nature of money itself lay at the heart of the credit problem. Deeming currency merely a representative sign of exchange that possessed no inherent worth as a material object, the commission argued that the greed and self-interest quintessential to the current capitalist system necessitated recourse to metallic form. Here, money could do nothing but act as a kind of pledge between rival interests. When society had reached an elevated state of socialist harmony, however, paper money would be issued by a state bank in a plan that sounded vaguely like that of John Law in the eighteenth century. "A time will doubtlessly come," the commission's report read, "where simple *promises* will be worth at least as much as *realities*." However, "at present, we should make due with the only credit possible, the credit based on *things*, while waiting for the time to come to accord trust in *people*."[50] True credit was to be based on a harmonious social order where trust reigned among all equal citizens. Yet, short of this ideal state of affairs, the commission had few radical answers to the credit problem. They approved of the warrant system and advocated the creation of a bank specifically designed to aid small business, artisans, and workers.

Credit continued to be associated with the left through the Second Republic, even after the June Days had all but destroyed hopes for the right to work. In 1849, for example, the Montagnard faction, under the leadership of Alexandre Ledru-Rollin, maintained that the state should provide credit rather than work.[51] Pierre-Joseph Proudhon famously attempted to establish a working bank of exchange, called Banque du Peuple, early in 1849. Despite attracting some 13,000 adherents, mainly from the working class, the bank's capital remained minimal and the enterprise faltered, much to the glee of political satirists.[52] Other proposals made by Proudhon in the National Assembly with the intention of rectifying what he saw as the unjust relationships between debtors and creditors and paving the way for a mutualist system of credit proved equally unsuccessful. Yet the significance of Proudhon's visions, as well as those of the other thinkers cursorily explored in this section, testify not only to the left's engagement with the reform of the credit system but also to a heightened awareness of the political and social ramifications of financial obligations.

Events Unforeseen

Even as the republicanization of credit evoked the positive potential of monetary relations to transform society, the financial crisis, which had only worsened since February 1848, brought home the decidedly less utopian and more harrowing consequences of financial interconnectedness. Potentially disastrous debt loomed after decades of economic expansion. As one newspaper put it, the dizzying growth of railroads, joint-stock companies, and the stock market in the previous years had meant that "the savings of the *rentier* or the small property owner, the economies of the waged laborers" became connected to larger speculations. "Today commerce has penetrated everywhere," the newspaper declared, and "if we wouldn't go so far to say that everyone is a trader in the full sense of the word, we can at least affirm . . . that everyone has commercial interests."[53] When commerce suffered, the results could send ripple effects throughout the entirety of French society.

Commerce was indeed hard hit in the first few months of the Second Republic. In late March 1848, the Paris Commercial Court estimated that somewhere between 6,000 and 8,000 businessmen in Paris alone had suspended payments with perhaps 4,000 more bankruptcies on the immediate horizon if the situation did not improve.[54] Nationwide, somewhere between 24,000 and 30,000 enterprises could not pay their creditors.[55] Legislators warned that even these dark figures did not fully capture the impact of the looming crisis. Workers employed by distressed companies and shareholders with significant investments in a failing business, for example, could be ruined by a company's demise. "Creditors and debtors," declared one representative, "all are intertwined, everyone is involved in the bankruptcy of his neighbor."[56]

Given this sobering situation, on March 20, 1848, the provisional government decreed a three-month delay for pursuits by creditors on unpaid debts.[57] Drowning out the concerns of the ever-cautious chambers of commerce and commercial courts, letters from pursued and distressed businessmen demanding such a decree flooded in from all over France.[58] Some writers bolstered their requests for delays with an implicit analysis of the political situation at stake. One petition signed by nearly fifty businessmen in the town of Blanc in Indre blamed the difficulties encountered by artisans and small business people in reimbursing their debts to the lack of capital at the small banks on which many such individuals depended. These banks, claimed the businessmen, had fallen victim to capitalists who withdrew their capital out of either fear or calculation.[59] Other writers stressed that the need to pay workers with actual money to stave off riots made the extension of credit for other transactions even more urgent.[60] In underscoring their sympathies to the workers or denouncing the machinations of the elite, the writers hoped to persuade the Assembly of the political soundness, as well as the economic necessity, of delays on repayment.

Even while decreeing these delays, the provisional government recognized that such a measure could be only a temporary palliative for a much deeper problem. The National Assembly put off legislation for several months, as the government struggled with numerous other problems, including its own survival after the closure of the workshops and the ensuing violence in June 1848. In the meantime, the public grappled with how a republican regime should handle defaulted debt. Several petitioners argued that the general collapse of the credit networks had created virtual anarchy in the marketplace. While good-hearted creditors extended delays on engagements, recognizing their debtors' good faith and the hard times, a single obdurate and ruthless creditor who pushed a debtor too hard to get back his own money might provoke other lenders to do likewise. Not only was this harmful to the revival of commerce, but such behavior also reflected a more profound breakdown in the rule of law. Petitioners demanded that the government respond by easing legislation on debtors; as early as April 1848, there were demands to facilitate the creation of *concordats*.[61] Among the more powerful proponents of such measures were the Chamber of Commerce of Le Havre and numerous stockholders of large, troubled firms. For example, the bank of Gouin, Ganneron, and Baudon in Saint-Germain-en-Laye, one of the largest of these, asked that those businesses whose distress was provoked by the Revolution be allowed to liquidate company assets while remaining exempt from normal bankruptcy penalties.[62]

Many of the petitioners linked the need for government action to republican goals. In various letters to the National Assembly, writers juxtaposed republican promises with the realities of debt. Businessmen like Emmemond Blanc, who owned a hauling company, stressed the suffering that would be inflicted on workers if businesses were forced into the costly and time-consuming process of bankruptcy. The republican government professed to care about the plight of the working class. Yet, if employers went bankrupt, Blanc prophesied, "unemployment will be long, damaging for public order, and perhaps for the Republic."[63] Hailing the new regime's expansion of the franchise to all men regardless of property, pamphleteers pointed out that men whose businesses failed owing to the Revolution remained as powerless as they would have been before the Revolution.[64] Writers often depicted banks, discounters, and other third-party bill holders as powerful and sinister forces who conspired to threaten the debtor with bankruptcy.[65] Through debt, wealth under the young republic amassed in increasingly few hands.

Such concerns weighed increasingly heavily on the minds of legislators. When the new Assembly was elected in May, its constituency was far more conservative and protective of property rights than the provisional government had been. Only a minority of around one hundred delegates could be considered committed republicans or socialists. On June 21, 1848, the Assembly's conservative majority voted to abolish the system of national workshops, which they perceived as wasteful and ineffective in alleviating unemployment. Thousands of workers, suddenly thrown off government support, joined by radical agitators, took to the streets during the June Days. The three-day uprising was brutally crushed by General Cavaignac, invested by the Assembly with dictatorial powers. More than a thousand combatants died, and thousands more were deported.

In this atmosphere, the ongoing debates concerning private debt took on substantial political ramifications. The June Days heightened the deep divisions between moderates, who wished only to protect and possibly enlarge political participation, and more radical members of the Assembly, who sympathized with the workers and believed that the government should intervene in private affairs to create economic justice. Both sides utilized the lingering threat of wide-scale unemployment and worker unrest to justify the need for their policies. As Victor Considerant put it, reformers marched at the head of a "great battalion of debtors" to meet the equally "great battalion" of creditors resistant to any change in the bankruptcy code. The overriding question, according to Considerant, was not to count the heads of each army but "know whose interests are the weightiest, the most important, the most sacred."[66] The tragedy of the June Days for the small shopkeepers was all about debt. Marx and Engels famously observed in *Class Struggles in France* that while these men had rushed to the aid of the government against the workers, fighting "for the salvation of property and the restoration of credit," they were in for a rude awakening at the end of the battles. Marx and Engels memorably described the aftermath of the fight: when "the barricades were thrown down and the workers were crushed and the shopkeepers, drunk with victory, rushed back to their shops, they found the entrance barred by a savior of property, an official agent of credit, who presented them with threatening notices: Overdue promissory note! Overdue house rent! Overdue bond! Doomed shop! Doomed shopkeeper!"[67] Particularly because of their important role in the June Days, these small merchants refused to allow creditors to seize their property without a fight. In the first few days of July 1848, over a thousand small traders and independent craftsmen gathered in the Stock Exchange and demanded that all businessmen who could trace their difficulties to the Revolution be allowed a delay on payments and exemption from bankruptcy penalties.

Within the space of a month, the legislators Jules Favre and Jacques-François Dupont independently proposed two different bills aimed at creating forced friendly arrangements (*concordats à l'aimable*). Jules Favre, a moderate left deputy from a merchant family in Lyon, proposed the granting of a *concordat* to any debtor who obtained two-thirds of his creditors on three-fourths of his outstanding debt.[68] This private settlement, accredited by the commercial court, bypassed many of the most deleterious aspects of bankruptcy for the debtor—including the delays and registration fees as well as the sequestration of his property. The debtor could formally arrange with his creditors while avoiding even a temporary loss of management. The more left wing Dupont, whose views on commercial failure were undoubtedly shaped by his experiences handling financial disputes for the banker Jacques Laffitte, proposed that a debtor should have his case reviewed by a council of five individuals, including both commercial judges and his creditors.[69] If the council ruled in favor, the debtor would be allowed an official liquidation, similar to Favre's proposal, overseen by a commercial court official. Favre and Dupont both sought to create an official path for arrangements that had previously been granted legitimacy only if ratified by all creditors.

Dupont, Favre, and their supporters believed the need for such regularization to be undeniable. They calculated that if all the suspensions of payments among businesses became actual bankruptcies in the following months, courts would be swamped with cases. In Paris alone, twenty-five commercial judges would be expected to oversee 6,000 or 7,000 bankruptcies.[70] Additionally, creditors would lose millions of francs in registration fees, which averaged over 1,000 francs per bankruptcy.[71] Merchandise, liquidated in auctions, would lose up to half its value. Dividends would be reduced by as much as two-thirds. The value of the bankrupts' landed property, much of which was mortgaged, would depreciate.[72] Most seriously, for Dupont and Favre, the prolonged arbitration process could entail massive unemployment among the laboring classes, inviting the danger of a reprise of the June Days.

Indeed, the fate of workers was a top priority for men like Favre and Dupont who deemed bankruptcy as damaging for the working class as for the merchants. Earlier reform efforts more specifically focused on improving the lot of workers in bankruptcies had met with little success. In July 1848, three leftist deputies, Louis Marius Astouin, Gustave Laboulie, and Démosthène Ollivier, had proposed new legislation that not only increased the amount of wages owed to workers in case of a bankruptcy but also moved employees to first in line among privileged creditors.[73] While Astouin, Laboulie, and Ollivier's bill failed, similar sentiments underlay the proposals to reform the *concordats*.

Careful to appeal to as broad an audience as possible, Dupont and Favre largely stayed away from the rhetoric of Astouin, Laboulie, and Ollivier's proposal and instead argued that their projects merely formalized what had become a ubiquitous and socially accepted reality over the previous months. Yet their fundamental claim was at its heart far more radical: the February Revolution, they argued, had inaugurated an unparalleled period of crisis in which responsibilities toward obligations could no longer be fulfilled as they had been before the Revolution. In the words of one pamphlet:

> Specie escapes and deserts its social function—transactions no long have an agent—the sign of exchange disappears—one no longer gets money from taking out a first lien.
>
> The discounting branches collapse one after the other—one no longer negotiates a bill even as a favor or as an exception.
>
> The French Treasury finds itself reduced to the necessity of suspending its payments and of demanding a forced conversion, in order to liberate itself from its creditors.
>
> The Bank of France, our first-order financial establishment, finds itself reduced to the necessity of invoking its power, force, in order to dispense with honoring its signature, of reimbursing the bills it has created, payable on sight.
>
> And one seriously demands whether *force majeure* has penetrated the commercial order![74]

As we have explored, the term *force majeure* had appeared before in discussions of bankruptcy and the intention to fail.[75] *Force majeure* explained how a perfectly competent and honorable business could go bankrupt. In 1848, however, *force majeure* was applied to the entirety of French society. After the February Revolution, the state had declared *force majeure* on its own contracts. Logically, proponents asked, "Is it not just to accord to all industry the simplest means of liquidation?"[76]

The bill's critics denied the applicability of *force majeure* to individual bankruptcy. To them, the state's position could not be compared to that of a private borrower. France, that "debtor who never dies, who cannot die," could not be allowed to go bankrupt, for this "would be odious, it would be a mortal blow to the Republic."[77] Only creditors themselves, however, could choose to forgive the obligations of their debtors. Some insisted that creditors themselves already recognized *force majeure* and had not pursued their debtors to bankruptcy.[78] Others saw revolutionary *force majeure* as a critical element of the risk undertaken in any capitalist venture.[79] A speculation always relied on aspects of the future that could not be predicted. Just as the speculator alone reaped the profits of his luck, so he alone must shoulder the losses when fortune did not smile in his favor.[80]

No opponent of the Favre and Dupont bills proved so forceful as Pierre-Claude Bravard-Veyrières, a highly respected commercial law professor at the University of Paris. Since his election to the Assembly as a representative for Puy-du-Dôme, Bravard-Veyrières had defended some of the most conservative causes put before the body with a legal acumen envied by many of his peers.[81] In the case of the forced friendly agreements, Bravard-Veyrières argued that laws could not be made for exceptional circumstances, and that to do so would permanently damage France's credit abroad. Such reforms, he insinuated, continued the war on industry perpetrated by the June riots in the name of "what is pompously called the right to work."[82] He denied that failure to meet obligations was the direct or inevitable consequence of the Revolution. Of the approximately 24,000 registered businessmen in Paris, he noted, less than a third had suspended payments. Bravard-Veyrières warned of embracing the perceived weakness of the American model of bankruptcy law and lauded his country's tradition of self-sacrifice in the face of potential dishonor. The rigor of bankruptcy must be preserved in order to avoid "a plague that ruins everyone from the capitalist to the laborer." Indeed, for Bravard-Veyrières, the Dupont and Favre bills symbolized the dangerous excesses of democracy.

The Bank of France aligned itself with Bravard-Veyrières and the opponents of the friendly forced agreements. Governor Antoine Maurice Apollinaire D'Argout noted while 543 bankruptcies had been declared in the first five months of 1847, only 280 had taken place in the first five months of 1848.[83] He furthermore suggested that most of these bankruptcies in fact began long before the Revolution and warned that the pathetic situation of a few honest men should not be allowed to override the products of experience.[84] The Bank of France officials denied the utility of forced friendly agreements. While hardly helpful to debtors, such measures would kill credit by compelling lenders to refrain from lending or to raise their rates.[85] Investors would subsequently rush to place their funds abroad, and the bank itself would be forced to profoundly change its relatively generous discounting policy.[86] Instead, D'Argout insisted that generosity should be left to private initiative. At the helm of the bank, he insisted that such forgiveness was already underway: although the bank's vaults held over 64 million francs' worth of unpaid commercial effects, it had not pressed a single debtor into bankruptcy since February 1848.[87]

Although Dupont and Favre portrayed the Bank of France as serving a greedy cabal of wealthy capitalists indifferent to the plight of small commerce, D'Argout's skepticism seems to have been broadly shared in the business community.[88] The Chamber of Commerce of Paris provided seven reasons for their opposition to the legislation, including that it "substituted hidden bankruptcy for public bankruptcy" and that the "truly cruel and humiliating necessity" that bankruptcy posed for the merchant should not obscure the fact that most of those who filed for bankruptcy deserved to undergo such humiliation.[89] Armand Pinard and Hippolyte Biesta, speaking for the administration of the National Discounting Bank, not only reiterated the doubts expressed by bank officials but worried that Favre's and Dupont's projects undermined the meaning of bankruptcy itself. They stressed the importance of honor, for both bankrupts and their families, and feared that the new legislation would fatally undermine it.[90]

The business press, applauding Pinard and Biesta's intervention, professed shock and revulsion that "these two lawyers [Favre and Dupont], complete strangers to the science of commercial affairs," found fit to meddle in such matters.[91] The chambers of commerce, consulted about the proposal in June 1848, were almost unanimously hostile.[92] The Reims Chamber of Commerce declared that the bills entailed "nothing more than that the government destroy credit and favor fraud."[93] Calling the "multiplicity of guarantees" the most "active and powerful stimulant of credit," the chamber of commerce argued that the moderate interest rates preceding the Revolution had been secured by the pillars of stringent bankruptcy law and debt imprisonment.[94] Now that debt imprisonment had been abolished, Dupont and Favre proposed to remove most of creditors' remaining guarantees: publicity, surveillance, and the verification of creditors. Indeed, several chambers of commerce urged the Assembly not just to reject Dupont's and Favre's projects but to reinstate *contrainte par corps* as well. Members of the chamber of commerce in Saint Quentin demanded immediate reestablishment of *contrainte par corps* and rejection of Favre's and Dupont's bills on *concordats à l'aimable*.[95] The commercial courts were no more favorable. François Jules Devinck, speaking as president of the Paris Commercial Court, agreed that some bankrupts deserved special treatment in terms of their legal incapacities but denied that any of the procedures should be changed to accommodate them and insisted that it was always "necessary to doubt new legislation."[96]

The debates on the forced arrangements dragged on for thirty-one sessions of the National Assembly.[97] In the course of these proceedings, one newspaper commented, this "great social question" devolved into a "dispute among businessmen" based on their "personal positions."[98] By the time a bill emerged in late August 1848 it was of an entirely different nature than the original proposals. After the subcommittees thoroughly criticized the original bills and the Assembly rejected them by a vote of 428 to 338, reformers scrambled to find alternatives more palatable to conservatives. These included one drafted by the Committee on Commerce and Industry, which had come to agree that "the shock that the February revolution has wreaked on commercial affairs has been too violent and its results too terrible that the case of *force majeure* should not be manifest to all eyes."[99]

The bill that emerged from this drawn-out process essentially negated everything for which the small businessmen had picketed in early July 1848. Rather than allowing debtors to continue at the head of their business operations if they obtained the consent of a majority of their creditors, the new legislation granted something called *liquidation judiciaire*. Under this process, commercial courts could allow a debtor, provided he obtained the agreement of the majority of his creditors, to avoid the label of bankrupt and many of the attendant losses of civil and political rights. It merely mandated that those suspensions of payment that had occurred since February 24 would not be called bankruptcies unless the *concordats* were not accredited or if the commercial court did not choose to free the debtor from the title of bankrupt. It also provided a process of liquidation that allowed a debtor to dispense with an inventory and seals if he could obtain adherence from at least three-fourths of his creditors. The debtor kept the administration of his estate and liquidated his assets under the surveillance of a judge.[100]

Supporters of the new legislation argued that the state could rightfully interfere only in matters of public law, determining who was allowed to participate in the political sphere, and should leave private law, including the relations of private creditors and debtors, to the courts and to private conscience.[101] *Force majeure* was not ultimately considered a good enough reason to let debtors out of their property relations to creditors. It was, however, sufficient to alleviate, at least with the proper approval, the shame that such failure normally entailed.[102] The head of the legislative committee, André Dupin, proclaimed triumphantly that the republic had heeded the calls of those "debtors who are unfortunate but in good faith" by "saving you from bankruptcy, preserving you from the incapacities attached to this title, you can continue to be jurors, officers of the national guard, continue to be representatives, continue lastly to enjoy all political rights." However, he added, "Let your creditors enjoy their civil rights!"[103] Members of the National Assembly applauded the speech loudly.

As the debate about *concordats à l'aimable* stretched on, legislators also reconsidered the fate of *contrainte par corps*. The provisional government's abolition of debtors' prison in March 1848 had awaited an official vote by the National Assembly. Before such a vote could be taken, however, the government itself had gradually mitigated the effects of the sweeping decree. On March 23, 1848, two weeks after the abolition, Minister of Justice Adolphe Crémieux declared that debts for criminal fines or expenses or for stellionates were necessarily fraudulent and therefore still entailed arrest.[104] A month later, the Executive Power Committee invoked *contrainte par corps* to punish unpaid customs, fishing and poaching fines, as well as some forms of taxes, arguing that those who committed such acts were frequently insolvent and could not be penalized at all without imprisonment.[105]

Business interests quickly reacted against what they saw as the government's hypocrisy. In Caen, wholesale dealers maintained that they needed *contrainte par corps* to restrain the bad faith of the small retailers. If debt imprisonment was to be permanently abolished, they asked for new laws granting permission to seize all a debtor's goods, including the dotal properties of his wife.[106] Other petitioners demanded that *contrainte par corps* be reestablished to punish powerful individuals. In November 1848 a businessman from Martin-et-Vignes wrote to the National Assembly that reinstating *contrainte par corps* would "put in prison all those railroad stock speculators who have decimated, by their infamous brand of commerce, an infinite number of small *rentiers*."[107] The Chamber of Commerce of Clermont-Ferrand claimed that the March 9 decree had already paralyzed numerous transactions in the town and that further delay in repealing it could render this damage permanent.[108] The chambers of commerce of Lille, Toulouse, Orleans, Reims, and Bastia issued similar demands.[109]

The notes on *contrainte par corps* drafted by the Bank of France's General Council demonstrate how important debt imprisonment was considered even at the very highest level of finance. The bank's General Council declared that the errors of the 1793 abolition could not be repeated.[110] Voting unanimously in favor of reinstatement, the council members listed admitted past abuses in the application of the laws but nevertheless held that the great majority of debt prisoners were dishonest businessmen, ready even to brave criminal pursuits if they existed, in order to exploit the trust of upstanding traders and merchants.[111] Although rarely used, the council members considered it a more effective guarantee than the confiscation of a debtor's goods.[112] While some on the council called for immediate reinstatement of the 1832 legislation, others favored slight improvements in the debtors' conditions.[113]

On August 12, 1848, Jean Labordère, a conservative deputy from the Somme, proposed the repeal of the March 9 decree on debt imprisonment.[114] Four days later, Hippolyte-Baudel Durand, a moderate representing the Seine-et-Oise and the head of a five-person legislative committee, supported Labordère's proposal. In September 1848, the National Assembly voted to reinstate *contrainte par corps* by a vote of 456 out of 693.[115] Few of the modifications proposed by opponents of *contrainte par corps* to alleviate the rigors of the law were adopted when a final bill was passed some months later. Indeed, the final version of *contrainte par corps* passed by the National Assembly on December 14, 1848, expanded the scope of the law by extending debt imprisonment to other government officers.

Conclusion

During the session of November 7, 1849, Bravard-Veyrières declared the official end of the law on *liquidation judiciaire* that he had disliked from its inception. Annoyed by what he described as the abuse of the law's generosity by debtors still claiming that their troubles had begun in the early months of 1848, the law professor asked that no more merchants be allowed to file for protection. He briefly reflected on the law's history. Although he admitted that it had been "beneficial in a certain number of situations worthy of interest," he asked whether it was "equally useful to the great majority of business people." He doubted this.[116] Bravard-Veyrières's suggestion was heeded without much discussion from the Assembly.[117] The resulting decree provided businessmen with only three days from the date of its application to say that they had actually ceased payments between February and August 1848.

By November 1849, even some of its initial supporters had become disillusioned with *liquidation judiciaire*. It seemed to them to have disproportionately benefited big business and finance to the detriment of smaller enterprises. While assessing the empirical reality of this claim is problematic, it does appear that the commercial courts may have been hesitant to allow small debtors out of the penalties attached to *faillis*, something that they accorded far more willingly to larger enterprises. Of the 860 *liquidations judiciaries* appearing on register with the Archives de Paris as being accredited by the Paris commercial tribunal from August 22, 1848, through November 12, 1849, the tribunal chose to free only 265 from the qualification and penalties accorded to a *faillite* at the time of the accreditation. Of the eighteen companies who reported assets above 1 million francs, a full fourteen of them were released from the title of bankruptcy. At the other end of the spectrum, among of the thirty-four businesses with assets reported at less than 5,000 francs, only one was granted freedom from the qualification and penalties of bankruptcy. This pattern seems to be consistent across the board: of the 115 *faillites* on the lower end of the spectrum, with assets less than 10,000 francs, only 16 were freed from the qualification of *faillite*.[118] "The honor of a small merchant!" remarked one newspaper concerning this

TABLE 6. *Liquidations judiciaires* in Paris, 1848–49

TOTAL ASSETS (FRANCS)	TOTAL NUMBER OF LIQUIDATIONS	NUMBER GRANTED REPRIEVE FROM BANKRUPTCY STIGMA (*AFFRANCHISEMENT*)
<5,000	31	1
5,000–9,999	84	16
10,000–19,999	121	24
20,000–29,999	107	30
30,000–39,999	70	22
40,000–49,999	60	14
50,000–99,999	137	44
100,000–249,999	118	56
250,000–499,999	52	20
500,000–99,9999	33	20
1 million +	18	14

Source: AP D13 U3 1, *Liquidations judiciaires*, 1848–49.

phenomenon, "What's that? But the honor of a big banker, that is something else altogether, my God."[119] It was a bitter, if predictable, irony, the newspaper continued, that under the former monarchy, every bankrupt lost his rights no matter his social class or previous standing, yet under a democracy touting universal manhood suffrage and egalitarian ideals, bankers and big businessmen escaped the consequences of speculation in stocks and bonds while the poor trader remained hounded by his failure.[120] By the time Bravard-Veyrières called for an end to the August 22 decree, *liquidation judiciaire* had outlived its initial popularity and cast a shadow on subsequent Second Republic discussions of bankruptcy reform.[121]

From the onset of the Revolution, the problem of credit was integrally linked to the creation of a new republican social order. The right and the left, the working class and the banking elite alike tried to reinstate faith in the financial system, although in a variety of ways and for a variety of ends. Talk of republicanizing credit transcended ideological boundaries, manifesting a broad consensus on the use of government power to stave off complete financial collapse. Yet beyond such generally shared conceptions, opinions and plans differed enormously. Some proposed not only creating new institutions of credit but making credit the heart of a new conception of society in which citizens would associate on a more egalitarian basis. More conservative elements worried that such change would entail too much disruption of the legal order on which commercial credit had always depended. The tentative abolition of *contrainte par corps* and the debates over the forced friendly agreements demonstrated the importance of credit not only as the basis of personal reputation and individual collateral but as a collective and social good that should be accessible to all. As dreams of social democracy in the Second Republic increasingly ceded to pressure from reactionaries, such a vision of credit, and the laws based on it, faded.

Liquidation judiciaire, which grew out of leftist notions of reorganizing credit, seems to have overwhelmingly benefited large merchants. Yet despite its failings or even because of them, the *liquidation judiciaire* was indeed revolutionary. Bankruptcy from the Commercial Code of 1807 through 1848 was deeply tied to the "person" of the debtor, a person understood as a physical, moral, and social entity. Notions of disgrace and criminality were attached even to perfectly innocent bankrupts. In 1848 private credit became a matter of urgent political attention and explicitly linked to public credit. Credit not only symbolized the tyranny of the old order, but also promised a way of reorganizing society on a just basis. Pushed by small shopkeepers and artisans fearful of losing their economic independence through bankruptcy, reformers proposed "forced friendly arrangements" to reshape the relationship between contractual obligation and political economy. Ironically, these ideas, which began on the left, gave birth to the *liquidation judiciaire*, which separated the person from the failure but preserved the creditors' rights to property. Yet in so doing they created a notion of business failure in which the process of debt collection was separated from the dishonoring of the debtor. Although the ameliorations ultimately implemented in the *liquidation judiciaire* were of most immediate benefit to the elite, they reflected a new, more abstract understanding of the personal as it related to commercial practices.

Pamphleteers, once so exuberant in their proposals for republicanized credit, bemoaned the failure of credit to reform the social order. In one 1850 pamphlet, *Guerre au crédit ou Considerations sur les dangers de l'emprunt*, a self-identified banker declared that "credit and public credit are such dangerous expressions that they should be banished from all commercial dictionaries as well as the language of economists; not only as dangerous but also as false."[122] By focusing on the cultivation of private credit, individuals were actively distracted from the cultivation of public credit: men and states alike became so consumed with future calculations and with the borrowing necessary to ensure these speculations that they ultimately narrowed their ability to act in the future by becoming overly entangled with debt.

While resonating with long-standing critiques of mobile property, the author's criticism also revealed a bitter disillusionment with the promises of the Second Republic. Ultimately, declared the banker, credit was incompatible with the ideals of republican citizenship: "To a nation engaged in the ways of credit, you do not speak of progress toward the future, of bettering the lot of the poor, of a more just distribution of social burdens. She only has eyes and ears for her book of due dates, and from the head of the government to the last small shopkeeper, the only preoccupation is to know whether one is able to—tomorrow, the day after tomorrow, forever—honor his signature. Oh, the bold citizens this forms!"[123] Indeed, while the idealism surrounding credit largely faded by the end of the Second Republic, many of the institutions founded by the revolutionaries took on new life under the man who ended the republic, Emperor Napoleon III. Sometimes called "Saint-Simon on horseback," the new emperor surrounded himself with men who put the institutions of 1848 to the service of financial modernization.

Epilogue

In the fourth volume of his exhaustive *Grande dictionnaire universel du 19e siècle,* Pierre Larousse provided a definition for the phrase *contrainte par corps.* After delving into its long history from Roman law through contemporary legislation, Larousse ended the entry on philosophical lines: "What is liberty? Is it among the objects that enter into commerce? Is it weighed in gold, and, if so, how much gold is it worth? In order to enforce its laws, society can seize the very bodies of its citizens . . . but can society divest itself of this high prerogative and give it instead to the first individual who shows up [*le premier venu*]?"[1] For Larousse, the time had come when the answer to this last question was a definitive "no." The volume in which the definition of *contrainte par corps* appeared was published in 1869, two years after Napoleon III's Corps Législatif had voted to abolish debtors' prison for the third time. While its recent history could have given Larousse pause in hastily writing an obituary, for him, the end of *contrainte par corps* was just, timely, and in a fashion preordained, an inevitable victory for the government over the forces of both commerce and of private arbitrary law.

Having posed his question about the meaning of liberty, Larousse affirmed that under a modern state, debt imprisonment became a kind of embodied contradiction. It constituted a kind of "preventative alienation of human liberty by the sole fact of a pecuniary obligation"; it formed thus "a constraint and rigor that is personal, arbitrary, discretionary, from one man to another man without the intervention of public authority: in short, a double violation of the social contract and of the essential right whereby is constituted the human personality."[2] The entry on *contrainte par corps* ended by opining that in a people "close to barbarity" such abuses of liberty were justifiable. In this state, "general principles of public law" remained primitive and the needs of commerce could be "pressing." However, Larousse continued, "today, public authority, jealous of its high prerogative, is highly developed." Since the state provided adequate protection for the needs of commerce through laws and institutions, it could no longer tolerate the direct violation of its monopoly of power over its citizens' bodies embodied in the debtors' prison.

Larousse's celebration of the simultaneous victory of liberty and of the state monopoly over incarceration was widely shared among contemporary observers. As one like-minded writer put it, in abolishing debt imprisonment France rid itself of "yet another remnant of the old belief that the State should put its shield and its sword at the service of private interests."[3] With the abolition of debtors' prison, creditors lost their power over the borrower's body. In place of this privilege, legislators and writers insisted, lenders would have to rely on careful assessments of the debtor's character and resources and on the increasing capacity of institutions, from banks to credit unions, to manage the risk of loans. "It is to the exterior situation that one lends," declared one legislator, "to a borrower's good name, to his intelligence, to his morality, to his hard work, to his credit: in a word, one lends *to* the person and not *on* the person."[4]

The year 1867 marked a crossroads in the deconstruction of a certain idea of legal personhood and of the idea of commerce linked to this conception. It was a crossroads long in the making. This book has explored the logic of the person as it related to notions of commerce, honor, and punishment in the post-Revolutionary period. It has followed how this vision was transformed in the aftermath of the Revolution of 1789. The endurance of this third and final abolition, as opposed to the earlier abortive attempts, must be attributed in part to the impressive growth of alternative mechanisms and institutions for handling the risks of debt. In contrast to the abolition of debt imprisonment in 1793 and 1848, the commercial community did not erupt in outcry against the new legislation nor did the Bank of France personally intervene to reestablish a law it deemed necessary to commerce. Not only did the Revolution of 1848 create a new network of financial institutions, it also popularized the idea of credit as both an economic necessity and a human right. Under Napoleon III, France witnessed a rapid and intense increase in the pace of economic development, including a profound reconstruction of the credit system.[5] By the end of the Second Empire, when debt imprisonment was abolished, France was still largely agricultural and its industrial base comparatively small-scale, but it was a very different country from the one in which debt imprisonment had been reinstated in 1797 or even in 1848.

Earlier that July, Napoleon III's Corps Législatif had passed critical legislation relaxing government authorization on the creation of joint-stock companies.[6] In moving to abolish *contrainte par corps*, government officials acted on a vision of France's future dominated by such developments. For those in power at least, a new vision of legal personhood, abstract and not corporally liable for debts, was clearly ascendant. Minister of Justice Eugène

FIGURE 10. Response to the abolition of debtors' prison from Daumier in *Le Charivari*. "A Usurer's Office: 'No, young man, I will discount nothing for a 'fils de famille'—the bill of exchange is nothing more now than a dead letter. To be reimbursed I could only content myself with your word of honor and that doesn't satisfy me at all." (Robert D. Farber University Archives & Special Collections, Brandeis University)

Rouher, connecting the abolition of *contrainte par corps* with the proliferation of limited-liability firms, declared that "all big, powerful commerce operates with the aid of joint-stock companies, with limited liability, and all the men who, under this form, perform commercial acts cannot be imprisoned for debts, while the unfortunate shopkeeper will be detained when he doesn't fulfill his engagements."[7] Two decades later, in 1888, a process of *liquidation judiciaire*, similar in some respects to the bankruptcy discharge proposals of 1848, enabled businessmen to liquidate their assets without bankruptcy.[8] Nor were such innovations confined to France. By 1900 debt imprisonment had been abolished or profoundly modified in the majority of European states, with France ending imprisonment for private debts in 1867, followed by Belgium (1868), Austria and the Northern German Confederation (1869), England (1869), Italy (1877), and Sweden (1879).[9] Moreover, across the industrialized world, modifications of bankruptcy law facilitated the liquidation process and reduced the penalties for failure.

Rather than perceiving in the new vision of commercial personhood emerging in the nineteenth century only a sanguine reassessment of the possibilities of risk, it is more useful to think of it as creating a bifurcated system. Certain types of risks, largely those incurred by large businesses, were justified and even encouraged by the broadened and more abstract meaning of commercial entities. Other risks, largely those taken by smaller merchants, subjected their takers to oversight and discipline. Whereas imprisonment had formerly served multiple purposes—including humiliation, detainment, security, and leverage, as well as punishment—distinctions were now drawn between securing debts and punishing debtors. The prison became seen as a mechanism for discipline rather than shame. Yet even in 1867, many merchants still believed the prison to be such a multifaceted place. The lowest levels of the urban trades and the newly formed *chambres syndicales* of small, independent artisans strongly disagreed with the government's dismissal of *contrainte par corps* as a remnant of the past. For these men and women, who comprised most of the incarcerated and most of the incarcerators, debt imprisonment provided not only a means of ensuring their loans against malfeasance but also an access to credit, as several tradesmen proclaimed to the legislatives commissions in 1867.

We often think of the rise of capitalism as encouraging new possibilities and new kinds of risks. Yet in 1867, certain possibilities previously enabled by the prison were occluded. For both supporters and opponents of debt imprisonment, the prison emerged as an institution entirely dedicated to

FIGURE 11. "Marius, Garde du Commerce," Cham. A commercial guard grieves. (Author's collection)

punishment. The 1867 debate was fought, this time almost solely, in the language of crime and punishment. In arguing against abolition, legislators in 1867, reaffirming their arguments of the past seventy years, stressed the exceptional nature of commerce and reconciled its anomalous legal standing with the notion of the public good. "For the priest, for the soldier, for the *commerçant*, it's the same law," argued one legislator, explaining that each of these groups, while serving a public purpose, needed to be held to a higher legal standard than an ordinary citizen.[10] Yet while stressing the exceptional nature of commercial law, they framed this exceptionality in the discourse of crime and punishment. Even if a commercial debtor committed no actual infraction in his failure to fulfill his engagement, they argued, nonpayment constituted a kind of quasi infraction, given that "an individual, who at the very least through imprudence, has exposed his creditor to all the inconveniences, all the misfortunes, and all the losses that can follow the refusal to execute a commercial engagement."[11] By 1867, even those who supported *contrainte par corps* saw in the debtors' prison, whether

TABLE 7. Incarcerated debtors in France, 1824–33 and 1857–66

YEAR	DEBTORS
1824	2,734
1825	2,621
1826	2,513
1827	2,858
1828	3,128
1829	3,265
1831	2,829
1832	2,004
1833	1,961
1857	1,975
1858	2,131
1859	2,081
1860	1,947
1861	1,701
1862	1,794
1863	N/A
1864	1,676
1865	1,482
1866	1,510

Sources: Bayle-Mouillard, *De l'emprisonnement pour dettes* (1824–33); and *Compte général* (1857–66).
Note: Bayle-Mouillard's figures, which were calculated by subtracting the number of prisoners for whom the state did not supply food from the total number of prison inmates, include all "debtors to private individuals." The *Compte général* included all debtors "for civil, commercial, and public belonging debts." Commercial debtors undoubtedly composed the largest number of debtors in both the earlier and later periods.

consciously or not, a punitive institution. The question was whether it was the best way to correct.

Abolitionists still believed that the prison had a large role to pay in maintaining commercial honor and securing property rights. The government, in promoting the abolition of *contrainte par corps* for commercial debts, adamantly upheld its necessity for debts resulting from unpaid fines and as compensation in situations such as fishing, poaching, and customs violations. Bayle-Mouillard, now in the role of Napoleon III's state councillor, argued that abolition should not apply to the "citizen debtor," a man or woman who had merely fallen behind in his payments to a private creditor, but only to the debtor whose unwillingness to pay rendered him or her a "rebel against the order of the law."[12] Using language that harkened back to the restoration of debt imprisonment in 1797, Bayle-Mouillard changed the logic of the message. While Revolutionary legislators had argued that failing to pay private debts rendered one a bad citizen who broke contracts to others, Bayle-Mouillard insisted that these debts had no bearing on citizenship status, which would be determined by relationship with the state alone. The ability to incarcerate, moreover, should be a tool in the hands of the state, not in the hands of private individuals.[13]

Can we then look at 1867 then as a point of rupture, as a year signifying the end of an old order and the beginning of a new regime? This book has cautioned against treating the persistence of debt imprisonment or the punitive nature of bankruptcy in the early nineteenth century as atavistic remnants of some vaguely understood "moral economy" fated to destruction before the onset of capitalism. The continual reworking of bankruptcy and debt imprisonment during this period testifies to their dynamism and adaptability. They formed, on one hand, an integral part of a highly complex fabric of legal mechanisms and customary usages that ordinary people utilized for ends that were both social and financial. On the other hand, they constituted an important part of the imaginary presented by "market culture"—the laws on debt, as they emerged from the Revolution, upheld a certain ideal of the market actor as an independent, solitary figure who was guided by rational self-interest but only to the extent that he would pursue virtuous means in achieving these ends.[14] Yet lurking behind this ideal of contractual individualism was the resort to coercion, manifested by debt imprisonment, as well as the realities of social inequalities and emotional considerations. As this book has shown, in the decades following the Revolution this vision became complicated by the very nature of economic practice itself. Ultimately, 1867 can be seen as part of a gradual reworking of the law that understood personhood in a new, more abstract way. The abolition of debt imprisonment, combined with changes to bankruptcy law and the authorization of joint-stock companies, engendered a world where, as Nadine Levratto has put it, the "enterprise could be detached from the entrepreneur."[15]

The story of commercial debt and personhood in the French context suggests profound developments in notions of agency that transcend ostensibly separate political and economic changes of the period. The French Revolution of 1789 had justified the possession or acquisition of wealth and property by means of merit and labor. The tiny minority of voters was selected on the basis of their possession of property. In the democratic order, fortune bestowed on a person not only social value but also, after a fashion, moral worth. However, it had long been widely recognized that the nature of commercial activity made commercial property subject to forces beyond individual control. For this reason, legislation in France and throughout the West had treated merchants differently when it came to debts. Yet all the same, bankruptcy and debt imprisonment highlighted the shaky underpinnings of the supposedly stable association between fortune and social and moral value. The nightmares of financial ruin that loomed large for any merchant or trader grew out of the fact that, through mere accident, one could lose all that had given him or her standing in the community.

Debtors were treated to harrowing consequences for their failure to reimburse not because they had necessarily done anything wrong but because the act of failure was considered shameful in and of itself and their person had been bound up with this act. Yet many of these individuals appeared to be "punished" for acts they had not intended, a reality that profoundly contradicted the ideals of the Revolution inscribed into the Napoleonic codes. Some observers sought to justify the lot of debtors by blaming them for their failure, turning to the language of punishment to explain the results of fortune. Bankruptcy and debt imprisonment were often attributed to unsuccessful attempts at social climbing wherein borrowers sought easy social mobility by undertaking foolhardy risks with other people's money. Other commentators took an even darker view, finding in both the debtors' prison and bankruptcy a convenient means to hide assets and thus augment a fortune. Others recognized that the Revolution and emergent capitalism had created circumstances in which basically all could find themselves insolvent debtors, yet not all were subjected to the law. It follows then that bankruptcy and debt imprisonment became pivotal to depictions of the emergent capitalist economy as inherently criminal and unjust.

The anxieties about debt imprisonment and bankruptcy in the post-Revolutionary era derived from the solidification of borders between property rights and penal law and between the realm of the economy and the realm of state more generally. In pre-Revolutionary law, notions of discredit and notions of crime, commonly seen in relation to their effect on the social order as a whole, had been closely intertwined. Before the rise of modern penal ideologies that severed the formerly indissoluble link between disgraceful activities and criminal activities, institutions that today seem punitive were in fact much more multifaceted places that not only curtailed some possibilities for their actors but also enabled others. With concepts of honor granted little public role in the new regime, writers increasingly framed risk in purely economic terms or in purely criminal ones, with less tolerance for the gray area in between.

The new regime of risk that solidified around commercial debt by the mid-nineteenth century created two different risk regimes. On one hand, the types of risk undertaken by large firms pooling the capital of multiple investors were given more security by the detachment of debt from the physical and moral person of the borrower. With collateral instead based on the property of fictitious and abstract entities, trust in these new institutions was encouraged. Meanwhile, for small borrowers at the other end of the spectrum, the demise of a commercial debt regime backed by concrete personhood was at best a mixed blessing. Over the course of the previous decades, reformers had critiqued the access to the credit market enabled by the economy of concrete personhood, which they saw as encouraging dangerous speculation by individuals—women, lazy masterless poor merchants, and feckless aristocrats—who did not belong in their idealized notions of an economy. Although these individuals no longer languished in debtors' prisons for transactions gone awry, this also meant that they could no longer borrow on the assets of their bodies. Furthermore, reformers increasingly called for laws that subjected inappropriate risk taking to the regime of surveillance and chastisement.

On the other hand, recent events might lead us to question whether have we really changed all that much since debtors' prison was outlawed in the 1860s. At a certain level the answer is definitely not. Whether one is battling with a creditor face-to-face or with the impersonal bureaucracy of Chase Manhattan, debt still elicits mixed and complicated feelings of shame, anger, hurt, despair, and dependence, as the dramatic denouements of various recent debt crises, from the US mortgage crisis to the Greek default, have demonstrated. Although laws today in most industrialized countries distinguish much more clearly between financial loss and white-collar crime, public outrage can still be generated by the hanky-panky of Wall Street hedge fund managers. The line between unethical behavior and unlawful behavior can still seem pretty blurry, particularly for those not initiated into the arcana of derivatives and mortgage-backed securities. And while we live in a world where limited-liability corporations have achieved legal parity with physical persons in a number of important respects, this equality of rights has yet to firmly attach itself to our commonsense understanding of the world.

This brings us back to the difficulty of erasing the physical remnants of the debtors' prison.[16] The ninety-seven prisoners incarcerated in Clichy on July 23, 1867, had waited, suitcases in hand, for the "blessed hour" of their release, namely midnight, July 24. Meanwhile, outside the prison walls, their friends and families brought "bottles of good wine" to greet their loved ones and toast the legislators who had voted to repeal the law.[17] At midnight, with the concierge's announcement that the debtors were officially free, they poured out along the rue Clichy and went separate ways, leaving only six men behind, serving time for debts incurred through criminal and correctional charges.[18] The physical remains of the prison itself, however, proved more difficult to manage than the bodies of the debtors who had been incarcerated there. When the government put the former prison up for sale in June 1869, one commentator wrote that the purchaser who "wishes to make it into an agreeable residence will have some terrible evenings. The horrible nightmares will start troubling his sleep. He will hear the imprecations of raging debtors against the creditors who have put them under lock and key!"[19] Another paper quipped that the debtors' prison should be made into a boarding house or seminary, since "no one will know the difference."[20] A play joked that the state should turn Clichy into "a most princely hospital for all the creditors whom the law makes ill."[21] One reformer suggested that it house Paris's prostitutes.[22] Initially put on sale for 1.5 million francs in July 1869, the Hôtel de Clichy attracted no buyers.[23] Rumors in the years the followed held that the former prison had been bought by speculators who aimed to turn it into a "market like that of Saint-Honoré," "a magnificent city," "a school and a market," and a "private residence."[24] In 1875 a developer bought the prison's lands for 800,000 francs.[25] Clichy prison, the former home of Paris's uncooperative or unlucky debtors, was quickly demolished.

NOTES

Introduction

1. Balzac, *Eugénie Grandet*, 70–71.

2. A useful summary of the resulting consensus on French economic development can be found in Crouzet, "The Historiography of French Economic Growth." See also Horn, *The Path Not Taken*. This revised consensus on the nature of French capitalism is reflected in Thomas Piketty's *Capital in the Twenty-First Century*, which draws on French data to argue for trends in the evolution of the modern industrialized world's economies, placing France at the center, rather than the periphery, of the development of the character of nineteenth-century economies. See Piketty, *Capital in the Twenty-First Century*, trans. Arthur Goldhammer (Cambridge, MA: Harvard University Press, 2014).

3. On the punitive history of debt, see David Graeber, *Debt: The First 5000 Years* (Brooklyn: Melville House, 2011).

4. See Balleisen, *Navigating Failure*; Ditz, "Shipwrecked"; Mann, *Republic of Debtors*; Sandage, *Born Losers*.

5. On the long history of debt imprisonment and bankruptcy, see Pomykala, "The Division and Destruction of Value"; and Thiveaud, "L'ordre primordial de la dette."

6. *Séances et travaux de l'Académie des sciences morales et politiques, compte rendu* (Paris: Felix Alcan, 1847), 11:213. This is an excerpt from Troplong's published *De la contrainte par corps en matière civile et de commerce: Commentaire du titre XVI, livre III, du Code civil* (Paris: Felix Alcan, 1847).

7. On the early history of debt imprisonment, see Claustre, *Dans les geôles du roi*.

8. Kessler, *A Revolution in Commerce*.

9. As Kessler notes, there is very little historical evidence to support the idea of a transnational merchant law and much more evidence that emphasizes national legal context. Ibid., 97–101.

10. Desan, *The Family on Trial*; and Blaufarb, *The Great Demarcation*.

11. Claire Lemercier, "Discipliner le commerce."

12. Blaufarb, *Great Demarcation*.

13. AN F 12 192, "Procès-verbal du Conseil géneral du commerce 10 Thermidor An XI."

14. See Spieler, *Empire and Underworld*.

15. Stanziani, *Rules of Exchange*, 44.

16. Code de Commerce Livre III, Article 586 ff.

17. See Peter Linebaugh, *The London Hanged: Crime and Civil Society in the Eighteenth Century* (Cambridge: Cambridge University Press, 1992); Ian Taylor, ed., *Crime and Political Economy* (Brookfied, VT: Ashgate, 1998); Douglas Hay, *Albion's Fatal Tree: Crime and Society in Eighteenth-Century England* (New York: Pantheon Books, 1975); Ignatieff, *A Just Measure of Pain*.

18. Foucault, *Discipline and Punish*.

19. On prisons in nineteenth-century France, see Michelle Perrot, *L'impossible prison*; Petit, *Ces peines obscures*; Petit, Castan, Fogeron, *Histoire des Galères*, esp. 45–167; and O'Brien, *The Promise of Punishment*.

20. Saint-Hilaire, *L'art de payer ses dettes*, 35.

21. This literature include Fontaine, *L'économie morale*; Hardwick, *Family Business*; Luckett, "Credit and Commercial Honor"; Crowston, *Credit, Fashion, Sex*.

22. Blaufarb, *The Great Demarcation*.

23. Crowston, *Credit, Fashion, Sex*, 3.

24. Nye, *Masculinity and Male Codes of Honor*.

25. Reddy, *The Invisible Code*.

26. See Kessler, *Revolution in Commerce*; Shovlin, *Political Economy of Virtue*; Jay M. Smith, "Social Categories."

27. Thompson, *The Virtuous Marketplace*.

28. For more on the importance of disgrace to the practice of criminal punishment in modern France, see Whitman, *Harsh Justice*. Anne Simonin, in *Le déshonneur dans la République*, has pointed to the tension between indignity, with its roots in the private and familial order before the Revolution, and the equality of rights guaranteed by the concept of citizenship.

29. John Smail has discussed the links between concrete substantiations of mercantile honor and ideals of mercantile honor in "Credit, Risk and Honor in Eighteenth-Century Commerce." For social relations and credit in nineteenth-century France, see Hirsch, *Les deux rêves du commerce*.

30. The distinction between promissory notes and bills of exchange rests in the numbers of parties technically involved as well as the requirement that bills of exchange be drawn between different places. For more on negotiable instruments, see De Roover, *L'évolution de la lettre de change*.

31. For a particularly successful example of this narrative of credit, see Jay M. Smith, "No More Language Games." Laurence Fontaine posits a similar story, wherein "merchant credit," which during the early modern period coexisted with "aristocratic credit" although obeying a different economic logic, ultimately grows to surpass the latter. Fontaine, "Antonio and Shylock." In Craig Muldrew's account of credit relations in early modern England, this transformation takes place earlier, as transactions previously settled informally instead become the subject of litigation. Muldrew, *The Economy of Obligation*.

32. See Lemercier and Zalc, "Pour une nouvelle approche."

33. Crowston, "Credit and the Metanarrative of Modernity"; Finn, *The Character of Credit*; Spang, *Stuff and Money*; Hoffman, Postel-Vilnay, and Rosenthal, "Information and Economic History."

34. Poovey, *Genres of the Credit Economy*.

35. Reddy, *The Rise of Market Culture*, 1.

36. On the contradictions to liberalism posed by debt law, see Suter, "Debt and Its Attachments."

1. Hard Contracts and Hard Money

1. *Appel à l'honneur*, 25.

2. Ibid., 76.

3. Ibid., 93–94.

4. Hoffman, Postel-Vilnay, and Rosenthal, *Priceless Markets*, 17.

5. Crowston, "Credit and the Metanarrative of Modernity," 7–19.

6. Spang, *Stuff and Money*, 275.

7. Livesey, *Making Democracy in the French Revolution*, 48–87.

8. On the use of the death penalty as a means of propping up the circulation of currency in the Financial Revolution, see Carl Wennerlind, *The Casualties of Credit: The English Financial Revolution, 1620–1720* (Cambridge, MA: Harvard University Press, 2011), 123–59.

9. Simonin remarks upon this tension between the equality of rights enjoyed by citizens and the degradation of honor befalling those who transgress the laws, in *Le déshonneur*, 196.

10. See Paul Cheney, *Revolutionary Commerce: Globalization and the French Monarchy* (Cambridge, MA: Harvard University Press, 2010).

11. Baron de Montesquieu, *L'esprit des lois* (Paris: Didot frères, fils et cie, 1860), 279. Montesquieu's comments on *contrainte par corps* were applauded by none other than one of debt imprisonment's most ardent foes, Jean-Paul Marat, whose *Eloge de Montesquieu* agreed that "commerce should be free: but at the same time this liberty does not permit businessmen to do whatever they want: they should be harassed, but only for the benefit of commerce. The exactitude with which they must fulfill their engagements demands *contrainte par corps*" (Marat, *Eloge de Montesquieu*, ed. Arthur de Brezetz [Libourne: G. Maleville, 1883], 43).

12. Montesquieu, *L'esprit des lois*, 282.

13. See Céline Spector, "Honor," trans. Philip Stewart, in *A Montesquieu Dictionary*, directed by Catherine Volpilhac-Auger, ENS Lyon, September 2013, http://dictionnaire-montesquieu.ens-lyon.fr/en/article/1376474900/en.

14. See Kessler, *Revolution in Commerce*, esp. 188–237.

15. For the application of *dérogeance*, see Matthieu Marraud, "Dérogeance et commerce: Violence des constructions socio-politiques sous l'Ancien Régime," *Genèses* 95, no. 2 (2014): 2–26.

16. Kessler, *Revolution in Commerce*, 18.

17. See Hirschman, *The Passions and the Interests*.

18. Coyer, *Développement et défense*, 137.

19. Shovlin, "Toward a Reinterpretation of Revolutionary Anti-nobilism."

20. Jay Smith, "Social Categories," 339–74.

21. *Journal de la Commerce et de l'Agriculture*, December 1760, 44–45; quoted in Luckett, "Debate on Debt Imprisonment," 166.

22. Ibid., 34–35; quoted in Luckett, "Debate on Debt Imprisonment," 166.

23. Ibid., 51–52; quoted in Luckett, "Debate on Debt Imprisonment," 166.

24. Closel d'Arnery, *Abus et dangers*, 6.

25. Ibid., 24–27.

26. Ibid., 11–12.

27. Ibid., 11.

28. Spang, *Stuff and Money*, 33–34.

29. Ibid., 36.

30. Sewell, *Work and Revolution*, 129.

31. Closel d'Arnery, *Abus et dangers*, 11.

32. See Kessler, *Revolution in Commerce*, 188–237.

33. Closel d'Arnery, *Abus et dangers*, 6.

34. Ibid., 10.

35. See Shovlin, *Political Economy of Virtue*.

36. See Sonenscher, *Before the Deluge*; Kaiser, "Money, Despotism, and Public Opinion"; Crowston, *Credit, Fashion, Sex*, 56–95.

37. Goldstein, *The Post-revolutionary Self*, 46–52.

38. *Archives parlementaires de 1787 à 1860: Recueil complet des débat législatifs et politiques des chambres françaises, Tome LXXII* (Paris: Paul Dupont, 1907), 8:230 (July 13, 1798).

39. Ibid., 8:112 (June 15, 1789).

40. Nye, *Masculinity and Honor*, 33.

41. *Archives parlementaires*, 8:337 (October 4, 1789).

42. Ibid.

43. Spang, *Stuff and Money*, 162–63.

44. See Miller, "Des contrats sous tension."

45. These being the laws of April 11, 1793, and September 5, 1793, respectively.

46. *Archives parlementaires*, 77:197–98.

47. Pierre-Joseph Cambon, "Rapport sur la dette publique," *Archives parlementaires*, 77:201.

48. The Cahier de tiers-état de Paris asked that *contrainte par corps* not be exercised for debts under 100 *livres*. See *Cahier du tiers-état*, 38.

49. Luckett, "Debate on Debt Imprisonment," 168.

50. Quoted in Petit, *Ces peines*, 47.

51. Indeed, the most contested, and ultimately undecided, part of the abolition involved whether public servants—specifically tax officials—should also be freed from *contrainte par corps* for money owed to the state. *Moniteur Universel*, March 11, 1793, 321.

52. Quoted in Braudel and Labrousse, *Histoire économique*, 53.

53. Quoted in in Crouzet, *La grande inflation*, 453.

54. Braudel and Labrousse, *Histoire économique*, 151. See also Taws, "Trompe-l'oeil and Trauma."

55. See Roussel, *Le système des mandats territoriaux*, 23.

56. On the abolition of the guilds, see Kaplan, *La fin de corporations*; Fitzsimmons, "The National Assembly"; Liana Vardi, "The Abolition of the Guilds during the French Revolution," *French Historical Studies* 15 (1988): 704–17.

57. See Jarvis, "Exacting Change."

58. See the police reports from years IV and V printed in Aulard, *Paris pendant la réaction thermidorienne*, vol. 3, esp. 12.

59. Vermale, "Les dettes privées sous la Révolution," 164.

60. Quoted in Marion, *Histoire financière de la France*, 365.

61. Mercier, *Le nouveau Paris*, 2:692.

62. In accordance with the law of 5 Thermidor An IV (July 23, 1796), loans made during the period of paper money had been stipulated with reimbursement payable in "money in use."

63. See AN DXXXIX n. 15, "Addresse aux citoyens répresentants du peuple formant le Conseil de Cinq Cents," 1 Germinal An V. This is the main point in Basin, *Dialogue sur les transactions*.

64. On the creation of the tables of depreciation, see Miller, "The Aftermath of the Assignat."

65. Valente, "Usury in France."

66. *Moniteur Universel*, July 24, 1795, 567.

67. When the Bourse was reopened, the law of 13 Fructidor An III forbade all speculation other than that in the Bourse, under threat of having a placard on one's chest reading *agioteur* (stock-jobber). See Marion, *Histoire financière*, 359.

68. "Considerations sur le Mont-de-Piété et sur les maisons dites Caisse auxiliare, Lombards et autres maisons de prêt sur nantissement," quoted in Danieri, "Credit Where Credit Is Due," 140.

69. Lefebvre, *La France sous la Directoire*, 143.

70. Mercier, *Le nouveau Paris*, 2:602.

71. AN F15 134, "Le Ministre de la Police générale de la République, au Ministre de l'Interieur," 17 Frimaire An V, Cochon.

72. Mallet du Pan, *Correspondance*, 2:176.

73. See Marion, *Histoire financière*, 365–66. The *patente* was instituted 5 Thermidor An III, creating a graduated code of taxes necessary to practice business. Four thousand livre would buy a general *patente* covering all trades, while small amounts paid for specialized *patente* varied depending on the size of the town. Fines were to be levied to merchants found practicing without a *patente*.

74. AN F 12 2469 mélanges: commerce, "Discours des Ministère de Finance et Ministère de l'Interieur," 6 Nivôse An V.

75. *Le Sentinelle*, November 29, 1796. See also Lefebvre, *France sous le Directoire*, 139.

76. AN F 12 2469 mélanges: commerce, "Députés extraordinaires du commerce au Ministère de Finance," 10 Nivôse An V.

77. Ibid.

78. AN F 12 2469 mélanges: commerce, "Lettre écrite au Ministère des finances par les députés extraordinaires du commerce le 18 Nivôse de l'An V."

79. On previous plans for a bank, see Marion, *Histoire financière*, 442–48.

80. On the impact of John Law, whose disastrous attempt to finance royal debt came to symbolize the evils of a speculative economy in French discourse for the next 150 years, see Spang, "The Ghost of Law."

81. "Lettre des députés extraordinaires du commerce, au Ministère des finances," published in *Moniteur Universel*, January 20, 1797, 481.

82. *Moniteur Universel*, July 26, 1795, 1241.

83. *Moniteur Universel*, August 16, 1795, 1324. For more *on patentes*, see Koepke, "The *loi* des *patentes* of 1844."

84. One representative even suggested extending *contrainte par corps* to citizens who did not pay their taxes or contribute to the forced loan. See "Opinion de Dubois-Crancé, sur les moyens de restauration du crédit public: séance du 7 ventôse, l'an IVe" (Paris: Imprimerie nationale, 1796).

85. Quoted in Livesey, *Making Democracy*, 64. It is highly unlikely that Robespierre said anything of the sort.

86. White, "The French Revolution," 248–50.

87. AN III 35 folio 123, Anonymous petition dated 8 Pluviôse An VI.

88. *À l'Assemblée des négocians convoqués à Paris par le gouvernement* (Paris: Imprimerie de Desenne, 1796), 4.

89. Ibid.

90. *Moniteur Universel*, February 24, 1797, 697. The last part of this proposition may appear slightly opaque but has to do with the constrained nature of civil debts to be judged *contrainte par corps*.

91. *Moniteur Universel*, March 2, 1797, 647.

92. See Miller, "Property in the Aftermath of the Assignat," 70–91.

93. See Luckett, "Debate about Debt Imprisonment," 169.

94. For the ambiguous Revolutionary relationship to property, see Blaufarb, *Great Demarcation*; B. Smith and Kelley, "What Was Property?"; and Callaway, "Revolutionizing Property."

95. *Moniteur Universel*, March 2, 1797, 647.

96. *Moniteur Universel*, March 16, 1797, 702.

97. *Moniteur Universel*, March 13, 1797, 692.

98. *Moniteur Universel*, March 2, 1797, 647.

99. *Moniteur Universel*, March 12, 1797, 687.

100. *Moniteur Universel*, March 13, 1797, 692.

101. Ibid.

102. *Moniteur Universel*, March 16, 1797, 702.

103. Ibid.

104. *Moniteur Universel*, March 13, 1797, 692.

105. *Moniteur Universel*, March 18, 1797, 709.

106. Ibid.

107. *Moniteur Universel*, March 18, 1797, 717. For the widespread brigandage in the countryside and high crime rates in the cities in the Directory, see Lyons, *France under the Directory*, 80–81; and Brown, *Ending the French Revolution*.

108. *Moniteur Universel*, March 18, 1797, 715.

109. *Moniteur Universel*, March 13, 1793, 692.

110. *Moniteur Universel*, March 19, 1797, 719.

111. *Moniteur Universel*, March 13, 1793, 694.

112. On the legal status of women and children as *commerçants*, see Szramkiewicz, *Histoire du droit des affaires*, 172–73.

113. The Code de procedure civile (1807) and the law of September 13, 1807, which regulated debt imprisonment for foreigners, provided additional explanations of *contrainte par corps*. *Bulletin des lois*, An VI 1 semestre n. 1795, "Loi relative à la contrainte par corps."

114. "Rapport du Bureau central du 10 ventôse AN V" (AN BB3 85), printed in Aulard, *Paris pendant la réaction thermidorienne*, 3:773.

115. Alhoy and Lurine, *Les prisons de Paris*, 57.

116. In particular, the former Parisian *gardes du commerce* used the reestablishment of *contrainte par corps* to push for the reestablishment of their order, arguing that the *huissiers* were too busy to adequately handle the caseload and that this in turn contributed to the slowness. See petitions 11 and 13 Brumaire An VI, 16 Frimaire An VI, AN AF III 123 dossier 35.

117. *Sur la contrainte par corps pour dettes*, 5.

118. Gorneau, *Révisions du projet de Code du Commerce*, 8.

119. AN F 12 192, *Procès-verbal du Conseil géneral du commerce*, 10 Thermidor An XI.

2. The Blessing of Being Judged

1. AN F 12 971 B dossier 7, folder 1, Letter from police bureau of Marseille to Minister of the Interior, 19 Brumaire An XII.

2. AN BB 18 193 n. 636, General police commissioner of Marseille, to the Minister of Justice, 19 Brumaire An XII.

3. See Louis Bergeron and Guy Chaussinand-Nogaret, *Les "masses de granit": Cent mille notables du Premier Empire* (Paris: Éditions de l'École des hautes études en sciences sociales, 1979).

4. "Exposé des motifs du livre III du Code du commerce, presenté au Corps legislative par M. Ségur, pour une portion, et M. Treilhard, pour l'autre portion séance 3 septembre 1807," in *Code du Commerce servant de supplement au procès-verbal des séances du Corps législatif September 1807: Exposés des motifs par les orateurs du gouvernement* (Paris: Hacquart, 1807), 72.

5. "Exposé des motifs, des titres I à VII, inclusivement, du livre 1er du Code de Commerce, presenté au Corps Législatif séance 1 septembre 1807," in *Code de Commerce*, 75.

6. On this lengthy and delicate process, see Jean-Louis Halpérin, *L'impossible Code civil* (Paris: Presses universitaires de France, 1992).

7. See Halpérin, *Histoire du droit privé*; and Xavier Martin, *Mythologie du Code Napoléon: Aux soubassements de la France moderne* (Paris: Dominique Martin Morin, 2003).

8. See Desan, *The Family on Trial*; and Michael Lucy, "Legal Melancholy: Balzac's Eugénie Grandet and the Napoleonic Code," *Representations* 76, no. 1 (2001): 1–26, doi: 10.1525/phr.2007.76.2.312.

9. Hilaire, *Introduction historique*, 90.

10. Hilaire notes: "The Commercial Code as such participated in the legal system coming out of the Revolution. It takes part in the mythology of a legislative work simulatenously exhaustive, clear, solidly founded and defying time. It constituted, however, the weakest part, being only a simple, timid, and botched revision of the Ordinance of 1673" (ibid., 79). While Halpérin dismisses it as "not very innovative," and at times "restrictive and illogical" (*Histoire du droit privé*, 35–36). Szramkiewicz, in *Histoire du droit des affaires* (274–77), shares Hilaire's opinion.

11. Hilaire, *Introduction historique*, 80–82.

12. Brown, *Ending the French Revolution*, 69.

13. Ibid., 68.

14. Roux, *De l'influence du gouvernement*, 390.

15. Denise Z. Davidson, "Local Identities and Internal Migration: Networking as Survival Strategy in Revolutionary and Post-revolutionary France," in *Place and Locality in Modern France*, ed. Patrick Young and Philip Whalen (London: Bloomsbury, 2014), 155.

16. Roux, *De l'influence*, 393.

17. Hilaire, *Introduction historique*, 85.

18. Rosanvallon, *The Demands of Liberty*,126.

19. See in particular AN F 12 971 B dossier 7, folder 1, Letter from the Prefect of the Department of the Meurthe to the Minister of the Interior, 28 Ventôse An XIII; and AN AF III 35, dossier 123, 14 Nivôse An VII, "Observations sur les causes des banqueroutes."

20. AN F 12 971 B folder 1, Letter from the prefect of the Department of the Aude to the Minister of the Interior, 20 Frimaire An XIV.

21. Thomas Luckett provides the following data on bankruptcies in Paris: 1797 (66 bankruptcies), 1798 (160), 1799 (317), 1800 (160), 1801 (190), 1802 (239), 1803 (346), 1804 (201), 1805 (293), 1806 (346), 1807 (280). This was a dramatic increase from the amount of bankruptcies during the period of paper currency: 1793 (44), 1794 (12), 1795 (5), 1796 (4), but also slightly lower than ancien regime levels, which Luckett arrives at by counting both private settlements and official bankruptcies. For example, in 1772 Luckett estimates the total number of actual bankruptcies at around 351, but by 1776 this number was around 447, in 1777, 465, and in 1778, 408, with a slight decrease in the years immediately preceding the Revolution. See Luckett, "Credit and Commercial Society," 98.

22. AN BB 18 191 n. 6973, Letter from Pierre Giraud to the Minister of Justice, 18 Messidor An XI.

23. AN BB 18 339 n. 2691 A3, Letter from M. Saillaid to the Minister of Justice, March 31, 1807.

24. AN BB 18 219 n. 1187, Letter from assorted businessmen to Napoleon Bonaparte, 27 Nivôse An X.

25. Ancien négociant, *Observations sur le projet de code du commerce*, 15.

26. AN BB 18 219 n. 864, Letter from M. Chancel to the Substitute Government Commissioner of the Criminal Court of Charente, 23 Nivôse An XI.

27. ADBdR 2 U 2 2543, Letter from the Mayor of Eyguières to the Justice of the Peace, Pluviôse An XII.

28. AN BB 18 273 n. 654 A3, Letter from the public prosecutor of the Haut-Garonne to the Minister of Justice, April 22, 1806.

29. AN AF III 35 dossier 123, Citizen Legras, "Project d'un Code des faillites, surseances, cessions judiciaries, et banqueroutes," 3.

30. AN F 12 971 B dossier 7, folder 1, Letter from Morize, citizen of d'Eveaux to the Minister of the Interior, 1 Germinal An VII. On the use of yellow hats in medieval and early modern punishments of debtors, see Beachy, "Bankruptcy and Social Death," 340.

31. AN F 12 971 B dossier 7, folder 1, Letter from Labonadière the Older to the Minister of the Interior, 12 Pluvôse An IX.

32. AN F 12 501 A, Letter from Vauchelet to Minister of the Interior, September 6, 1807.

33. AN F 12 866, Response from the Chambre de Commerce de Toulouse, July 21, 1806.

34. On sentiment toward the guilds among Napoleon's elite, see Sibalis, "Corporatism after the Corporations." For the continuing difficulty in regulating commerce without corporations and the role of the law in so doing, see Lemercier, "Discipliner le commerce sans corporations."

35. See Chambre de Commerce de Paris, *Rapport sur les jurandes et maîtrises*, 99.

36. AN F 12 971 B dossier 2, "Mémoire sur la question de savoir si l'état actuel du commerce, le défaut de confiance et de circulation et la necessité de trouver une ressource présente et certaine pour empêcher au moins diminuer le nombre des faillites qui désolent le commerce et pour détruire l'usure . . ." (anon, n.d.)

37. Roux, *De l'influence*, 403.

38. On the backgrounds of these men, see Szramkiewicz, *Histoire du droit des affaires*, 270–72.

39. *Projet de Code du commerce*, 26.

40. Gorneau, *Révision du projet de Code du commerce*, 148

41. See *Observations des tribunaux de cassation et d'appel, des tribunaux et conseils de commerce, &. sur le projet de code du commerce* (Paris: Imprimerie de la République, 1802), 1:427–28, 2:66–68, as well as AN F 12 543–46, responses from the chambers of commerce.

42. For this financial crisis, caused by the failure of the banker-brokers Négociants Reunis, see Pierre Branda, *Le prix de la gloire: Napoéon et l'argent* (Paris: Fayard, 2007), 258–80; Bergeron, *Banquiers, négociants*, 147–60.

43. Quoted in Madelin, *Histoire du Consulat*, 323.

44. AN F 12 971 B (III), Circular from the Ministry of Interior, June 18, 1806.

45. See Madelin, *Histoire du Consulat*, 205–6, 259–61. Police reports from Thermidor An XIII through VendémiaireAn XIV testify to the staggering number of

people forming lines outside banks to retrieve their money in the panic. See Ernest d'Hauterive, *Le police secrète du Premier Empire: Bulletins quotidiens addressés par Fouche à l'Empereur, Vol. II, Juillet 1805–Septembre 1806* (Paris: Librairie academique Perrin, 1913).

46. AN F 12 866, Response from the Chamber of Commerce of Le Havre, July 23, 1806.

47. AN F 12 866, Letter from the Chamber of Commerce of Bayonne to the Minister of the Interior, July 12, 1806.

48. AN F 12 866, Letter from the Chamber of Commerce of Toulouse, June 18, 1806.

49. Ibid.

50. Locré, *La législation civile*, 98.

51. Ibid., 105.

52. Ibid., 461.

53. Ibid., 68.

54. See Serge Chassagne, "Faillis en Anjou au XVIIIe siecle: Contribution à l'histoire économique d'une province," *Annales ESC* 2 (1970): 477–79; and Pierre de Saint Jacob, "Histoire économique et sociale dans les archives de la jurisdiction consulaire de Dijon (1715–1789)," *Bulletin de la Société d'Histoire Moderne* 12, no. 4 (1961): 13–38. This abuse was a common source of complaint among legal thinkers.

55. Claude Dupouy uses factums and the ambiguous wording of Title IX of the Ordinance of 1673—which employs the word *débiteur* rather than *marchand débiteur* to argue for the flexibility of old regime rulings. See Dupouy, *Le droit des faillites*.

56. *Code de commerce* (Paris: Chez Clement Frères, 1808), 122. On the novelty of this point, see Hilaire, *Introduction historique*, 183.

57. Locré, *La législation civile*, 79.

58. In areas without commercial courts, the *Code de commerce* ordered that bankruptcies were to be handled by civil courts.

59. AN F 12 192, Minutes of the General Commercial Council, 10 Thermidor An XI.

60. *Code de commerce*, 1.

61. Locré, *La législation civile*, 63. For additional information, see Freedeman, "Joint-Stock Business Organization."

62. *Code de commerce*, 122.

63. "Motifs exposés de M. Treilhard," in *Code de commerce*, 444.

64. *Code de commerce*, 119.

65. Locré, *La législation civile*, 151.

66. Ibid., 88.

67. Ibid., 79.

68. Ibid., 305–7.

69. Ibid., 297.

70. Ibid., 305–7.

71. *Code de commerce*, 145.

72. *Code de commerce*, 10. Of course, females very much did act as merchants and did undergo bankruptcy. On female bankrupts, see Crowston, *Credit, Fashion, Sex*, 195–245.

73. AN F 12 971 B dossier 7, folder 1, Letter from Lucien Bonaparte to the Minister of Commerce, 18 Ventôse An VIII.

74. Locré, *La législation civile*, 479.

75. Ibid., 486.

76. On the importance of dotal properties to businesses in the eighteenth and nineteenth centuries, see Stanziani, *Rules of Exchange*, 77–82.

77. Locré, *La législation civile*, 483.

78. *Code de commerce*, 149.

79. Articles 551–53, *Code de commerce*, 149.

80. AN BB 18 197 n. 2113, Letter from the Chamber of Commerce of Marseille to the Duke of Massa, March 3, 1812.

81. AN BB 18 197 n. 2113, Letter from the Minister of Commerce to the Minister of Justice, April 4, 1812.

82. AN BB 18 197 n. 2113, Letter from M. Arnaud to Minister of Justice, May 5, 1812.

83. AN BB 18 162 n. 1097, Letter from Fabre, public prosecutor of the Imperial Court of Montpellier, to the Minister of Justice, September 9, 1811.

84. AN BB 18 221 n. 1274, Letter to the Minister of Justice, August 12, 1811.

85. AN BB 18 134 n. 876, Letter from Public Prosecutor in Metz to the Minister of Justice, August 19, 1813.

86. AN BB 18 265 n. 5437 A3, Letter from a judge of the Criminal Court of the Dordogne to the Minister of Justice July 7, 1809.

87. AN BB 18 162 n. 4508, Letter from the Bishop of Carcassonne to the Minister of Justice, October 31, 1814.

88. AN BB 18 162 n. 8288, Letter from creditor of Jean-Pierre Giraud to public prosecutor, October 28, 1809.

89. AN BB 18 314 n. 8963, Letter from the public prosecutor of Finistère to the Minister of Justice, July 31, 1810.

90. For the treatment of white-collar crimes during this period, see Donovan, *Juries and the Transformation of Criminal Justice*, 200.

91. AN BB 18 339 n. 2691 A3, Letter from M. Roque to Minister of Justice, May 1807.

92. AN BB 18 162 n. 25, Letter from M. Vidal to the Minister of Justice, April 25, 1811.

93. AN BB 18 290 n. 2827 C2, Letter from Grégoire Saint-Hélène to Minister of Justice, February 24, 1808.

94. AN BB 18 162 n. 5332, Letter from M. Valentin to Minister of Justice, July 30, 1814.

95. See the file on the Oduard case in AN BB 18 282 n. 4733 A4.

96. AN BB 18 266 n. 5367, Letter from M. LaBroissière to the Minister of Justice, October 9, 1810.

97. AN BB 18 795 n. 7652, Letter from creditors of the Compagnie Godard to the Minister of Justice, 1811.

98. AN BB 18 235 n. 8843, Letter from public prosecutor of Corrèze to the Minister of Justice, February 12, 1811.

99. AN BB 18 795 n. 271 A4, Letter from the Imperial Prosecutor to Minister of Justice, March 19, 1811.

100. AN BB 18 795 n. 178 A4, Request in intervention for François-Philippe Mondot-Lagorge to the Appeals Court, February 22, 1811.

101. AN BB 18 219 n. 864, Letter from M. Chancel to the Substitute Government Commissioner of the Criminal Court of Charente, 23 Nivose An XI.

102. AN BB 18 250 n. 2076, Report presented to the Minister of Justice by the public prosecutor of Dijon (1816?).

103. AN BB 18 795 n. 748 A4, Letter from the Procurer General to the Minister of Justice, February 14, 1812.

104. See BB 18 273 n. 2363 and BB 18 338 N. 8404 A2, which detail the cases of André Cochet, a traveling salesman who fled to Switzerland, and Jean Guillaume Lérat, a broker who fled to Spain, allegedly taking 400,000 francs of his clients' money.

105. BB 18 294 n. 5453, Letter from the Procurer-General of the Département of Doube to the Minister of Justice, November 2, 1808.

106. AN BB 18 250 n. 2025, Letter from Nicolas Chevallot to Emperor Napoleon, April 17, 1812.

107. AN BB 18 792 n. 6538, Letter from Femme Paris to Minister of Justice, April 19, 1809.

108. AN BB 18 795 n. 8174, Letter from Magistrat of Surety to Minister of Justice, February 15, 1810.

109. AN BB 18 275 n. 17, Letter from Jean-François Kraus to Minister of Justice, April 1813.

110. AN BB 18 293 n. 8068, Letter from Alphonse Lesage to Napoleon, April 10, 1810.

111. AN BB 18 250 n. 1430, Letter from Nicholas-François Japiot to Minister of Justice, November 11, 1811.

112. AN BB 18 796 n. 1706, Report of the imperial prosecutor of Paris on *faillites* and *banqueroutes*.

113. Ségur, "Exposé des motifs du livre III du Code du commerce, presenté au Corps legislative par M. Ségur, pour une portion, et M. Treilhard, pour l'autre portion séance 3 septembre 1807," in *Code du commerce servant de supplement*, 73.

114. M. Fréville, "Discours prononcé par M. Fréville, l'un des orateurs du Tribunat, et au nom des sections de Législation et de l'Interieur, sur le IIIe Livre du Code de Commerce 12 September 1807," in *Code du Commerce servant de supplement*, 95.

3. Risky Business

1. *Gazette des Tribunaux*, June 7, 1828, 505. Litigation over the appellation of *banqueroutier* was hardly new. Julie Hardwick notes a case in Lyon in 1707 where a plaintiff pressed similar charges against an acquaintance for a similar thing. See Hardwick, *Family Business*.

2. Barbier, *Droit commercial*, 47.

3. *Moniteur Universel*, March 29, 1838, 720. As several debtors were to learn to their chagrin, this only applied to prior commercial debts. Other kinds of debts could still

entail imprisonment. See *Gazette des Tribunaux*, March 9, 1839, 471, and October 2, 1839, 1214.

4. AN BB 30 279 folder: Chambres de Commerce, Response from the Dijon Chamber of Commerce.

5. Geoffroy, *Le Code pratique*, X.

6. Tocqueville, *Democracy in America*, 731.

7. See Hautcoeur and Levratto, "Petites et grandes entreprises."

8. Kete, "Stendhal and the Trials of Ambition," 468.

9. Goldstein, *Console and Classify*, 160.

10. See Martin, "Le commerçant."

11. Crouch, "The Petite Bourgeoisie of Paris," 64.

12. AN F 20 722–23, folder *faillites statistiques*, 1820–49.

13. Hautcoeur and Levratto, "Petites et grandes entreprises."

14. Collingham, *The July Monarchy*, 44.

15. Palmade, *French Capitalism in the Nineteenth Century*, 80.

16. See Hoffman, Postel-Vinay, and Rosenthal, *Priceless Markets*.

17. For banking in nineteenth-century France, see Braudel and Labrousse, *Histoire économique et sociale de la France 3*, vol. 1; Robert Bigo, *Les banques françaises au cours du XIXe siècle* (Paris: Recueil Sirey); and Gille, *La banque et le crédit en France*.

18. For such credit networks, see Crossick and Haupt, *The Petite Bourgeoisie*, 182–86.

19. For legal restriction on usury in the early nineteenth century, see Vause, "A Subject of Interest"; and Valente, "Usury in France."

20. Lebaudy, *Réflexions sur la banque générale*, 18–19; Lamouroux, *De quelques griefs de l'industrie*, 19. An 1830 pamphlet, for instance, estimated that most small manufacturers were unable to find discount rates much below 12 to 15 percent. Another pamphlet alleged that a third of small- and medium-size businesses couldn't find anyone willing to discount their paper at all, another third went through extreme difficulty to find discounters, and the rest faced discount rates ranging from 6 to 10 percent depending on the particularities of their situation and location. Morin, *Le petit commerce*, 15. On discounting, see also Gille, *La banque et le crédit*, 100–110.

21. Crowston, *Credit, Fashion, Sex*.

22. For a discussion of the link between macroeconomic events and bankruptcies, see Marco, *La montée des faillites*, 150–60.

23. Saint-Hilaire, *L'art de payer les dettes*, 33.

24. See Thierry Nootens, "Fous, prodigues et faibles d'esprit: L'interdiction et le conseil judiciaire dans le tribunal de première instance d'Angers 1820–1835, 1880–1883," *Déviance et Société* 24, no. 1 (2000): 47–67.

25. Geoffroy, *Code pratique*, X.

26. LaMarre, *Au Roi*, 15–16.

27. AP 2ETP/3/3/80 1, folder 722, Report by the Paris Chamber of Commerce, September 1827.

28. AN C 767 3, February 1835, Letter from Fleury in Paris to Chamber of Deputies.

29. AP 2ETP/3/3/80 1, folder 723, *Giraudeau Mémoire sur les moyens de prévenir les fraudes en matière de faillites* (Paris: Imprimerie de Goetschy, 1829), 1–2.

30. Geoffroy, *Code pratique*, X.

31. *Moniteur Universel*, March 18, 1838, 645.

32. Roret, *Code de commerce*, 129.

33. Ibid., 15–16.

34. Ibid., 252–54.

35. Ibid., 19.

36. Ibid., 18.

37. Ibid., 14.

38. Ibid., 25.

39. Ibid., 217–22.

40. Boulay-Paty, *Traité des faillites et banqueroutes*, XXVI.

41. Ibid., XXVI.

42. Ibid., XXVIII.

43. *Moniteur Universel*, April 3, 1838, 774.

44. "Resumé statistique du tribunal de commerce de la Seine, pendant l'année judiciare 1838–1839," *Gazette des Tribunaux*, August 31, 1839, 1103.

45. Ibid.

46. "Audience d'installation des nouveaux juges et juges suppléants: Tribunal de commerce de la Seine," *Gazette des Tribunaux*, August 25, 1844, 1049–50.

47. "Addresse de Pepin Lehalleur, président du Tribunal de Commerce," *Gazette des Tribunaux*, August 29, 1841, 1145.

48. "Séance d'installation des nouveaux juges et juges suppléants," *Gazette des Tribunaux*, August 30, 1846, 1371.

49. AN BB 30 279, folder: Chambres de Commerce, Response from the Metz Chamber of Commerce.

50. *Gazette des Tribunaux*, July 22–23, 1839, 969.

51. At the installation of the new commercial judges at the Paris Commercial Court in August 30, one presiding judge declared that of the 931 bankruptcies declared in Paris in the business season between 1844 and 1845, 172 were wine merchants, caterers, lodgers, or restaurant owners; 45 tavern keepers (*limonadiers*); and the same number of grocers. See "Séance d'installation des nouveaux juges et juges suppléants," *Gazette des tribunaux*, August 30, 1846, 1371.

52. AP D 11 U3 81 D. 6722, dossier Agnes Ribot

53. See AP D11 U3 76 D. 6564, dossier François Noel.

54. *Gazette des tribunaux*, November 6, 1842, 22.

55. "Repression de la banqueroute," *Gazette des Tribunaux*, October 15, 1845, 1201.

56. Ibid.

57. See Donovan, *Juries and the Transformation of Criminal Justice*, 200.

58. AP D8 U3 8, Letter from the Chamber of Commerce of the Rhône to the trustees of the Leroux Bankruptcy, July 1811.

59. ADBdR 2 U 2 2548, Indictment against Jean-Joseph Guiraud, 1813.

60. *Gazette des Tribuanux*, May 24, 1828, 489, and December 12, 1828, 1089.

61. *Gazette des Tribunaux*, September 2–3, 1833, 897.

62. *Gazette des Tribunaux* September 29, 1847, 1204.

63. Perre, *À messieurs le président, 10–11.*

64. Fourcher, *Deuxième mémoire.*

65. ADBdR 2 U 2 2548, dossier Jacques Giraud négociant de Marseille 1813, Indictment against Joseph-Jacques Giraud.

66. Ibid.

67. Sauvayre, *Mémoire pour Joseph-Marie Sauvayre*, 13.

68. Chassaing, *Mémoire justicatif pour le sieur Brassier*, 14.

69. Fourcher, *Deuxième mémoire*, 46.

70. ADBR 2 U 2 2548, Louis Lambert, Agent of the *faillite* of J. J. Guiraud, to Monsieur the imperial prosecutor, July 7, 1813.

71. See Baudry, Duparc, and Milliard, *Rapport de Mssrs. les syndics.*

72. Twenty-nine creditors were successfully prosecuted, including Denis Lallemand, Demiannay's brother-in-law, who had been given 50,000 francs. Yet legal costs taken out of Demiannay's assets came to 80,000 francs. See ANMT Papiers Thuret 68 AQ 12, letters from Lemarchand dated August 29, 1832, and December 28, 1832. Most of the paid creditors were able to use the Commercial Code to claim that their payments were valid given that they had acted in good faith and in ignorance of the true state of Demiannay's discredit. See Commercial Code 1807, Book III, Articles 442–47.

73. For marital property law and debt, see Darrow, *Revolution in the House*, 56–85; and Desan, *The Family on Trial*, chap. 4.

74. See Baudry, Duparc, and Milliard, *Rapport de Mssrs. les syndics provisoires.*

75. *Journal de Rouen*, June 17, 1836, 2; and *Gazette des Tribunaux*, June 17, 1836, 756.

76. See C.-D. Demiannnay, *Mémoire au Roi Pour Demiannay ainé*, 3; ANMT 68 AQ 8, Narcisse Lebas, "Réport aux Msrs. Le président et judges composant le tribunal de Commerce de Rouen Juge-commissaire," July 4, 1831, 2.

77. *Affaire Demiannay: Contient l'acte d'accusation et les audiences des 23 au 28 mai 1836 devant la Cour d'assises de Rennes* (n.p., n.d.), 47. See also AP D11 U3 79, dossier James Rollac.

78. On the 158 charges that pended against the nine, see "Cour de Rennes," 1–22.

79. *Gazette des Tribunaux*, September 21, 1834, 852.

80. "Affaire Demiannay," *Journal de Rouen*, July 5, 1836, 3.

81. "Affaire Demiannay," *Journal de Rouen*, July 16, 1836, 2.

82. *Affaire Demiannay*, 159.

83. Ibid., 161.

84. Quoted in C.-D. Demiannay, *Au Roi*, 4.

85. *Cour de Rennes*, 21.

86. *Gazette des Tribunaux*, June 10, 1836, 754.

87. See *Gazette des Tribunaux*, May 30–31, 1836, 711; *Affaire Demiannay*, 177; *Journal de Rouen*, May 31, 1836, 2.

88. *Journal de Rouen*, July 16, 1836, 1.

89. *Le Droit*, July 2, 1836, 736, italics in original.

90. Rollac, *Affaire Demiannay*, 5.

91. F. Demiannay, *Mémoire pour François Demiannay*, 23. The charge was lodged against him by one M. Lasnon and was judged in Demiannay's favor. See C.-D. Demiannay, *Réponse pour le sieur*. Demiannay's past reputation as a usurer was brought up quite regularly as a means of discrediting him. See ANMT 68 AQ 8, "Renseignments fournis par M. Thuret qui font partis des interrogatories à Rennes." This was discussed as reason for moving the trial, in *Gazette des Tribunaux*, September 21, 1834, 985.

92. F. Demiannay, *Mémoire pour François Demiannay*, 23.

93. Ibid., 4.

94. See ANMT 68 AQ 8, "Renseignments fournis par M. Thuret qui font partis des interrogatoires à Rennes"; and F. Demiannay, "Mémoire pour François Demiannay."

95. *Affaire Demiannay*, 178–79.

96. Rollac, *Affaire Demiannay*, 28.

97. ANMT 68 AQ 9, Letter from Thuret to M. Cheron, March 1843. The expert Leprevost was accused of similarly profiting from the bankruptcy's extension, which had won him a position at the Rouen Tribunal of Commerce and "earned him a living off the 13,000 accusations."

98. "Affaire Demiannay," *Journal de Rouen*, July 7, 1836, 2.

99. "Audience de 28 juin," *Le Droit*, July 2, 1836, 736.

100. C.-D. Demiannay, *Au Roi, pour Demiannay*, 5.

101. For the role of *force majeure* in French law, see J. D. Smith, "Impossibility of Performance."

102. *Le Droit*, July 2, 1836, 736.

103. Ibid.

104. "Affaire Demiannay," *Journal de Rouen*, July 16, 1836, 1.

4. A Palace of Debt

1. These versions included *Pauvre Jacques: Journal philosophique, anecdotique et littéraire de Sainte-Pélagie* (March 18, 1829, to June 15, 1829); *Pauvre Jacques: Journal de Sainte-Pélagie* (June 20, 1829, to August 30, 1829); *Pauvre Jacques: Journal de Sainte-Pélagie et des maison de detention pour dettes* (May 30, 1830, to July 27, 1830); *Pauvre Jacques: Journal Philanthropique* (August–October 1830); *Pauvre Jacques: Journal Populaire* (January 3, 1832, to December 29, 1833); *Gazette de Sainte-Pélagie et de toutes les maisons de detention* (November 30, 1834, to February 21, 1835); *Pauvre Jacques, Journal des Prisons, philosophique, anecdotique, littéraire* (March 1835); *Pauvre Jacques* (September 1838). While most of these were written from inside the prison, *Pauvre Jacques* in 1838 appears to have been edited by Maurice Alhoy after he left Clichy.

2. *Pauvre Jacques*, January 3, 1830, 2.

3. Foucault, *Discipline and Punish*, 235.

4. Ibid., 236.

5. *Gazette des Tribunaux*, February 7, 1829, 331.

6. I speak here of those arrested for *contrainte par corps* for private debts.

7. While debt prisoners tried to lobby prison reform organizations, like the Société royale des prisons, for ameliorations in their circumstances, the early prison reformers demonstrated little specific interest in debtors. See Société royale pour l'amelioration des prisons, "Rapport fait au conseil général des prisons dans sa séance du 2 juin 1819 par la commission nommée dans son sein par S. Ex. Le Ministre de l'Interieur, pour les instructions religieuses et morales des Prisons," 1. See also "Nouvelle supplique des prisonniers pour dettes au roi et aux deux chambres, à S. A. R Mgr. le duc d'Angoulême, Président de la Société royale pour l'amelioration des prisons, et à S. Exc Mgr. le Ministre de l'Interieur, Président; M . . . Vice-President, et autres membres du Conseil général des prisons, May 1819" (Paris: De l'Imprimerie de Anthe Boucher, 1819).

8. Wright, *Between the Guillotine and Liberty*, 48.

9. Petit, Castan, and Fogeron, *Histoire des Galères*, 45–63.

10. Ibid., 63–80.

11. O'Brien, *The Promise of Punishment*, 23.

12. See Spieler, *Empire and Underworld.*

13. O'Brien, *The Promise of Punishment*, 75–108.

14. Closel d'Arnery, *Abus et dangers*, 3.

15. Crivelli, *De la contrainte par corps*, 42.

16. Ibid.

17. Loubens, *De la contrainte par corps*, 24.

18. Pirmé, *De la nécessité*, 21.

19. ADHR Y 83, Direction générale de l'administration départmentale de la police Bureau des batiments civils et prisons Circulaire n. 88, November 16, 1820; and Ministère de l'Interieur direction générale de l'administration communale et départmentale Bureau des Prisons Circulaire n. 3, December 13, 1819. The widespread abuses noted in this inquiry, of which debt imprisonment was only one part, led to the creation of a permanent Royal Prison Society to oversee conditions in the prisons. On this, see Wright, *Between the Guillotine and Liberty*, 55–56.

20. ADHR Y 83, Decree of the Minister of Interior, November 4, 1820 (Paris: Imprimerie royale, 1820).

21. Bayle-Mouillard, *De l'emprisonnement pour dettes*, 139

22. Ibid., 332.

23. Vingtrinier, *Notice sur les prisons*, 23.

24. ADHR Y 83, "Réponse de Mairie du Colmar de Ministère de l'Interieur Direction générale de l'administration communale et départmentale Bureau des prisons circulaire N. 3 13 Dec 1819," question 10; *Le Pauvre Jacques Lyonnais*, December 26, 1830, 5.

25. See ADL Y 114, Letter to the Prefect of the Rhône, May 2, 1843.

26. *Gazette des Tribunaux*, April 28–29, 1835, 629.

27. According to Ouvrard, the money he paid for one room allowed a former lodger to reimburse his creditor and leave the prison. See Ouvrard, *Mémoires sur sa vie*, 3:102–3.

28. "Société de la Morale Chrétienne: Comité des Prison quatrième rapport sur les prisons de la Seine," *Gazette des Tribunaux*, April 5, 1829, 523.

29. Gallois, *Promenade à Sainte-Pélagie*, 61.

30. Ibid., 64.

31. Liancourt, *Le rideau levé*, 62.

32. Moreau-Christophe, *De l'état actuel des prisons*, 30.

33. Ibid.

34. Mayret, "La nouvelle prison," 339.

35. Ibid., 342.

36. "Reglement du 13 October 1841," reprinted in Cadrès, *Code manuel de la contrainte par corps*, 255–64.

37. See, e.g., the letters from debt prisoners written to the Corps Législatif in the 1860s collected in AN C 1115 dossier 44, Archives du Corps Législatif: Session 1867, Contrainte Par Corps.

38. Finn, *The Character of Credit*, 109.

39. Innes, "The King's Bench Prison."

40. See Woodfine, "Debtors, Prisons, and Petitions."

41. APP DA 233, folder: Petite Dettes à Sainte Pélagie, Letter to the Count of Anglas, Minister of State and Prefect of Police, January 22, 1819.

42. Pradel, *Les amis de Bordeaux*, 31.

43. ADO 1 Y 999, registre de délibérations de la commission de prisons de Beauvais, February 23, 1821.

44. ADL 1 Y 114, Letter from several prisoners to the subprefect, August 3, 1845.

45. Appert, *Journal des prisons*, 1:190.

46. Debt prisoners of Paris, "Reclamation des détenus pour dettes contre une inadvertence des législateurs de 1832" (Paris: Schnieder et Lagrand, May 10, 1846), 3.

47. Alhoy and Lurine, *Les prisons de Paris*, 252.

48. Gallois, *Promenade*, 61. The pittance became less frequently handed out to debt prisoners in the 1830s, probably because the increased alimentation allowed for the purchase of more food. See Mayret, "La nouvelle prison," 349.

49. Appert, *Journal des prisons*, 1:190.

50. *Gazette des Tribunaux*, May 15, 1839, 715.

51. See Mayret, "La nouvelle prison," 4:336.

52. APP DA 233, folder: Petite Dettes à Sainte Pélagie, Letter to the Prefect from the debt prisoners of Sainte-Pélagie, October 19, 1821.

53. Alhoy and Lurine, *Les prisons*, 247.

54. *Gazette des Tribunaux*, September 16, 1831, 987; March 10, 1839, 476; June 6, 1840, 767; October 29, 1846, 1001.

55. *Pauvre Jacques*, January 11, 1837, 3.

56. *Gazette des Tribunaux*, April 8, 1832, 345.

57. Moreau-Christophe, *De l'état actuel*, 32.

58. Bayle-Mouillard, *De l'emprisonnement*, 262.

59. *Pauvre Jacques*, January 24, 1830, 3.

60. APP DA 233, folder: Petite Dettes à Sainte Pélagie, Letter from Prefecture of Police dated October 24, 1818.

61. Ibid., petition, June 4, 1819.

62. AP D2 U4 16, Papiers Jean-Baptiste Adam, Letter from Jean-Baptiste Adam to Intendant-General of the King's Household, May 14, 1830.

63. APP D/A 233, folder: Petite Dettes à Sainte Pélagie, Letter from the Prefect of the Police, January 10, 1818.

64. G. Touchard Lafosse, *De la contrainte par corps en matière civile et commerciale in Loubens et Bourbon Leblanc suivie de Considerations morales, historiques et descriptives sur le même sujet* (Paris: L'Huillier, 1829), 310–13.

65. See APP DA 233, folder: Petite Dettes à Sainte Pélagie, Letter from the Prefect of the Police, January 10, 1818.

66. Ibid., Letter to the Baron Paquet, Prefect of Police, by the prisoners, February 14, 1811.

67. Ibid.

68. APP DA 233, folder: Petite Dettes à Sainte Pélagie, Report on the General Administration of Police in the Kingdom, June 28, 1814.

69. Ibid., Song enclosed in letter from Sainte Pélagie concierge to Prefect of Police, August 9, 1815.

70. O'Brien, *Promise of Punishment*, 14.

71. The example of Rouen mentioned above is the only one I can find in which debt prisoners were included in workshops.

72. ADL 1 Y 114, Letter to Prefect, December 8, 1842.

73. Ibid., Letter to Prefect, November 16, 1842.

74. Ibid., Letter to the Prefect, December 28, 1842. Apparently Fancon had been allowed the partial remuneration for his labor regularly given to prisoners. See Petit, *Ces peines obscures*, 172–73.

75. Ibid.

76. Alhoy and Lurine, *Les prisons*, 244.

77. Appert, *Journal des prisons*, 451. For canteens in penal institutions, see O'Brien, *Promise*, 159–60.

78. DA 233, folder: Petite Dettes à Sainte Pélagie, September 30, 1824.

79. *Gazette de Sainte-Pélagie et de toutes les maisons de detentions*, January 3, 1833, 3.

80. Ibid., May 6, 1833, 1.

81. *Pauvre Jacques*, December 12, 1830, 4.

82. APP D/A 233, folder: Petite Dettes à Sainte Pélagie, Letter to prefect of the police, June 10, 1811.

83. Alboize de Pujol and Maquet, *Les prisons de l'Europe*, 228.

84. Gallois, *Promenade*, 358–59.

85. Ouvrard, *Mémoires*, 105.

86. APP D/A 233, folder: Petite Dettes à Sainte Pélagie, Letter from concierge to Prefect of Police, December 24, 1811.

87. Ibid., Letter from concierge to Prefect of Police, June 24, 1814.

88. Ibid., Letter from concierge to Prefect of Police, October 19, 1821.

89. Ibid., Letters from prefect of police, June 4, 1832 and July 15, 1834.

90. Ibid., Letter from concierge to Prefect of Police, September 14, 1819.

91. *Gazette des Tribunaux*, February 17, 1831, 367.

92. Ibid., May 12, 1831, 657.

93. See APP D/A 234, prisons: Actes de bienfaisance. See also "De tout ce qui s'est passé," 4.

94. *Journal des Debates*, February 6, 1820, 4.

95. *Pauvre Jacques*, February 21, 1835, 3.

96. Pradel, *Les amis de Bordeaux*, 52–53.

97. See ADR 1 Y 42, folder Don Martin; and *Les Détenus pour dettes à Lyon aux prises avec la contrainte par corps en presence de la répresentation nationale et de leur concitoyens* (Lyon: Imprimerie de Th. Lépagnez, 1845).

98. Bayle-Mouillard, *De l'emprisonnment*, 160.

99. *Pauvre Jacques Lyonnais*, December 5, 1830, 4. This was apparently true of such donations more broadly. Indeed, outside donations were often viewed as means by which usurers expected to be paid. See similar charges made in Gallois, *Promenade*, 75.

100. *Pauvre Jacques Lyonnais*, December 5, 1830, 4.

101. ADL 1 Y 114, Letter from the Prefect of the Loire to the Deputy Prefect of the Loire, October 1, 1843.

102. APP D/B 233, folder: Petite Dettes à Sainte Pélagie, Report on the general administration of police in the kingdom, June 28, 1814.

103. Ibid.

104. Alboize de Pujol and Maquet, *Les prisons de l'Europe*, 228.

105. *Gazette de Sainte-Pélagie et de toutes les maisons de détention*, January 3, 1833, 4.

106. *Pauvre Jacques*, December 13, 1834, 4.

107. APP D/A 233, folder: Petite Dettes à Sainte Pélagie, Letter to the Prefect of Police, April 1831.

108. For more on the life of James Swan, see Rice, "James Swan."

109. *Gazette des Tribunaux*, July 23, 1829, 890.

110. Ibid., September 2, 1830, 1004.

111. James Swan, "À Messieurs de la Chambre des Députés" (Paris: Chez l'auteur, 1817), 4.

112. *Gazette des Tribunaux*, July 23, 1829, 890.

113. Ibid.

114. James Swan, *Réflexions adressées aux deux chambres relativement à la contrainte par corps dont sont passibles les étrangers, suivies d'une lettre ou sont développées des considerations politiques sur la même sujet* (Paris: Imprimerie Pihan Delaforest, 1829).

115. The most complete rendition of the colorful but largely apocryphal life of James Swan can be found in H. W. Small, *The History of the town of Swan's Island, Maine*, 1898, accessed at http://www.swansisland.org/swan.pdf, 31–38. Many of these anecdotes are corroborated by the anecdotal evidence in the French records, including his return to debtors' prison following the Revolution of 1830. See *Le Tocsin National: Journal des Libertés politiques, commerciales et littéraires*, July 5, 1830, 3.

116. *Pauvre Jacques*, June 20, 1830.

117. For Swan's requests to take up shooting and visit the spa, see the letters from the prefect of Paris dating June 15, 1816, and June 20, 1811, in APP D/A 233, folder: Petite Dettes à Sainte Pélagie.

118. AP D2 U4 16 consists of an entire dossier of Adam's letters, petitions, and poetry.

119. AP D2 U4 16, Papiers Jean-Baptiste Adam, Letter from Jean-Baptiste Adam to the Prefect of the Seine, July 22, 1821.

120. Ibid., Letter to the Good Works Committee in Ste Pélagie, 1822.

121. Ibid., Letter from Jean-Baptiste Adam to Charles X, May 1, 1830.

122. Ibid., Letter from Jean-Baptiste Adam to Intendant-General of the King's household, May 14, 1830.

123. In ibid., there are rent slips for these amounts.

124. *Gazette des Tribunaux*, September 20, 1834, 897.

125. *Le Droit*, March 19, 1838, 8.

126. APP D/B 132, "Considerations générales sur l'execution des contraintes par corps dans le département de la Seine."

127. Hulot, *Mémoire d'un prisonnier*, 3–4.

128. Blache, *Coup d'oeil*, 18.

129. Loubens, *De la contrainte par corps*, 52.

130. *Moniteur Universel*, March 25, 1828, 291.

131. *Pauvre Jacques*, January 3, 1830, 2.

132. *Pauvre Jacques: Journal Populaire*, March 29, 1829, 3.

133. *Pauvre Jacques*, December 20, 1829, 3.

134. *Pauvre Jacques*, September 27, 1829, 2.

135. *Gazette de Sainte-Pélagie et de toutes les maisons de détentions*, January 24, 1833, 3.

136. *Pauvre Jacques*, January 16, 1834, 3.

137. *Gazette de Sainte-Pélagie et de toutes les maisons de détentions*, January 17, 1833, 1.

138. *Pauvre Jacques*, January 3, 1830, 2; and February 7, 1830, 3.

139. See *Pauvre Jacques*, July 5, 1829; November 29, 1829; March 1, 1830.

140. *Pauvre Jacques*, June 6, 1830.

141. *Pauvre Jacques*, August 29, 1830.

142. Hulot, *Mémoire d'un prisonnier*, 8.

143. *Pélagiana ou le détenu pour dettes, petit poème en un chant* (Paris: Chez les Libraries du Palais Royal, 1816), 20.

5. The Economy of Discredit

1. Bayle-Mouillard, *De l'emprisonnement*, 4.

2. Ibid., 129.

3. Ibid., 136.

4. Ibid., 3.

5. See Hautcoeur, "La statistique et la lutte."

6. Between 1816 and 1832, for example, surviving pamphlets include M. A. B., *Abus de la contrainte par corps* (Paris: Delaunay, 1816); Saint-Aubin, *Essai sur la contrainte*

par corps; Burg, *Considérations sur la contrainte parcorps*; Claveau, *Réflexions sur le régime*; Chevalier, *Lettre à Me Claveau*; Anonymous, *Lettres d'un ancien avocat à un député sur la contrainte par corps* (Paris: Dentu, 1821); Boileau, *Contrainte par corps*; Huet, *Observations sur l'éxercice du droit*; Auguste Bonnal, *Pétition à la Chambre des Députés*; Leroy, *Observations pratiques*; Joyau, *Discours sur les abus*; Leblanc fils, *Observations sur l'esprit et les imperfections de nos lois relatives à la contrainte par corps en matière civile* (Paris: Eymery, Fruger et Cie, 1828); Loubens, *De la contrainte par corps*; Pirmé, *De la nécessité*; Anonymous, *Réfutation proposition par proposition de l'exposé des motifs du projet de loi sur la contrainte par corps, par un légiste* (Paris: Sellique, 1829); Crivelli, *De la contrainte par corps*; Salel, *Bombe lumineuse*; Anonymous, *Pétition à MM. de la Chambre des pairs au sujet de la contrainte par corps* (Saint-Denis: Imp. de Prevost, 1830); Anonymous, *Le cri du peuple, ou La liberté conquise en juillet 1830, et la contrainte par corps rétablie avec le règne de la tyrannie en janvier 1832* (Paris: Impr. de Carpentier-Méricourt, 1832); Foelix, *Commentaire sur la loi*; Pance, *De la contrainte par corps*.

7. Claveau, *Réflexion sur le régime*, I.

8. Coleman, *Debtors and Creditors in America*, 268.

9. Finn, *Character of Credit*, 152–96.

10. Peebles, "Washing Away the Sins of Debt."

11. See Hautcoeur, "La statistique et le lutte," 170.

12. *Journal des Débats Politiques et Littéraires*, December 31, 1816, and November, 21, 1830, 2.

13. Hautcoeur, "La statistique et la lutte," 174.

14. Bayle-Mouillard, *De l'emprisonnement*, 4.

15. Porter, *Trust in Numbers*, 82.

16. See, e.g., Ratcliffe, "Classes laborieuses."

17. Scott, *Gender and the Politics of History*, 115.

18. The passion for statistics in early nineteenth-century France is well documented in numerous books, most notably Hacking, *The Taming of Chance*; and Porter, *The Rise of Statistical Thinking*.

19. See Piers Beirne, "Adolphe Quetelet and the Origins of Positivist Criminology," *American Journal of Sociology* 92, no. 5 (1987): 1140–69; and Porter, *The Rise of Statistical Thinking*, 40–55.

20. Thompson, *Virtuous Marketplace*, 26.

21. "Les déténus pour dettes," in *Les français peints par eux-mêmes: Encyclopédie morale du dix-neuvième siècle* (Paris: L Curmer, 1840–42), 4:45.

22. *Moniteur Universel*, March 24, 1821, 400.

23. Hilaire, *Introduction historique*, 137–47.

24. A particularly cogent reflection on this theme can be found in P. E. Potier's 1851 work *De la contrainte par corps sous le régime républicain*, wherein, commenting on different commercial and appeals court decision, the author questioned why millers were treated differently than bakers and why inn keepers were "sometimes considered *commerçants* and sometimes not according to the nuances of their practice" (11–12).

25. Burg, *Considerations sur la contrainte par corps*, 100–101.

26. *Moniteur Universel*, May 9, 1829, 707.

27. *Moniteur Universel*, May 14, 1829, 739–42.

28. *Journal des Débats Politiques et Littéraires*, March 3, 1818; and *Moniteur Universel*, March 24, 1821, 398.

29. This was specified in Article 4 of the law of April 17, 1832. For a particularly trenchant critique of this, see Foelix, *Commentaire sur la loi*, 34–39.

30. Bayle-Mouillard, *De l'emprisonnement* 227.

31. Ibid., 201

32. Ibid., 203.

33. Ibid., 195.

34. Ibid., 160–61.

35. Ibid., 202.

36. Bayle-Mouillard's information here seems to have been largely what he pieced together from his personal impressions of the prisons. Most registers gave little detailed information about the profession of debtors or creditors. For example, in his statistics on the professions of provincial prisoners, the majority (some 161 of the 306 he reported) were simply titled "businessmen without other specification" or "merchants without additional specification." Likewise, of the 1,232 debtors on the internment records in Paris between the years 1831 and 1833, 161 were listed simply as "businessmen," 272 as merchants, and 105 as "*industriels*" (manufacturers or artisans) and artists.

37. Bayle-Mouillard, *De l'emprisonnement*, 202.

38. Ibid., 206.

39. Mary Lynn McDougall, "Consciousness and Community: The Workers of Lyon, 1830–1850," *Journal of Social History* 12, no. 1 (1978): 129–45.

40. Bayle-Mouillard, *De l'emprisonnement*, 356.

41. Ibid., 332, 336.

42. Louis-René Villermé, *Rapport à l'Académie des sciences morales et politiques sur l'état physique et moral des ouvriers, employés dans les fabriques de soie, de coton et de laine* (Paris: Mémoires de l'Académie des sciences morales et politiques, 1839), 349.

43. ADR 2 Y 284, Entry July 20, 1836, and ADR 2 Y 285, Entry November 11, 1837.

44. Kessler, "A 'Question of Name,'" 54–55.

45. Plessis, "Les banques locales," 204.

46. ADR 2 Y 285, Entry September 14, 1839.

47. ADR 2 Y 284, Entry April 23, 1835.

48. ADR 2 Y 285, Entry November 11, 1836.

49. William Reddy, *The Navigation of Feeling: A Framework for the History of Emotions* (Cambridge: Cambridge University Press, 2001), 259.

50. See Joan Landes, *Women and the Public Sphere in the Age of the French Revolution* (Ithaca: Cornell University Press, 1988).

51. See Sharif Gemie, "Balzac and the Moral Crisis of the July Monarchy," *European History Quarterly* 19, no. 4 (1989): 469–94.

52. See Hirschmann, *The Passions and the Interests*, 115–36.

53. Bayle-Mouillard, *De l'emprisonnement*, 123.

54. Ibid., 202.

55. Ibid., 111–12.

56. Ibid., 270.

57. Ibid.

58. Ibid., 149. The lottery would be abolished in 1836, the year Bayle-Mouillard's text was published.

59. Ibid., 232.

60. See, e.g., Léon Gozlan, *Nuits du Père La Chaise* (Paris: A. Lemerle, 1845); Xavier de Montépin, *Les Pécheresses: Pivoine* (Paris: A. Cadot, 1849); and E.-L. Guérin, *Magdeleine la Repentie, roman intime* (Paris: C. Lachapelle, 1837).

61. Alhoy, *Physiologie du créancier*, 14.

62. The novel, published in 1824, takes liberties in depicting the courtesan as a *femme commerçante*.

63. Bayle-Mouillard, *De l'emprisonnement*, 120.

64. Ibid., 258.

65. *Code civil*, Article 1158.

66. While Bayle-Mouillard offered little concrete evidence to prove that such alienations were in fact commonplace, some anecdotes emerged in trials which reveal that such an act may have been somewhat regularly undertaken. In one court case, after one Gontier of Caen was imprisoned and recommended by one Fromage for a 6,000-franc debt, his wife obtained authorization to take some property from her dowry to satisfy Sr Fromage and free her husband. *Gazette des Tribunaux*, January 26, 1840, 303.

67. *Moniteur Universel*, March 24, 1816, 3.

68. Bayle-Mouillard, *De l'emprisonnement*, 259.

69. Ibid.

70. Ibid., 231.

71. Ibid., 282.

72. Ibid., 318.

73. Ibid.

74. Ibid., 316.

75. Charles Vergé, *Séances et travaux de l'Académie des sciences morales et politiques, compte rendu* (Paris: Félix Alcan, 1847), 11:294.

76. Moreau-Christophe, *De l'état actuel des prisons*, 12.

77. Ibid., 37.

78. Decourdemanche, *Aux industriels*, 2.

79. Ibid., 8.

80. Ibid., 38.

81. Ibid., 46.

82. Ibid., 44.

83. Potier, *De la contrainte par corps*, 11.

1. This case is told from the following factums, mainly filed by Honoré Ardant, held by the Bibliothèque Nationale Francaise: "Cour Royale 3eme Chambre: Courte replique pour M. Ardant, appellant: Contre Mme Ve Genthon et ses syndics, intimés" (Paris: Imprimerie de J. R. Mevrel, 1836); "Note pour Le Sieur Ardant contre 1. Le Sieur Leborgne 2. La demoiselle Morvan 3. Le Sieur Dréan" (Paris: Typographie de A. Pinard, 1838); "Tribunal de Commerce. Faillite Genthon. Lettre de M. Ardant, négociant à Paris à Lemercier, évêque de Beauvais, se disant créancier de ladite Faillite" (Paris: Imprimerie A. Appert, 1834); "Tribunal de Commerce. Faillite Genthon. 2e Lettre de M. Ardant, négociant à Paris à Lemercier, évêque de Beauvais, se disant créancier de ladite Faillite" (Paris: Tribunal de Commerce, 1834); "Faillite Genthon: 3eme Lettre. À Monsieur l'évêque de Beauvais, se disant créancier de cette faillite plainte à M. le Procureur du Roi contre la veuve Genthon, contre M. Callou, avoué etc" (Paris: Imprimerie de J.-R. Mevrel, 1835).

2. "Note pour le Sieur Ardant," 16.

3. "Cour Royale 3me Chambre," 11.

4. Balzac, *César Birotteau*, 230.

5. *Journal de Rouen*, January 13, 1835, 3.

6. Ibid.

7. On ideas about competition and the potential for fraud, see Stanziani, *Rules of Exchange*, 115–44.

8. The folder AN BB 30 279 contains hundreds of responses to these circulars.

9. Examples of this include Alhoy, *Physiologie du créancier*; Maxim James, *Mémoires de mes créanciers, moeurs parisiennes* (Paris: Dufey et Vézard, 1832); Armand-Séville, "Le débiteur à la mode," in *Chansonnier de momus ou recueil de chansons inédites par MM. les membres des dîners du vaudeville, du caveau moderne et des soupirs de momus pour 1823* (Paris: T. Grandin, 1823), 159–60; Etienne-François Bazot, "Un tour de débiteur," in *Nouveaux contes en vers* (Paris: Cadot 1841), 102–4; Saint-Hilaire, *L'art de payer ses dettes*.

10. These dossiers can be found in the Archives de la Seine AP D11 U3 65–92.

11. Groult, *Exposé de quelques-uns des griefs*.

12. AP D11 U3 67 D. 6294, dossier Jacques Bestgen.

13. In the case of the dressmaker Alexis Languier, the trustees were chastised by the commercial court for their failure to do this. AP D11 U3 70 D. 6391, dossier Alexis Louis Languier.

14. AP D11 U3 67 D. 6288, dossier Marie Flory and Eugéne Flory.

15. Before the law of 1838, debtors had to be granted a safe-conduct pass by their creditors in order to be released from *contrainte par corps* and allowed to attend the affairs of their bankruptcy. Generally, most creditors would relent, acknowledging the need for debtors to assist the trustees. However, clashes could result between those who wished to keep the right of *contrainte par corps*.

16. D11 U3 85 D. 6869. See similar dossiers D11 U3 69 D. 6329, dossier Dame Lefebvre; and D11 U3 90 D. 7022, dossier Le Beau.

17. For example, following the death of her husband, Madame Noualhier managed 241,861 francs on behalf of her five minor children with only a usufruct over this property until they reached adulthood. When she went bankrupt in 1831, her creditors realized that they had a mortgage both on any sale of her estate up to this amount and on any product that came from its use. AP D11 U3 88 D. 6967, dossier Veuve Noualhier et Cie.

18. *Code civil*, Article 2101.

19. AP D11 U3 76 D. 6568, dossier Elisabeth Grim. A company's *fonds (de commerce)* refers not only to its assets but also to its clientele lists and the reputation enjoyed in the community. Early nineteenth-century companies regularly sold and mortgaged the *fonds* as an asset. See Stanziani, *Rules of Exchange*, 80–86.

20. AP D11 U3 76 D. 6567, dossier Chrétien Broder.

21. Marchant-Duroc, *L'art de s'enricher*, 29–30.

22. Balzac, *César Birotteau*, 231.

23. *Moniteur Universel*, March 29, 1838, 719.

24. Ibid.

25. On the preference for *concordats* in the first part of the nineteenth century, see Hautcoeur and Levratto, "Legal vs. Economic Explanations," 16–17, graph on 26.

26. AP D11 U3 88 D. 6958, dossier Adolphe François Cailleux and Auguste Henry Lefevre.

27. Ibid.

28. "Compte-rendu de la justice civil pendant l'année 1842," *Gazette des Tribunaux*, August 3, 1844, 973.

29. AP D11 U3 85 D. 6856, dossier Simon François Auberton.

30. Ibid.

31. *Gazette des Tribunaux*, August 25, 1844, 1050.

32. Balzac, *César Birotteau*, 42.

33. *Gazette des Tribunaux*, March 30, 1834, 197.

34. AP D11 U3 69 D. 6332, dossier Louis Ferdinand Blanchard.

35. *Gazette des Tribunaux*, April 24, 1827, 465.

36. *Gazette des Tribunaux*, February 17, 1842, 515.

37. "Résumé statistique du tribunal de commerce de la Seine, pendant l'année judiciare 1838–1839," *Gazette des Tribunaux*, August 31, 1839.

38. Chambre de Commerce de Marseille, "Observations de la Chambre de commerce de Marseille sur la législation relative aux faillites et banqueroutes" (Marseille: A. Ricard, 1827), VI.

39. AN BB 30 279, folder: Chambres de Commerce Response: Chamber de Commerce de Boulougne-sur-Mer.

40. Ibid., Chambre de Commerce de Dijon.

41. Ibid., Chambre de Commerce de Metz.

42. *Gazette des Tribunaux*, August, 29, 1830, 678.

43. *Moniteur Universel*, January 27, 1836, 152.

44. Ibid.

45. *Moniteur Universel,* March 18, 1838, 645.

46. Ibid.

47. AP 2ETP/3/3/80 1 Faillite 1804–1911, "Rapport presenté à la chambre des députés, dans la séance du 17 mars, par M. Quénault, député de la Manche."

48. Ibid.

49. *Moniteur Universel,* April 5, 1838, 453.

50. *Gazette des Tribunaux*, August 28, 1842, 1213.

51. See AP D11 U3 68 D. 6320, dossier Charles and Julienne Martin.

52. AN BB 29 280, "Déliberations du commission sur la projet sur les faillites et banqueroutes," 25.

53. AP 2ETP/3/3/80 1 Faillite 1804–1911, folder 721, "Circulaire du ministère de la justice aux tribunaux, chambres de commerce, etc au subject des modifications à supporter à la législation des faillites," May 22, 1827.

54. AN BB 29 280, "Déliberations du commission," 27.

55. Ibid.

56. Ibid., 32.

57. *Gazette des Tribunaux*, April 26, 1835, 432.

58. *Moniteur Universel,* March 28, 1838, 702.

59. *Gazette des Tribunaux*, November 7, 1839, 19.

60. Guérin-Chassi, "Exposé," 45–48.

61. AP D11 U3 91 1 D. 6365, dossier François-Émile Lecamus.

62. *Gazette des Tribunaux*, August 21, 1844, 1033.

63. Kessler, *Revolution in Commerce*, 141–42.

64. As Charles Freedeman notes, a disproportionately high number of directors sported the aristocratic prefix "de," whether they came by it honestly or not. This appeal to nobility supposedly lifted the esteem, and thus the credit, of the company in the eyes of investors. Freedeman, *Joint-Stock Enterprise*, 104.

65. Ibid., 8.

66. Between 1826 and 1837, 1,779 *sociétés en commandite par actions* were registered in France, nearly two-thirds of which were in Paris. The number of companies increased dramatically in the 1830s. In Paris in 1833, 55 companies, with a combined capital of 15 million francs, were registered by the Commercial Court of the Seine. Four years later, there were 288 companies with capital of 361 million francs. Freedeman, *Joint-Stock Enterprise*, 53.

67. Barthe, quoted in ibid., 59.

68. Wolowski, *Des sociétés par actions*, 47.

69. *Gazette des Tribunaux*, May 8, 1841, 691.

70. *Moniteur Universel,* March 17, 1838, 648.

71. *Gazette des Tribunaux,* January 28 and 29, 1839, 321–22.

72. *De la faillite d'Ibarrart: Des motifs qui ont determiné sa provocation et de ses suites probables* (Nantes: Imprimerie du Commerce, V. Mangin et W. Busseuil, 1841).

73. *Gazette des Tribunaux,* June 4, 1840, 753.

74. Ibid.

75. See *Gazette des Tribunaux*, April 29, 1841, 649.

76. See, e.g., M. Delangle, "Opinion de M. Delangle, avocat général la Cour de cassation sur la question de savoir si les créanciers d'une Société en faillite, répresentés par leurs syndics, ont une action directe contre les commanditaires en payment de leur mise" (Paris: Imprimerie de Madame Veuve Bouchard Huzard, 1844).

77. See *Gazette des Tribunaux*, March 14, 1844, 460; March 3, 1842, 567; April 29, 1841, 649.

78. For société anonyme, see Anne Lefebvre-Teillard, *La société anonyme au XIXe siècle: Du Code de commerce à la loi de 1867 histoire d'un instrument juridique du development capitaliste* (Paris: PUF, 1985).

79. Twenty companies were granted this status from the implementation of the Commercial Code in 1808 to the fall of Napoleon in 1815, 33 between 1815 and 1820, and 119 between 1820 and 1833. Freedeman, "Joint-Stock Business Organization," 201.

80. Ibid., 14.

81. *Gazette des Tribunaux*, November 2–3, 1843, 5.

82. *Gazette des Tribunaux*, January 18, 1838, 285.

83. Ibid.

84. Horace Émile Say, *Avant-propos*, 30.

85. Ibid., 42.

86. Ibid., 56.

87. Laviron, *Observations sur les faillites*, 39–40.

88. Ibid., 9–10.

89. Ibid., 50.

90. Ibid.

91. On this trope, see Schreiber, "Les Juifs."

92. Toussenol, *Les Juifs*, 1:172.

93. Ibid., 1:173.

94. "Discours du président of the Tribunal de Commerce de la Seine," *Gazette des Tribunaux*, August 30, 1840, 1060.

95. Hautcoeur and Levratto, "Petites et grandes entreprises," 206.

7. A Discount on the Future

1. Villain, *Récit exact et détaillé*, 7.

2. *Le Constitutionnel*, February 25, 1848, 1; Golovin, *L'Europe révolutionnaire*, 72.

3. Indeed, debt prisoners were freed by passing Revolutionary mobs in the Revolution of 1830. Luckett notes that during the French Revolution of 1789, debt prisoners were spared the September Massacres. See "Debate about Debt Imprisonment," 174.

4. L. Blanc, *Le socialisme*, 38–39.

5. L. Blanc, *Organisation du travail*, 145.

6. Considerant, *Le socialisme devant le vieux monde*, 5.

7. Decree of March 9, 1848, *Bulletin des lois*.

8. See *Le Droit*, March 16, 1848, 283.

9. For an overview of the financial crisis in 1848, see Gille, *La banque et le crédit*, 356–69.

10. See Marquess of Normanby, *A Year of Revolution*, 1:212–13.

11. See Palmade, *French Capitalism*, 117.

12. Hubert Bonin, "France, Financial Crisis and the 1848 Revolutions," accessed August 10, 2010, at http://www.ohio.edu/chastain/dh/franfin.htm.

13. AN F 12 6835 A: crises économiques, dossier 1: Décrets 1848, folder: Effets de commerce, comptes de retour, March 21, 1848, Lettre de Banque de France à la Chambre de Commerce de Toulouse, August 14, 1848.

14. *Le Droit*, March 17, 1848, 268.

15. *Le Droit*, March 4, 1848, 222.

16. Daniel Stern (Marie d'Agout), *Histoire de la Révolution de 1848*, 311.

17. Ibid., 312.

18. See AN F 12 6835 B, dossier 1: Projet de moratoire des effets de commerce.

19. *Bulletin des lois*, law of March 23, 1848.

20. M. Smith, *The Emergence of Modern Business Enterprise*, 69.

21. *Gazette des Tribunaux*, April 21, 1831, 603.

22. Palmade, *French Capitalism*, 125.

23. See the government circulars from AN F 12 6835 A: 1848 crises économiques, dossier 2: Comptoirs d'escompte et magasins de dépôt 1848.

24. See "Demande immediate de la nation française à retenir la crédit," March 17, 1848, AN F 12 6835 A: 1848 crises économiques, dossier 2: Comptoirs d'escompte et magasins de dépôt 1848. One letter writer, calling himself a *rentier*, proposed that commissions be nominated to collect money from households for the sake of commerce.

25. *Le Droit*, March 23, 1848, 297.

26. These inconveniences were the bases for reforms of the warrant system in 1858. For more on the warrant system, see Bruno M.-J. Dubron, *Étude juridique et économique sur les magasins généraux, les récépissés et les warrants* (Paris: L. Larose, 1898).

27. *Le Droit*, March 26, 1849, 297.

28. *Le Droit*, April 2, 1838, 322.

29. *Le Droit*, March 16, 1848, 283.

30. Ibid.

31. AN 67AP 11, quoted in Nicholas Stoskopf, "La fondation du comptoir national d'escompte de Paris, banque révolutionaire," *Histoire, Économie et Société*, no. 3 (2002): 408–9.

32. *Le Droit*, April 2, 1848, 322.

33. *Le Constitutionnel*, March 23, 1848, 3.

34. Darlot, *Économie politique et populaire*, 4.

35. My counts indicate eleven banks or credit institutions were proposed in 1848, whereas the period from 1830 to 1848 also had eleven. In all, thirty banks were proposed between 1848 and 1852. This is taken from the dossiers of banks and credit institutions provided in AN F 12 6776–79 and F 12 6825–31.

36. For land-backed banks, see pamphlets such as Coulombe, "Exposé des motifs suivi de trois projets de décret: demandant 1, ouverture d'un grand livre d'inscriptions

hypothécaires, 2, établissement d'une banque nationale foncière, 3, extension des attributions de la Banque de France actuelle" (Paris: Bouchard-Huzard, 1848); E. Dutreih, "Lettre sur la nécessité, le mode de création et les résultats d'une banque immobilière en France: adressée aux représentants du peuple: 22 mai 1848" (Paris: N. Chaix, 1848); and J. B., ex-agent-de-change à Lyon, *Observations présentées au citoyen Cavaignac, Chef du Pouvoir exécutif, sur les effets de la création d'une banque hypothécaire foncière* (Lyon: Dumoulin et Ronet, 1848).

37. There are numerous examples of pamphlets proposing various bank projects with the goal of alleviating the financial situation and bettering the situation of the working class. These plans differed widely in nature. For a few of the hundreds published that year, see J.-B. Cluzel, *Fusion des intérêts territoriaux et commerciaux, ou, Nouveau système de crédit applicable, par le commerce, à la propriété foncière et aux . . .* (Paris: Reynard, 1848); Johan C. Bijleveld, *De l'organisation du travail par un meilleur système de crédit* (Paris: Guillaumin, 1848); Victor Dégenétais, *La triple réorganisation du crédit, des richesses, du travail, par l'agriculture, l'industrie, la navigation, et le commerce, pour plus de 24 millions de travailleurs de 100 professions différentes* (Paris: Garnier, 1848); J.-B. Delcros, *Suppression de la Banque de France, création d'une banque nationale* (Paris: V. Magen, 1848); Edélestand Du Méril, *Organisation financière de la république* (Paris: Guillaumin, 1848); Lamennais, *Projet de constitution du crédit social.* For popular enthusiasm for such projects, see the numerous petitions sent to the legislative committee in spring 1848 in AN C 2241, including Citizen Martin, *Pétition aux citoyens représentants de l'Assemblée constituante pour la creation d'une banque nationale ouvrière* (Paris: Imprimerie de Vinchon, 1848).

38. Considerant, *Le socialisme*, 106.

39. Ibid.

40. Lamennais, *Projet de constitution du crédit social*, 5–6.

41. Coulombel, *La vérité sur la crise financière et sociale: Au Chef du pouvoir exécutif et à l'Assemblée nationale: État de la société et des ressources* ([Paris?]: 1848), 5.

42. *Les aberrations de m. Thiers: Projet de réforme financière propre à venir au secours de l'état, de la propriété et du commerce dans la situation* (Paris, 1848).

43. Fontarive, *Révolution sociale*, 15.

44. Avril, *Histoire philosophique du credit*, 1:vi–vii.

45. Langlois, *Du crédit privé*, 5–6.

46. Alphonse Jobez, *Une préface au socialisme, ou, Le système de Law et la chasse aux capitaliste* (Paris, 1848).

47. Audiffret, *La crise financière de 1848*, 58.

48. Gustave Puynode, *Lettres économiques sur le proletariat* ([Paris?], 1848), 167.

49. See Benjamin Delessert, *De la situation financière: Le ministre et le Comité des finances* (Paris: Bureau de la Revue des deux mondes, 1848), 12–15; and Gustave Barsalou-Fromenty, *Études sur le passé et sur l'avenir des travailleurs industriels* (Agen: P. Noubel, 1848), 143–44.

50. "Exposé général de la Commission de Gouvernment pour les travailleurs," in Louis Blanc, *La Révolution de Février au Luxembourg* (Paris: Michel Lévy, 1849), 125–26.

51. Anonymous, "Constitution de la République Française d'après l'texte official adopté par l'Assemblée nationale: Déclaration au peuple par les représentants s de la Montagne" (Paris: Chez Gosset, 1848), 12.

52. See, e.g., Cham, *La Banque-Proudhon et autres banques socialistes* (Paris: Bureau du Journal de Charivari, 1849).

53. *Journal du Tribunal de Commerce et de la Bourse de Paris*, November 26, 1848, 1.

54. *Moniteur Universel*, August 18, 1848, 2049.

55. Ibid.

56. *Moniteur Universel*, August 21, 1848, 2106.

57. See AN C 921 dossier 343, "Abrogation du décret du 20 mars 1848 qui a accordé un sursis judiciaire aux commerçants poursuivis" (Ordre du jour 27 novembre 1848).

58. See AN F 12 6835 B, dossier 1, folder: Projet de moratoire des effets de commerce.

59. AN F 12 6835 B, dossier 1, folder: Faillites sursis "Les commerçants de la ville de Blanc (Indre) aux citoyens membres du gouvernement provisoire," March 30, 1848.

60. AN F 12 6835 B dossier 1, folder: Projet de moratoire, especially "Déliberation de la Chambre de commerce de Saone et Loire," March 30, 1848, and Mallet Pointevin(?), "Lettre au Citoyen Bethmont, ministre de commerce à Paris," March 13, 1848.

61. See AN F 12 6835 A 1848: Crises économiques, dossier 1, folder: concordats aimables.

62. Ibid., Letter from shareholders of the Maison Baudon, Ganneron and Gouin Saint-Germain-en-Laye to the Minister of Finance, April 18, 1848.

63. E. Blanc, "La vérité sur la position commerciale." This one-sheet petition was credited with having started the debate on contracts *à l'aimable*. See *Journal des économistes: Revue mensuelle de l'économie politique, des questions agricoles, manufacturieres et commerciales* (1848), 168.

64. See AN C 2241, particularly the letters from Colette Aîné of Rouen to the legislative committee, June 1, 1848, and from Daniel de Costera, May 29, 1848.

65. Ibid.

66. *Moniteur Universel*, August 19, 1848, 2062.

67. Karl Marx, *Class Struggles in France, 1848–1850*, 33.

68. On Jules Favre, see Robert, Bourloton, and Cougny, *Dictionnaire des Parlementaires*, 2:618–20.

69. On Dupont, see ibid., 2:500–501.

70. *Moniteur Universel*, August 18, 1848, 2046.

71. Ibid.,

72. See *Gazette des Tribunaux*, July 27, 1848, 935.

73. See AN C 921 dossier n. 344, Privilege des ouvriers, en cas de faillites pour leurs salaires.

74. E. Blanc, *Note des délégués du commerce de Paris*, 3.

75. See J. D. Smith, "Impossibility of Performance."

76. *Moniteur Universel*, August 18, 1848, 2046.

77. Ibid., 2050. The term used is *banqueroute*.

78. *Moniteur Universel*, August 19, 1848, 2064.

79. See *Dictionnaire des Parlementaires*, 1:492.

80. *Moniteur Universel*, August 19, 1848, 2063.

81. See *Dictionnaire des Parlementaires* 1:473–74.

82. *Moniteur Universel*, August 12, 1848, 1986.

83. ABF 1069200401/218 dossier: contentieux: concordats aimables 1848–1918, Argout, "Observations sommaires sur les propositions soumises à l'Assemblée Nationale, par MM. Jules Favre et Dupont de Fussac, sur les concordats forcés," 9.

84. AN F 12 6835 A 1848: Crises économiques, dossier 1, folder: concordats aimables, Letter from the Governor of the Bank of France to the Minister of Agriculture and Commerce, August 10, 1848.

85. Ibid.

86. AN F 12 6835 A dossier 1, Governor of the Bank of France to the Minister of Agriculture and Commerce, September 10, 1848.

87. Argout estimated the amount involved to be between 52 and 64 million francs. ABF 1069200401/218 dossier: contentieux: concordats aimables 1848–1918, pièce Argout, "Observations sommaires."

88. *Moniteur Universel*, August 17, 1848, 2050.

89. AP 2ETP/3/3/80 8 Concordat 1848–1961; assurances contre la faillite, 1808–1860 Chambre de Commerce de Paris; Legentil, Horace Say, and Lanquetin, "Mémoire contre l'adoption des projets de décrets relatifs aux concordats aimables" (Paris: Plon Frères, July 6, 1848).

90. AN F 12 6835 dossier 1 A, Pinard and Hippolyte Biesta, "Observations présentés à l'Assemblée nationale par le comptoir national d'escompte de Paris sur les projets de décrets relatifs aux concordats amiables proposés par citoyens Jules Favre et Dupont (de Bussac)" (Paris: Paul Dupont, 1848), 4.

91. ABF 1069200401/218 dossier: contentieux: concordats aimables 1848–1918, "Des concordats forcés," *Gazette des Affaires*, July 8, 1848.

92. The Lyon Chamber of Commerce pushed its commercial court to accredit all concordats that unified the majority of creditors and where fraud was not suspected. See ABF 1069200401/218 dossier: contentieux: concordats aimables 1848–1918, "Concordats forcés," *Gazette des affaires*, July 22, 1848.

93. AN F 12 6835 A 1848: Crises économiques, dossier 1, folder: concordats aimables, Response of the Reims Chamber of Commerce, June 16, 1848.

94. Ibid.

95. See AN F 12 6835 A 1848: Crises économiques, dossier 1, folder: concordats aimables, "Lettre des membres de la chambre consulaire des arts et manufacturers de St. Quentin au Ministre," June 22, 1848.

96. ABF 1069200401/218 dossier: contentieux: concordats aimables 1848–1918, pièce 29, "Opinion émise au nom de tribunal de commerce par M. Devinck, president, sur les propositions de Jules Favre et M. Dupont de Bussac."

97. *Moniteur Universel*, August 20, 1848, 2077.

98. "Concordats aimables," *Gazette des Tribunaux*, July 30, 1848, 954.

99. "Avis du commité du commerce et de l'industrie sur les question des concordats aimables et les diverses propositions qui lui ont été soumises," reprinted in *Moniteur Universel*, August 12, 1848, 1987. Also AN C 921 dossier 342, "Accreditation

des concordats aimables réunisssant l'adhesion de deux tiers des créanciers," Décret du 22 Août 1848, doc. 3, "Projet sur les concordats aimables adopté par le comité du commerce et de l'industrie." Printed in *Moniteur Universel*, August 12, 1848, 1987.

100. *Bulletin des lois*, "Décret relative aux concordats amiables," August 22, 1848.

101. *Moniteur Universel*, August 22, 1848, 2110.

102. Ibid.

103. Ibid., *Moniteur Universel*, 2109.

104. Potier, *De la contrainte par corps*, 9.

105. ACC III 2.43 (Contrainte par corps), "Rapport du Commission du pouvoir exécutif," May 19, 1848.

106. AN C 2238 n. 354, "Aux citoyens membres de l'Assemblée Nationale à Paris."

107. AN F 12 6835 A dossier 1 (décrets et arrets 1848), folder: décret du 9 mars 1848, demandés du rétablissement de la contrainte par corps en matière commercial, letter from *négociant* from Martin-et-Vigne, November 16, 1848.

108. Ibid., "Extrait des registres de deliberations de la chambre de commerce de Clermont-Ferrand," October 28, 1848.

109. Ibid., Responses to Letter of Minister of Commerce and Agriculture, July 11, 1848.

110. ABF 1069200401/218 dossier: contrainte par corps, n. 34, "Conseil général 19 June 1848–22 June 1848."

111. Ibid.

112. The Bank of France's council also pointed to the relatively minimal use of *contrainte par corps*, estimating that while the number of *commerçants* in Paris was somewhere around 500,000 to 600,000 including foreigners, Clichy housed only 140 debtors at a time even though there were 40,000 or 50,000 judgments annually by the Paris Commercial Court that contained orders of *contrainte par corps*. ABF 1069200401/218 dossier: contrainte par corps, n. 34, "Conseil général 19 June 1848–22 June 1848."

113. Ibid.

114. "Rapport fait par le citoyen Hippolyte Durand, sur la proposition du citoyen Labordère, tendant au rétablissement de la contrainte par corps," *Moniteur Universel*, August 20, 1848, 2084.

115. Ibid., 2262.

116. *Moniteur Universel*, November 9, 1849. See also AN C 994 dossier 808, Cessation de l'application du décret du 22 aout 1848 sur les concordats aimables (Loi du 12 Novembre 1849), "Exposé des motifs et texte de la proposition présentée par M. Bravard-Veyrières."

117. AP D1 U3 48 Assemblée Nationale Legislative n. 456, "Rapport fait au nom de la Commission chargée d'examiner la proposition tendant a mettre terme . . . ," November 7, 1849.

118. See AP D13 U1 1, Liquidations judiciaires 1848–49.

119. *Journal du tribunal de commerce et de la bourse*, November 26, 1848, 2.

120. Ibid.

121. See AN C 994 dossier 809, "1. La Régularisation des concordats par abandon 2. dépôt au greffe de tout projet de concordat et du compte à rendre par les syndics, en cas d'union 3. système plus complet de publicité en matière de faillite: Exposé des motifs et texte de la proposition de M. Bravard-Veyrières"; and dossier 810, "Dispositions législatives à ajouter au code de commerce pour acceler la marché des faillites et assurer le paiement des dividendes revenant aux créanciers: Texte de la proposition présentée par MM. de la Boulie et Paul Sevaistre."

122. *Guerre au crédit*, 8.

123. Ibid., 59–60.

Epilogue

1. Pierre Larousse, "Contrainte par corps," in *Grand dictionnaire universel du XIXe siècle français, historique, géographique, mythologique, bibliographique* (Paris: 1866–67), 4:1101.

2. Ibid.

3. Eugène Paignon, "Question du jour, Paris 21 janvier: La contrainte par corps," *La Presse*, January 22, 1866, 1.

4. *Moniteur Universel*, July 17, 1867, 958.

5. M. Smith, *Emergence of Modern Business Enterprise*, 70.

6. A mere seven years after its enactment, there were to be more joint-stock companies formed in Paris alone than in the entirety of France in the previous sixty-year period in which authorization had been required. Freedeman, *Joint-Stock Enterprise*, 144.

7. *Gazette des Tribunaux*, November 2–3, 1843, 5.

8. See Sgard, "Do Legal Origins Matter?"

9. As Margot Finn has argued in her analysis of British debt imprisonment in *The Character of Credit*, the 1869 reform still allowed poor debtors to be imprisoned for their "unwillingness" to pay debts.

10. *Moniteur Universel*, July 18, 1867, 977.

11. *Moniteur Universel*, July 17, 1867, 918.

12. *Moniteur Universel*, July 7, 1867, 880.

13. *Moniteur Universel*, March 30, 1867, 385–86.

14. A similar story about the "collectivization of risk" can be found in Ewald, *L'état providence*, in which the completely responsible individual agent of the Civil Code gives way to the welfare state where all risk is assumed collectively. The genealogy I trace here, however, differs considerably from Ewald's.

15. Levratto, "Abolition de la contrainte par corps," 238.

16. *Moniteur Universel*, April 16, 1867, 469.

17. Ibid.

18. APP E/B 86, *Le Monde Illustrée*, August 2, 1867.

19. APP E/B 96, *L'Opinion Nationale*, June 24, 1869.

20. APP E/B 96, *Le National*, July 18, 1869.

21. Bernard and Clairville, *Feu la contrainte par corps*.

22. APP E/B 96, *Paris Journal*, June 22, 1870.

23. APP E/B 96, "Proceedings of Conseil General de la Seine 30 Avril 1872," 14–19.

24. APP E/B 96, *Le Corsaire*, May 3, 1872; *Le Rappel*, April 17, 1872; *Le Rappel*, July 26, 1869.

25. Anonymous, *Histoire de Paris, l'ancien et le nouveau. Les mystères de la préfecture de police. Les prisons de Paris. Le Châtelet et ses souterrains . . .* (Paris: S. Lambert, 1879), 167.

BIBLIOGRAPHY

Archival Sources

Archives Nationales (AN)

AD IX 541–45 papier-monnaie, assignats 1789–1815

AD XI 58–59 agents de change, banqueroutes faillites

AF III 35 dossier 123 questions du droit commercial et tribunaux de commerce

BB 18 162, 191, 193, 197, 204, 208, 211, 212, 219, 221, 235, 245, 246, 250, 265, 266, 273, 274, 275, 282, 287, 296, 314, 324, 748, 787, 789, 790, 792, 793, 795, 796, 797, 802

Correspondance générale de la division criminelle

BB 29 381 projet de loi sur banqueroutes et faillites

BB 30 279 projet de loi sur banqueroutes et faillites

F 12 501 A lettres et pétitions soumis au Ministre du Interieur où au Secretaire générale du minister 1792–1816

F 12 523 séances du Conseil général du commerce

F 12 796 projets et réflexions de particuliers sur les monnaies, les assignats les faillites 1790–An X

F 12 798B monnaie metallique et monnaie du papier

F 12 543–46 Code du Commerce An X–1808

F 12 866 banqueroutes et faillites 1806–11

F 12 971 B faillites contrainte par corps An IV–1815

F 12 2194 mémoires sur la commerce

F 12 2193 Code du commerce

F 12 2337–38 notes sur état d'industrie 1848 and avances aux ouvriers saisies-arrêts

F 12 2401 mémoires et notes sur les moyens de favoriser le commerce

F 12 2403 demandes et réclamations

F 12 6835 1848 crise économique: correspondence et législation, banques, effets du commerce, concordat à l'aimable, contrainte par corps, caisse d'escompte

F 70 pétitions Seconde Empire

271 AP 2 BB 10 Papiers Odilon Barrot: Correspondence: Affaire Demiannay

Archives Nationales Centre du Monde du Travail (ANMT)

68 AQ 8–18 Fonds Thuret: Affaire Demiannay
2003 060 371–77 Fonds Thuret: Affaire Demiannay

Archives de la Prefecture de Police de Paris (APP)

D/A 233 prisons: détenus pour dettes 1798–1834
D/A 234 prisons: actes de bienfaisance
D/B 27 huissiers
D/B 132 contrainte par corps
D/B 362 gardes du commerce
E/B 52 Tribunal du Commerce
E/B 86 Clichy
E/B 92 Sainte-Pélagie
Carton I Tribunal du Commerce
Carton V prisons

Archives de la Banque de France (ABF)

1069200401/218 dossier: concordats aimables 1848–1918
1069200401/218 dossier: contrainte par corps
1710199101/21 dossier: contentieux: faillites

Archives Departmentales

ARCHIVES DU RHONE (ADR)

1 Y 34 détenus pour dettes: reports
1 Y 42 détenus pour dettes: donation Martin
2 Y 485 détenus pour dettes: registre d'écrou

ARCHIVES DE L'HAUT-RHIN (ADHR)

1 Y 83 détenus pour dettes: enquête (1819–67)

ARCHIVES DU BOUCHES DU RHONE (ADBDR)

2 U 2 1132–2552 dossiers de justice: banqueroute

ARCHIVES DE L'OISE (ADO)

1 Y 705	contrainte par corps: circulairs
1 Y 706	contrainte par corps: prisons, enquêtes
1 Y 999	contrainte par corps
1 Y 1598	Compiegne: prisonniers pour dettes, enquête 1819

ARCHIVES DE LA LOIRE (ADL)

1 Y 114	detention des dettes, contrainte par corps

ARCHIVES DE PARIS (AP)

2ETP/3/2/00 4	Chambre de Commerce de Paris: contrainte par corps
2ETP/3/3/80 1	Chambre de Commerce de Paris: Faillite 1804–1911
2ETP/3/3/80 8	Chambre de Commerce de Paris: Concordat 1848–1961; assurances contre la faillite, 1808–60
D2 U4 16	Jean Baptiste Adam, marchand d'objets, détenu pour dettes 1820–21
D2 Y13 344	registre d'écrou Clichy 1837–46
D1 U3 48–49	Circulaires, correspondence, tableaux Ans V, IX, 1823–80 faillis
D8 U3 1–10	Tribunaux de Commerce: faillites, saisies etc.
D11 U3 65–92	Dossiers de faillite 1830–31
D11 U3 107–9	Dossiers de faillite 1848
D14 U3	Dossiers liquidations judiciaries 1848–49

Newspapers and Periodicals

Those without dates indicate journals consulted over several nonconsecutive years.

Archives Parlementaires

Le Charivari

Le Constitutionnel

Le Droit

Le Garde du Commerce: Journal des Renseignements Mutuels La Gazette des Tribunaux (1826–48)

Gazette de Sainte-Pélagie et de toutes les maisons de detention (1834–35)

Journal de Commerce

Journal de Debats Politiques et Littéraires

Journal de Rouen (1834–36)

Journal du Tribunal de Commerce et de la Bourse de Paris (1848)

Le Moniteur Universel

Pauvre Jacques: Journal philosophique, anecdotique et littéraire de Sainte-Pélagie (1829–33, 1835, 1838)

Le Pauvre Jacques Lyonnais (1830–31)
La Presse (1848)
La Sentinelle (1797–1807)
Le Tocsin du Commerce: Journal Administratif de Renseignements et de Garanties

Legal Codes and Annuals

Bulletin des lois
Civil Code (1804)
Civil Procedure Code
Code of Commerce (1807)
Compte général de l'administration de la justice criminelle en France Dictionnaire des Parlementaires (Paris: Bourloton, 1889–91)
Recherches statistiques sur la ville de Paris et le département de la Seine

Printed Sources

Alboize de Pujol, Jules-Édouard, and A. Maquet. *Les prisons de l'Europe*. Paris: Librairie théâtrale, 1851.
Alhoy, Maurice. *Physiologie du créancier et du débiteur*. Paris: Lavigne, 1842.
Alhoy, Maurice, and Louis Lurine. *Les prisons de Paris: Histoire, types, moeurs, mystères*. Paris: G. Havard, 1846.
Ancien négociant. *Observations sur le projet de code du commerce, présenté au gouvernement, le 13 frimaire an 10, par le ministre de l'Intérieur, et envoyé aux Tribunaux et Conseils de Commerce, avec invitation de transmettre au gouvernement leurs remarques*. Paris, 1802.
Antier, Benjamin, Jean Amand Lacoste Saint-Amand, and Alexandre Chapponier. *L'auberge des Adrets*. Grenoble: Roissard, 1966.
Antonov, Sergei. *Bankrupts and Usurers of Imperial Russia: Debt, Property, and the Law in the Age of Dosteovsky and Tolstoy*. Cambridge, MA: Harvard University Press, 2016.
Appel à l'honneur ou Les remboursements en assignats: Drame en III actes. Paris: Chez J. J. Fuchs Librairie, 1797.
Appert, Benjamin. *Journal des prisons, hospices, écoles primaires et établissements philanthropiques*. Paris: Chez Baudouin Frères, Libraires, 1825.
Audiffret, Charles-Louis-Gaston. *La crise financière de 1848*. Paris: Amyot, 1848.
Aulard, Alphonse, ed. *Paris pendant la réaction thermidorienne et sous le directoire: Recueil de documents pour l'histoire de l'ésprit public à Paris*. Paris: Librairie L. Cerf, 1899.
———, ed. *Paris sous le consulat: Recueil de documents pour l'histoire de l'ésprit publique à Paris*. Paris: Librairie Cerf, 1923.
Avril, Victor. *Histoire philosophique du crédit*. Paris: F. Alcan, 1849.
Balleisen, Edward J. *Navigating Failure: Bankruptcy and Commercial Society in Antebellum America*. Chapel Hill: University of North Carolina Press, 2001.

Balzac, Honoré. *César Birotteau*. Translated by Robin Buss. New York: Penguin Books, 1994.

———. *Eugénie Grandet: Scènes de la vie de Province*. Charleston: Biblio Bazaar, 2007.

Barbier, Victor. *Droit commercial: De la banqueroute frauduleuse*. Strasbourg: Imprimerie de E. Huder, 1859.

Basin. *Dialogue sur les transactions entre un créancier et un débiteur d'assignats*. Paris: De l'Imprimerie de Tarlier, 1797.

Batbie, Anselme. "La liberté économique dans la législation: Les sociétés commerciales et la contrainte par corps." *Revue des Deux Mondes* 73 (1868): 1025–41.

Baudrillart, Henri. *Chronique économique*. Paris: P. Rossi, 1865.

Baudry, Duparc, and Milliard. *Rapport de Mssrs. les syndics provisoires de la faillite Demiannay l'ainé lu à l'assemblée générale des créanciers le 14 février 1837*. Rouen: F. Baudry, 1837.

———. *Tableau justicatif du préjudice éprouvé par les créanciers Demiannay l'ainé, de Rouen*. Lyon: Imprimerie de Nigon, 1843.

Bayle-Mouillard, Jean-Baptiste. *De l'emprisonnement pour dettes: Considération sur son origine, ses rapports avec la morale publique et les intérêts du commerce, des familles, de la société; suivies de la statistique de la contrainte par corps*. Paris: Imprimerie royale, 1836.

Bazot, Étienne-François. *Nouveaux contes en vers*. Paris: Cadot, 1841.

Beachy, Robert. "Bankruptcy and Social Death: The Influence of Credit-Based Commerce on Cultural and Political Values." *Zeitsprünge: Forschungen zur Frühen Neuzeit* 4, no. 4 (2000): 329–43.

Beirne, Piers. "Adolphe Quetelet and the Origins of Positivist Criminology." *American Journal of Sociology* 92, no. 5 (1987): 1140–69.

Bergeron, Louis. *Banquiers, négociants et manufacturiers parisiens du Directoire à l'Empire*. Paris: EHESS, 1978.

———. "Profits et risques dans les affaires parisiennes à l'époque du Directoire et du Consulat." *Archives Historiques de la Révolution Francaise* 185 (1966): 359–89.

Bernard, Victor, and M. Clairville. *Feu la contrainte par corps*. Paris: Librarie Dramatique, 1867.

Bertrand, Clément. *Pourquoi la contrainte par corps doit être aboli suivi de: Nos bons huissiers, curieux details!!!* Paris: Chez l'auteur, 1867.

Bièville, Edmond de. "Du rétablissement de la contrainte par corps." PhD thesis, Université de Paris–Sorbonne, 1904.

Bigo, Robert. *Les banques françaises au cours du XIXe siècle*. Paris: Recueil Sirey, 1947.

Blache, Joseph-Virgile. *Coup d'oeil rapide sur la contrainte par corps*. Paris: Chez les principaux librairies et marchands de nouveautés, 1821.

Blanc, Emmemond. *Note des délégués du commerce de Paris: Des vraies raisons de decider dans la question dite des concordats aimables*. Paris: Imprimerie centrale de Napoléon Chaix et Cie, 1848.

———. *La vérité sur la position commerciale: Aux électeurs de la Seine*. Paris: Plon, 1848.

Blanc, Louis. *Organisation du travail, 5. éd., revue, corrigée et augmentée d'une polémique entre m. Michel Chevalier et l'auteur, ainsi que d'un appendice indiquant ce qui pourrait être tenté dès à present*. Paris: Au bureau de la Société de l'industrie fraternelle, 1848.

———. *Le socialisme: Droit au travail: Réponse à m. Thiers*. Paris: M. Lévy, 1848.

Blaufarb, Rafe. *The Great Demarcation: The French Revolution and the Invention of Modern Property*. New York: Oxford University Press, 2016.

Boileau, Marie-Louis-Joseph de. *Contrainte par corps, abus à réformer: Appel à S. M. Louis XVIII et au Corps législatif*. Paris: Chez l'auteur, n.d.

Bonin, Hubert. *La banque et les banquiers en France: Du Moyen Age à nos jours*. Paris: Larousse, 1992.

Bonnal, Auguste. *Pétition à la Chambre des Députés, pour l'amélioration de la contrainte par corps en matière commercial*. Paris: Imprimerie de A. Égron, 1823.

Bonnier, Édouard. *Éléments de procédure civile*. Paris: Plon frères, 1853.

Bosher, John. *French Finance, 1770–1795: From Business to Bureaucracy*. Cambridge: Cambridge University Press, 1970.

Boulay-Paty, Pierre-Sébastien. *Traité des faillites et banqueroutes: Suivi de quelques observations sur la déconfiture*. Paris: Videcocq, 1849.

Bourbon-Busset, Gabriel de. *De la contrainte par corps en matière civile et commerciale*. Paris: L'Huillier, 1829.

Braudel, Ferdinand, and Ernest Labrousse, eds. *Histoire économique et sociale de la France, Tome III/1, L'avènement de l'ère industrielle (1789–années 1880)*. Paris: Presses universitaires de France, 1976.

Brolles. *Aperçus nouveaux sur la contrainte par corps: Son rétablissement ou suppression de la faillite*. Paris: E. Dentu, 1868.

Brown, Howard. "A Discredited Regime: The Directory and War Contracting." *French History* 4, no. 1 (1990): 48–76.

———. *Ending the French Revolution: Violence, Justice, Repression*. Charlottesville: University of Virginia Press, 2006.

Brown, Howard, and Judith Miller, eds. *Taking Liberties: Problems of a New Order from the French Revolution to Napoleon*. Manchester: Manchester University Press, 2002.

Bruguière, J.-Thomas. *Discussion politique sur l'usure et le prêt sur gages, adressée aux Consuls de la République*. Paris, 1802.

Bruno, M.-J. Dubron. *Étude juridique et économique sur les magasins généraux, les récépissés et les warrants*. Paris: L. Larose, 1898.

Burg, Michel. *Considérations sur la contrainte par corps en matières de dettes dites commerciales, suivies du tableau alphabétique des incarcérateurs*. Paris: Delaunay, 1820.

C, T de. *Pélagiana ou Le détenu pour dettes, petit poème en un chant*. Paris: Chez les librairies du Palais Royal, 1816.

Cadrès, Émile. *Code manuel de la contrainte par corps et l'emprisonnment pour dettes (en matière civile, commerciale, criminelle, correctionelle et de police)*. Paris: Chez l'éditeur, 1853.

Cahiers du tiers-état de la ville de Paris. Paris: Méquignon, 1789.

Callaway, Hannah. "Revolutionizing Property: The Confiscation of Émigré Wealth in Paris and the Problem of Property in the French Revolution." PhD thesis, Harvard University, 2015.

Chaïbi, Olivier. "Entre crédit public et crédit mutuel: Un aperçu des théories du crédit au XIXe siècle." *Romantisme* 151, no. 1 (2011): 53–66.

Chaline, Jean-Pierre. "La banque à Rouen au XIXe siècle." *Revue d'Histoire Économique et Sociale* 52, no. 2 (1974): 390–402.

———. *Les bourgeois de Rouen: Une élite urbaine au XIXe siècle*. Paris: Presses de la Fondation nationale des sciences politiques, 1982.

Chambre de Commerce de Paris. *Rapport sur les jurandes et maîtrises; et sur un projet de statuts et règlemens pour MM. les Marchands de vin de Paris*. Paris, 1805.

Chambre de Commerce de Toulon et du Var Extrait des Registres de Déliberations. Toulon: Imprimerie, lithographie et librairie civiles et militaires de Ch. Mihière, 1874.

Chambre syndicale de la joaillerie, bijouterie, orfèvrerie et horlogerie. *Note adressée par la Chambre syndicale de la Joaillerie, Bijouterie, Orfèvrerie et Horlogerie au nom de tous les commerçants qu'elle représente à monsieur le président et à messieurs les membres de la commission de la loi sur la contrainte par corps*. Paris: Imprimerie Dupont, 1866.

Chassaing. *Mémoire justicatif pour le sieur Brassier, père, habitant la ville de Clermont-Ferrand, accusé, contre M. le Procureur-général près la Cour royale de Riom, poursuivant, en presence et contre plusieurs de créanciers du sieur Brassier-Bernard, son fils, parties civiles*. Clermont-Ferrand: Impr. J.-J. Vaissière, 1829.

Chevalier, A. P. *Lettre à M. Claveau, au sujet de ses réflexions sur la contrainte par corps*. Paris: J. Crémière fils, 1820.

Claustre, Julie. *Dans les geôles du roi: L'emprisonnement pour dette à Paris à la fin du Moyen Âge*. Paris: Sorbonne, 2007.

Claveau, L. J. *Réflexions sur le régime de la contrainte par corps à l'occasion des changemens demandés*. Paris: Chez les marchands de nouveautés, 1820.

Closel d'Arnery, Claude Gaspard. *Abus et dangers de la contrainte par corps*. Paris: Royez, 1788.

Cobb, Richard. *Terreur et substances 1793–1795*. Paris: Librairie Clavreuil, 1968.

Cobban, Alfred. "The 'Middle-Class' in France, 1815–1848." *French Historical Studies* 5 (1967): 41–52.

Code du Commerce servant de supplement au procès-verbal des séances du Corps legislatif September 1807: Exposés des motifs par les orateurs du gouvernement. Paris: Hacquart, 1807.

Coleman, Paul. *Debtors and Creditors in America: Insolvency, Imprisonment for Debt, and Bankruptcy, 1607–1900*. Madison: University of Wisconsin Press, 1974.

Collingham, H. A. C. *The July Monarchy: A Political History of France, 1830–1848*. New York: Longman, 1988.

Considerant, Victor. *Le socialisme devant le vieux monde, ou, Le vivant devant les morts suivi de Jesus-Christ devant les conseils de guerre*. Paris: Librairie phalanstérienne, 1848.

Constitution de la République française d'après l'texte official adopté par l'Assemblée nationale: Déclaration au people par les représentant de la Montagne. Paris: Chez Gosset, 1848.

Cour de Rennes: Affaire Demiannay. Rennes: Imprimerie de Marteville, [1836?].

Cour Royale 3me Chambre: Courte réplique pour M. Ardant, appellant: Contre Mme Ve Genthon et ses trustees, intimés. Paris: Imprimerie de J. R. Mevrel, 1836.

Coyer, Gabriel Francois. *Développement et défense du système de la noblesse commerçante*. Paris: Chez Duschesne, 1757.

Le cri du peuple, ou La liberté conquise en juillet 1830, et la contrainte par corps rétablie avec le règne de la tyrannie en janvier 1832. Paris: Imprimerie de Carpentier-Méricourt, 1832.

Crivelli, Joseph-Louis. *De la contrainte par corps considérée sous les rapports de la morale, de la religion, du droit naturel et du droit civil, et dans l'intérêt de l'humanité en general*. Paris: G. Pissin, 1830.

Crossick, Geoffrey, and Heinz-Gerhard Haupt. *The Petite Bourgeoisie in Europe, 1780–1914*. New Brunswick, NJ: Routledge, 1997.

Crouch, Charles. "The Petite Bourgeoisie of Paris during the Bourbon Restoration, 1814–1830: A Prosopographical Inquiry into the Political and Economic Integration of the Parisian Lower Middle Class." PhD thesis, University of Illinois, Urbana-Champaign, 1991.

Crouzet, François. *La grande inflation: La monnaie en France de Louis XVI à Napoléon*. Paris: Flayard, 1993.

———. "The Historiography of French Economic Growth in the Nineteenth Century." *Economic History Review* 56, no. 2 (2003): 215–42.

Crowston, Clare. "Credit and the Metanarrative of Modernity." *French Historical Studies* 34, no. 1 (2011): 7–19.

———. *Credit, Fashion, Sex: Economies of Regard in Old Regime France*. Durham, NC: Duke University Press, 2013.

———. "Family Affairs: Wives, Credit, Consumption and the Law in Old Regime France." In *Family, Gender, and Law in Early Modern France*, ed. Susanne Desan and James Merrick, 62–100. University Park: Pennsylvania State University Press, 2009.

———. "The Queen and Her Minister of Fashion: Gender, Credit and Politics in Pre-revolutionary France." *Gender & History* 14, no. 1 (2002): 19–44.

Danieri, Cheryl. "Credit Where Credit Is Due: The Mont-de-Piété of Paris 1777–1851." PhD thesis, University of California, Irvine, 1981.

Darlot, G. *Économie politique et populaire: Le crédit, les banques, la Banque de France*. Paris: Imprimerie de V. Barbier, 1895.

Darrow, Margaret. *Revolution in the House: Family, Class, and Inheritance in Southern France, 1775–1825*. Princeton: Princeton University Press, 1990.

Davidson, Denise Z. *After the Revolution: Urban Life, Gender, and the New Social Order*. Cambridge, MA: Harvard University Press, 2007.

Débiteur. *Physiologie de l'argent*. Paris: Desloges, 1841.

Decourdemanche, Alphonse. *Aux industriels: Lettres sur la législation dans ses rapports avec l'industrie et la propriété*. Paris: Le Globe, 1831.

Demiannay, Charles-Denis. *Au Roi, pour Demiannay, ainé ancien banquier à Rouen*. Paris: Imprimerie de Felix Malteste, 1836[?].

———. *Mémoire au Roi pour Demiannay ainé, ancien banquier*. Paris: Imprimerie de Felix Malteste, 1836.

———. *Réponse pour le sieur Demiannay aux deux libelles signés Henry Lasnon*. Rouen: Imprimerie N. Périaux le jeune, 1829.

Demiannay, François. *Mémoire pour François Demiannay neveu, première partie*. Rouen: Imprimerie de Mégard, 1832.

Dennery, M., and E. Grange. *À Clichy: Épisode de la vie d'artiste*. Paris: Michel Levy Frères, 1855.

De Roover, Raymond. *L'evolution de la lettre de change, XIVe–XVIIIe siècles*. Paris: Armand Colin, 1953.

Desan, Suzanne. *The Family on Trial in Revolutionary France*. Berkeley: University of California Press, 2006.

———. "Reconstituting the Social after the Terror: Family, Property and the Law in Popular Politics." *Past and Present* 164 (1999): 81–121.

De Santos, Antonio. "Les conflits de compétence entre jurisdiction consulaire et jurisdictions ordinaries en matière de faillite: Le role de la chambre de commerce de Guyenne." In *Les Tribunaux de commerce: Genèse et enjeux d'une institution*, ed. Pascal Clément, 55–66. Paris: Association française pour l'histoire de la justice, 2007.

Deshusses, Frédéric. "Mésurer l'insolvabilité?: Usages statistiques des dossiers de faillite (1673–1807)." *Histoire et Mésure* 23 (2008): 19–41.

De tout ce qui s'est passé au moment du depart du convoi de S.A.R. le duc d'Orleans pour se rendre à Dreux. Ce qui a eu lieu à Versailles, Sevres, Passy etc. Autres details de l'arrivée du convoi à Dreux, ou se trouvaient LL MM le Roi, la Reine et tous les Princes. Paris: Imprimerie de Chassaignon, 1842.

De Vries, Jan. "The Industrial Revolution and the Industrious Revolution." *Journal of Economic History* 54 (June 1994): 249–70.

Deymes, Louis. "L'évolution de la nature juridique de la contrainte par corps." PhD thesis, Université de Toulouse, 1942.

Ditz, Toby L. "Shipwrecked; or Masculinity Imperiled: Mercantile Representations of Failure and the Gendered Self in Eighteenth-Century Philadelphia." *Journal of American History* 81, no. 1 (1994): 51–80.

Donovan, James. *Juries and the Transformation of Criminal Justice in France in the Nineteenth and Twentieth Centuries*. Chapel Hill: University of North Carolina Press, 2010.

Duffy, Ian. *Bankruptcy and Insolvency in London during the Industrial Revolution*. New York: Routledge, 1985.

Dumas, Alexandre. *The Count of Monte Cristo*. Translated by Robin Buss. New York: Penguin Classics, 2003.

Dupouy, Claude. *Le droit des faillites en France avant le Code de commerce*. Paris: Librairie générale de droit et de jurisprudence, R. Pichon et R. Durand-Auzias, 1967.

Duveau, Georges. *1848: The Making of a Revolution*. Translated by Ann Carter. New York: Pantheon Books, 1967.

Ewald, François. *L'état providence*. Paris: Grasset, 1986.

Exposé de quelque-uns des griefs de M. Martin Groult, ancién négociant à Rouen contre M. Auguste Delalande, fabricant à Elbeuf. Rouen: Imprimerie N. Périaux le jeune, 1829.

Faillite Genthon: 3me Lettre à Monsieur l'Évêque de Beauvais, se disant créancier de cette faillite plainte à M. le Procureur du Roi contre la veuve Genthon, contre M. Callou, avoué etc. Paris: Imprimerie de J-R Mevrel, 1835.

Fairchilds, Cissie. "The Production and Marketing of Populuxe Goods in Eighteenth-Century Paris." In *Consumption and the World of Goods*, ed. John Brewer and Roy Porter, 228–48. New York and London: Routledge, 1993.

Farr, James R. "The Death of a Judge: Performance, Honor, and Legitimacy in Seventeenth-Century France," *Journal of Modern History* 75 (March 2003): 1–22.

Ferreira, Nathalie. "Crédit et monnaie sociale chez P.J. Proudhon (1809–1865)." *Revue de Philosophie Économique* 12 (2011): 91–116.

Finn, Margot. *The Character of Credit: Personal Debt in English Culture, 1740–1914*. Cambridge: Cambridge University Press, 2003.

Fitzsimmons, Michael. *From Artisan to Worker: Guilds, the French State, and the Organization of Labor, 1776–1821*. Cambridge: Cambridge University Press, 2010.

———. "The National Assembly and the Abolition of Guilds in France." *Historical Journal* 39, no. 1 (1996): 137–52.

Fleury, Jules. *De la contrainte par corps: Études économiques*. Paris: Auguste, 1863.

Foelix, Jean-Jacques-Gaspard. *Commentaire sur la loi du 17 avril 1832 relative à la contrainte par corps*. Paris: G. Pissin, 1832.

Fontaine, Laurence. "Antonio and Shylock: Credit and Trust in France, c. 1680–c. 1780." *Economic History Review* 54, no. 1 (2001): 39–57.

———. *L'économie morale: Pauvreté, crédit et confiance dans l'Europe pré-industrielle*. Paris: Gallimard, 2008.

———. *A History of Pedlars in Europe*. Durham, NC: Duke University Press, 1996.

———. *Les personnes aux institutions: Réseaux et culture du crédit du XVIe au XXe siècle en Europe; actes du colloque international centenaire des FUC*. Louvain-la-Neuve: Bruylant-Academia, 1996.

Fontarive, Leo. *Révolution sociale: Bases du crédit positif, institutions de garantisme, organisation du travail, des armées industrielles, colonization*. Paris: Librairie phalanstérienne, 1848.

Ford, Richard. "Imprisonment for Debt." *Michigan Law Review* 25 (November 1926): 24–49.

Foucault, Michel. *Discipline and Punish: The Birth of the Prison*. Translated by Alan Sheridan. New York: Vintage Books, 1995.

Fourcher, M. L. "Deuxième mémoire pour M. L. Fourcher, défendeur, accusé de banqueroute frauduleuse contre les parties civiles plaignantes." Paris: Imprimerie de Paul Dupont, 1838.

Freedeman, Charles. "Joint-Stock Business Organization in France, 1807–1867." *Business History Review* 39 (Summer 1965): 184–204.

———. *Joint-Stock Enterprise in France, 1807–1867: From Privileged Company to Modern Corporation*. Chapel Hill: University of North Carolina Press, 1979.

Friedland, Paul. *Seeing Justice Done: The Age of Spectacular Capital Punishment in France*. New York: Oxford University Press, 2012.

Gallais-Hamonno, Georges, and Pierre-Cyrille Hautcoeur. *Le marché financier français au XIXe siècle*. Paris: Sorbonne, 2007.

Gallois. *Promenade à Sainte-Pélagie ou petit manuel à l'usage des journalists, des hommes de lettres, de tous ceux qui font des dettes*. Paris: A. Leroux, 1823.

Gens de banque et de finance vus au XIXe siècle. Paris: Les Éditions Errance, 1984.

Geoffroy, Louis. *Le code pratique des faillites*. Paris: Durand, 1853.

Gérard, F.-C. *Les trois amis, ou le Prix du travail*. Rouen: Mégard, 1853.

Gille, Bertrand. *La banque en France au 19e siècle: Recherches historiques*. Paris: Droz, 1970.

———. *La banque et le crédit en France de 1815 à 1848*. Paris: Presses universitaires de France, 1959.

Giraudeau. *Mémoire sur les moyens de prévenir les fraudes en matière de faillites*. Paris: Imprimerie de Goetschy, 1829.

Goldstein, Jan. *Console and Classify: The French Psychiatric Profession in the Nineteenth Century*. Cambridge: Cambridge University Press, 1987.

———. *The Post-revolutionary Self: Politics and Psyche in France, 1750–1850*. Cambridge, MA: Harvard University Press.

Golovin, Ivan. *L'Europe révolutionnaire*. Paris: Capelle, 1849.

Gontard, Maurice. *La Bourse de Paris (1800–1830)*. Aix-en-Provence: Edisud, 2000.

Gorneau, Philippe-Joseph. *Révision du projet de Code du commerce, précédée de l'analyse raisonnée des observations du Tribunal de Cassation, des tribunaux d'appel et des tribunaux et conseils de commerce*. Paris: Imprimerie de la République, 1803.

Guérin-Chassi. *Exposé pour le sieur Guérin-Chassi, marchand de Bois, à Nantes*. Nantes: Imprimerie de Veuve Mangin, 1828.

Guerre au crédit: Ou les dangers des l'emprunt. Paris: Videcocq Fils, 1850.

Gueslin, André. "Aux origines de l'État-providence: La mise en place du modèle français des caisses d'épargne." *Revue d'Histoire Moderne et Contemporaine* 38, no. 2 (1991): 231–50.

Haagan, Paul. "Imprisonment for Debt in England and Wales." PhD thesis, Princeton University, 1986.

Halpérin, Jean-Louis. *Histoire du droit privé francais depuis 1804*. Paris: Presses universitaires de France, 1996.

Hardwick, Julie. "Banqueroute: La faillite, le crime et la transition vers le capitalisme dans la France modern." *Histoire, Économie & Société* 30, no. 2 (2011): 79–93.

———. *Family Business: Litigation and the Political Economies of Daily Life in Early Modern France*. New York: Oxford University Press, 2009.
Harris, S. E. *The Assignats*. Cambridge, MA: Harvard University Press, 1930.
Hautcoeur, Pierre-Cyrille, ed. *Le marché financier français au XIXe siècle*. Paris: Sorbonne, 2007.
———. "Les transformations du crédit en France au XIXe siècle." *Romantisme* 151, no. 1 (2011): 23–38.
———. "La statistique et la lutte contre la contrainte par corps: L'apport de Jean-Baptiste Bayle-Mouillard." *Histoire et Mésure* 23, no. 1 (2008): 169–89.
Hautcoeur, Pierre Cyrille, and Nadine Levratto. "Legal vs. Economic Explanations of the Rise in Bankruptcies in XIXth Century France." Paper presented at the conference "Not Just Firms: History, Law, and Economics," Paris, March 2007.
———. "Petites et grandes entreprises face à la faillite en France au 19e siècle: Du droit à la pratique." In *Le capitalisme au futur antérieur: Crédit et spéculation en France, fin XVIIIe–début XXe siècles*, ed. Nadine Levratto and Alessando Stanziani, 199–265. Brussels: Émile Bruylant, 2011.
Herland, Michel. "Perpetuum mobile et crédit gratuit: Deux propositions oubliées pour améliorer le fonctionnement d'une économie monétaire." *Revue Économique* 28, no. 6 (1977): 938–73.
Hilaire, Jean. *Introduction historique au droit commercial*. Paris: Presses universitaires de France, 1986.
Hirsch, Jean-Pierre. *Les deux rêves du commerce: Entreprise et institution dans la région lilloise, 1780–1860*. Paris: EHESS, 1991.
———. "Revolutionary France, Cradle of Free Enterprise." *American Historical Review* 94, no. 5 (1989): 1281–89.
Hirschman, Albert O. *The Passions and the Interests: Political Arguments for Capitalism before Its Triumph*. Princeton: Princeton University Press, 1997.
Hoffman, Philip T., and Jean-Laurent Rosenthal. "New Work in French Economic History." *French Historical Studies* 23, no. 3 (2000): 439–53.
Hoffman, Philip T., Giles Postel-Vilnay, and Jean-Laurent Rosenthal. "Information and Economic History: How the Credit Market in Old Regime Paris Forces Us to Rethink the Transition to Capitalism." *American Historical Review* 104, no. 1 (1999): 69–94.
———. *Priceless Markets: The Political Economy of Credit in Paris, 1660–1870*. Chicago: University of Chicago Press, 2000.
———. "Private Credit Markets in Paris, 1690–1840." *Journal of Economic History* 52, no. 2 (1992): 293–306.
Hoppitt, Julian. "Attitudes to Credit in Eighteenth-Century England." In *Business Life and Public Policy: Essays in Honour of D. C. Coleman*, ed. Neil McKendrick and R. B. Outwaithe, 64–78. Cambridge: Cambridge University Press, 1986.
———. *Risk and Failure in English Business, 1700–1800*. Cambridge: Cambridge University Press, 1987.
Horn, Jeff. *The Path Not Taken: French Industrialization in the Age of Revolution, 1750–1830*. Cambridge, MA: MIT Press, 2008.

Huet, Nicolas-Francois. *Observations sur l'exercice du droit de contrainte par corps envers l'indigence et la vieillesse, pour dettes commerciales ou supposées telles*. Paris: Imprimerie de A. Boucher, n.d.

Hulot, Jean Etienne. *Mémoire d'un prisonnier pour dettes détenu à Sainte-Pélagie*. Paris: Poussin, Imprimeur, 1831.

Ignatieff, Michael. *A Just Measure of Pain: The Penitentiary in the Industrial Revolution, 1750–1850*. New York: Pantheon Books, 1978.

Innes, Joanna. "The King's Bench Prison in the Later Eighteenth Century: Law, Authority and Order in a London Debtors' Prison." In *An Ungovernable People: The English and Their Law in the Seventeenth and Eighteenth Centuries*, ed. John Styles and John Brewer, 250–98. New Brunswick, NJ: Rutgers University Press, 1980.

Jacquemont, André. *Escrocs et demi-escrocs: Étude pratique de l'escroquerie et du dol*. Paris: Pierre Rogers & Cie, Editeurs, 1855.

Jarvis, Katie L. "Exacting Change: Money, Market Women, and the Crumbling Corporate World in the French Revolution." *Journal of Social History* 115 (2016). doi: 10.1093/jsh/shw115.

Johnson, Christopher. "The Revolution of 1830 in French Economic History." In *1830 in France*, ed. John Merriman, 139–80. New York: New Viewpoints, 1975.

Jones, Colin, and Rebecca Spang. "Sans-culottes, sans café, sans tabac: Shifting Realms of Necessity and Luxury in Eighteenth-Century Paris." In *Consumers and Luxury: Consumer Culture in Europe, 1650–1850*, ed. Maxine Berg and Helen Clifford, 37–62. Manchester: Manchester University Press, 1997.

Joyau, F.-J. *Discours sur les abus de la contrainte par corps en matière de lettres de change et sur les moyens d'y remédier sans porter atteinte à la prospérité du commerce, prononcé le 5 novembre 1827 à la rentrée solennelle de l'Académie universitaire de Caen*. Caen: Imprimerie de A. Le Roy, n.d.

Kadens, Emily. "The Last Bankrupt Hanged: Balancing Incentives in the Development of Bankruptcy Law." *Duke Law Journal* 59, no. 1 (2010): 1229–1319.

Kaiser, Thomas E. "Money, Despotism, and Public Opinion in Early Eighteenth-Century France: John Law and the Debate on Royal Credit." *Journal of Modern History* 63, no. 1 (1991): 1–28.

Kalifa, Dominique. *Naissance de la police privée: Détectives et agences de recherches en France, 1832–1942*. Paris: Plon, 2000.

Kaplan, Steven. *La fin de corporations*. Translated by Beatrice Vierne. Paris: Fayard, 2001.

Kessler, Amalia D. "Enforcing Virtue: Social Norms and Self-Interest in an Eighteenth-Century Merchant Court." *Law and History Review* 71 (Spring 2004): 74–118.

———. "A Question of Name: Merchant Court Jurisdiction and the Origins of the *Noblesse Commerçante*." In *A Vast and Useful Art: The Gustave Gimon Collection on French Political Economy*, ed. Mary Jane Parrine. Stanford: Stanford University Press, 2004.

———. *A Revolution in Commerce: The Parisian Merchant Court and the Rise of Commercial Society in Eighteenth-Century France*. New Haven: Yale University Press, 2007.

Kete, Kathleen. "Stendhal and the Trials of Ambition in Postrevolutionary France." *French Historical Studies* 28 (Summer 2005): 467–95.

Koepke, Robert. "The *loi des patentes* of 1844." *French Historical Studies* 11 (1980): 398–430.

Kwass, Michael. *Contraband: Louis Mandrin and the Making of a Global Underground*. Cambridge, MA: Harvard University Press, 2014.

———. "Saving and Spending in the Enlightenment." *Historical Reflection/Reflexions Historiques* 31 (Spring 2005): 49–70.

Lacan, Laure. "Les dossiers de contentieux des banques: Observatoire privilégié de l'endettement." *Entreprises et Histoire* 59, no. 2 (2010): 122–25.

Laly. *Adresse au Roi, tendante à l'abolition de la contrainte par corps*. Paris: Imprimerie de Bellemain, n.d.

Lainné, A. F. *Examen du projet de loi sur les faillites et banqueroutes: Présenté à la Chambre des députés, le 9 février*. Paris: L'auteur, 1835.

LaMarre, L.E. *Au Roi en faveur des négocians commercans banquiers etc*. Paris: Le Normant, 1814.

Lamennais, Félicité Robert. *Projet de constitution du crédit social*. Paris: Au Bureau du people Consitutant, 1848.

Lamouroux, Charles. *De quelques griefs de l'industrie*. Paris: Chez DeLangle, Librarie, 1830.

Landes, David S. "French Entrepreneurship and Industrial Growth in the Nineteenth Century." *Journal of Economic History* 9, no. 1 (1949): 45–61.

Langlois, Louis. *Du crédit privé dans la société moderne et de la réforme des lois qui doivent le constituer: Réforme du régime hypothécaire et organisation du crédit foncier: Du projet de crédit du Comité d'agriculture et du crédit foncier, avec cours forcé: Contre-projet sans cours force*. Paris: Joubert, 1848.

Larousse, Pierre. *Grand dictionnaire universel du XIXe siècle français, historique, géographique, mythologique, bibliographique*. Paris: Larousse, 1866–67.

Laviron, A. F. *Observations sur les faillites et banqueroutes, et sur le dernier projet de loi présenté aux Chambres, ou Recherches sur les réformes à opérer dans la législation commerciale*. Paris: Renard, 1837.

Lebaudy. C. *Réflexions sur la Banque générale de commerce et d'industrie sous la raison J. Lafitte et Cie*. Paris: Dupont, 1837.

Lefebvre, Georges. *La France sous la Directoire 1795–1799*. Paris: Messidor Éditions Sociales, 1989.

Lemercier, Clare. "La Chambre de commerce de Paris comme corps intermédiaire, des origines aux années." In *La Chambre de commerce et d'industrie de Paris (1803–2003), II: Études thématiques*, ed. P. Lenormand, 33–54. Geneva: Droz, 2008.

———. "Discipliner le commerce sans corporations: La loi, le juge, l'arbitre et le commerçant à Paris au XIXe siècle." *Le Mouvement Social* 224 (2008): 61–74.

———. "The Judge, the Expert and the Arbitrator: The Strange Case of the Paris Court of Commerce (ca. 1800–ca. 1880)." In *Fields of Expertise: A Comparative History of Expert Procedures in Paris and London, 1600 to Present*, ed. Christelle Rabier, 115–45. Newcastle: Cambridge Scholars Publishing, 2007.

———. "Liens privés et régulation de l'économie: La famille et l'institution (Paris, XIXᵉ siècle)." *Revue d'Histoire du XIXe siècle* 33, no. 2 (2006): 23–53.

———. *Un si discret pouvoir: Aux origines de la chambre de commerce de Paris, 1803–1853*. Paris: La Découverte, 2003.

Lemercier, Claire, and Claire Zalc. "Pour une nouvelle approche de la relation de crédit en histoire contemporaine." *Annales: Histoire, Sciences Sociales* 67, no. 4 (2012): 979–1009.

Leroy. *Observations pratiques sur l'exercice de la contrainte par corps*. Paris: Imprimerie de Pollet, n.d.

Lettres d'un ancien avocat à un député sur la contrainte par corps. Paris: Dentu, 1821.

Lescure, Michel, and Alain Plessis, eds. *Banques locales et banques régionales en France au XIXe siècle*. Paris: Albin Michel, 1999.

Leuchter, Tyson, "The Most Sacred Right of All: Property, Public Debt, and the Law at the Paris Stock Exchange, 1793–1825." PhD thesis, University of Chicago, 2017.

Levratto, Nadine. "Abolition de la contrainte par corps et évolution du capitalisme au XIXᵉ siècle." *Economie et Institutions* 8, no. 2 (2009): 221–49.

Livesey, James. *Making Democracy in the French Revolution*. Cambridge, MA: Harvard University Press, 2001.

Locré, Jean-Guillaume. *La législation civile, commerciale et criminelle de la France, ou, Commentaire et complément des codes français*. Vol. 19. Paris: Treuttel et Würtz, 1827–32.

Loubens, J.-M. *De la contrainte par corps en matière civile et commercial*. Paris: L'Huillier, 1829.

Luckett, Thomas. "Credit and Commercial Honor in France, 1740–1789." PhD thesis, Princeton University, 1992.

———. "The Debate about Debt Imprisonment in the Eighteenth Century." In *Les personnes aux institutions: Réseaux et culture du credit du XVIe au XXe siècle en Europe; Actes du colloque international centenaire des FUC*, ed. Laurence Fontaine, Gilles Postel-Vinay, Jean-Laurent-Rosenthal, and Paul Servais, 163–74. Louvain-la-Neuve: Bruylant-Academia, 1996.

Lyons, Martyn. *France under the Directory*. Cambridge: Cambridge University Press, 1975.

Madelin, Louis. *Histoire du Consulat et de l'Empire*. Vol. 2. Paris: Éditions Robert Laffont, 2003.

Mallet du Pan, Jacques. *Correspondence du Mallet du Pan avec la cour de Vienne (1794–1798)*. Edited by André Michal. Paris: Librarie Plon, 1884.

Mann, Bruce. *Republic of Debtors: Bankruptcy in the Age of American Independence*. Cambridge, MA: Harvard University Press, 2002.

Marchant-Duroc, A. *L'art de s'enrichir par la faillite: Tableau satirique et moral*. Bordeaux: Imprimerie de Ve N. Duviella, 1845.

Marco, Luc. *La montée des faillites en France, XIXe–XXe siècles*. Paris: Harmattan, 1989.

Marion, Marcel. *Histoire financière de la France depuis 1715*. Vol. 3. Paris: Rousseau, 1925.

Markham, Lester V. *Victorian Insolvency: Bankruptcy, Imprisonment for Debt, and Company Winding-Up in Nineteenth-Century England.* Oxford: Clarendon Press, 1995.

Martin, Jean-Clement. "Le commerçant, la faillite et l'historien." *Annales E S C* 6, no. 18 (1980): 1251–68.

Marx, Karl. *Class Struggles in France, 1848–1850.* New York: International Publishers, 1964.

Mayret, Jules. "La nouvelle prison pour dettes." In *Paris, ou Le livre des cent et un.* Vol. 15. Paris: Ladvocat, 1831–34.

Maza, Sarah. *The Myth of the French Bourgeoisie: An Essay on the Social Imaginary, 1750–1850.* Cambridge, MA: Harvard University Press, 2003.

Mélesville and Vanier. *L'art de payer ses dettes.* Paris: Riga, 1832.

Mémoire justificatif de Michel-Antoine Baudouin fils, en réponse aux accusations portées contre lui. Paris: De l'Imprimerie d'Everat, 1815.

Mémoire pour M. Thuret contre les syndics definitifs de la faillite Demiannay. Lyon: Imprimerie de Dumoulin, Ronet et Sibuet, 1840.

Mercier, Sebastien. *Le nouveau Paris.* Edited by Jean-Claude Bonet. Paris: Mercure de France, 1994.

Miller, Judith. "The Aftermath of the Assignat: Plaintiffs in the Age of Property, 1794–1804." In *Taking Liberties: Problems of a New Order from the French Revolution to Napoleon*, ed. Howard Brown and Judith Miller, 70–91. Manchester: Manchester Univesity Press, 2002.

———. "Des contrats sous tension: Rétablir la propriété après la Terreur." *Annales Historiques de la Révolution Française* 352 (April–June 2008): 241–62.

Mitchell, Léonie M. "The British Conception of Negotiable Instruments v. the French." *Journal of Comparative Legislation and International Law* 10, no. 4 (1928): 237–47.

Moreau-Christophe, Louis-Maturin. *De l'état actuel des prisons en France consideré avec la théorie pénale du code.* Paris: A. Desrez, Librarie, 1837.

———. "Les détenus pour dettes." In *Les français peints par eux-mêmes: Encyclopédie morale du dix-neuvième siècle*, 4:44–49. Paris: L. Curmer, 1840–42.

Morin, C. M. *Le petit commerce et le commerce intermediare affranchis ou institution, par association mutuelle, d'un comptoir de crédit consolidé et de garantie d'escompte, pour Paris.* Paris: Imprimerie Le Normant Fils, 1830.

Muldrew, Craig. *The Economy of Obligation: The Culture of Credit and Social Relations in Early Modern England.* New York: St. Martin's Press, 1998.

Noël, Tangi. "La notion de *'commerçant'* d'après les procedures de faillite devant les tribunaux de commerce de Bretagne au XIXe siècle." In *Les Tribunaux de commerce: Genèse et enjeux d'une institution*, ed. Pascal Clément, 55–66. Paris: Association française pour l'histoire de la justice, 2007.

Nord, Philip. *Paris Shopkeepers and the Politics of Resentment.* Princeton: Princeton University Press, 1986.

Normanby, Marquess of. *A Year of Revolution from A Journal Kept in Paris in 1848.* London: Longman, Brown, Green Longmans and Roberts, 1848.

Note pour Le Sieur Ardant contre 1. Le Sieur Leborgne 2. La demoiselle Morvan 3. Le Sieur Dréan. Paris: Typographie de A. Pinard, 1838.

Note pour MM. Mellet, Henry, Servestre et Bernage, actionnaires et créanciers appelants, contre 1° les trustees de la Société anonyme du chemin de fer de la Loire, 2° M. de Favières. Paris: Imprimerie de A. Belin et Compagnie, 1838.

Nouvelle supplique des prisonniers pour dettes au roi et aux deux chambres, à S. A. R Mgr. le duc d'Angoulême, President de la Societe royale pour l'amelioration des prisons, et à S. Exc Mgr. le Ministre de l'Interieur, President; M . . . Vice-President, et autres membres du Conseil general des prisons, May 1819. Paris: De l'Imprimerie de Anthe Boucher, 1819.

Nye, Robert. *Masculinity and Male Codes of Honor in Modern France*. New York: Oxford University Press, 1993.

O'Brien, Patricia. *The Promise of Punishment: Prisons in Nineteenth-Century France*. Princeton: Princeton University Press, 1982.

Observations des tribunaux de cassation et d'appel, des tribunaux et conseils de commerce sur le projet de code du commerce. Paris: Imprimerie de la République, 1802.

Ouvrard, Gabriel-Julien. *Mémoires sur sa vie et ses opérations financières*. Paris: Moutardier Librarie, 1827.

Palmade, Guy P. *French Capitalism in the Nineteenth Century*. Translated by Graeme Holmes. London: Barnes and Noble, 1972.

Pance, B. *De la contrainte par corps*. Paris: Tenon, 1832.

Peebles, Gustav. "Washing Away the Sins of Debt: The Nineteenth-Century Eradication of the Debtors' Prison." *Comparative Studies in Society and History* 55, no. 3 (2014): 701–24.

Péraud, Alexandre. "La comédie humaine comme mise en texte de l'imaginaire social du crédit." In *Les Français et l'argent: Entre fantasmes et réalités*, ed. Alya Aglan, Olivier Feiertag, and Yannick Marec, 235–50. Rennes: Presses Universitaires de Rennes, 2011.

———. "La panacée universelle, le crédit' (César Birotteau): Quelques exemples d'inscription narrative du crédit dans la littérature du premier XIXe siècle." *Romantisme* 151, no. 1 (2011): 39–52.

Perre, Gustave. *À messieurs le président et les conseillers composant la chambre des mises en accusation en cour de Nîmes pour Gustave Perre, . . . prévenu de banqueroute . . .* Nîmes: Imprimerie de veuve Gaude, 1845.

Perrot, Michelle. *L'impossible prison*. Paris: Seuil, 1980.

Petit, Jacques-Guy. *Ces peines obscures: La prison pénale en France, 1780–1875*. Paris: Fayard, 1990.

Petit, Jacques-Guy, Nicole Castan, and Claude Fogeron, eds. *Histoire des galères, bagnes et prisons XIIe–XXe siècles: Introduction à l'histoire pénale de la France*. Toulouse: Bibliothèque historique Privat, 1991.

Pétition addressée par des habitants de Paris à Mm. les pairs et Mm. les deputés sur la contrainte par corps. Paris: Imprimerie Edouard Proux, 1845.

Pétition à MM. de la Chambre des Pairs au sujet de la contrainte par corps. Saint-Denis: Imprimerie de Prevost, 1830.

Pinard, A., and Hipp. Biesta. *Observations présentés à l'Assemblée nationale par le comptoir national d'escompte de Paris sur les projets de décrets relatifs aux concordats amiables proposés par citoyens Jules Favre et Dupont (de Bussac)*. Paris: Paul Dupont, 1848.

Pinkney, David. *Decisive Years in France, 1840–1847*. Princeton: Princeton University Press, 1986.

Pirmé, Victor. *De la nécessité, dans l'intérêt du commerce, de l'industrie et de la morale, de l'abolition de la contrainte par corps, au lettre à M. le duc de Cazes*. Paris: Delauny, 1829.

Plessis, Alain, *La Banque de France sous le Second Empire*. Paris: Droz, 1985.

———. "Les banques locales, de l'essor du Second Empire à la 'crise' de la Belle Epoque." In *Banques locales et banques régionales en France au XIXe siècle*, ed. Michel Lescure and Alain Plessis. Paris: Albin Michel: Paris 1999.

———. "La révolution de l'escompte dans la France du XIXe siècle." *Revue d'Histoire du XIXe Siècle* 23 (2001): 143–63.

Pocock, J. G. A. *Virtue, Commerce and History*. Cambridge: Cambridge University Press, 1985.

Pomykala, Joseph. "The Division and Destruction of Value: An Economic Analysis of Bankruptcy Law." PhD thesis, University of Pennsylvania, 1997.

Poovey, Mary. *Genres of the Credit Economy: Mediating Value in Eighteenth- and Nineteenth-Century Britain*. Chicago: University of Chicago Press, 2008.

Porter, Theodore. *The Rise of Statistical Thinking, 1820–1900*. Princeton: Princeton University Press, 1986.

———. *Trust in Numbers: The Pursuit of Objectivity in Science and Public Life*. Princeton: Princeton University Press, 1995.

Potier, P. E. *De la contrainte par corps sous le régime républicain*. Paris: Chez l'auteur, 1851.

Pradel, E. C de. *Les amis de Bordeaux ou Le prisonnier pour dettes*. Paris: À la librarie française de l'advocat, 1821.

Projet de Code du commerce presenté par la commission nommée par le gouvernement le 13 Germinal An 9. Paris: Baudouin, Garnery et Randonneau, 1803.

Proudhon, Pierre-Joseph. *Organisation du crédit et de la circulation, et solution du problème social*. Paris, 1848.

Rappaport, Erika. "'A Husband in His Wife's Dresses': Consumer Credit and the Debtor Family in England, 1864–1914." In *The Sex of Things: Gender and Consumption in Historical Perspective*, ed. Victoria de Grazia and Ellen Furlough. Berkeley: University of California Press, 1996.

Ratcliffe, Barrie. "Classes laborieuses et classes dangereuses à Paris pendant la première moitié du XIXe siècle?: The Chevalier Thesis Reexamined." *French Historical Studies* 17, no. 2 (1991): 542–74.

Réclamation des détenus pour dettes contre une inadvertence des legislators de 1832. Paris: Schnieder et Lagrand, 1846.

Reddy, William. *The Invisible Code: Honor and Sentiment in Postrevolutionary France, 1814–1848*. Berkeley: University of California Press, 1997.

———. *The Rise of Market Culture: The Textile Trade and French Society, 1700–1900*. Cambridge: Cambridge University Press, 1984.
Reffait, Christophe. *La bourse dans le roman du second XIXe siècle: Discours romanesque et imaginaire social de la spéculation*. Paris: Honore Champion, 2007.
Réfutation proposition par proposition de l'exposé des motifs du projet de loi sur la contrainte par corps, par un légiste. Paris: Sellique, 1829.
Reybaud, Louis. *Jérôme Paturot à la recherche d'une position sociale*. Paris: Dubochet, 1846.
Reynard, Pierre Claude. "The Language of Failure: Bankruptcy in Eighteenth-Century France." *Journal of European Economic History* 30, no. 2 (2001): 355–90.
Rice, Howard C. "James Swan: Agent of the French Republic 1794–1796." *New England Quarterly* 10, no. 3 (1937): 464–86.
Riviale, Philippe. *Fourier et la civilization marchande: Egarement du libéralisme*. Paris: L'Harmattan, 1996.
Robert, Adolphe, and Gaston Cougny. *Dictionnaire des parlementaires français . . . depuis le 1er Mai 1789 jusqu'au 1er Mai 1889*. Paris: Bourloton, 1889.
Rollac, James. *Affaire Demiannay: Premier mémoire presenté par James Rollac à la chambre d'accusation de la cour royale de Rennes*. Paris: Imprimerie Decourchant, [1836?].
Roret, Jacques-Pierre. *Code de commerce, manuel complet d'industrie commerciale, contenant les lois, règles, applications et exemples de l'art de gagner sa vie, et de faire fortune le plus honnêtement possible dans tous les états*. Paris: J. P. Roret Editeur, 1829.
Rosanvallon, Pierre. *The Demands of Liberty: Civil Society in France since the Revolution*. Cambridge, MA: Harvard University Press.
Rougement, M. de. *Une heure à Sainte Pélagie: Comedie en un acte*. Paris: Chez Martinet, 1822.
Roussel, P. L. *Le système des mandats territoriaux: 1796–1797*. Paris: L. Tenin, 1920.
Roux, Vital. *De l'influence du gouvernement sur la prospérité du commerce*. Paris: Chez Fayolle, 1800.
Safley, Thomas. "Bankruptcy: Family and Finance in Early Modern Augsburg." *Journal of European Economic History* 29, no. 1 (2000): 53–76.
———, ed. *The History of Bankruptcy: Economic, Social and Cultural Implications in Early Modern Europe*. New York: Routledge, 2013.
Saint-Aubin, Camille. *Essai sur la contrainte par corps, à l'occasion du projet de loi soumis en ce moment à la Chambre des Pairs*. Paris: A. Bailleul, 1819.
Saint-Hilaire, Emile. *L'art de payer ses dettes et de satisfaire ses créanciers sans debourser un sou*. Paris: Imprimerie de Balzac, 1832.
Salel, Jean-Joseph. *Bombe lumineuse, ou Abolition de la contrainte par corps, opuscule dédié aux deux Chambres législatives de la session de 1830*. Paris: Delaunay, 1830.
Sandage, Scott. *Born Losers: A History of Failure in America*. Cambridge, MA: Harvard University Press, 2005.
Sargent, Thomas J., and Francois R. Velde. "Macroeconomic Features of the French Revolution." *Journal of Political Economy* 103, no. 3 (1995): 474–518.

Sartre-Salis. *La prison pour dettes*. Toulouse: De l'imprimerie de Bellegarrigue, Librarie, 1826.

Sauvayre, Joseph-Marie. *Mémoire pour Joseph-Marie Sauvayre, prévenu de banqueroute simple, contre le Ministère publique*. Nyons: De l'Imperimerie de Gros, 1825.

Say, Horace Émile. *Avant-propos à la discussion d'une nouvelle loi sur les faillites*. Paris: Guillaumin, 1837.

Say, Jean-Baptiste. *Traité d'économie politique; ou, Simple exposition de la manière dont se forment, se distribuent, et se consomment les richesses*. Paris: Chez Deterville Libraire, 1803.

Schnerb, R. "La depression économique sous le Directoire après la disparation du papier-monnaie." *Archives Historiques de la Révolution Française* 11 (1934): 27–49.

Schreiber, Jean-Philippe. "Les Juifs, rois de l'époque d'Alphonse Toussenel, et ses avatars: La spéculation vue comme anti-travail au XIXe siècle." *Revue Belge de Philologie et d'Histoire* 79, no. 2 (2001): 533–46.

Scott, Joan Wallach. *Gender and the Politics of History*. New York: Columbia University Press, 1995.

Sée, Henri. *La vie économique sous la monarchie censitaire (1815–1848)*. Paris: F. Alcan, 1927.

Sewell, William H., Jr. *Work and Revolution in France: The Language of Labor from the Old Regime to 1848*. Cambridge: Cambridge University Press, 1980.

Sgard, Jérôme. "Do Legal Origins Matter? The Case of Bankruptcy Laws in Europe 1808–1914." *European Review of Economic History* 10, no. 3 (2006): 389–419. doi: 10.1017/S1361491606001808

Shovlin, John. *The Political Economy of Virtue: Luxury, Patriotism, and the Origins of the French Revolution*. Ithaca: Cornell University Press, 2006.

———. "Toward a Reinterpretation of Revolutionary Anti-nobilism: The Political Economy of Honor in the Old Regime." *Journal of Modern History* 72, no. 1 (2000): 35–66.

Sibalis, Michael David. "Corporatism after the Corporations: The Debate on Restoring the Guilds under Napoleon I and the Restoration." *French Historical Studies* 15, no. 4 (1988): 718–30.

Simonin, Anne. *Le déshonneur dans la République: Une histoire de l'indignité, 1791–1958*. Paris: Bernard Grasset, 2008.

Smail, John. "Credit, Risk and Honor in Eighteenth-Century Commerce." *Journal of British Studies* 44, no. 3 (2005): 439–56.

Smith, Bonnie, and Donald Kelley. "What Was Property? Legal Dimensions of the Social Question in France (1789–1848)." *Proceedings of the American Philosophical Society*, 128, no. 3 (1984): 200–230.

Smith, J. Denson. "Impossibility of Performance as an Excuse in French Law: The Doctrine of Force Majeure." *Yale Law Journal* 45, no. 3 (1936): 452–67.

Smith, Jay M. "No More Language Games: Words, Beliefs, and the Political Culture of Early Modern France." *American Historical Review* 102, no. 5 (1997): 1413–40.

———. "Social Categories, the Language of Patriotism, and the Origins of the French Revolution: The Debate over *Noblesse Commerçante*." *Journal of Modern History* 72, no. 2 (2000): 339–74.

Smith, Michael. *The Emergence of Modern Business Enterprise in France, 1800–1930*. Cambridge, MA: Harvard University Press, 2006.

Sonenscher, Michael. *Before the Deluge: Public Debt, Inequality, and the Intellectual Origins of the French Revolution*. Princeton: Princeton University Press, 2008.

Spang, Rebecca. "The Ghost of Law: Speculating on Money, Memory and Mississippi in the French Constituent Assembly." *Historical Reflections/Réflexions Historiques* 31, no. 1 (2005): 19–27.

———. *Stuff and Money in the Time of the French Revolution*. Cambridge, MA: Harvard University Press, 2014.

Spieler, Miranda. *Empire and Underworld: Captivity in French Guiana*. Cambridge, MA: Harvard University Press, 2012.

Stanziani, Alessandro. "Les deux sens de la speculation au XIXe siècle." In *Les Français et l'argent: Entre fantasmes et réalités*, ed. Alya Aglan, Olivier Feiertag, and Yannick Marec, 267–80. Rennes: Presses universitaires de Rennes, 2011.

———. *Rules of Exchange: French Capitalism in Comparative Perspective, Eighteenth to Early Twentieth Centuries*. Cambridge: Cambridge University Press, 2012.

Stern, Daniel (Marie d'Agout). *Histoire de la Révolution de 1848*. Paris: Éditions Balland, 1848.

Sue, Eugène. *Les mystères de Paris*. Paris: C. Gosselin, 1843.

Sur la contrainte par corps pour dettes telle qu'elle a été etablie par la loi du 15 Germinal An VI par. M. L.P.d.L.F. (ancient jurisconsulte). Paris: Chez la fille d'auteur, 1803.

Suter, Mischa. "The Boundaries of Debt: Bankruptcy between Local Practices and Liberal Rule in Nineteenth-Century Switzerland." In *The Cultural History of Money and Credit: A Global Perspective*, ed. Chia Yin Hsu, Thomas Luckett, and Erika Vause, 51–66. Lanham, MD: Lexington Books, 2016.

———. "Debt and Its Attachments: Collateral as an Object of Knowledge in Nineteenth-Century Liberalism." *Comparative Studies in Society and History* 59, no. 3 (2017): 1–28.

Swan, James. "À Messieurs de la Chambre des Députés." Paris: Chez l'auteur, 1817.

Szajkowski, Zosa. *Agricultural Credit and Napoleon's Anti-Jewish Decrees*. New York: Éditions Historiques Franco-Juives, 1953.

Szramkiewicz, Romauald. *Histoire du droit des affaires*. Paris: Montchrestien, 1989.

———. "Les tribunaux de commerce: Une longue histoire dans la justice économique." *Justices* 1 (1995): 7–14.

Taws, Richard. "Trompe-l'Oeil and Trauma: Money and Memory after the Terror." *Oxford Art Journal* 30, no. 3 (2007): 353–76.

Taylor, George. "Noncapitalist Wealth and the Origins of the French Revolution." *American Historical Review* 72, no. 2 (1967): 469–96.

———. "The Paris Bourse on the Eve of the Revolution, 1781–1789." *American Historical Review* 67, no. 4 (1962): 951–77.

———. "Types of Capitalism in Eighteenth-Century France." *English Historical Review* 79, no. 312 (1964): 478–97.

Thiveaud, Jean-Marie. "L'ordre primordial de la dette: Petite histoire panoramique de la faillite, des origines à nos jours." *Revue d'Economie Financière* 25 (1993): 67–106.

Thompson, Victoria. *The Virtuous Marketplace: Women and Men, Money and Politics in Paris, 1830–1870*. Baltimore: John Hopkins University Press, 2000.

Thuillier, Guy. *La monnaie en France au début du XIX siècle*. Paris: Champion, 1983.

Thuret, Pierre. *Histoire et généalogie des Thuret*. Paris: Chez Pierre Thuret, n.d.

Tocqueville, Alexis de. *Democracy in America*. Translated by Arthur Goldhammer. New York: The Library of America, 2004.

Touchard Lafosse, G. *De la contrainte par corps en matière civile et commerciale Loubens et Bourbon Leblanc suivie de considerations morales, historiques et descriptives sur le même sujet*. Paris: L'Huillier, 1829.

Toussenel, Alphonse. *Les Juifs, rois de l'époque: Histoire de la féodalité financière*. Paris: C. Marpon et E. Flammarion, 1847.

Tribunal de Commerce. *Faillite Genthon. Lettre de M. Ardant, négociant à Paris à Lemercier, évêque de Beauvais, se disant créancier de ladite faillite*. Paris: Imprimerie A Appert, 1834.

———. *Faillite Genthon. 2e Lettre de M. Ardant, négociant à Paris à Lemercier, évêque de Beauvais, se disant créancier de ladite faillite*. Paris: Tribunal de Commerce, 1834.

Turgot, Anne-Robert-Jacques. *Mémoires sur le prêt à intérêt et sur le commerce des fers*. Paris: Froullé, 1789.

Valente, Fabien. "Contribution à l'histoire de la codification du droit commerciale: Le projet de la chambre de commerce de Paris (1804)." *Revue Historique de la Droit* 82, no. 1 (2004): 79–96.

———. "Les jurisdictions consulaires dans le Code de commerce napoléonien." In *Les Tribunaux de commerce: Genèse et enjeux d'une institution*, ed. Pascal Clément, 112–19. Paris: Association française pour l'histoire de la Justice, 2007.

———. "Usury in France in the Nineteenth Century." In *Private Law and Social Inequality in the Industrial Age: Comparing Legal Cultures in Britain, France, Germany and the United States*, ed. Willibald Steinmetz, 437–55. London: Oxford University Press, 2000.

Van Voorhis, Robert Henry. "Borrowing Our Way to Socialism: The Economic Thought of Pierre-Joseph Proudhon." PhD thesis, Duke University, 1944.

Vause, Erika. "'The Business of Reputations': Shame, Secrecy, and Social Standing in Nineteenth-Century French Debtors' and Creditors' Newspapers." *Journal of Social History* 48, no. 1 (2014): 47–71.

———. "Disciplining the Market: Debt Imprisonment and the Making of Commercial Actors in Revolutionary France." *Law and History Review* 32, no. 3 (2014): 647–82.

———. "'He Who Rushes to Riches Will Not Be Innocent': Commercial Honor and Commercial Failure in Post-revolutionary France." *French Historical Studies* 35, no. 2 (2012): 321–49.

———. "A Subject of Interest: Usurers on Trial in Nineteenth-Century France." *Financial History Review* 24, no. 1 (2017): 103–19.

Vermale, François. "Les dettes privées sous la Revolution: Les remboursements en assignats." *Annales Historiques de la Révolution Française* 10, no. 56 (1933): 160–66.

Villain, Alexis. *Récit exact et détaillé des évènements qui ont eu lieu à Paris pendant les 3 immortelles journées des 22, 23 et 24 février 1848, narration circonstanciée et puisée à des sources authentiques de toutes les luttes soutenues contre un pouvoir liberticide par la population héroïque de Paris*. Sedan: Laroche-Jacob, 1848.

Villemarest, Maxime de, and James Rousseau. *Mémoires de mes créanciers, moeurs parisiennes*. Paris: Dufey et Vezard, 1832.

Vingtrinier, A.-B. *Notice sur les prisons de Rouen*. Rouen: F. Baudry, Imprimeur du Roi, 1826.

Walton, Charles. *Policing Public Opinion in the French Revolution: The Culture of Calumny and the Problem of Free Speech*. New York: Oxford University Press, 2009.

Wennerlind, Carl. *The Casualties of Credit: The English Financial Revolution, 1620–1720*. Cambridge, MA: Harvard University Press, 2011.

Whitman, James. *Harsh Justice: Criminal Punishment and the Widening Gap between Europe and America*. Oxford: Oxford University Press, 2005.

Wolloch, Isser. *The New Regime: Transformations of the French Civic Order, 1789–1820s*. New York: W. W. Norton, 1994.

Wolowski, Louis. *Des sociétés par actions*. Paris: Révue de législation et de jurisprudence, 1838.

Woodfine, Philip. "Debtors, Prisons, and Petitions in Eighteenth-Century England." *Eighteenth-Century Life* 30, no. 2 (2006): 1–31.

Wright, Gordon. *Between the Guillotine and Liberty: Two Centuries of the Crime Problem in France*. Oxford: Oxford University Press, 1983.

Yates, Alexia. "'C'est comme ça que vous entendez les affaires?': Gogos and the Moral Parameters of Commercial Life in Nineteenth-Century France." *Proceedings of the Western Society for French History* 36 (2008): 149–65.

Ymbert, J. G. *L'art de faire des dettes et de promener ses creanciers, par un homme comme il faut dedié aux gens destitués, réformés; aux amateurs des plaisirs de la vie; aux victimes des révolutions et des changemens de ministères*. Brussels: J. M. Lacrosse Librairie, 1834.

INDEX

Italicized page numbers refer to illustrations; "t" following a page number refers to tables.